SHAZ KAHNG'S

THE CLOSER

Beverly Hills Book Award Finalist 2017

Selected as one of Bustle's "*9 Fall Book Debuts By Women You're Going to Want to Read Immediately*"

"*Unreservedly recommended...An original and compelling novel about a woman who must compete in what has traditionally been a 'man's world', The Closer reveals author Shaz Kahng as an impressively skilled storyteller who is able to entertainingly engage her readers from cover to cover.*" - **Midwest Book Review**

"*The Closer is an inspiring and fun take on women in business, with plenty of ceiling smashing along the way. Shaz Kahng's fast-paced, sports-focused The Closer is timely and refreshing, a novel that exposes the difficulties that women face in industries that are dominated by men. Vivien Lee is a thoroughly likable lead...even faced with manipulation and outright lies, Vivien typically picks the higher road. The story takes some inspiring turns, including Vivien's participation in a Wharton-founded secret club, the Ceiling Smashers, which functions as a place to maintain alliances with other women in business. Anecdotes about women's experiences at those meetings read as realistic and give credence to the bonds of sisterhood highlighted throughout.*" - **Foreword Reviews**

"The Closer gives women the heroine for whom they have been looking."
- **BOSS Magazine**

"From the first page of The Closer, readers are thrown into Vivien's world...We really don't see many female characters like Vivien. It's not until you read Vivien's story that you begin to feel inspired by the type of female role model she is: a strong businesswoman who side steps any "stereotypes" placed on women in positions of power...Shaz's creation of Vivien as a strong character capable of weathering brutal situations speaks volumes--not just about the person she's loosely based on, but also about the deeply ingrained stereotypes that persist today, both in fictional constructs of female characters and real women."
- **Women's Running Magazine**

"The book is the first in a series designed to keep the momentum going in destroying stereotypes that nice women finish last."
- **Good Sports Magazine**

"Insightful and inspirational." - **Renowned Silicon Valley Entrepreneur and Venture Capitalist**

"Exciting and relevant narrative- Kahng has a gift for storytelling."
- **Hollywood Producer**

"Couldn't put it down." - **Former Nike Female Senior Executive**

"Business savvy and entertaining all in one... I am definitely recommending this book to all of the women in my life who are smashing the ceilings themselves." - **Amazon Reviewer**

CEILING SMASHERS: BOOK 1

THE CLOSER

SHAZ KAHNG

CEILINGSMASHERS.COM

OLOM
PRESS

~

To my darling daughters, Gemma and Zoe,
who are already proving to be strong, savvy women.

~

PART ONE

CHAPTER 1: SHADOW DAY

The torture was unending. Vivien fought for each breath as she sprinted through the icy, chest-high water. She gasped as her legs churned against the heaviness of the frigid liquid.

A stern voice prodded her. "Had enough?"

Vivien shot her tormentor a look of defiance.

Smiling, the man pressed some buttons on a remote, increasing the speed of the submerged treadmill and raising the incline. "Let's see if this is better."

Focus and breathe.

At long last the session came to an end. Vivien swam over to the side of the huge pool and stood on legs that wobbled like jelly.

"You're pure evil, Doc Z." Vivien sputtered as she struggled to catch her breath. "Even if you are the best physical therapist in the country."

He helped her out of the pool. "I love compliments like that!" Doc Z threw his head back and laughed. "Seriously, Vivien, you put in the effort and it really paid off–fastest recovery from an ACL surgery I've ever seen. Great job!" He high-fived her. "My work here is done."

She thanked him with a hug and glanced at the clock. Better get moving so she could make it to work on time.

After showering and getting dressed, Vivien hustled through the comfy waiting area of the elite physical therapy center and noticed basketball player Dwyane Wade sitting in a plush leather chair...Doc Z's next victim–er, patient, no doubt.

"Thanks for visiting the Game Ready clinic, Vivien! Take care." The receptionist gave a wave.

Feeling reenergized, Vivien waved and bolted out the door.

3

It was a typical sweltering summer day in New York City. On that sticky day in early August, Strategic Consulting Partners was conducting its annual Shadow Day. During the first week of new-hire orientation, each new consultant shadowed one of the firm's partners for an entire day. A long-standing tradition at SCP, it engaged the new hires by showing the partners in action.

Vivien barely had time for a few sips of coffee before a newly promoted partner, Mahesh Chatterjee, knocked on the door to her office. "Good morning! I've got your new recruit here." He spoke in a lilting British accent and smiled, his brilliant white teeth contrasting with his smooth, dark skin. He wore a crisply starched, windowpane-patterned shirt and charcoal trousers.

"Thanks, Mahesh, please come in."

He ushered in the new hire, Jodie. She stood at over six feet and sported blond hair and sincere gray eyes that carried an open and curious expression. "Jodie, I'd like to introduce you to Vivien Lee, one of our senior partners and my mentor since day one. You'll be tagging along with her for your Shadow Day and I guarantee it will be memorable."

Vivien rose up to welcome Jodie, feeling unaccustomed to being a couple of inches shorter than any female.

Jodie said, "I'm excited to be here and to spend the day with you, Vivien."

She held out her hand. "I think we'll manage to have some fun, Jodie. Shall we head out?"

✳

A blast of hot air assaulted Vivien and Jodie as they exited the revolving doors of the office building.

"Okay, Jodie, here's our schedule." Vivien walked at a good clip along the bustling city sidewalk. "First we'll head downtown to a retail client meeting along with Harry, an SCP manager, and his team. After that we'll head back to midtown for a leadership conference. Then everyone will reconvene at the end of the day for a celebration at the office. Sound good?"

"Can't wait. Anything I can do to help or should I just observe?"

"It's meant to be a learning day for you, Jodie, so just drink it in. I'm happy to share any tips so feel free to ask questions along the way." Despite the heat and humidity, Vivien strode at so rapid a pace that even Jodie with her long legs had difficulty keeping up. "Sorry, Jodie, I walk fast, talk fast, pretty much do everything with a good amount of speed. Patience is not a virtue of mine." Vivien laughed.

"Things move so quickly around here," Jodie said. "I love the energy of New York. Grew up in San Francisco, though–totally different."

They arrived at the downtown offices of the client, a global retailer with stores and kiosks in airports and hotels. Harry and the SCP team stood when they entered the lobby. After introducing Jodie and greeting her team warmly, Vivien got a quick debrief.

"We're three weeks into assessing their business performance problems. The company's revenue has been declining steadily over five years, so they really do need help. Today they want an update on progress and specifically requested that you attend." A look of concern came across Harry's face. "Our problem is the chief financial officer. His buddy's a partner at a rival consulting firm, and he's been lobbying to bring them in and replace us. He's a classic bully and I don't trust the guy. The rest of the executives seem really supportive, though."

"Good to know, Harry. What's on the agenda? I looked over the presentation deck you sent me last night. That's what we're reviewing?"

"Yes. Attending the meeting today will be the CEO, CFO, head of merchandising, head of store operations, and a few others."

She looked at her watch. "Let's head on up. Harry, why don't you and the team present your work and I'll add color commentary when needed, okay?"

He nodded, looking relieved to have Vivien there.

On the top floor of the Manhattan skyscraper an executive assistant ushered them into a newly renovated, swanky conference room with a panoramic view of the city.

Vivien said quietly to her team, "For a company that's losing money they're certainly not too thrifty."

The executives entered and greeted the consultants. Once everyone was seated Harry started presenting their analysis of the client's business. As expected, the management team was receptive to the material, except for the cantankerous CFO.

Dick, the CFO, said, "You've been studying our business for weeks now, and while this work isn't bad, I don't see how you can help us. I've been with this company for twenty years, and let me tell you, this business is so complex it will take you years to understand it." He seemed prepared for a battle and glared at Harry, who shifted uncomfortably.

Harry glanced over at Vivien, who calmly said, "I understand, Dick. It's not uncommon for a client to say their business is unique or complex. Our job is to look at it with fresh eyes."

"Yeah, you're learning our business on our dime," Dick grumbled.

James, the CEO, shot Dick a look of caution over his disrespectful behavior.

"That's true of any consulting firm you'd hire," Vivien said, unfazed. "It seems to me there are two questions we need to answer here, Dick. The first is, can this company improve its performance?" The CFO nodded yes. "The second is, do you need our help? Of course, you could have chosen any consulting firm, but you've selected us. To set your mind at ease, if you feel dissatisfied with us at any point you can terminate the project."

Dick said sharply, "And we wouldn't hesitate to do that."

Harry, the team, and Jodie all sat holding their breath, hoping Vivien would figure out some way to appease the combative CFO. *Poor guy, he must be under a lot of pressure to turn things around. No wonder he's so stressed out,* Vivien thought. "We would expect nothing less," she said. "At the same time we like our clients to be receptive to our ideas, so the relationship needs to be collaborative. We've only been at this for three weeks and Harry and his team have done great work so far–"

The gruff CFO cut her off. "I bet you can't tell me anything about our business that I don't already know. You're the all-knowing partner, Vivien. Why don't you tell me something new about our business? Go on, one thing," Dick demanded.

Beads of sweat formed on Harry's forehead. He had only sent Vivien the deck last night.

Vivien maintained her positivity. "*All-knowing.* Wow, thanks for the compliment, Dick." She laughed, injecting some much needed levity into the room, and people chuckled in relief. "You know, I believe I can share something that you might find helpful." She stated, "You've got the wrong products in the wrong store locations." Vivien sat back, awaiting the response.

"What? What are you talking about?" Dick protested. "That can't be right."

Finally the CEO, James, spoke up. "Vivien, what makes you say that? We work very hard to ensure our merchandising strategy is effective." He looked quizzically at his head of merchandising, who shrugged his shoulders.

"Let me explain, James." Vivien stood up and went to the whiteboard at the front of the conference room. It was always better to visually walk a client through a problem. She drew a diagram of an airport terminal with X's to denote the client's store locations and a stick figure to illustrate a passenger. "Forgive my rudimentary drawings, but here's a typical passenger's journey through the airport. First they

check in here, get through security, and then rush to find their gate."
She showed the path of the passenger with dashed lines. "What's their
frame of mind here, just past security?"

"They're in a rush," James said. "Probably worried about making it
to the gate on time."

"Right. And here"–Vivien drew a dotted line to show the passenger's
movement–"when the passenger finally reaches their gate. How are
they feeling now?"

"Probably looking for something to eat or read before getting on
the plane," Harry said, drawing from his own travel experience.

"That's right. Now, let's take a look at what the stores are carrying,"
Vivien said. "Here are your stores just past the security gates. None
of them are performing well…what's in them? We've got postcards,
plush toys, perfume, jewelry, scarves, souvenirs, stationery, magazines,
drinks, etc. Harry, would you please pull up slide number twelve so we
can see the performance of each product category at these locations?"

"Knowing the frame of mind of the harried passenger, it's not
surprising to see that no one buys anything in the gift, souvenir, or toy
categories at this point in the terminal." She pointed out the terrible
sales numbers. "Now look at the stores close to the gates. Harry, slide
thirteen, please. The performance of these categories is significantly
better. Why? Think about it. The passenger has reached their gate;
what's their mind-set?"

The head of merchandising offered, "They're more relaxed and
open to shopping."

"Exactly. They have time to browse and that makes it the perfect
opportunity to guilt them into buying gifts and toys for their family."
Vivien drew a smiley face on the passenger stick figure. "But on page
eighteen of the presentation, it's evident that we don't have enough
of the right merchandise in those stores. In fact, we're experiencing
stock-outs. That translates to lost sales." She added a fistful of dollars
to the hand of the stick figure. "For a company that's losing money,

well, you can't afford to lose sales. You're leaving money on the table."

Vivien popped the cap back on the marker. James's eyes widened in comprehension.

"Today you've got working capital tied up in inventory in locations where it will never sell," Vivien summarized, "and you have a shortage of items in the places where they will sell. That's not investing your money in the most effective way. I also did a back-of-the-envelope calculation, and if we expand food and drink options at the right locations, we could increase average spend by six fifty per transaction, but Harry and his team can confirm that."

"My goodness, you've been looking at our business for just a few weeks, yet you've shared insights that have escaped us for years. I'm impressed," James marveled.

"You've pointed out things we've overlooked," the head of merchandising said "and given us a new way of thinking about our customer. This has been incredibly helpful. If we can increase the average transaction by six fifty that would be fantastic!"

Begrudgingly, Dick said, "I guess it's an interesting way of looking at the business."

Vivien sensed a shift in Dick's demeanor as she moved back to her seat. "It's more than just *interesting*, Dick, because these insights translate into specific actions. Actions that will improve your store performance and your revenues. Your business issues are fixable, and we can help you solve them. Harry and his team are among our best and brightest. They have many ideas on how to boost your sales. If we work together we can turn your business around. So, are you with us?"

The clients' heads nodded, and then Vivien put the icing on the cake to make sure the CFO was happy. "Dick, when we finish our work here, your shareholders will be amazed with the results you've delivered." She and her team would make him look like a superstar. For the first time the grumpy old CFO cracked a smile. "Now, that I'd like to see."

They finished their presentation and the meeting broke up, with the consultants heading to another conference room for a working session over lunch.

Harry pulled Vivien aside. "It's not like I haven't seen you in action before, but I can't believe how you won over Dick. You always deliver under pressure–thanks for your help."

Vivien smiled. "Harry, you're going to do a great job with this client. Just keep the team focused and moving forward."

After wolfing down lunch and strategizing with the team on additional analyses, Vivien and Jodie said good-bye to head to midtown. They took sanctuary from the brutal midday heat inside a well-air-conditioned taxi.

As they snaked their way through traffic, Jodie took full advantage of their time together. "I know you've been with SCP for ten years and worked with premier retail, apparel, and consumer brands. Mahesh mentioned you were the youngest person and the first woman of color to make partner in the firm's hundred-year history. That's incredible."

"Oh, um, thanks," Vivien said, shifting uncomfortably. A decade in consulting…was it because she enjoyed it so much or was she putting off what she really wanted to do?

"What's the one thing that has made you so successful?"

Vivien sat back, thinking. "Well, first of all I really love strategy consulting. I love solving problems and helping clients." She blew a stray hair from her face. "But I've definitely had some challenging experiences over the years. I learned that the most important quality for succeeding in business–scratch that; for succeeding in life–is resilience. No matter what you've accomplished in the past, your future success depends upon your ability to bounce back from adversity and recover your spirit, strength, and good humor quickly."

Soon enough the taxi pulled up in front of the Waldorf Astoria, the perfect location for a prestigious leadership conference that gathered Fortune 500 CEOs. Vivien rushed in with Jodie in tow and scanned the huge ballroom. An elegant-looking man with perfectly coiffed hair waved her over.

"Oh my gosh, is that David Burkhart IV, CEO of Burk's Department Stores?" Jodie whispered. "He's like the most respected executive in all of retail."

"Yup, that's Dave all right," Vivien said. "He's awesome." The admiration in her eyes was evident. "He's giving the keynote speech today, which I helped him write." For most of her career Vivien had toiled behind the scenes to help her clients shine, never seeking out the spotlight for herself.

Dave gave Vivien a warm hug and introduced himself to Jodie. "I can't thank you enough, Vivien. My speech is a hundred times better with your input. Hopefully I won't screw it up." He winked and then nudged her gently. "You should be the one up there giving speeches, Vivien. When are you going to go for it?" That was the million-dollar question, all right...

Dave knew her dreams all too well.

✳

It was ten years ago that Vivien first met Dave Burkhart. She'd been a twenty-four-year-old, new consultant with SCP assigned to work on a project with a partner named Gerard Needham. They were tasked with analyzing Burk's Department Stores' business and helping refine their strategy.

At a two-day off-site in rural Pennsylvania, they would present their work and secure the company's agreement on a go-forward plan. Attending the meeting at the fancy private country club were the board of directors, senior executive team, Gerard, and Vivien.

The first day of meetings went well, followed by cocktail hour. While everyone else went up to the bar, Vivien stayed downstairs preparing for the next day. Soon enough, she headed upstairs and walked into the bar to see everyone chatting, drinks in hand. Gerard hovered near Dave Burkhart, attempting to engage him in discussion. Vivien recalled vividly the masculine dark wood and requisite dead animal heads adorning the walls of the bar. She stepped up to the highly polished bar and politely ordered a drink. Then the oddest thing happened.

The bartender looked up and appeared startled. He said, "I'm sorry, miss, but you're not allowed in here." Vivien thought it was a joke, so she laughed and assured him she was of legal drinking age. She repeated her drink order. Again the bartender said, "Sorry, you can't be here."

Although she'd heard him clearly, she couldn't comprehend what he was saying. Sheepishly he pointed to a sign above the door that read, "Gentlemen Only."

Vivien said, "Are you kidding? That sign's not an antique?"

He shook his head and gave a shrug, as if to say, *Hey, lady, I don't agree with the sign, I'm just doing my job.*

Vivien was in shock. Of the nineteen people attending the off-site, she was the only female, the only minority, and evidently the only one not allowed in the bar. She did not like being the center of this kind of attention. By then, all conversation had ceased and nineteen pairs of expectant eyes (the bartender's included) were upon her.

Vivien glanced imploringly at Gerard, who avoided eye contact and gazed at the floor. She could have used his help, but he didn't want to leave his client. Apparently she'd have to fend for herself.

Finally she turned to the bartender and said, "Okay, here's what we'll do. I'd like for you to make my drink, please, which I will then take outside and enjoy. Thank you." Turning to the roomful of men, she said in a slightly louder voice, "Well, we've been cooped up all day, so I'm going outside to enjoy the sunset. If anyone would like to join me on the terrace, you are welcome." She forced a confident smile while she waited for a response. Any response. Crickets. She grabbed her drink and left the bar.

Her cheeks burned with anger and embarrassment as she walked down the long dark hallway. Her tense grip on her glass caused even the ice cubes to tremble with rage. Out on the sprawling stone terrace she reflected, *This is the nineties; how could this kind of treatment be possible?* She plopped down on a chaise lounge and in the absolute stillness had never felt more alone.

After a while she picked up her head and looked around. The scenery was gorgeous, with verdant trees, rolling green hills, and cotton-candy wisps of clouds floating across a magenta sky. *Just enjoy this moment of peace. You're in a gorgeous setting, plus you've got a cocktail.*

A deep voice behind her said, "Is this a private sunset or may I share it with you?" The voice belonged to Dave Burkhart.

"This is an equal-opportunity sunset, Dave," Vivien said. "Pull up a chair."

She felt grateful to him for coming outside to keep her company; it was an act of kindness she'd never forget. It was no mystery why he was so highly regarded.

Dave sat down and said, "I like the way you handled yourself back there, Vivien. I'm sorry about that silly rule. I promise to get them to change it."

All of a sudden it dawned on her...this was a golden opportunity. She had a private audience with the CEO. They soon became so engrossed in conversation Vivien barely noticed the procession of executives trickling out over the next fifteen minutes. Like lemmings, all the executives–and Gerard–left the bar to follow their leader and the great example he'd set.

The next day the group was discussing the new business strategy when Dave asked to take a break to confer with "his consultant." At that point Gerard (whom by then Vivien had nicknamed Gerard Don't Needham) eagerly ran over to the CEO. Dave waved him off, saying, "Actually, I wanted to consult with Vivien. Alone." Gerard backed off.

Dave said, "Based on our discussion last night about my leadership philosophy, do you still think these recommendations will work for Burk's?" Huh? This famous business leader was asking the opinion of a twenty-four-year-old consultant?

Vivien paused. "I would say no, Dave. You told me that rather than fire the bottom ten percent of employees, you want your top performers to mentor those at the bottom, lifting the performance of everyone in your company. I admire that approach and it makes your company unique. I think we need to rework our recommendations so they make sense for your culture."

Then she explained exactly how. Dave was a man who focused only on getting the best ideas, no matter the source. He thanked her and they concluded their tête-à-tête, but not before Vivien seized upon the opportunity to ask Dave to be her mentor. "You know what, Vivien? I'll bet we can mentor each other," Dave responded. What a class act.

✳

Dave Burkhart stood in front of a rapt audience, mesmerizing them with his (actually, Vivien's) powerful words. "The key to building an enduring enterprise isn't simply to try to survive…"

Vivien mouthed the words as Dave spoke them aloud. Her eyes sparkled with respect for the man.

"…but to thrive. That means valuing your customers, your employees, and your community. Yes, businesses are meant to make a profit, but who says they can't also make a positive impact in this world?"

The entire audience of CEOs gave Dave a standing ovation.

"Great speech, Vivien." Jodie grinned as if she had won the Powerball lottery. "I can see you up on that stage someday."

Vivien smiled and sighed. Someday. But first someone had to give her a chance.

✳

Shadow Day culminated in a meeting in the main conference room at the SCP office for a wrap-up and celebration. Vivien headed back to her office briefly while Jodie ran into Mahesh.

"You weren't kidding, Mahesh, I had a fantastic day with Vivien!"

He smiled. ""Of course. What were the highlights?"

Jodie filled him in. The rest of the room grew louder as partners and new hires traded anecdotes about their day. A giant spread of fruit and cheese platters sat on a side table along with bottles of chilled water. Vivien raced back in, pausing to grab some water and a slice of cheese. Mahesh, who was in charge of organizing the Shadow Day program, stood at the front of the room.

"Welcome back, everyone. I trust you all had a brilliant Shadow Day?"

The entire room hooted in approval. He called on a few people to share their experiences, some of which were highly entertaining. Everyone laughed heartily, including the current CEO and chairman of the firm, Arthur Hartmann.

Arthur had been boss and mentor to Vivien for the past decade, and she was one of the few allowed to call him "Art." Brilliant and elegant yet understated, Arthur spoke eloquently in a British accent and came across as a nerdy James Bond. He was the human equivalent of osetra caviar: posh and a little nutty.

Arthur stood up, welcomed the new hires, and spoke about their choice of career. "We help the most fascinating companies in the world and work alongside their people to implement ideas for improvement–it's a role of which you can be proud. Each of you was handpicked with the expectation that you'll not only make excellent strategy consultants but perhaps become great business leaders. Now I'd like to share one of my Shadow Day experiences with you, because it shows the power of potential, the potential in each of you."

The room grew silent as everyone's curiosity was piqued.

"One Shadow Day I was partnered with a new hire we now call TC. We were going to meet with Colgate-Palmolive's board of directors in the hopes of selling strategy work. As we waited in the lobby TC reviewed the presentation and asked some questions. I said, 'Don't worry about the details–I've got this covered. This meeting has been months in the making and I'm determined to close this sale today.' We were led into the mahogany-paneled boardroom with handcrafted Italian calfskin chairs. It was a classic beauty contest, where the client was choosing between us and two other consulting firms. I've given hundreds of presentations without incident. However, on that particular day something felt off. TC and I introduced ourselves to the board and I gave our pitch. Halfway through, I had trouble catching my breath and felt pain radiating down my left arm."

Arthur was universally adored at the firm and as his story unfolded concerned looks came across people's faces.

"I ignored the signs and pressed on–you know, stiff upper lip. Next thing I remember is waking up in a hospital bed with all sorts of tubes coming out of my body. I learned that I'd suffered a massive heart attack requiring emergency triple-bypass surgery. Perhaps even more shocking was what happened at that meeting. During the presentation, as I talked through some numbers, I said, 'Beg your pardon, I need some help.' TC whipped out her HP 12C and looked up, ready to help with any calculations. Steadying myself against the conference table, I gasped, 'Not that kind of help,' and collapsed onto the floor like a felled redwood. The entire board of directors sat stunned. Meanwhile TC jumped up and rushed to my aid. She started CPR immediately and in between breaths asked the chairman to call 911."

The audience was shocked. Who could imagine something like that on their Shadow Day?

"The paramedics arrived and got me stabilized and into the ambulance. TC asked which hospital they were headed to and called my assistant Laura. TC explained what happened and asked her to call my wife. Laura said, 'You sound like you're running.' TC said, 'I feel sick to my stomach, but I'm heading back up to the meeting anyway.' She returned to the boardroom, adjusted the focus on the projector, and said to the board, 'Let's continue.' All the executives marveled that TC could handle so dramatic a situation with that level of professionalism. She not only sailed through the rest of the presentation but single-handedly closed the sale. The chairman was so impressed he insisted that TC work on the project. Not only did she save my life that day, but she closed the biggest sale we'd had up to that point. Remember, this was her *second day* on the job. And that, ladies and gentlemen, is the story of how Vivien Lee got her nickname, 'the Closer,' or as we affectionately call her, 'TC.'" His eyes grew misty.

All heads turned in Vivien's direction and a beaming Jodie gave her a thumbs-up. Vivien's cheeks reddened as she waved off the applause. Janice, a partner seated next to her, playfully elbowed Vivien in the ribs.

Arthur wrapped up, "It also shows how anyone can make a significant contribution to the firm, even in their early days. You have a great opportunity in front of you, so please keep that in mind. Welcome to SCP." The meeting started to break up.

Vivien felt her cell phone buzzing. She looked at the area code of the caller and raced to her office to take the call. "Hello? Yes. Oh, really? Absolutely. I'm thrilled. Thank you." It was the shortest and most pivotal conversation of her entire career. Her heart was thumping. She stood at her desk murmuring, "Oh my god, oh my god," not noticing Mahesh standing in her doorway.

"Everything okay, TC?" His brow was furrowed.

Wide-eyed, Vivien said, "My life is about to change."

CHAPTER 2: THE GIANT STRIDE

Michael Jordan held her gaze, eyes gleaming with the ever-present confidence of a champion.

"What would you do, MJ? You'd go for it, right?" Vivien asked the basketball legend. "Of course you would."

Had she forgotten she was talking to the man whose athletic skill and balletic grace on the court soared above those of all others? The athlete who led his Chicago Bulls to three NBA titles and then retired at the apex of his career...only to take on the next challenge of playing professional baseball? Who does that? MJ was the guy who demanded the ball in a tied championship game with two seconds left on the shot clock. He took risks. He hungered to prove himself again and again. Vivien found inspiration in her sports hero's example. She was reflecting upon her own major decision when a rap on the door interrupted her consultation with the sports champion.

Mahesh stuck his head in the door, only to see his mentor gazing at a life-size cardboard cutout of Jordan. "Heading over soon, TC?"

Vivien turned to the cutout. "MJ, I think it's time you found a new home with Mahesh. Here you go, my friend." She picked up the cardboard image (autographed by the athlete himself) and handed it ceremoniously to an astonished Mahesh.

"Really? Wow, thanks so much!"

"He's all yours; take good care of MJ. I'll be done in ten minutes and meet you there," Vivien said.

Ten years' worth of memories took just thirty minutes to pack up. She was leaving many files behind and only needed five boxes for her books and most cherished items. Three nearly identical plaques hung on her wall. *Highest Sales...Highest Client Evaluation Scores... Outstanding Global Partner.* All with her name. Arthur said she was the only partner who'd ever won all three in one year. Vivien stacked the awards carefully and put them in the box with the rest, plus her sports memorabilia.

Arthur appeared at Vivien's office door as she finished packing up her boxes to be shipped. "Well, my dear, shall we wander over to the restaurant together? The cocktail hour will be starting shortly."

Suddenly she felt unsure. "Art, I've loved every minute of working here. Am I making the right choice, trying something I've never even done before?"

His eyes twinkled. "Vivien, you're destined to do great things, about that I have no doubt. But if you want to achieve your dreams you must take a chance. Nothing will happen if you do not try. I know it's daunting, but I believe in you."

Vivien smoothed her long glossy black hair and adjusted her summer-weight Armani suit. With a sigh she switched off the lights and walked out of the SCP offices for the last time. The evening air felt balmy, the city's normal humidity taking a break for the night. Her life had been on fast-forward in the two weeks since she'd made her big decision. She just needed a moment to take it all in. Arthur seemed to sense her pensive mood and they strolled together in silence.

*

The host at the posh restaurant directed them to the private party room, a large glass-enclosed area overlooking the main part of the restaurant. Elegant jazz music played on a piano in the background combined with the sound of clinking glasses. This partners' dinner was a classy affair but tinged with sadness as they were saying farewell.

Vivien and Arthur joined the group already partaking of the cocktails and hors d'oeuvres. A favorite colleague, Brad, rushed over to give her a hug. A big bear of a man with a thunderous laugh, he was always ready with a joke or clever retort.

"TC, you've come a long way since I recruited you from Wharton."

"Gosh, that was ages ago, Brad."

"Where did the time go?" Brad said, then brightened up. "Well, at least now I can share my favorite TC story, about a certain infamous poker game."

Joining them, Mahesh said, "Don't think I've heard that one."

Brad's eyes brightened. "It was TC's first partners' meeting. As usual that night, we had our after-dinner poker game with a small group. Two newly promoted partners joined us for the game, TC and Miles Zabriskie. Miles, overconfident as usual, started trash-talking about how he intended to wipe us all out. TC had never played before but was willing to try."

Vivien glanced around to see the other partners laughing and enjoying themselves. Waiters in crisply starched uniforms moved silently in the background, making sure cocktail glasses were filled and appetizers offered freely.

Brad continued, "I briefly explained the rules of poker and the value of the different hands. TC jotted them down on a cocktail napkin and said, 'All right, I'm ready.' As the game progressed she kept a watchful eye on everyone, as if she were making detailed mental notes. I'm sure you've seen her do that before."

Mahesh and Arthur nodded.

"I figured out later that TC was analyzing everyone's 'tells.' She was learning, based on those tics, who had a good hand or not. At the end of the evening a huge pile of money sat in the middle of the table. It was down to the last hand with two players remaining–TC and Miles. We all know how Miles likes to one-up TC, so it was a tense moment." Brad lowered his voice even though Miles, who stood at the opposite end of the room, couldn't possibly hear him. "Miles sniffed and placed his bet. TC looked at her cards and said solemnly, 'I'll see your fifty, Miles, and I'll raise you everything I've got. That's called "going all in," isn't it, Brad?"'

Arthur interjected, "Ahh, yes. I remember saying, 'TC, that's a bloody boatload of cash. You sure you want to do that?'"

Eyes wide, Mahesh said, "She bet it all?"

Brad smirked. "TC said, 'Just a sec,' and looked at her cocktail napkin notes, then back at her cards. Then she said, 'Absolutely.' Miles sat there adjusting his glasses, his eyes moving between TC and the mountain of money. Finally he said, 'Well, I've already won plenty tonight and I want to keep my money. I'm out.' He folded."

"So TC won?" said Mahesh.

"The entire lot! I said, 'TC, you must have had a killer hand.' She just gave me a little wink as she raked in the loot. Later, at the bar, I bugged TC to tell me what cards she had. She whispered, 'Okay, it was a pair of twos. I figured if I showed a lot of confidence Miles would fold, so I went for it.' 'What? You were bluffing?' I couldn't believe it. TC told me I had to keep it a secret, but now that she's leaving the firm I can finally tell the story. Ha ha!" Brad gave Vivien a hearty slap on the shoulder.

Mahesh stole a glance at Miles, who was still parked in a corner across the room checking emails on his smartphone as the four of them cracked up.

Arthur put his arm gently around Vivien's shoulder. "We have so many fond memories of you, my dear. You know you'll be missed terribly."

Since day one Vivien had made something clear to Arthur–her dream was to someday run a business. Over the years Arthur had ensured that she got the experience and developed the skills to become a well-rounded executive. Now that Vivien was making her big move, her mentor had some wisdom to impart.

"I've always known you to be ethical, kind, and trusting, TC. But corporate America is different–the politics can be treacherous, and I'm afraid that could be a blind spot for you."

"All right, Art, I promise to be careful. Thanks for the advice."

One of the smartest and most straight-talking SCP partners, Pete, chimed in and put it bluntly. "Listen, TC, I've been in three senior executive positions where despite doing a great job I got shoved aside or fired because of internal politics. It's an old boys' club out there, and sometimes even if you *are* an old boy you're still not in the club!"

Vivien and the others cackled.

Pete cautioned, "Be prepared to get kicked in the ass when you least expect it. You're too trusting of other people. You think everyone is good at heart. I think you're gonna be shocked at how nasty people can be."

"Okay, Pete," Vivien replied. "Anything else?"

"On the bright side, you're great under pressure. A lot of people in industry can't think as fast as you and can't make good decisions quickly. That'll be an advantage for you."

Mahesh pulled Vivien aside for a quiet chat. "After ten years in consulting you're finally going after your dream. I'm so excited for you. But are you ready for all the change? Moving to a new city, new industry, new company–that's got to be unnerving."

"It is a lot to take in, Mahesh," she said. "I'm sure it'll be tough, but hopefully fun, as well. By the way, would you please take Jodie under your wing and mentor her?"

"Like you've done for me and so many others? Of course. I've learned from you what it means to be a great coach. I've also learned from you how to be on your game. At any moment you could ask me how I'd solve a problem, so I felt like my brain had to be firing on all cylinders at all times. It was great training, but exhausting!" Mahesh laughed, then started to tear up. "I'm really going to miss you, TC." Vivien hugged him.

She made her way around the room to say a few words of appreciation to every partner, coming at last to the corner where Miles Zabriskie stood waiting.

Miles was an intelligent man but had an irrepressible need to be the smartest person in the room. Hence his annoying habit of incorrectly correcting people. An undercurrent of competitiveness had always run between them, and Vivien guessed that Miles felt gleeful about her departure. His straight hair was precisely parted and a crisp pocket square peeked out from his seersucker suit. His round, solemn face was adorned with pursed lips, as was typical for him.

"Hi there, Miles."

"Vivien." He was the only person in the firm who refused to use her nickname. Miles adjusted his round wire-rimmed glasses by pushing them up at the bridge of the nose with his middle finger. Was this a furtive insult or was he doing it unawares? "Enjoying the party in your honor?"

"Sure, it's been fun listening to the anecdotes people are sharing. I'd forgotten so many."

"Yes, a couple of the *antidotes* were quite amusing."

Ugh, there he goes again.

"It's going to be so different for you out there, Vivien. Here you're popular, admired, and well-known, but once you enter a new company you'll be starting from scratch. I can't believe you're willing to walk away from all this." The corners of his mouth turned up a little. "You're certainly in for a change."

"I understand that, Miles. I don't expect it to be easy."

He gave a little snort. "You know, out there in the real world as a female senior executive you're always going to have people who don't like you. Plus you've picked an industry that isn't welcoming of women or outsiders. That makes the risk of failure even higher."

Jeez, Miles was such a downer, but Vivien had to admit there was a grain of truth to what he said. "Well, I'm not out to win any popularity contests. I just want to be respected for what I can accomplish."

"You sound pretty confident, Vivien."

"I think you have to put yourself in situations outside of your comfort zone. That's what builds confidence, Miles. You have to take risks if you want to succeed. Anyway, I'm sure I'll make plenty of mistakes along the way."

Miles scoffed, "What, the great Vivien Lee is actually showing vulnerability?"

Vivien sighed, "Oh, Miles, a person can show strength and be vulnerable at the same time, can't they?" Normally a kindhearted person, Vivien found it challenging to be nice to Miles.

"Yeah. Well, good luck. I'll be rooting for you," he said dryly. His eyes drifted away.

Before Vivien could question his sincerity, their conversation was mercifully cut short. Arthur clinked his wine glass lightly with his fork, indicating that it was time for dinner. Vivien moved to the other side of the room and took a seat among friendlies. She savored the delicious meal, fine wine, and scintillating conversation. Finally, the dessert course came, and that meant it was time for Arthur's toast. Her separation from the firm was now official and Vivien felt her stomach tense up. Was she really leaving behind all these great people and the reputation she'd worked so hard to build?

Arthur stood up. "As you all know, TC is leaving the firm to embark on a new adventure and go after her dream of running a business. Over the years we've all worked closely with TC and have become familiar with her endearing quirks: her impatience, which occasionally lands her in hot water; her stubbornness, which can be an asset we call perseverance; and her virtue, which can make it difficult for her to see it lacking in others. Despite her many successes, TC has always maintained her humility and has made success look so easy. But most importantly, she's made a positive impact on so many of us in the firm, and for that I am truly grateful." Arthur turned to Vivien and said, "Care to say a few words, my dear?"

Vivien smiled appreciatively and stood up. "I've been reflecting upon my time here at the firm and all the experiences we've shared.

I've had the great fortune of learning from each of you and having the gift of your friendship. For a lot of people what they do is just a job, the source of a paycheck. Yet, I find myself getting quite sentimental about leaving this place and the people here. This job has meant so much more than a paycheck; it's been a source of pride. I'm proud of the work we've done and how well we work together. A piece of advice my father has always given me is 'Be great and be good.' To me that means having the confidence to do your best and conducting yourself with honor. And that brings me to Arthur..."

Arthur looked up, surprised to hear his full name.

"It's been a true pleasure and privilege to work with someone with such a brilliant mind, keen wit, and noble principles. Not only have I learned so much about business from you, but you taught me about being a better person. Knowing all of you fine people has been a huge factor in shaping the person I am today and I can't thank you enough. Cheers to you."

The sound of clinking glasses brought the dinner to a close, though some stayed on.

Amid parting hugs and a few tears Vivien said her good-byes. She was leaving behind a hard-earned legacy as the Closer. She was an avid scuba diver and she was about to take what in diving terms was called a giant stride, where a diver takes a huge step forward and leaps off the boat. Vivien was taking a giant stride into the unknown. Exhausted and emotionally spent, she gave a wave as she walked out.

✳

Back inside the restaurant, her former colleagues huddled together.

"I'm excited for her, but also nervous. How do you think our friend will fare out there?" Mahesh asked as he stood near Arthur and Janice.

Janice grinned. "TC's a rebel; the guys in her new company aren't going to know what hit 'em. She's bright, hardworking, and has the determination of a pit bull."

Mahesh giggled, "You mean she's a bit stubborn?"

"Yes," Janice said, "but that's what helps her succeed. She's strong but also one of the nicest, most honorable people I know."

"Like a nun with a switchblade, eh?" Arthur laughed. "As long as she stays true to herself and trusts her instincts, I'm sure she'll be just fine."

CHAPTER 3: ON YOUR MARK, GET SET

In typical New York fashion, the predawn mechanical grinding of the garbage trucks smashing the city's refuse woke Vivien. It was Saturday morning and construction work outside her Murray Hill apartment building added jackhammering to the cacophony of city sounds.

Vivien snuggled up to her fiancé, Clay. She kissed him and whispered, "I'll be back in a couple of hours, honey." Half-asleep, he gave her a quick peck and opened one eye. "Okay, babe, see you soon. Hey, don't forget I head off to London tonight." He turned onto his side and resumed snoring. They'd been up most of the night packing up her apartment. Vivien rolled out of her warm bed and moved quickly across the cool hardwood floors in bare feet, navigating around the stacks of boxes and sports equipment. After splashing some cool water on her face and doing her daily fifty push-ups and fifty curl-ups, she dressed for her run.

Struggling to pull her racer-back sports bra over her head and shoulders, she wondered why no one had created a better design. Any physically active woman owned multiple sports bras and continued to purchase them over time, so there was a built-in market. It was a huge oversight that while many athletic apparel companies made sports bras, they were universally poorly designed. Hmm, maybe that presented an opportunity she could capitalize on.

Before heading out the door she glanced back at Clay. She was still incredulous that they were engaged.

She'd met Clayton Finch three years earlier at a Wharton/Harvard MBA alumni mixer. He breezed into the room as if he had just come from a photo shoot for *GQ* magazine–tall, golden blond, strong jawed, with sparkling blue eyes. He surveyed the room and fixed his gaze on Vivien. Flustered, Vivien averted her eyes and turned to her friends. Clay walked directly over, introduced himself, and asked her out. Despite his abundant confidence and handsome looks, she didn't bite thinking, *Anyone who looks that good probably doesn't try too hard.* But Clay pursued her with the intensity of a hungry cheetah stalking a gazelle, sending her a love sonnet and bouquet of flowers every week. He wasn't necessarily her type and his Boston accent was a bit jarring, but after several romantic meals together she succumbed to his charm.

Boyfriend Résumé on Clay
Name: Clayton Finch
Description: Vivien's boyfriend of nearly three years who proposed on Valentine's Day with a five carat diamond ring.
Occupation: Investment banker for a prestigious firm.
Education: Undergrad in political science from Brown University and a Harvard MBA.
Personal Traits: Tall, gorgeous, and self-assured. Great basketball player. Extremely close with his mother. Always has redundant systems, especially for his favorite things, like shoes, clothes, and cufflinks.
Personal Life: Prior to Vivien his former flame was Elizabeth Atwood, a coanchor for a morning news program. Clay comes from the storied Finch family of Boston, who made their fortune running Finch Investments.

One of Vivien's favorite running paths snaked up along the West Side Highway, which was where she usually ran with her best friend, Coop. After making a quick call to let him know she'd be at his place in fifteen minutes, she set out.

Stepping off the elevator and into the white marble lobby of her building, Vivien was greeted by the ever-cheerful doorman sitting at his post like a king on his throne, surveying his domain. "Good morning, Abraham. What's going on this time?" She motioned outdoors.

"Good morning, Vivien. Today? Either the water pipes or Con Ed." A frown showed his irritation at the regular sight of a repair crew. He straightened his spotless, pressed uniform.

Vivien said good-bye and ran at a good warm-up pace across town. The early morning sun shone fiercely, but the summer air still felt comfortably cool.

Coop lived in a brick apartment building in Chelsea sandwiched between a Citarella gourmet market and a J Crew, covering all the essentials for a gay man. He was nowhere to be seen so she asked his doorman to buzz him.

Coop answered the intercom somewhat sluggishly–never a good sign.

"Hey, Coop, I'm here and ready to roll," she said.

"Okay, sweetie. I'll be down in two minutes."

Twenty minutes later Coop, always lovable but never punctual, arrived in the lobby looking sporty and ready to run. Coop hadn't been on time for anything since their undergraduate days at Cornell. As they progressed toward the running path Coop said reflectively, "Sweetie, do you realize how long we've been running together? What am I going to do now that you're moving?"

Vivien and Coop had been running buddies in college and continued after graduation when they both took jobs in Manhattan. They'd kept up their Saturday morning runs while attending business school together at Wharton and since graduating. In fact, the only break they'd ever taken was to accommodate the time Vivien needed to rehab her knee. Barring illness or travel they rarely missed a run together, as it was their special time to share what was going on in their lives.

Friend Résumé on Coop
Name: Gary Edward Cooper, or "Coop" for short. Bonded instantly with Vivien over their movie star names.
Occupation: Certified public accountant for a large accounting firm; specializes in forensic accounting.
Education: Undergrad in accounting and economics from Cornell University, MBA from the Wharton School.
Personal Traits: Fun-loving, joyful, and universally well liked. Height: five foot nine. Honest. Youthful looking, but tends to lie about his age and does so inconsistently, so even his best friends get tripped up when asked the age of their friend. Collects and disperses inspirational quotes.
Personal Life: Cautious, exhibits sound judgment in all areas... except his love life. Maintained a disastrous dating track record over the years and has not dated anyone seriously in ages.

That bright August morning Coop and Vivien kept up a steady pace on the trail along the West Side Highway. "I'm on pins and needles about the promotion council meeting this week," Coop said. "If I don't make partner this time I'll just die." He had worked for the same accounting firm since graduating from Wharton and was betting everything on making partner.

"Are you getting some signs it'll happen this time?" Vivien said, trying to mask her concern.

"Last year when I was finally put up for partner my boss said, 'Don't worry, you're a shoo-in, Coop.' When I didn't get the promotion I was devastated. Remember that? My boss said I should just be patient. 'Keep on doing what you're doing and it will happen for you,' was his advice."

"You deserve to be made partner, Coop. You've earned it a few times over by now. *Ten years* at the same accounting firm–you've sold more work, managed more project revenue than anyone. Lead forensic accountant on every high-profile account. I can't imagine why they wouldn't promote you. But just in case, you might want to start looking around at other opportunities. You have too much talent to be stuck at a place that doesn't value you." Did Coop's sexual orientation have anything to do with his being held back? That accounting firm was so conservative...if that was why he was being passed over, it would not likely change with time.

The slight breeze off the water felt good and despite the odor from the Dumpsters containing the city's marinating trash, it was a pleasant run. They worked up to a good pace.

"Yeah, you're right, you're right," Coop said, breathing hard. "But I really like the firm and most of the people, even though it can be pretty stodgy. I'm leading a great team. People I care about are depending on me. I'd like to stick it out."

That was his tactical error. He wasn't making the partners sweat even a bit. To them Coop seemed like a lifer, and why should they hurry up and promote someone who was going to stick around anyway? No, their strategy made good business sense. String Coop along and squeeze better performance out of him, while not giving him what he deserved because he was willing to wait. Vivien knew sometimes the only way to move up in a firm is to threaten to move out, but that lesson seemed lost on her friend.

Coop slowed his pace, looked over at Vivien tenderly, and threw his arms around her, letting out a huge sigh. "Oh, sweetie, I'm going to miss you so much. This is happening too fast. I can't believe you're leaving me to move to Oregon, of all places!"

"Don't worry, Coop. You'll always be in my life. It's weird, but it's hard for me to believe this is happening, too."

"Promise me you'll come back so we can go see Hugh Jackman on Broadway–rumor is he's previewing a one-man show sometime soon," Coop said.

Vivien laughed, "Come on, would I miss a chance to see Hugh

Jackman?"

It wasn't an easy call to leave her father, her friends, and the city she loved, but she had put a great deal of consideration into this decision. Vivien was closing in on the age her mother had been when she died, and that brought home the lesson that life was short and unpredictable. A sense of urgency compelled Vivien to go after her dreams.

After their run, they stopped at their favorite breakfast spot. She was going to miss her life in New York. Was she crazy, moving to Portland, Oregon, for her career?

"And how's the fiancé handling your big move? Is he going to join you?" Coop said.

"You know Clay, he's a city boy. I can't say he's thrilled about Oregon. The trip down to my place from his Upper East Side apartment is a taxing enough journey for him."

"But you're going to be married soon, sweetie. Married couples live together, you know."

"Well, since this is so new we agreed to commute on weekends for the first six months or so, then figure out where to live. Things are going well for Clay at his banking firm and I think he'd like to put in a few more years there. Anyway, I'll have to be back here a lot to plan the wedding."

Coop took a sip of orange juice. "You are so much braver than I am, moving across the country to a city where you don't know a soul. I could never do that."

Vivien toyed with her bagel, smoothing the layer of cream cheese. "Hopefully I'll make some new friends. With Clay staying back here I'll pretty much be on my own. But we'll make it work somehow." Vivien tried to sound convincing.

CHAPTER 4: THE CEILING SMASHERS

That evening Vivien knocked on the door of her friend Sofia's Upper West Side apartment and heard Grace's voice saying, "It must be Vivien, I'll get it!" The door swung open and Grace gave Vivien a big hug. "Come on in. Sofia's in the kitchen talking to her parents and julienning carrots. I don't know how she does it so fast. I'd have lost a limb by now."

Vivien laughed, knowing the truth of that statement. A modern sofa the color of espresso faced a large picture window looking out on the New York skyline. The city lights sparkled all the way down Broadway. Hard to believe she wouldn't be seeing that view regularly anymore. Vivien set her purse down on the sofa and walked over to the granite counter separating the kitchen from the living room. She sat down on one of the bar stools and blew a kiss to Sofia, who waved from the kitchen. The consummate multitasker, Sofia was preparing dinner while having a phone conversation with her parents via her Bluetooth headset. She moved effortlessly from English to Spanish to French and around again. With surgical skill, Sofia thrust a fork into the shell of a jumbo shrimp to remove it and then swiftly deveined it. Grace looked on in awe and then poured a glass of champagne for Vivien. She took the stool beside her friend.

<u>Friend Résumé on Grace</u>

Name: Grace King

Occupation: Brand strategist, CMO.

Education: Undergraduate degree from Northwestern University in mechanical engineering, MBA from Wharton.

Personal Traits: Tall, blonde Midwesterner with a calm personality, but capable of fighting fiercely when needed. Played basketball with Vivien on the intramural team at B-school. Owns a well-stocked toolbox and can fix just about any piece of broken machinery. An exceptional brand expert. Confident in her capabilities.

Personal Life: Wants to get married and have a family, but just too busy to date.

"Cheers, Vivien. I think it's so cool that you are doing this and I know you're going to do a fantastic job. How are you feeling about it all?"

They clinked glasses.

"I'm excited…and nervous. Not really sure what to expect."

Grace grabbed a cracker off the cheese board and spread a generous amount of brie on it. "Well, you'll be the only senior woman in a male-dominated company in a male-dominated industry. Not exactly a cakewalk. And, oh, by the way, you'll have a lot of people watching you."

"Mmm-hmm." Vivien munched on a handful of Marcona almonds.

"But you know that the Ceiling Smashers are here to support you, especially me and Andi. Sofia is resisting your move to Portland, but she'll come around. So don't be shy about asking any of us for help. That's the reason we started the group in the first place, right?"

*

The Ceiling Smashers was a secret society the four friends had founded during their first year as MBA students at Wharton. Vivien had envisioned that the Ceiling Smashers would serve as a personal board of directors for its network of talented women in their future careers. The Smashers were optimists but pragmatic; they knew there would be times when they'd need each other for counsel, support, and empathy. Vivien incorporated her father's advice, "Be great and be good" into her founding philosophy for the Smashers: their aim would be not only to achieve success, but to motivate others by conducting themselves with honor. Membership was kept to twenty women, a mix of MBAs and women from other University of Pennsylvania graduate schools. Every other month they'd get together for dinner in New York and would hold strategizing conference calls whenever a member needed focused advice to solve a problem.

*

Having wrapped up her call and marinated the shrimp, Sofia joined her friends at the counter. The champagne glass with the red lipstick mark belonged to her. She was a stylish, graceful woman who was always camera ready. The soft halogen lights above the counter shone on Sofia's luminous skin, which was the color of rich caramel and seemed to match her inner glow.

"Oh, Vivi, we're going to miss you so much. I hate to think of you being so far away and all on your own in Portland. Why couldn't you just find a good job here in New York?"

"I know, I'll miss you guys. But at least I'll still get to see you every day on TV, Sofia."

Friend Résumé on Sofia

Name: Sofia LaForte

Occupation: Financial analyst/reporter on CNBC.

Education: Tulane undergrad degree in mathematics with a minor in romance languages (speaks five languages fluently), MBA from Wharton's Lauder Institute international program.

Personal Traits: An excellent head for figures, but also an artistic soul. Her love of languages stems from her half-French, half-Nigerian jazz musician father and Spanish mother, a documentary film maker. Sophisticated and worldly. Possesses a maturity beyond her years. Has a knack for getting inside people's heads.

Personal Life: States adamantly that she has no interest in marriage and prefers to focus on her career. Not dating anyone currently.

Sofia, who was adept at reading people and understanding politics, offered her friend some sage advice. "I don't want you to go, but I do want to see you succeed. You will need to quickly identify key people you can trust at multiple levels in the organization. I'm sure that after a brief honeymoon period you'll be fighting some political battles and will need people who support you and what you're doing."

"Yes, I'll do that, Sofia. First I'll need to figure out whom I can trust." Vivien took a sip from her glass.

Grace nodded and stuffed more cheese and crackers into her mouth.

"Keep in mind, Vivi, some of the superstars of the company are going to be intimidated by you. They've probably never worked with someone with your brains and experience. You're bringing new approaches that will shake things up. The headline is these folks are going to feel threatened and when people feel threatened they close their circle to protect those who belong."

Vivien considered what Sofia had told her. "So what you're saying is just focusing on the work isn't going to be enough to make me successful in this role."

"Exactly. Don't make the same mistake that so many women do. Don't just keep your head down, do great work, and expect that to be enough to succeed. You're in a highly visible role. It's a potentially vulnerable situation, so cultivating strong relationships is key."

"Have I ever *not* built strong relationships?"

"True, but watch your back regarding Charl Davis, the guy you're replacing, especially since he'll be reporting to you. I can't imagine the blow to that guy's ego." Sofia moved back into the kitchen to toss the salad.

Grace paused before slicing a hard cheese. "Do you think you'll be able to trust this guy Charl and form a bond with him? If that's not possible then you're going to have to clear the decks. Keeping someone around who wants to put a knife in your back is a bad idea." She gestured with the cheese knife for effect. "You always expect the best from people, Vivi, and that could be dangerous."

Sofia piped up. "I almost hate to say this, but you've also got to be careful of any underhanded women who appear to welcome you while they really see another female as competition. You know what I'm talking about. Even more so in the sports industry; the few women there may see things as a zero-sum game where they need to eliminate any talented women so they can keep moving up." Sofia looked at her watch, annoyed. "And where in the world is our friend Andi?"

As if on cue there was a crashing sound followed by a forceful knock at the door. Grace ran to answer it. Andi stood on crutches, trying to maintain her balance, while her purse and computer bag lay in a heap on the floor. She was a pretty, petite brunette with a muscular build. While Andi was extremely athletic, she was also a terrible klutz. Grace grabbed her friend's belongings off the floor and stepped back to take a look. "Oh my gosh, Andi, what happened to you this time?"

Friend Résumé on Andi

Name: Andrea Andiamo, Andi for short.

Occupation: Wall Street investment banker and one of the top performers at Goldman Sachs.

Education: UC Berkeley undergrad degree in microbiology, MBA from Wharton.

Personal Traits: Direct and straightforward almost to a fault. Grew up with four older brothers and developed a love of sports, an intense competitiveness, and a natural ease in dealing with men. Does not suffer fools gladly, particularly long-winded fools. Her reply to a lengthy voice mail might sound like, "Twelve basis points; yes, I agree; Tuesday's good; Geneva; and thirty-five percent."

Personal Life: Seven years ago Andi married an Italian man, Luca, whom she happened to meet in line at a Starbucks. He has an MBA, MD, and PhD, and his job is thinking up questions for Educational Testing Service in Princeton, New Jersey. They have twin three-year-old boys, Antonio and Francesco.

A look of chagrin came across Andi's face and her hazel eyes moved down to her foot. In her alto, slightly gravelly voice reminiscent of Lauren Bacall, she said, "Antonio and Francesco were playing around with a ten-pound dumbbell this morning and tossed it right onto my foot. I've got broken bones in three places. Can you believe this?" Despite her pain Andi gave a hearty laugh.

Vivien ran over to greet Andi. She set up a comfortable seat on the sofa and propped her friend's foot up on a pillow. "I swear, Andi, next to you even I look like Darci Kistler!"

Andi chuckled. "A ballerina I'm not."

Vivien laughed. "Other than that, how are the boys doing?"

"Just great. They're a lot more fun now that they're talking so much. Having a family is wonderful, but twins are just exhausting."

"I hear that," Grace said, handing her some champagne.

Sofia came over and gave Andi a small plate of snacks. She returned to the kitchen to pop dinner in the oven. Meanwhile Vivien set the dining table.

"Oh god, am I dreading tomorrow," Andi groaned. "A colleague of Luca's at ETS is having a brunch party. His coworkers are okay, but the party conversation usually devolves into testing out new SAT or MCAT questions on the guests. Great way to clear a room. Not how I want to spend my Sunday morning. Oh well." Andi took a drink and turned to face her friend. "Listen, Vivien, I've been thinking. You're about to encroach upon the last bastion of male territory, the sports industry. Some guys might be open to a bright woman with great ideas, but I'll bet a lot of them will resent it and try to protect their turf."

"I know." Vivien leaned up against the dining table. "But I have a some great ideas."

"Sure you do. But you not only have to show them you bring value, you also have to win them over. Don't overwhelm them with all your great ideas at once. That'll just freak 'em out. Get buy-in to a few ideas first. Move fast to get some points on the board with your business and get results. If you show them you can get the W, they'll want you on their team." Andi hungrily attacked her plate of cheese and crackers. She was always talking in sports speak, but Vivien knew a "W" was a win. "You've got to build up trust with these folks–and that goes both ways. You can't work with people you don't trust. Right?"

Andi had faced similar challenges building her career in the testosterone-filled banking industry, so Vivien recognized that her friend was sharing smart advice. "Yes, we were just talking about all the things I need to do in my new role."

Grace said, "Did I tell you I know the head of marketing you'll be working with, Steele Hamilton? We were at Kraft Foods together years ago. What a weasel. I can't believe he landed such a primo job."

"What was your experience like with him?" Vivien said.

"Well, one day we were in a Cheese Spread Team meeting–"

Andi snorted some champagne out of her nose. "Hang on, are you kidding? You had something called a 'Cheese Spread Team meeting'?" Sofia helped clean up her friend and then ushered everyone over to the table for dinner.

"Yes, Andi," Grace said patiently as she served the salad. "We were trying to come up with new brand-positioning concepts. I wanted to make the packaging more microwave friendly. Steele and I had a heated debate about changing the packaging and it got to the point where he was literally shouting at me. He got quite nasty. I finally stood up and said, 'Folks, let's put this into perspective. We're not talking about curing cancer here, we're talking about Cheez Whiz.' The team had a good laugh and then agreed with my idea. After the meeting Steele said, 'You know what your problem is, Grace? You think you're better than you really are.'" Grace held the salad tongs like a dagger, mimicking Steele's pointed finger.

"Asshole," Andi said, digging into her salad.

"Yeah. I told him, 'Steele, the idea I shared is exactly what's needed to move this brand forward. And I'm not sure what you're referring to as a 'problem.' I'd rather have more confidence in myself than think I'm only half as good.'"

"Sounds like he was threatened by you," Sofia observed. She hustled back into the kitchen to retrieve the main course and veggies.

"Well, watch out for him, Vivi. Steele has a high opinion of himself and doesn't know when to quit. He kept pestering me about the packaging change until one day I said, 'Steele, back off. I'm not going to argue with you anymore about pasteurized, processed cheese spread! And, oh, by the way, sales are up two hundred sixty percent since we changed the packaging.'" Grace smiled and shrugged her shoulders proudly.

"Good for you, Grace." Vivien high-fived her friend. "You've come a long way. From cheese spread victor to the chief marketing officer who led the revival of the Burberry brand. What a success."

"What about you, Vivi? You've never had anything but success," Grace said, tilting her head up. "As a matter of fact, in all the years I've known you I can't think of a single time you've failed at something."

Vivien held up her hand. "Oh, don't be silly, I'm sure that's not true."

"Actually, it is true," Sofia said. "You've never failed."

Andi nodded in agreement while she chewed.

"Guys, I know you're worried about me but this is my big break." Vivien exhaled. "On the one hand, I've never run a business before, so who knows if I can even do it. But on the other hand, if I don't go for it I'll always regret it."

The topic of failure was only making her feel anxious, so Vivien quickly changed the subject. Throughout the rest of the dinner the four women shared memories and lots of laughs. Andi, Grace, and Sofia were doing their best to delay the inevitable good-bye.

"Ahh, this is so civilized. Best friends, wonderful food, and excellent wine. I'm so relaxed." Grace sighed.

"Now that you've started your sabbatical from work, are you going to tell us how you plan on spending your free time?" Sofia's investigative reporting skills were evident.

"After all the grueling European travel and long hours I'm just going to take a year off and enjoy myself," Grace said.

Vivien raised an eyebrow. Grace King was not one to sit idle.

"And I'm working on a book about branding."

"Oh, that sounds great!" Andi said in an unusually supportive tone. "With Vivien off on her new adventure and Grace working on a business book, I should figure out what I want to do next. I've about had enough of I-banking."

"What about me?" Sofia said.

"You're already famous and on CNBC every day interviewing business moguls. What more could you want?" Vivien teased.

"Love," she said. "Just not marriage." Her friends chuckled. "And Clay, he's okay with traveling to Portland every other weekend?"

"Honestly, I thought we'd live in New York forever. I was this close to moving in with Clay." Vivien squinted through pinched fingers. "Never considered relocating until this opportunity came along. But Clay seems fine with it…probably because he thinks I'll be back here in a year's time."

"Nice. How supportive." Andi huffed.

Grace said, "Oh, Vivi, our regular Friday night gatherings won't be the same without you. But you'll be three hours behind so at least we can Skype with you every week."

"Sounds like a plan. Thanks for the fantastic dinner, Sofia."

Over a final glass of wine, her evening with the founders of the Ceiling Smashers came to a heartrending end. Sofia's eyes filled with tears as she hugged Vivien. Andi gripped her in an embrace so strong Vivien felt certain she heard a couple of her vertebrae crack. After Grace gave her a hug she said, "Remember, we're here for you." Vivien was starting to get choked up. Saying good-bye to her Smasher friends was harder than she'd ever expected. This new job had damn well better be worth it.

✳

Her final good-bye was, of course, the most difficult.

As per their usual Sunday morning ritual, Vivien visited her father's apartment in Kips Bay for brunch; later the two of them would hop a cab across town to hit balls at the Chelsea Piers driving range. Her father's apartment was in the same building as his thriving dental practice. As Vivien pushed the buzzer she realized with great sadness that this would be the first time they'd be separated by so many miles. She balanced the weight of her Sunday golf bag across both shoulders.

"Hi, Dad!"

"Come on up, Vivi!" Her father's voice was always cheerful and melodic. He threw open the door and gave her a big smile, revealing perfect white teeth. "Ahh, my darling daughter." Tall for a Korean man, Dr. Lee stood eye to eye with Vivien as they hugged. His black hair was graying at the temples but he was still as vibrant and handsome as ever.

They had their typical brunch conversation about sports, politics, and favorite recent meals. Vivien noticed her father avoided any talk about her impending move, trying to keep things light. Before they headed out to the range he pressed a package into her hands.

"What's this?"

"A six-month supply of toothbrushes, tongue scrapers, and floss. Now, don't forget your oral hygiene when you're out in Oregon!" He wagged a finger and winked. "These extra-soft toothbrushes are gentler on the gums, really excellent."

"Oh, Dad. Thanks." Vivien chuckled softly and placed the package in her golf bag.

*

Checking in at the driving range, Dr. Lee ordered two $50 golf cards. He spoke with the diction of someone raised in Connecticut, belying the years of hard work it had taken to perfect his English. Determination was a trait her father had most certainly passed on to his daughter.

"Wow, that's like two hundred balls each, Dad! We're going to be here awhile."

"Yes, but I want to test out my new driver. Look at this, isn't it gorgeous?" He beamed as if he were showing off a newborn.

After hitting one hundred balls each, they took a breather and sat sipping cool water in the shade. Dr. Lee looked out into the distance and, as if recalling his own journey from being a boy in South Korea to leading a successful life in America, he spoke softly. "This is your time, Vivi. I'm so proud of you for going after your dreams." He patted her knee. "America is the greatest country in the world because anyone can achieve their dream simply by working hard. "

Vivien had heard this lecture so often during her upbringing she wondered if her father was on the payroll of the US tourism board. "Yes, Dad, this is my chance to finally do what I've been working toward. Hopefully I'll make the most of it."

"I wish your mother was here to see the person you've become. Remember, Vivi…"

Anticipating his words, Vivien said, "I know, Dad. Be great and be good. Right?"

"No." He looked at her with moist eyes. "I was going to say remember every day when you're out there on your own how much you are loved."

Getting choked up, she had to look away for a second. "I love you more, Dad. I'll call you every Sunday."

PART TWO

CHAPTER 5: A SERIES OF FIRSTS

Zero dark thirty. The military term for the time of day before even the sun has woken up. It was four thirty Monday morning when Vivien awoke to get ready for her flight to Portland, Oregon.

Was she really moving to Portland? She'd asked the question multiple times over the weekend.

Her new employer had arranged all the details of her trip. A car service picked her up at five fifteen a.m. sharp and took her to Teterboro Airport in New Jersey. Her ride to the airport was so fast she barely managed a sentimental backward glance at the skyline of the city.

While Vivien had literally flown millions of miles on commercial airlines, this would be her first trip on a private jet. Bright and early, the limo glided to a stop at the security booth at the airport. The driver gave the tail number of the corporate jet and Vivien's name, and they were cleared through the gates. As soon as the car pulled up to the curb two uniformed personnel ran out to greet her and retrieve her bags from the trunk. The copilot assured Vivien that he would put her computer bag on the plane in an accessible spot. Her luggage was whisked away to the waiting jet while Vivien was escorted to the departure lounge and offered gourmet coffee and freshly baked muffins. It was the first time she'd traveled carrying nothing but her purse.

After letting Vivien enjoy the comfy chairs and coffee, the copilot came over to say, "The jet is ready to board whenever you like."

Vivien walked out onto the tarmac. The gleaming white Gulfstream jet awaited her with the company logo on the side. As she walked up the steps of the jet she noticed the Smart Sports torch logo emblazoned on each one. A cheery flight attendant greeted her, offering a chilled or room-temperature bottle of water. Aboard the empty plane Vivien asked how many other passengers would be making the trip.

"This plane is just for you," was the response. "Are you a professional athlete?"

Vivien shook her head no.

"Oh, usually when the Smart brothers send the jet it's for an athlete."

"I'm just doing some consulting work," Vivien said, as the company founders had instructed her to do. "They probably just let me catch the return flight from someone else's trip."

The flight attendant smiled politely, looking unconvinced.

Vivien made her way toward the back of the jet and picked a seat facing forward. The seats were cushiony and made of soft leather the consistency of butter. Plush leg rests made of sheepskin popped up at the touch of a button. Vivien sank into the luxurious seat, feeling uncharacteristically giddy. The décor on the inside of the plane was modern and clean, with polished wood, carbon fiber, and brushed steel accents. Even the air coming through the vents was crisper and more refreshing than the purest mountain air. She inhaled deeply, taking in the scent of money. This was the way to travel. No check-in, no long lines, no hassles. Pure luxury. *I could get used to this.*

Vivien was no stranger to Portland. She and her team had worked on a project for Nike, focusing the product line and improving their execution at retail. Phil Knight had offered her a job and she had considered it, but Nike lacked the entrepreneurial spirit and growth prospects she wanted. She'd waited a long time for the perfect opportunity to come along.

The perky flight attendant continued her cross examination. "Which business are you going to be consulting on?"

An unskilled liar, Vivien decided to play dumb. "I'm not really sure yet, I'll learn more once I get there."

The Smart brothers wanted to keep the announcement of Vivien's hiring quiet until she was introduced at the company meeting later that day. That meant she had to keep mum about the new job. With her colleagues at SCP she'd only shared that she was joining the private company Smart Sports in an executive role. Of course her family and closest friends knew about her job, but they were sworn to secrecy.

Vivien wasn't sharing any further intel and focused her attention on her book, so the flight attendant left her alone and set about performing her in-flight duties.

Upon finishing her gourmet hot breakfast, Vivien stretched out and leaned back in her seat. She reflected upon the dinner conversation with her Ceiling Smasher buddies, especially their comment about her never experiencing failure. Fear suddenly gripped her as she realized…the decision was irreversible. Vivien would become either the most remarkable female executive in the industry, or the biggest failure. Was this all a mistake? If she failed, would she be letting a lot of women (and men) down? Her mind was swirling but she finally lapsed into a peaceful slumber.

The plane touched down on the landing strip at Hillsboro Airport, jolting Vivien awake. She took a deep breath and looked out the window to see a lush blanket of evergreen trees covering the hillsides in all directions. Vivien was about to enter the unknown.

✳

The Smart brothers had sent a car to pick up Vivien at nine a.m. Portland time. The driver greeted her, introduced himself, and took her bags. "So, you're coming from New York City? I hope you like Portland, it's such a great place."

The Northwest weather was cool, dry, and comfortable. "Wow, no humidity; it feels wonderful. Does it get pretty warm during the day?"

"Summers in Portland are the best-kept secret. Yeah, we get rained on throughout the year, but summertime here is awesome. Dry as a bone. Cool mornings and then it warms up throughout the day. Great golfing weather. Hottest time of day is five p.m. and then it cools down again so it's comfortable for sleeping." The driver, Logan, chatted freely, unlike the limo drivers back in New York. "So, you're going to be working for Smart Sports? That's exciting. I've driven Alex and Malcolm Smart to their jet before; I can't tell the twins apart. Can you?"

"Yeah, they really are identical. But with Alex's background in engineering and biomechanics and Malcolm's degrees in design and business they're the perfect pair to have founded a sports company."

Logan nodded. "They were the first sports company to focus on lightweight running shoes that strengthen the foot muscles. This town skews heavily toward Nike, but I will only run in Smart Sports shoes."

Vivien started to relax. That didn't last long.

"Anyhoo, what are you going to be doing for Smart Sports? There's been talk that they're making some changes at the executive level. Maybe replacing Charl Davis, the president of the women's apparel business…you involved in any of that?"

Her heart about thudded to a stop. Portland was already feeling like a really small town. That the limo driver seemed to have detailed files on her was kind of freaky. Vivien deflected his questions. She quickly learned from Logan that there was one main car service in town and they drove around all the executives from all the sports companies, so these drivers were privy to many conversations held in the car and on the phone en route to the airport. That explained why Logan was so well informed.

The car pulled up to the guard booth at the Smart Sports campus and Logan said, "We have Ms. Vivien Lee to see the Smart brothers." The guard checked his list and said, "Good morning, Vivien. They're expecting you over at the executive building." He radioed the guard at the executive building and then waved them through. This was

THE CLOSER

Vivien's first visit to the Smart Sports campus, which was set along the banks of the Willamette River and was even more impressive than it was in photos. Throughout the interview process the Smart brothers had either met her in New York or flown to a location outside of Portland to keep her hiring under wraps.

Heading toward the executive building, they drove past the heart of the complex, the Stadium. It was made of twisted sheets of gleaming metal and glass spiraling up to the top of the building, which sported a graceful curved glass torch–Vivien recognized the Smart Sports icon immediately. To her it represented a soaring competitive spirit. The sunlight danced off the top of the torch in all directions. As the driver navigated through the beautiful campus, Vivien took in her surroundings. Two teams were jostling for the ball on an expansive soccer field, and a few runners populated a running track. She heard the distinctive thwap of a tennis ball and saw four tennis courts were filled with grunting players. Even the basketball courts and beach volleyball pits sported many muscular, fit bodies in motion. Looking up at the glass-enclosed fitness center, Vivien saw it was teeming with employees doing every kind of sport imaginable. This was an athlete's nirvana and she could practically smell the sweat drifting across the gorgeous green campus. She noted the main building, which contained the commissary and employee store; an apparel building; and the footwear building; and finally they came to the executive building.

*

A security guard was waiting to take her luggage and escort her into the building. He smiled and assured her he'd keep her things safe. "You can head up to the fourth floor to meet the Smart brothers."

Vivien stepped off the elevator, where Alex Smart was waiting.

"Welcome, Vivien!" He pumped her hand. "We're excited to have you on the team. Let's spend some time together with Malcolm to get you oriented before we introduce you to the company."

"I'm thrilled to be here, Alex. I can't wait to meet everyone and get started."

They walked to the conference room that sat in between the brothers' offices.

For years Smart Sports had seen consistent and steady growth in revenues and profits, which allowed them to expand into new markets and new product areas. And to build such a fabulous headquarters. The interior was bright and airy, with bamboo flooring and modern finishes.

The Smart brothers were poised to take the company public, which was a huge enticement for Vivien to join. The stock options she would be given could be worth a bundle in time. They had a simple organizational model–the brothers were co-CEOs and they had four presidents running the company: one each for men's footwear, women's footwear, men's apparel, and women's apparel.

In her first touch-base with Alex and Malcolm Smart, Vivien learned some news that had not been shared with her during the interview process and she got a better sense of the strengths of each of the brothers. They were indeed identical twins, and the only way to tell them apart was by their dress and the fact that Malcolm wore a goatee. Vivien had noticed in the times they had met that Alex favored golf shirts while Malcolm preferred button-down shirts; both wore jeans and Smart Sports sneakers.

"Vivien, as we mentioned during the interview process things are going poorly with our apparel business." Malcolm fidgeted with a pen. "Now that you are an employee we can tell you that apparel is a money-losing business for us." He looked away. " As you can imagine, the team is demotivated."

Alex leaned forward. "Not only are we losing money, in all the years we've been in business, we have never made a dime on apparel. It's been a head scratcher for us given the explosive growth in activewear. Footwear is highly profitable, and those profits have been carrying apparel. We need you to assess the segment and let us know if this is even a business we should be in. My gut tells me we should be, but honestly–we don't know crap about how to run it successfully. If we can't turn it around in three years, then we should decide if we should just cut it loose."

So she was inheriting a troubled business, and the Smart brothers were giving her only three years to turn it around.

Malcolm nodded and stroked his goatee. "One of the biggest challenges is getting the team back on track and bought into a vision they can believe in. The lack of clear vision or strategy frustrates many of them. Also, it's pretty clear that Charl isn't too pleased about stepping down, so you will need to see if you two can establish a productive working relationship. If not, you'll have to decide how you want to handle having him on the team."

Interesting. Alex focused on numbers, while Malcolm focused on people. Good to know. "I'll need a little time to get up to speed–what's working, what isn't, what's missing–and then sketch out a vision and strategy." Vivien opened her laptop. "Something I plan on doing with my team as a starting point is a strategic war game–a simulation game that will help us anticipate what is going to happen in the industry over the next three to five years. It will take some time to assess the talent and culture of the team. As we discussed when I took the job– and I want to make sure we are still in agreement on this–I'll be able to make any changes to the team that I see fit, right?"

"Yes, we agree," Malcolm said. "It's your team. You make the changes you see fit. Just touch base once you've made your decisions, to keep us in the loop."

Vivien made a note of that. "What's the most important objective for you both? Is it to turn around the business? Make a profit? Fix the business strategy? Create a stronger vision? Improve the product? Inject more innovation? Grow revenues? Ensure the team is functioning well?"

Both Malcolm and Alex nodded. "All of the above," Alex said. "But the main thing is to get the business profitable so we have proof that it's a segment we should be in. We need to act quickly, but we understand you'll need to get up to speed first. It's a complex business so make sure you take the time to get a solid foundation. And please feel free to come to either of us as you have questions or observations. I'd wager it'll be a good six months before you get your arms around the business."

After a pause Malcolm spoke. "Vivien, a couple of watch-outs we want to discuss with you. You are the first female president here, and frankly, it's about time. But it may be rough going with some of the boys. There are cliques, even though we try to discourage that, but don't let that bother you. The sports industry is notorious for not having enough talented senior women and we want to change that."

She put down her pen. "I appreciate that."

"The average tenure of a senior hire in this sector is less than a year," he said. "We've given our guys some coaching to let them know we have a new person coming whom we believe in and that we fully expect them to support you. You should let us know if you run into any issues. Alex and I assume you've dealt with challenges before and can rise above. That, plus the talent and ideas you bring, is why we wanted you."

"Don't worry about me, guys, I'll be fine. I intend to focus on what needs to get done. If I need you to run interference I'll ask, but I can handle difficult situations on my own." She glanced at her notes. "Malcolm, I will need a little help learning the culture and politics. I want to understand how to be most effective at Smart Sports. Is there a well-entrenched person you recommend I get to know who can show me the ropes?"

"Sure thing. Let's get you set up with someone whom you can ask questions that you don't feel comfortable asking your team or your peers. We should keep it an informal coaching relationship...we'll call them your 'ghost mentor.' And please know I'm always here for you. Also, let's discuss what you might like to cover when you are unveiled at the company meeting."

"We can't wait to see what you can do with the business, Vivien," Alex reiterated. "You have our full support to do what you need to and turn the business around."

Vivien took the opportunity to show them her ninety-day plan and explain her approach to understanding the business.

"This is terrific, Vivien." Alex let out a long breath of relief. "I think we're finally going to get this business fixed."

"Thank you." She knew that social time was fundamental to raising people's comfort level, so she closed her laptop and leaned back. "Well, I'm looking forward to getting to know Portland, trying some Oregon Pinots, and playing some golf occasionally, so if you're up for any of that, it would be great."

"Portland summers are the absolute best in the country." Alex grinned. "That's why we do all our recruiting and hiring this time of year. It takes a while to get used to all the rain here, but it's worth it. You'll see."

"I believe it," she said, smiling in return.

"We'll let you get settled in and find a temporary place to live this weekend, but let's plan on having you over to my place next weekend for dinner, Vivien. Alex is a mean griller." Malcolm shot a smile at his brother.

"Sounds great. My fiancé, Clay, will be out here for a visit." Things were off to a good start.

Malcolm got up to ask his assistant something and came back. "Listen, I have the perfect person to be your ghost mentor. Penny's calling him now."

A slight commotion was heard outside. "Don't tell me these guys are making a last-minute change to the company meeting agenda," a voice said in an ornery tone.

"Doug, get in here. There's no changes to the agenda," Malcolm called out. "We just want to introduce you to someone."

A tall, lanky man with close cropped gray hair came in.

Alex slapped the guy on the back and brought him in closer. He looked like a Marine. "Doug, this is Vivien Lee, our first female president. She'll be–"

"Let me guess, running Women's Apparel."

Malcolm laughed. "That's right. Nothing gets past you, Doug. Vivien, this is Doug Hawke, infamous for being–"

"Yes, I know, employee number one at Smart Sports. It's great to meet you." Vivien held out her hand.

Doug had the imposing glare of a school principal as he looked her in the eye, and then his gaze dropped down to her feet. Then he smiled approvingly and said hello, grasping her hand. She had passed the first test.

Typical protocol in the footwear-dominated sports industry was to size up newcomers by what they wore on their feet. The footwear had to be the right brand (competitor brands were verboten) and the right style, and bonus points were awarded for wearing current-season shoes. Vivien had been thoughtful about her footwear choice for the first day on the job.

The Smart brothers pitched the idea to Doug of being a ghost mentor for Vivien. He pondered for a moment and said, "I don't know how much help I'll be, but sure thing. Happy to." She thanked him and sat down with all three men to discuss the company meeting agenda.

In a short while Vivien would be introduced to the entire company. She expected she'd encounter a somewhat antagonistic audience–after all, she was an outsider replacing one of their own. The typical ROS (run of show) for the company meetings was to kick things off with an inspiring "highlight reel" of great Smart Sports athletic moments. Then Doug would come out and share a story, typically in colorful language, to charge up the ranks. Next, Doug would introduce the co-

CEOs, the Smart brothers. Alex would give a brief update on the six-billion dollar business and Malcolm would highlight new products and give a nod to any major achievements from their people. The most exciting part followed: one of their sponsored athletes would appear onstage to say a few words and interact with the audience. The last order of business on that day would be to introduce Vivien.

Doug stood up. "Sounds good. Well, it's ten-forty-five; we better head over."

"You ready, Vivien?" Malcolm said.

"Let's do it." She smiled confidently, but her heart was already racing. *Can I really do this?*

✳

The key thing was for Vivien not to be seen. While the Smart brothers took the regular walking path to the Stadium, Doug whisked her down a back alley. It was a covert operation worthy of a Robert Ludlum spy novel. Just moments before the company meeting was to begin Doug swung open the back door to the Stadium and snuck Vivien through the series of catwalks backstage. Music pumped over the sound system, accompanying the images on the screen. Doug gave her a wink to say good luck and then he walked out onstage. Hearty applause from the employees was suddenly accompanied by a thunderous sound, like a stampede of buffalo across a vast plain.

Vivien peeked out from behind the curtain into the cavernous auditorium. The audience was giving Doug a standing ovation. The thunderous noise was the sound of the auditorium seats flipping up and hitting the backs of the chairs. That sound was magnified in another wave when the Smart brothers came out, confirming how much their employees cherished them. As the brothers addressed the audience, Vivien rehearsed in her head what she would say. Unlike many people, she enjoyed public speaking, but now her throat felt dry. The next twenty minutes would set the stage for her entire career.

Vivien felt the thrill of anticipation, like being at the top of a roller-coaster before the big plunge.

But first, they introduced Mackey Keeyes, a newly signed basketball player. After some banter with the company founders, Mackey was given the microphone. "What time is it?" He held his hand to his ear, waiting for a response, then he gave it. In a booming voice he said, "It's Mackey Time–yo, holla! Are y'all excited to have Mackey Keeyes in the house?" The audience laughed and applauded. Although he'd actually completed his degree at Duke, Mackey did not sound too scholarly right now. Perhaps he was trying too hard. "You may know me for my basketball skills, but I love all sports…except golf. Chasing around that little ball is hard work. Even worse, the last time I played a woman outdrove me. A woman. Outdrove me, Mackey Keeyes. Crazy! I don't like any sport where a woman can do better than a professional athlete. They oughta just ban women from golf…that's right, no more women on golf courses from now on. Now, that's what I'm talking about." His comments elicited some uncomfortable chuckles from the crowd. Vivien looked out and saw women in the audience with their arms crossed, not looking pleased.

Mercifully, Doug stepped up and said, "Let's have a round of applause for Mackey Keeyes. We can't wait to see the energy you'll bring to the basketball court this season." He deftly brought the focus back to Mackey's athletic accomplishments and escorted Mackey off to the side to take a seat on one of the bar stools. The Smart brothers returned to center stage to talk about the great history of the company.

"Still, we need to constantly improve and change things up to move the company forward," Alex said. He glanced at Malcolm.

"Right. And we have two· exciting announcements. First, as of August tenth, the anniversary of when we founded Smart Sports, we will officially become a public company traded on the New York Stock Exchange." Malcolm paused for the applause and cheers from the employees. "Very exciting times for all of us. Second, we are delighted to bring on the first female executive in the history of Smart Sports." As he ran down Vivien's background, low whistles of admiration came from the audience. "It is my great pleasure to introduce to you our first female president of Smart Sports Women's Apparel, Vivien Lee."

Heart thumping in her chest, Vivien stepped out from the wings and onto the stage. "Thank you, Alex and Malcolm, for this great opportunity." She invoked the words of baseball legend Lou Gehrig: "Today I consider myself the luckiest woman on the face of the earth." The audience, delighted by the witty sports reference, laughed warmly. Then Vivien dared to go off script. "I'm thrilled to be joining the Smart Sports team. But, sorry, I have to call an audible." Boldly, she turned to Mackey Keeyes. "Mackey, as much as I respect your athletic performance, on behalf of all women here I need to address your comment about not allowing women on the golf course. I disagree with you, so I'd like to challenge you to a round of golf. If I outscore you, you owe me and every woman in this company a drink. If you beat me, I'll make up a special apparel product just for you." She had caught a glimpse of Mackey's golf ability at a televised charity event and he didn't look like a threat.

Doug burst out laughing. "Mackey, if Vivien has the balls to challenge you to a game of golf, then you are toast, my friend."

The audience applause crescendoed, and the thunder clap of the auditorium seat backs demonstrated that people approved of her comments. Adrenaline pulsed through Vivien's veins.

Mackey smiled and shook his head. He mimed locking his lips and throwing away a key.

Now Vivien could concentrate on what she really wanted to say. By the time she finished speaking it appeared that she was starting to win over the normally tough crowd.

Doug wrapped up the meeting with a few more jokes and a comment about the upcoming golf match between Vivien and Mackey, and then the audience filed out.

As Vivien was making her way offstage a couple of people rushed to intercept her. "Hi, Vivien. My name's Aileen and I'm a designer on your apparel team. I just wanted to welcome you and say hello." The woman gave a big smile.

A man with bright eyes and a crew cut said, "J. J. Monroe, also on the Women's Apparel team. That was awesome, challenging Mackey to play. Can't wait to see that!"

She shook hands with them and regrouped with the Smart brothers. "You were terrific," Malcolm said, giving her a pat on the back, while Alex grinned. Vivien let out a long exhale. She felt good about clearing the first hurdle; now it was on to the next challenge.

Immediately after the company meeting everyone wanted to meet and speak with Vivien. She barely made it back to the executive building in time to attend the executive staff meeting.

CHAPTER 6: SURVIVING THE FIRST DAY

Vivien walked into the executive conference room and saw a tall man with silvery-blondish hair deep in conversation with a shorter, stocky guy with a shaved head. The tall guy's head was bowed and his back hunched over, arms crossed low about his midsection–his silhouette resembled a giant human question mark. He stood. "Hallo, Vivien, I'm Duncan Doric. Delighted to welcome you to the executive team. Anything I can do to help, and I mean anything, please let me know. Let's make sure to get a coffee together soon."

Duncan stood at about six foot two and had movie-star-thick hair that cascaded in waves, framing his face perfectly. He had a hawkish nose, pale blue eyes, thin lips, and a prominent dimple on his chin. Each feature in itself was not particularly attractive, but in combination with his confident attitude he seemed to have a magnetic effect on the other guys.

Vivien said hello, trying to decipher the origin of Duncan's odd accent–it sounded like a bad imitation of Monty Python. Although Duncan was the first president to welcome Vivien, her gut reaction to him was caution. She knew he was the head of Men's Footwear and had left Nike nearly a decade ago to join Smart Sports.

He snapped at the conference room attendant, "Excuse me, the meeting is starting. We need our lunch now. I'm bloody famished."

Vivien had always been taught to treat everyone with respect, so Duncan's rudeness did not sit well with her.

His sidekick introduced himself. "Hi there, Johnny O. Man, you're tall."

Not quite sure how to respond, she shook his hand, saying, "Thanks," and moved to the side of the room to get some coffee.

Someone sidled up to her. "Ah, hello, Vivien. I am Klaas van der Hooft, the chief financial officer."

She tried to place the accent. German? No, Dutch. She smiled.

Klaas towered over her looking like a Nordic god with a chiseled face, short blond hair, and pale eyes with a slightly cold expression. His round, steel-rimmed glasses only added to the austere look.

"I also come from a consulting background, but from Bain. Let me get something straight here. You made partner at SCP in less than four years, and you were called the Crusher?"

Vivien introduced herself and corrected him on her nickname.

"And now you're the youngest president at Smart Sports."

"Um, I guess so," Vivien answered slowly, uncertain of where Klaas was going.

"You must be some kind of superstar," he said flatly. "But you are new to this business. Let's see if you can do the job." He did not smile.

Unaccustomed to getting a compliment and a cutting insult simultaneously, she just chuckled and said, "Yes, let's see."

Vivien guessed that Klaas must be incredibly smart, a saving grace to balance out his utter lack of social skills. Vivien had worked with Dutch people in the past, and her experience was that while they didn't intend to hurt someone's feelings, their comments could be both brutally frank and accurate. Maybe as she worked with Klaas she'd find he was someone who could give it to her straight–that could be helpful.

*

The executive staff meeting, Vivien quickly learned, followed a set pattern. Alex and Malcolm opened the meeting with small talk about the latest box office grosses just to lighten the mood. Once everyone settled in they turned things over to the CFO, followed by a marketing update and an HR update, and then each of the presidents would talk about their business. Today's meeting would be the first opportunity for Vivien to meet her fellow presidents and see them in action.

"Okay, let's get started," Malcolm said. "Welcome, Vivien. Let's go around the table and introduce ourselves so she knows the cast of characters. We're missing our head of HR, Ron Billings, today. He returns next week after recovering from hip replacement surgery."

Duncan Doric was seated next to Alex Smart, wearing a V-neck T-shirt with sleeves shortened to just above his biceps. He nodded and placed a pair of black rectangular glasses on his nose. Next to Duncan was the president of Men's Apparel, Johnny O'Connell, who was called Johnny O by everyone. Then Charl Davis, the guy that Vivien would be replacing. Steele Hamilton, the chief marketing officer, was next, and then Klaas, the CFO. Last, was the president of Women's Footwear, Tim Kelley.

After everyone introduced themselves the Smart brothers ran through the regular agenda and then moved on to the updates from each president.

The Women's Footwear president, Tim Kelley, seemed like a no-nonsense, design-oriented guy. Tim had a typical runner's physique–average height and a slight, compact frame–and he exuded vitality. He did a little show-and-tell and gave a sneak peek at the newest women's running shoes. "They're the lightest yet sturdiest we've ever produced."

Vivien turned one over in her hand and noted the high-tech outsole and woven polymer upper that made it feel so light. "Wow, Tim, these are cool!"

"Thanks, Vivien, we're pretty stoked about this shoe. One of our female designers came up with this concept and did an awesome job executing it. Give me your size and I'll hook you up with a sample pair so you can tell me what you think about the shoe."

"Great, thanks. How are you going to market these?"

Steele, the CMO interjected, "That's my area, Vivien. We're still brainstorming, but I'm sure we'll come up with something fantastic."

"It might be interesting to highlight the extreme lightness of the shoe in a compelling way," she said. "Like maybe use an old-fashioned scale and put a shoe on one side versus a typical object that people know the weight of, like a banana, on the other so it's clear just how light these shoes are. Then you barely need any copy."

"I love it! That's exactly what we should do, Steele." Tim nodded.

"Great idea, Vivien." Malcolm also nodded. "Steele, can you and your team consider how you might execute it?"

"Absolutely, Malcolm. Thanks so much for the input, Vivien," Steele said, smiling a little too broadly.

Next, the president of Men's Apparel, Johnny O'Connell, gave his update. As was typical of high-testosterone cultures, Vivien noted the male bonding and requirement for a cool nickname. When Johnny O spoke it sounded as if he was intentionally lowering his voice a couple of octaves to sound more macho, but he came across like an old-time radio announcer. He was stocky guy with a shaved head–usually the sign of an attempt to cover up premature balding.

Charl Davis, the soon-to-be-ex-president of Women's Apparel, gave the last update. Vivien was struck by the fact that Charl looked like a miniature version of Duncan. He had a smaller and more perfect nose, but his head of black hair was styled exactly like Duncan's, and he wore black-framed eyeglasses like the ones Duncan used. Charl also was sporting Duncan's uniform of low-cut V-neck T-shirt and jeans. Vivien half expected him to pull out a fake English accent.

"I'm really proud of the work we've done," Charl began, "but a lot of outside forces have made it challenging for our business. I, for one, welcome some new thinking and look forward to working with you, Vivien." He was friendly enough, but Vivien would have been foolish to believe he was happy about being replaced. "Let me know when you want me to walk you through the business and I'll clear my schedule for you. I want this business to succeed and am happy to help in any way." He put on a good show.

"Thanks, Charl, I appreciate that and look forward to working together," Vivien said.

Alex gave a nod. "Okay, let's spend a few minutes talking about our IPO. Klaas, can you talk us through the process?"

"We've been working on the valuation of the equity shares," Klaas said, "based on a comparable industry sector P/E analysis. That means we've established a strike price for the shares. When our company goes public on August tenth, a market price for the shares will be established. Your profit on your stock options will be the market value minus the strike price. This is different from the stock compensation you received while the company was still private."

Heads nodded.

Alex spread his hands on the table. "To make these shares worth more we need to continue to build this company successfully. By the way, the vesting period for the stock options is only two years, so at that point you can exercise all or some of your shares."

Klaas gave each executive a manila folder with their name on it. "You'll need to carefully review and then sign this shareholder agreement." It was a long, detailed official document.

Duncan, in cavalier fashion, quickly flipped through the pages and just signed wherever required. He pushed the manila folder back at the CFO. Most of the other guys followed suit.

Not Vivien. Thorough by nature, she never signed a legal document without careful review. Tim Kelley slipped the manila folder into his computer bag and gave her a wry smile.

Vivien felt like things with Tim had clicked. He could become an ally. As the meeting broke up, she grabbed a moment with him. "Hey, Tim, know of any good running paths around here? I usually like to get in a run early."

"I'm happy to show you my favorite route. It's five point three miles along the river, perfect for a morning run. I can bring you the new shoes to try out."

"Sounds great. How about tomorrow? Six a.m. work for you?"

"Sure, let's lace up outside the footwear building."

As she walked swiftly down the hall she heard someone panting to keep up with her. "Hey, Vivien, wait up!" It was Steele. "I'd love to treat you to lunch. How about next week?" He seemed a little too eager. Was he on a reconnaissance mission to learn more about the new competition? Or did he like her marketing idea and want to suck more out of her?

Steele was the smallest guy out of all the other Smart Sports executives, standing at barely five foot seven, a few inches shorter than Vivien. He had light brown hair, which he spiked up in the front; grayish-green eyes; and a smattering of freckles dotting his face, which made him appear more youthful than he actually was.

"Lunch sounds good, let me check my schedule, Steele."

"You're going to love working here, Vivien. It's been such an awesome ride for me."

"Oh? How long have you been with the company?"

Instead of providing a simple number, Steele felt it necessary to share his résumé. "Well, my first job was at Kraft Foods. That was fun. I was responsible for Cheez Whiz. Made a packaging change that increased sales almost three hundred percent."

"Really? Impressive." Knowing the truth, she had to suppress a laugh.

"Then I got called up to HQ and worked for Philip Morris in marketing–handled all their events, even internationally. Got to do some NASCAR stuff, very cool. Then I reconnected with Duncan when he came over here and Smart Sports needed marketing help."

"So you knew Duncan from before?"

"Oh yeah, we met years ago at a sports event and kept in touch. Lots of folks around here go way back."

Vivien was starting to understand the intricate connections.

Steele yammered on, "Anyway, I've been here four years and it's been cool. We have a very talented executive team." He was including himself in the compliment, no doubt. "And, don't worry, you're going to enjoy working with Charl. He's a great guy."

"Good to hear. Then we should get along just fine. I'll let you know about lunch."

*

Malcolm Smart had set up Vivien's next meeting, which was with the leaders on her Women's Apparel team. As he introduced Vivien to the seven people, she noticed two of her direct reports were missing. People welcomed her and were polite, but not overly enthusiastic.

Vivien turned to J. J. Monroe, her head of sales. "We seem to be missing a couple of people, aren't we?"

"Charl and Rebecca, the head of product design and development—guess they had a meeting conflict," he said.

Malcolm's look darkened a bit. Vivien remained silent but thought it odd they couldn't rearrange their schedules to meet with their new boss. *Aren't they curious about what I have to say?* Was this a subtle sign of disrespect from Charl already? Vivien would need to quickly get the lay of the land and gain the support of her team, and spend time with Charl to review the business—which might be tough if he was trying to avoid her.

*

Pandy heard her new boss entering her office and she popped in. "Hi, Vivien, I'm your assistant, Pandy," she greeted her with a smile. She had no idea what to expect from this female executive from New York. Weren't New Yorkers supposed to be rude and snobbish?

Vivien smiled. "Hi Pandy, nice to meet you. That's an interesting name."

"Oh, it's short for Pandora."

"I like it. Listen, Pandy, I'm pretty low maintenance but perhaps we can sit down and chat about how we'd like to work together. I'd love to hear about your background, how long you've been with Smart Sports, etc. I'm sure you'll have some tips for me on how to be effective here. Can we do that tomorrow morning?"

Pandy was surprised that Vivien seemed so friendly. And down-to-earth. "That sounds great, I'll block some time on your calendar. I've worked for a few other execs who came in from outside the company and am happy to share any tips, Vivien. Also, I've printed out your schedule for the week: here it is." Pandy handed her a clear plastic folder containing Vivien's schedule–she prided herself on her organizational skills. "Anything I can do for you now?"

"Actually, there is." Vivien said, "I need to get some time set up with Charl, please."

"I'm on it." Pandy walked back to her desk. She returned to Vivien's office two minutes later with a sour expression. She hated to disappoint her boss already. "Charl's assistant says he's so overbooked he can't meet until next week."

Vivien looked up. "Is that so?"

Pandy relayed what Charl's assistant told her: "'What can I say? He's a popular guy.'" She bit the end of her pencil and gave Vivien an apologetic look. *Wow, it's her first day and she's already getting the runaround? These guys are not going to make it easy for her.*

*

Vivien gently smacked one fist into the palm of her other hand while she was thinking. The response from Charl was unacceptable and contradicted his generous offer to spend time with her when they were at the executive staff meeting. Rather than get angry, Vivien simply set a plan in motion.

She gave a smile to Pandy. "That's all right. Here's what we'll do. Would you please go to the cafeteria and get Charl's favorite caffeinated drink and drop it off as a gift? I'd also love a latte for myself–I've been up since one thirty a.m. Portland time. Here's a twenty, feel free to get a drink for yourself, too."

Charl was getting ready to move out of his office, which was within earshot of Vivien's office. What the heck kind of a name was Charl anyway? Shouldn't it be Charles or Charlie?" She had to mentally check herself from adding an *-es* every time she said his name.

About thirty minutes later, when she figured the diuretic effects of the caffeine were kicking in, Vivien listened for movement in Charl's office. When he walked out and around the corner to the men's room, Vivien stood there waiting. "Hi, Charl." Vivien smiled. "Do you have a few minutes?"

"Actually, I need to be somewhere in a few minutes." Charl smiled slightly but his pale skin showed a tinge of red. Now that she stood face-to-face with him–well, sort of, as he was slightly shorter–she could sense his aloofness.

"That's okay," she said, undaunted, "this will only take thirty seconds. We need to spend time together ASAP to review the business, so I'll have Pandy set that up. The main thing I wanted to say, Charl, is that you're an important part of this team and it's my hope and expectation we can work together effectively. I understand this must be awkward for you and the team. Let's collaborate so we can ensure as smooth a transition as possible. Everyone is looking to both of us to set the right tone here."

"Look, no offense, Vivien; I don't know you at all. It's not that I have a problem with you per se. It's just, I have tons of experience in the sports industry and have worked for this company for five years. I've done a lot of work that I am really proud of–I didn't luck into this role, I earned it." Charl's edgy tone and word choice were telling. "Was I happy with the recent org changes? Frankly, no. I can't understand how someone with no experience can be taking the business away from me."

Yep, just a bit bitter. Clearly, despite performance numbers that showed the contrary, Charl thought he had been doing a good job. He would be a challenge to deal with, but she'd give him a chance.

"Charl, I appreciate your candor. I know you have a lot of experience and I hope we can leverage that. And let me just clarify something. While I may not have many years of experience in the sports industry, I do bring some unique skills, and I'm just asking you to give me a chance. You may not like it, but you are reporting to me now. If, ultimately, you find that you can't follow my lead, then I'm happy to work with you and the Smart brothers to find you a role elsewhere. I'm hoping it won't come to that. I look forward to seeing you at the all-hands meeting tomorrow." Vivien turned and walked away feeling unsettled.

*

Vivien's last meeting of the day was with the head of recruiting–also the interim head of human resources–a showy character named Zac Archer.

"Vivien, thank god you're here," he said, his voice projecting loudly, as he breezed into her office and air-kissed her on both cheeks. "You certainly do improve the landscape. You've probably heard of me already, Zac Archer."

"Hello, Zac." His greeting was decidedly un-HR-like. What was his deal?

"Some folks around here call me Zac Lambo."

"Oh, why is that?" Vivien said, humoring him. Internally she groaned. *Enough with the nicknames, already.*

"Because I drive a Lamborghini Gallardo." Like a proud parent showing off his kids, he whipped out his smartphone to share a picture of his bright yellow car, and in it his darkly tanned self in a tank top leaning back and flexing his muscles. "I have to say, I have one of the coolest jobs in the world. You wouldn't believe how many people try to get time with me every day."

Zac's ego was as big as Mount Hood. He was so flamboyant she couldn't tell if he was straight and just really high on himself or gay and playing it super macho in this high-testosterone culture. His slicked-back brown hair with streaky highlights sported so much hair gel that it gave the plastic furniture covers used by grandmothers a reason for existence. His button-down shirt had a few too many buttons undone under a thin, buttery leather motorcycle jacket, and his jeans were so tight that even Vivien couldn't help but notice the bulge. Whether his tan was authentic or artificially bronzed, she couldn't tell. Zac seemed a little too Hollywood for Portland.

She threw him a bone. "Nice set of wheels, Zac. That would make a great New York taxi."

He looked a little hurt but then chuckled anyway.

"It would help if you can give me a rundown of the key players on my team and their skills and development opportunities as you see them. Shall we get started?" She already had the lowdown on her team from Malcolm but wanted to see if Zac could add any salient facts.

She quickly discovered that Zac was not a skilled assessor of the talent, but he was skilled at gossip, so the only thing he provided was color commentary. What exactly was he was doing in that job? Did he land this role through connections or dumb luck? In certain corporations the HR function was the graveyard for people who had few business skills but enough political connections to stay employed– was this the case at Smart Sports?

Zac droned on, his comments limited to people's length of service; how outgoing and attractive they were; if they had good "buzz"; how athletic they were; whether they were married; if not, whom they were dating; and some psychobabble about owning who they were…all of which he shared in a solemn, hushed tone.

Useless.

"I've been involved in all the key hires," he said at one point, "so

I have to say I was disappointed I was left out of the loop on the decision to hire you. In fact, I was the one who recruited Charl Davis to come here from Reebok, and that was a good get." So Zac admitted responsibility for a guy with a terrible track record and was boasting about his *good get*? "I think M and A"–it took her a second to figure out this was a reference to the Smart brothers– "must have known I was swamped with other searches and didn't want to overload me. To be honest, though, I don't know that I would've supported your hiring, given that you've only ever been a consultant." He said *consultant* as one might say *leper*. "You're so lucky, Vivien, scoring such a great job. In fact, the role is much higher-profile than the size of the business. And joining Smart Sports right before we go public, now, that is fortunate timing."

Vivien looked at Zac evenly and said, "Mmm-hmm."

He kept going. "And Charl. He's a great guy. Great guy. We lift weights together two, three times a week. I'm not totally sold that there needed to be a management change there. Let me offer you some advice, Vivien." Zac leaned in closer and pointed his finger in a manner that resembled a gun. "If I were you I would tread lightly."

Unintimidated, Vivien leaned forward. "What do you mean, Zac?"

"It sounds like in your first conversation with Charl you, shall we say, hinted that he could lose his job? Charl has a lot of supporters here so I wouldn't make any hasty decisions. He's friendly and well liked on campus." Zac bared his pearly teeth and flexed his pecs. "At any rate, you and I should get to know each other better–perhaps get together for happy hour?"

Zac didn't appear to have a clue about how to do his job, yet he dared to give her advice? His close relationship with Charl was probably the reason the Smart brothers had left him out of the hiring discussion.

She sweetly said, "Well, Zac, I'm sure we'll enjoy working together. As you begin to see what I can do, I'm confident your comfort level about my role here will increase. Charl seems like a pleasant guy with a lot of experience, so I'm looking forward to working with him. Anyway, I shouldn't keep you any longer. Thanks for meeting with me, Zac. And, sure, let's do happy hour sometime soon."

Zac appeared to want to chat further, but he got the hint and skulked out. "Oh," he said, almost as if it were an afterthought, "here's a packet of all your employment paperwork to fill out, and your contract. Oregon is an at-will employment state so that's reflected in the contract. Feel free to ask me any questions after you've looked it over."

At will. So he felt it necessary to remind her she could be let go at any time, for any reason, with no obligation of compensation. In her entire career Vivien had never even considered the possibility of being fired. She wasn't troubled by the employment contract she was about to sign. That the Smart brothers had intentionally left Zac out of the decision to hire her showed they lacked confidence in him. Maybe they were in the process of moving him out. She would have to get a better sense of Zac's standing in the eyes of her bosses.

CHAPTER 7: TEAM ENCOUNTERS
OF THE FIRST KIND

It was a sunny, slightly brisk morning as Vivien started off her five-mile run along the Willamette River with Tim Kelley. Today she'd be conducting an all-hands meeting with her Women's Apparel team so they could get a sense of their new leader. It was her first opportunity to meet the entire team and she was a bit jittery, which was unusual for her. Vivien spent part of the run just getting to know Tim. An Oregon native, he hailed from a dynasty of footwear designers, with his father at Adidas and sister at Nike. He came across as a person able to look past gender, race, and personalities to focus only on great ideas. That quality would make him a great collaborator, and Vivien made a mental note of it. Then their talk turned to business.

"Do you have any idea what part of England Duncan is from? I've worked with lots of Brits and his accent is unlike anything I've heard."

Tim shook his head and laughed. "Dunk grew up in Cleveland, Ohio. He spent a summer in England as a teen and then did a two-year stint there with Nike. Apparently when he returned to Portland he was speaking like an Englishman–or at least trying. I heard he even had a coat of arms designed around the Doric family name."

"Gee, can't wait to see that." Vivien was getting into a fast running pace with Tim.

"If you haven't noticed, Dunk is the big man on campus. His accent elevates his stature and allure. He's considered to be one of the smartest people around."

"He certainly seems tight with Johnny O, Steele, and Charl."

"Vivien, those guys go way back. One thing to remember is that connections here are deep, as are loyalties. Keep that in mind as you navigate Smart Sports. Also, people tend to judge new hires quickly, so the faster you can generate good buzz, the better." Her new running buddy also provided some nuggets about which sports each executive favored. Duncan's sport of choice was tennis. Interesting that only Johnny O had played a team sport–football.

Intent on experiencing all that this new city had to offer, Vivien asked him what she shouldn't miss during her time in Portland. Hiking around Mount Hood and the Japanese Garden were at the top of Tim's list. Vivien noticed he was wearing a wedding ring so she made a mental note to suggest they get together with their significant others for cocktails or dinner.

During her postrun stretch time she worked out what she wanted to say to her team and tried to anticipate any issues that might arise. First she'd meet the 115 people on the Women's Apparel staff who would be reporting to her, then she'd spend some time with the key members of her team. Some would be upset at her hiring and Charl's demotion, although with the business in such a sad state, there were probably people on the team who were ready for a change. She'd likely encounter some resistance at the all-hands meeting, so she had to show confidence. Then she had to get the team to reach the conclusion on their own that the business needed some major changes. That was not going to be an easy task, but in order for them to be open to a new leader and a new approach they had to admit the business was in trouble. Vivien was deep in thought as she jogged to the fitness center to shower.

✳

At eight thirty sharp, Vivien walked briskly into the main conference room of the apparel building, where the team was gathered. Normally the enormous room was sectioned off into thirds, but not today. At least 70 percent of the team was male. Clusters of people were huddled together chatting. She noted who was talking to whom.

The room fell silent as Vivien stood at the end of the long beech conference table, where some team members were seated while others stood around the room. She had declined the Smart brothers' offer to be there. Meeting her team on her own was a move that showed self-confidence, but the downside was she didn't have a top executive standing behind her for support when she might need it most. She was like a lone gladiator entering the Colosseum to face a horde of bloodthirsty combatants.

As she surveyed the room, some people smiled and looked curious, while a large number of eyes had an *impress me* glare to them.

She had to exude charm but also get these folks back on their heels a bit first.

"Hello, team, I'm excited to work with all of you to take this business to new heights. I believe we have a bright future ahead of us, but I'll get to that in a minute. First, I'd like to start off with a little quiz." People shifted uncomfortably. "Who can tell me who Leroy Smith is? Anybody?"

Crickets. Either no one knew or some knew and didn't want to volunteer the answer. This was not going to be easy.

"Okay, here's an easier one. Who is Michael Jordan?"

"The most amazing basketball player ever and the shooting guard for the Chicago Bulls," one of the guys shouted.

"Who said that?" Vivien scanned the room, resting her eyes on the person with his hand raised. "Good, you win a Starbucks gift card," she said, and tossed one to him. "Okay, now let's make things a little more challenging. How are Michael Jordan and Leroy Smith connected?"

A young woman raised her hand. "Did they play basketball together?"

"Yes, that is correct, you also win a Starbucks gift card." With a smile, Vivien tossed the card to the happy recipient, who waved it triumphantly. "We'll come back to Leroy Smith in a few minutes. Now let's turn our attention to the Smart Sports women's apparel business. As you get to know me you'll learn that I am a pretty direct person. So something I would like to understand from you is what you think of the business. What do you think needs to be changed?"

Silence.

Finally someone blurted, "Not that much. I think we are doing all right."

"Tell me, why do you say that?" Vivien asked the crowd. "Do many of you think business is going well enough that we don't need to do anything differently?"

A few people in the crowd mumbled, "Yeah, it's pretty good."

One guy said, "Come on, guys, there's always something we could do better."

Vivien stepped back, arms folded. "I see. So a lot of people here think things are good…who here would classify the business as successful? Raise your hands."

A number of hands went up, including Charl's. No surprise.

"That's interesting. In your opinion, what makes this business a success?"

"We introduce lots of new products every season–that shows that we are innovating," someone offered.

"Good. What else?" Vivien prodded.

"Our sales are improving over last year, percentage growth is good," another called out. "Seems people like our brand."

"We have a lot of talent on the team," Charl offered, "and we've done work we're really proud of."

Work I'm really proud of seemed to be Charl's go-to phrase.

"Let's come back to your comment later, Charl. So you're all telling me that lots of new products and year-over-year sales increases mean the business is successful. Do I have that right?"

The team who nodded in unison.

"Okay, here's where we disagree. I think in order to have a

successful business you must do four things, and do them all well."
Vivien walked to the whiteboard and sketched four pictures: a shirt, a
combination lock, a heart, and a dollar sign. "Number one, you have
to have unique products that consumers want and that perform well."
Vivien wrote *product* next to the shirt on the whiteboard. "Number
two, you need an ownable and protectable business strategy that's
difficult for competitors to copy." She wrote *strategy* next to the
combination lock. "Number three, you need a brand that people are
passionate about." Vivien wrote *brand passion* next to the heart. "And,
number four, you've got to make money." She circled the dollar sign.

Quite a few of the people in the room looked curious, scribbling
down what she'd said.

"Based on those four criteria for success, can we conclude this
business is doing well? Let's take a closer look. First, many of our
product designs seem to be borrowed heavily from competitors. Do
we own a distinct design aesthetic or technology? Not that I can see.
Also our product returns are some of the highest in the industry. That
tells me consumers aren't happy with our product once they've tried
it. Our repurchase rate is also low, so we don't have repeat customers
for women's apparel."

She stuck the marker back on the tray. "Let's turn to the business
strategy. Unfortunately, we don't seem to occupy a point of view in the
minds of consumers, which indicates lack of a distinct strategy. Based
on the latest brand awareness study, most people know Smart Sports
footwear, but there was very low unaided awareness that we even
offer apparel. The last point I want to make is important. I believe
in transparency...some of you may not know this, but the Women's
Apparel business is losing money."

Charl shifted uncomfortably. The looks of surprise around the
room revealed this was news to them.

"That's right. Not only that, we've never made a cent in the history
of the division. We're the smallest division at Smart Sports, and even

though our percentage sales increased over last year, that was from an incredibly small base. When you look at the net size of our business versus the competition it's nowhere near where it should be. So we are a small business that's not profitable, and we have a product, brand, and strategy that are not unique."

She looked around. "Given those facts, can we still say this business is successful?" She waited for a response. "Can we call this business a success?"

"Guess not."

"Nope."

"No way."

More than a few people mumbled.

"Shifting gears a bit, who can tell me what's our bestselling product?" Vivien asked.

"Our Stride Track pants," someone offered.

"Cool. How many Stride Track pants do we sell in a year?" Vivien asked the team.

There was a pause and some quick calculations, then someone offered up the number of annual units.

"Thanks for that information. Now who can tell me how many units of the bestselling Nike running pants are sold per year? Any guesses?"

More silence.

"Nike sells about forty times the volume of our bestselling product–and that's just in the US. What do you think about that?"

"Shoot, maybe we should just close up shop," someone said sarcastically.

"Quitting is an option. Go big or go home. Any of us here can choose to do either," Vivien countered. She was met with some chuckles. "I, for one, did not come here to close down this business. I think anyone who enjoys a little competition isn't going to give up that easily."

People around the room started nodding.

"This business is in a tough spot, and it probably took years to get to this point. I want to emphasize that it isn't any one person's fault. What's done is done. Moving forward, we all need to take responsibility for the direction of this division. What do we have that no one else has? Charl alluded to it a few minutes ago: talent. This is a good time to come back to Mr. Leroy Smith. Does anyone remember him? Leroy Smith was the six-foot-seven high school basketball player who was chosen for the varsity basketball team over a devastated Michael Jordan, who was only five foot ten at that time and put on the JV team." A surprised look came across many faces. Maybe they did not know that fact about the sports icon, or they were impressed that Vivien did. "Being cut from varsity was the thing that probably propelled Michael Jordan to greatness, because in addition to his talent, he put forth a supreme effort. More than having talented people, we need a team that functions well together, plus an intense desire to win. Talent, desire, and supreme effort will give us a great advantage. I understand that one of our product designers, Aileen, has been working on a special training collection that's the most technically advanced we've offered. Erika from product development has been investigating fabrics that can give our products new properties. And Angela from marketing has ideas for connecting more powerfully with our consumers." Erika and Angela looked a bit shocked, as they had not yet met Vivien in person but she seemed to know them.

Now they could see that Vivien had done her homework and that she understood the business and its problems better than anyone in the room. Even Charl.

"What we need is a unified vision we all work toward, directing our efforts to maximum impact. We have some kernels of innovation here, but we need to cultivate those ideas to make them ownable, powerful, and profitable. Think about this…we have a great opportunity here. No one in the industry considers us a threat. Even internally at Smart

Sports we're an afterthought. We have the potential to be a major player in the industry and contribute significantly to the growth of this company. I believe we can become the number one brand of sports apparel within the next five years."

Vivien saw people's eyes light up. Perhaps she'd lit a fire in them.

"First, we have to turn this business around. How often do you get the chance to change the destiny of your company?" She looked around. "Who's excited about that?"

A few murmurs and nods.

She leaned on the table, arms wide. "Together we can accomplish much. Are you with me? If so, then game on."

Heads were nodding all around. People actually started to look excited. Then they burst into applause.

Vivien drew back a bit, taking a deep breath to keep her calm. "Yes! Now I'd like to open it up to questions. Please tell me your name and what you do before you ask a question. That'll help me get to know you. Thanks."

The first question came from Aileen. "Are we planning on increasing the number of styles we offer? Because I think we need to understand the impact on our workload. We are pretty short-staffed here."

"Aileen, I believe in working smarter, not necessarily harder. We need to take a closer look at our product offering and see what's working and what isn't, what can be cut and what gaps we need to fill. My gut feeling is we're offering too many products and need to trim the line; that would leave more time for all the designers to do your jobs well."

Sam, a burly guy who headed up operations, asked about the strategy for changing the factory sourcing base. Vivien shared her philosophy but said she'd need to understand the pain points before making any major changes.

J. J., the head of sales, said, "I know your credentials are really impressive, and I don't mean any disrespect, but have you actually run this type of business before or turned a business around? With all our challenges it seems like it would be helpful to have someone lead the turnaround who has done this a few times before."

On the one hand it was a reasonable question, but on the other hand, she wondered if Zac Archer had already started to poison the well. Besides, had Charl turned around a business before? No. So why were people protecting their old, ineffective boss instead of giving her a chance? Because he was a "great guy"?

Vivien remained affable. "That's a fair question, J. J., although not necessarily the question that should be asked. No, I haven't been responsible for this type of business before, so I have a lot to learn. I'm counting on you guys to help me along the way. You have expertise that we need to leverage; that's why it's a team. Many here bring years of industry experience, and I'm sure that's been valuable. But industry experience alone will not solve the problems. So here's the question we should be asking, and I think my answer will set your minds at ease: what has prevented this business from being successful thus far? A turnaround needs a leader who can quickly fix the issues and build a vision, executing both well. I do know how to turn around a business and I do know how to turn around a brand. I've worked with some of the best companies out there–Target, Apple, Tiffany, Red Bull, Virgin, Mini Cooper–and have implemented some game-changing ideas. Most importantly, I know how to get results. But I'm not doing this all alone. We all need to pull together to succeed. You need to bring your A-game. Imagine what we can accomplish together when we approach the business more intelligently."

The power of Vivien's words and the strength of her personality achieved the desired impact. She'd sparked the team's imagination. Excited side conversations started to pop up.

A petite woman who had been sitting near Charl and conferring with him the entire time raised her hand. Her fingernails were glossy red against two thin Moleskine notebooks, one black and one pink, which she clutched in her hands. "Hi, Vivien, I'm Rebecca Roche director of product design & development. This may not be the right forum, but I would love to get your ideas on where we should be taking the design of our product."

Something about Rebecca immediately struck Vivien the wrong way and unsettled her. Rebecca sported a severe asymmetrical platinum-blond bob (most likely bottled) and a prominent bosom (most likely silicone). Perhaps more disconcerting, her choice of writing implement was a Hello Kitty pen with a heart on the top encasing a tiny bell that tinkled eerily when she wrote. Something about her was disturbingly familiar. Vivien wracked her brain. Rebecca Roche…Rebecca Roche. How did she know that name?

Within seconds, Vivien landed on the precise and horrifying recollection in her mental files. It was Becky Roche, the USC runner who'd given Vivien a black eye during a race. She winced at the memory. Despite the years and the cosmetic changes it was still mousy Becky Roche under that façade and the shiny fingernail daggers.

Rebecca appeared oblivious to any recollection of Vivien. Not a bad thing. She chose not to remind her of their prior association. "Actually, Rebecca, we need to do two major things. First, we need to look at the product offering together with merchandising. I'd like to understand the exact breakdown of our product portfolio and figure out where we need to migrate our offering. Do we have some sort of product pyramid?"

"I'm not exactly sure what you're asking for, but I'm sure we have it." Puzzling response. Rebecca wrote some notes in her pink notebook, her Hello Kitty pen tinkling. She tapped a single red dagger nail on the conference room table loudly.

"The second thing is we need better consumer insights into who we're targeting and what's important to them. Then we need to incorporate those elements into our design. I'd like to create a more distinct look, so from twenty yards away someone can identify a piece of apparel as a Smart Sports design. We'll have a chance to discuss this further in the coming days, Rebecca."

Vivien made a few concluding remarks and brought the meeting to a close.

Afterward, when the room had mostly cleared out, Rebecca came over and said, in a voice so sweetly artificial it was like human NutraSweet, "Vivien, can I tell you something? I am just so excited that we finally have a woman as president."

Hadn't Rebecca stuck to Charl like glue throughout the meeting? Would she turn on him so quickly? Unlikely.

"It's going to be so *exciting* having a leader who understands the women's market. I have a feeling you'll be great." She raised her fists up by her ears and said, "Yay!" She started to walk away but turned back. "Oh, I wanted to let you know we left a little surprise for you in your office, Vivien." Another sweet smile.

The heavyset woman hanging back and waiting for Rebecca couldn't be missed, so Vivien extended her hand and introduced herself. To shake Vivien's hand the woman had to set her giant-sized Jamba Juice smoothie down on the table–jeez, how much sugar was in one of those things? It turned out the woman was named Cat McClintock and was head of product development. Cat was five foot two in all directions and had a bright red bob that was similar to Rebecca's. It was curious that someone who didn't appear to exercise would choose a career working on sports apparel. In Vivien's experience, duplicitous people always had an evil sidekick, and in Rebecca's case it was clearly Cat.

"Thanks for your support, Rebecca." Vivien would need to handle her with caution. Her Ceiling Smasher friends had called it about a certain type of treacherous woman, and Rebecca's reputation fit the bill. Maybe she'd changed over the years and acquired some integrity… though it wasn't likely. After someone's early twenties their character was pretty much set in stone.

Rebecca asked in an innocent tone, "So, Vivien, what do you think of Charl and the team so far?" Clearly she was fishing for some dirt.

Vivien refused to fall for the trap. "We have some big challenges ahead, so I'm looking forward to working with the whole team."

"Well, you're going to love working with Charl, he's a great guy."

By now Vivien was tired of hearing that description.

When she finally got back to her office, it was like walking into a botanical garden. One beautiful floral arrangement was from the entire Women's Apparel team. Such a nice gesture. Another bouquet came from Art Hartmann and the SCP team, congratulating her on the new role. A gorgeous sculpted arrangement in a square glass vase was from Coop and the Ceiling Smasher founders. Her dad had sent a lovely purple orchid plant, and other flower arrangements from friends and former clients filled the room. Pandy had brought in some small decorative touches, but Vivien's spacious office was still pretty sparse, so all the flowers gave it a warmer feeling.

Vivien put her hand up and caressed her new necklace. Last night when she'd completed her marathon first day of work she'd wearily checked into the hotel. In her room a small Tiffany box was waiting on her nightstand. Inside was a little diamond pendant in the shape of a star and a sweet note from Clay. She called him to say thanks and tell him about her day. "Vivi, the star means this is your time to shine. Even though I wish you were back here, babe, I'm proud of what you're doing." Clay's gift and all the flowers served as a reminder–a lot of people were rooting for her success and she did not want to disappoint.

*

"How's it going so far?" asked Doug Hawke, her ghost mentor. As agreed, they'd meet for an early breakfast once a week until Vivien got up to speed.

"Pretty good. The Smart brothers gave me three years to turn around the business, but I'm guessing they won't wait that long. I'm aiming to do it faster." Vivien ate a forkful of scrambled egg whites.

"Smart. That division has been a dog for years. Alex, in particular, is impatient to see results." Doug spread some butter on his cinnamon raisin toast. "What's your plan of attack and how can I help?"

Vivien needed to quickly understand the problems so she could set about fixing them.

"First up–develop a two-pronged strategy. The first prong is to figure out what to do in the short term to stop the bleeding and turn the business around. The second prong is to simultaneously come up with a vision and action plan to propel the business forward. I'd love for you to participate in the second prong and will give you details later."

Doug nodded. "Sounds good. What's your take on your team so far?"

"I have to assess my team more closely to find out if we've got the right skills to get the job done." She talked through her take on each person, starting with the strongest.

J. J., in charge of sales–he just needed clearer direction and refinement in his approach to building the business.

Meredith, in charge of merchandising, was sharp, analytical, and had promise, but was a bit green and needed some guidance.

Angela, in charge of marketing, had the right instincts. Vivien could coach her on how to craft the marketing strategy and build the brand.

Sam, in charge of operations, had some issues, particularly with out-of-stocks and order fulfillment.

"That brings me to Charl, in charge of business development. I'm not really clear what his role is. Also he offered to get me up to speed on the business but has yet to make time for me."

"That's bullshit." Doug spat. A former New Yorker, he spoke with an unvarnished directness Vivien appreciated. "Welcome to the

Northwest. People don't confront each other. They say, 'For sure, let's get together and chat about it.' Then they avoid you and hope you'll forget about the issue. I prefer New Yorkers who say, 'I'm going to sue your ass and here's why.'"

"Any suggestions?"

"Go over and make friends with his assistant and she'll help you out. I swear the assistants around here are the ones with the hidden power, so it's worthwhile to get to know them. Okay, Vivien, who else are you worried about?"

"My biggest concern by far is product design and development, headed up by Rebecca Roche. Perhaps the job's just too big for Rebecca's skill set, but I need to determine this for sure. In trying on the product I can see a lot of obvious design and fit issues." Rebecca's sidekick, Cat, who led product development, typically said little except to echo Rebecca's comments and was potentially the source of the numerous fit problems. Vivien had learned that Cat's background was mostly in wovens, while 90 percent of Smart Sports' apparel was knits. And prior to joining Smart Sports, Rebecca had experience mainly in mass-market, casual apparel. The product design and development team did not seem to have the right skills at all.

"My only comment is that the entire time Rebecca's been in charge of product it's looked like crap." Doug shrugged. "My wife complains about it all the time."

"I'm also concerned about Gus, in charge of consumer insights. So far I haven't heard a single insight from him about the consumer. The rest of the functions–IT, finance, HR, innovation–all seem about average." Yeah, Gus was an issue. She'd heard rumblings from the team about his condescending attitude. And apparently he spent most of his time at work writing a blog about unusual bacon recipes.

"People will be watching the changes you make to the team. It's going to send a signal to the rest of the folks. If you've got some rotten apples, get rid of them fast. If you keep people around who don't deserve a spot, others will think you don't have the balls to make tough calls."

Vivien chuckled at his comments. Frankness was so refreshing. She looked at her watch.

"Thanks so much, Doug, this has been great. I have to meet Duncan for coffee, so I better run."

"Sure, see you later, Vivien."

✳

Duncan Doric was standing outside of the commissary talking on his cell phone when he saw Vivien. He waved her over.

"Right, Johnny O, catch you later."

Why was he on the phone with someone he saw many times a day?

"Good morning, Vivien, how are you?" Again, that weird British accent.

"Great, thanks. Beautiful day." She suggested they enjoy their coffee outside.

Duncan sat down. "Vivien, I know the transition to Smart Sports can be difficult. In our industry when an executive joins from the outside, turnover is quite high, with folks usually lasting only about ten months. So, I'm here to help you."

"Thanks, Duncan, I appreciate that. Why do you think people leave so quickly?"

"Dunno. Maybe new execs think they need to make their mark too fast. That's when they make mistakes or alienate people in the company." He flexed his bicep as he lifted his coffee cup to his lips. The hours he spent in the gym were evident. "As much as possible, Vivien, you should try not to do anything for the first three or four months. Just spend time getting to know the industry and the company. Of course your team will expect strong leadership but at multidivision meetings just listen and take it all in. Don't feel like you need to give an opinion on anything. Sometimes talking too early shows how green you are."

Really? She had been brought in to turn around a failing business, yet Duncan was telling her no one expected anything from her for the first four months? Odd. Yet, he seemed to be genuine in his desire to help her. They chatted for a bit and then Vivien had to get to her next meeting.

"Well, thanks for the coffee and the advice, Duncan," Vivien said.

"Feel free to come to me with any questions and I'll get you sorted." Duncan grinned. "Don't think we'll have to worry too much about you."

*

Nope, don't think we'll have to worry about you, Vivien Lee. As he watched her walk away Duncan sat back in his chair feeling supremely confident. He had seen this play out before, at both Nike and Smart Sports. A talented outsider with big ideas would get hired as a senior executive and through their own mistakes plus a little nudge from company insiders they'd flame out fast.

Duncan had the choreography all worked out. Be overly welcoming toward her in front of the Smart brothers, offer help and "advice." After a few months, along with Johnny O and Steele, express concerns about Vivien's competence to others. Repeat the basic questions she's asked. Encourage her to take risks and then intimate to Malcolm and Alex worries about her reckless decision-making—decisions made by someone too inexperienced in the industry. Watch her stumble. Make it impossible for Vivien to create a support system. Watch her implode. Agree with M and A that it was a good idea to hire her, but that it's just not working. Chip away at the confidence the Smart brothers had in Vivien. Soon she'd be history, like the other executives Duncan had worked to eliminate. He rubbed his hands together. It was fun to kill someone's career. And too easy.

"Hey, bud, how was coffee with the new girl?" Johnny O said, pulling up a chair.

"Went as expected. I'm sure she'll be following my great advice."

They both snickered.

Duncan said, "She's real easy on the eyes, man, too bad she won't be around long. I'm getting tired of staring at your bald head." He punched Johnny O playfully in the arm.

✳

Later that day, in a multidivisional meeting, Vivien followed Duncan's advice. She remained mostly silent throughout the meeting and just listened. Even at a critical moment when someone asked for her opinion, Duncan shot her a look of caution and she demurred, saying, "I'd like to understand the business a bit better before weighing in." Duncan and Johnny O smiled at each other and then looked at her approvingly. Things were off to a good start.

✳

A key tool that Vivien used with her leadership team was called an "expectations exchange." She set up one-on-one meetings with each individual so she could get to know them and use this tool. Her first meeting was with J. J., her head of sales.

"Here's how it works, J. J. First, I outline the five to seven things I expect from you over the next year in terms of responsibilities and behavior. Then you tell me what your expectations are of me as a leader."

J. J. stared at her. "You mean you want me to tell you what I expect of you as a boss? No one has ever asked me that before."

"To lead effectively, there has to be good two-way communication. So yes, I will commit to delivering on your expectations of me. Within reason." She winked.

He laughed.

Most of the team's requests of their boss were pretty simple: keep them informed, be honest with them, give them timely feedback, and set a consistent vision.

All things Vivien felt confident she could deliver.

∗

On Vivien's third day, Rebecca showed up at Vivien's office in the executive building with Cat in tow and presented Vivien with an obscenely large bouquet of flowers in a tasteful black vase. "This is a welcome gift from me and the Women's Apparel leadership team. We're so excited to have you here, Vivien!" Rebecca was all smiles, clutching her two notebooks, both with Hello Kitty stickers adorning the covers. She lightly stroked her cheek with one set of long red nails.

Cat smiled obsequiously. "So excited." Echo, echo.

As they chatted a bit, Vivien noticed that they readily agreed with everything she said. That meant either they truly did agree with her, or they had their own agenda and were just playing along.

Vivien was intent on working closely with these two women so she could get a better sense of why they were making decisions that had a negative business impact.

After they left, she had a quiet word with Pandy. "Would you please, in the most diplomatic way, ask the team to stop bringing me flowers?" For a business that was losing money, letting her team waste their budget on flowers for their boss did not send the right signal.

CHAPTER 8: FIRST IMPRESSIONS

One evening later that week, Vivien attended a sports industry function at the prestigious MAC Club in Portland. It was the one time executives from competing companies came together, to celebrate the greatest sports moments from the past year and the greatest achievements in the business. Insiders viewed it as the Oscar night of the sports industry, and it was a great way to see the most successful product launches across competitors. Executives from Nike, Adidas, Columbia, Smart Sports, and Under Armour as well as other brands were all in attendance.

Vivien found her way to the MAC Club and stepped into the grand ballroom. It was a massive cream-colored room with many windows, softly lit with crystal chandeliers and candelabras placed all around. Rather than blend in with the dark business suits, Vivien wore a tasteful red dress and three-inch heels. She looked around. Not only did she not know a single soul in the crowd, but she was the only woman there…at least the only female executive.

Being an unknown was foreign to her. At SCP everyone knew her, if not personally then by reputation. At company events she was always surrounded by people eager to speak with her. Some mornings she'd walk into the elevator and a new employee would say, "TC, you don't know me, but I've heard about you and wanted to introduce myself," and they'd shake her hand as if they were meeting a celebrity.

For the first time in a long time, Vivien Lee was in a professional setting where she felt completely anonymous. Liberating, but at the same time, a bit daunting.

She sauntered over to the bar, aware that her mere presence as a woman was catching glances from around the room. Clusters of men chatted loudly, drinks in hand, slapping each other on the back. The bartender asked, "Are you Michelle Wie?"

Vivien laughed. "No. I do play golf, but not that well."

A voice behind her said, "Well, hello. It's nice to see a pretty face in this crowd. How do you like the MAC Club?"

She turned. The voice came from a fiftyish guy with salt-and-pepper hair.

"Hello. It's my first time here. Looks like a beautiful club. By the way, what does 'MAC' Club stand for?"

"Multnomah Athletic Club."

"So it's called the 'Multnomah Athletic Club Club'? That's funny." Vivien snorted.

"I guess it's a bit silly." The man chuckled. "My name is Stevie. Are you involved in organizing this event?"

"No, Stevie, I'm here for work."

"Oh, then you must be with the catering staff?" It was half question, half statement.

Vivien blinked for a second. Was this guy for real? Even though this was the sports industry, was it that hard to believe that a woman attending this business function was not there to serve the food? Judging from his expression Stevie was in earnest. What a chauvinistic dope. She couldn't wait to share this story with her Ceiling Smasher friends.

First, she decided to have a little fun with it. "Why yes, I am with the catering staff. In fact, I'm responsible for that canapé you're eating now. The goat cheese crumbles were my idea. Like it?"

"It's delicious. Nice job!" Stevie smiled. "You know, I have a huge loft downtown and I host lots of social events. Anyone who is anyone in this town knows about my parties. Since I'm a single guy I always hire a caterer. Perhaps I should get your number so I can hire you."

What, so now he was hitting on her?

Best to cut the conversation off. "I'm sure your parties must be fun. Listen, Stevie, I need to make sure the hors d'oeuvres are coming out of the kitchen all right. Would you please excuse me?"

"Oh, of course, I understand. We'll talk more later. I'll come look for you."

Vivien disappeared into the crowd, losing Stevie. She resolved to quickly start building new business relationships. She saw Steele Hamilton, the Smart Sports CMO, speaking to someone intently. Although she caught his eye, he gave a brief wave and turned back to his buddy. A clear signal Steele did not want her to come over.

Over in the corner was a group of five guys engaged in animated conversation. They seemed jovial, so Vivien summoned up the courage to work her way into the group, smiling and saying hello. The men greeted her, then finished up the topic at hand and reached a lull in the conversation.

One of them asked, "What company are you with?"

"I'm a new employee at Smart Sports."

After a brief chat about her being new to Portland, to Vivien's horror, the guys moved on to the topic of football. Not American football, but European soccer. She was not a footballer and had little to add, so she listened politely and nodded. It was like they were speaking Swahili. She came over to converse with the men and now didn't have a single thing to say. Awkward.

Vivien tried to engage one of the younger-looking guys. His name was Christoph, and he had a bowl haircut and sported a hammered silver ring on his left middle finger. Although he didn't quite cut a dashing figure, Christoph made it clear in the first thirty seconds that he came from a wealthy family in Europe. In a German accent he spoke pompously to Vivien and one of the other guys about how he was restoring an antique Ferrari. Blah, blah, blah.

When Vivien tried to ask a question or make a comment, he looked at her blankly and resumed his monologue. Boring, and rude to boot.

Finally the other guys tired of soccer and the topic turned, thankfully, to work.

"One of the biggest puzzles for us has been understanding our consumer base. We have difficulty analyzing their spending patterns so we can plan our line better," a bald guy said in a clipped accent to the clean-cut guy next to him.

After a few weak suggestions from the others, Vivien took a deep breath and said, "Have you considered conducting consumer segmentation based on specific purchase drivers, then overlaying psychographic and demographic data? Once you have enough data by segment, you can plug it into an algorithm using a neural network that will give tremendous predictive ability about buying preferences."

There was a moment of confused silence as everyone stared blankly at her.

She was merely doing what came naturally to most consultants—solving a problem. Vivien couldn't help it. It was her nature.

Someone who had moments ago joined the group laughed, "How would you know about something like that? Did you overhear someone else say that?" Stevie.

Vivien chuckled. "Actually, I was a partner at a consulting firm for a while. I developed that technique for one of our clients, the Victoria's Secret catalog. I'm sure you guys have heard of it."

Dumbfounded, Stevie leaned in and took a closer look at the small lettering on Vivien's name badge, which indicated that she worked for Smart Sports. "You mean the goat cheese canapés weren't your idea?" The other guys just stood there, looking mystified by Stevie's question.

"Ah, Vivien, there you are," a voice called out. "I see you're hanging out with the Adi crowd," said Malcolm. "Looks like our German friends have met our new president, Vivien Lee."

She let out a small sigh. Finally she was in the company of someone she knew. She and Malcolm exchanged hugs.

The guys from Adidas snapped to attention, stepped back a bit,

and stood up straighter to greet Malcolm Smart. Stevie said, "Uh…
Vivien here was just mentioning that she used to work in consulting."

"Yes, Strategic Consulting Partners. Youngest partner in its history."

"Really? I've heard that to become a partner there, you not only
have to come up with great ideas, but you have to bring in a lot of new
clients. Did you sell a lot of work?" another asked.

"Well, yeah, I sold a bit." Vivien drew back, blushing. Now she was
the center of attention.

"Are you kidding? Her nickname at the firm was the Closer. What
do you think? Vivien sold more work than most senior partners–
kicking ass!" Alex Smart joined the group, bumping fists with the guys.

An audible gasp escaped one of the guys. "Oh. My. God. You're TC?"
he asked, nearly in a whisper. "My brother works in the SCP Frankfurt
office; I've heard stories about you. Like the one about a senior partner
having a heart attack in the middle of a client presentation, and you
saved his life and sold the project, too? And it was like your second
week on the job?"

"Try second *day*," Malcolm said.

How did Malcolm and Alex even know about her nickname or the
origin story? Clearly they had done their homework before hiring her.

Suddenly, the air around them was buzzing as the swarm of men
surrounding Vivien grew exponentially. She felt like a bare lightbulb
on a hot summer evening being bombarded by excited, clinging flies.
Questions were being flung at her from all sides.

Out of the corner of her eye she noticed Duncan, Johnny O, and
Steele huddled together at the bar watching her. Duncan was giving
her a salacious look. The three of them lowered their heads together.
Somehow she suspected they were talking about her, and it unnerved
her.

*

A double chime signaled the end of the cocktail hour–time to sit down for dinner and the awards presentation. The tables were organized by company, so all the Smart Sports executives sat together.

Phil Knight from Nike was being honored, so the festivities started with the presentation of his lifetime achievement award. As he accepted the award, he looked around the room. "Well, you're a sorry-looking bunch, but you clean up pretty good. It's great to see you guys and–oh, Vivien, is that you? Hi there." He waved.

With a tight smile, Vivien waved back. To be called out in front of that crowd by the Nike founder made her night. One of the things she admired about Phil was his quick wit. Malcolm leaned over and said, "Don't tell me Phil Knight tried to recruit you, too. Well, we got you." He grinned at his brother and nudged him.

"I did some project work for Nike a couple of years back." Vivien kept mum about the job offer from Nike. No need to brag.

A late arrival took the empty seat next to Vivien. It was a dapper-looking Tim Kelley, who winked at her and grabbed a roll from the bread basket.

The rest of the evening was a blur except for the most significant award of the evening, the Premier Product Award. This award was being presented by a special guest: basketball legend Michael Jordan, who walked out onstage grinning to thunderous applause.

Vivien put her hand to her chest, hyperventilating. "Oh my god, oh my god…"

"You okay, Vivien?" Tim asked.

She babbled, "It's him. Michael Jordan! I can't believe it. I've seen, like, all his games."

Malcolm said, "I guess you'd like me to introduce you to him after the ceremony?"

"What? That would be incredible!" Vivien was starstruck for the first time.

In his smooth baritone Michael announced the recipient of the Premier Product Award. His glowing smile was even more mesmerizing in person. The award went to Nike for their ingenious Flyknit Running Shoe that fit a foot like a second skin.

"Damn Nike," Steele muttered. "I'd sure like Smart Sports to win that award sometime."

Malcolm held his hands up to calm him. "Don't worry, we will."

Intrigued, Duncan said, "For what? What product will we win for?"

Gesturing to his team at the table, Malcolm said, "That's for you guys to figure out."

*

On Friday afternoon, her desk phone rang. With a click of a button she took the call on her headset so she could continue sorting papers into files while talking.

"How's life in the Wild Wild West, sweetie?"

"Oh, Coop, it's so great to hear your voice. Things are going well so far. I'm going shopping for a condo this weekend."

"A condo? I thought you weren't putting down roots there."

Vivien explained, "Well, the rental market here is nonexistent and real estate prices are good, so it makes more sense to buy, especially with the relocation benefits. Clay and I talked about it and I'm zeroing in on a few places. Work has been interesting, and I'm learning a lot, although things are way more political than I expected. How are you, Coop?"

"Same old same old. Just wrapping things up in the office. So, what is the company like, how are the people?"

"Everyone's really friendly. My peers seem pretty welcoming. I've been surprised; when I walk around on campus everyone remembers my name and says hi.

"Well, Vivi, didn't you get introduced at the company meeting?

Shouldn't everyone in the company know who you are?"

"Yes, but there are always new people being hired here, so I don't expect everyone to remember me."

"Sure, but how many presidents are there at Smart Sports?"

"Four."

"And how many of those are women?"

"One."

"So you're the only female Asian-American president there and you're surprised people know who you are?"

"Okay, I see your point. I guess I am easy to spot."

"How's your team? Do they seem pretty strong?"

"The team has some bright spots and some gaps. There's a guy in charge of consumer insights I may need to get rid of quickly. Oh my god, I almost forgot. Guess who else is on my team? A total blast from the past. Give you a hint–from my track days."

"A Cornell teammate?"

"Nope. Someone from another school. This person is infamous."

*

During their Cornell days Vivien was a middle-distance runner, while Coop played singles on the school tennis team. They ran together regularly. A bit of sports drama unfolded for Vivien during a track meet senior year.

"Oh, not her again," Vivien's coach said, motioning to a USC student named Becky Roche who had a reputation as a dirty racer.

Unremarkable in every aspect except for running ability, Becky was average height with average looks–a pale, freckled face and mousy brown hair. With her vanilla personality, she was the kind of person you'd forget even if you met her multiple times, but Vivien had good reason to remember Becky. Junior year during the fifteen-hundred-meter race, Vivien had been in the lead...until Becky tried passing her and jabbed Vivien in the eye with an elbow. Vivien finished with a black eye and second-place trophy.

Her coach gave her a nudge. "How are you feeling for the eight-hundred-meter, Vivi? You up for racing against Becky?"

"Try and stop me, Coach," a determined Vivien replied.

The racers lined up for the eight-hundred-meter race and as fate would have it, Becky Roche was in the lane beside Vivien. The gunshot sounded and Vivien knew to take the lead early to avoid any trouble from Becky. In the eight-hundred-meter race the first turn was protected, so runners had to stay in their designated lane for one hundred meters to avoid people getting jammed up too early. The protected turn was a hard and fast rule. Vivien hit her stride at about fifty meters, but someone tried to shove her way in front of her. Becky, again. Vivien maintained her footing and said, "Not happening, Becky," thrusting out her arm and giving her a Heisman while never breaking her stride.

Focus and run your race. It was Vivien's senior year and last chance to finish strong. The length of the race made it impossible to all-out sprint, but the shorter distance required an exact calculation on when to make a move. Vivien was breathing hard, her quads burning. Just then Becky inched ahead to take the lead. Forty meters left. Vivien risked it all–she ran full out, praying she'd have enough kick. She zoomed ahead of the field and crossed the finish line, victorious. Becky had dropped back to third place.

Instead of the race results flashing up on the scoreboard right away, there was an unusual delay as the officials conferred. Finally the names and times of the top three finishers appeared on the board. Vivien's name led the list, then two other racers were designated as second and third. Below their names it read, "Becky Roche, DQ'd." She had been disqualified for violating the protected turn rule. Becky let out a screech in protest and violently flung her water bottle onto the track.

✳

Sucking in a huge breath, Coop said, "No, not the evil Becky Roche!"

"Coop, at the first team meeting, I nearly fell over when I realized it was her. Man, she's had a lot of work done; you wouldn't recognize her. And she goes by Rebecca now."

"Jeez, you should fire that evil wench."

"I'm going to give her a fair shot to prove herself. She's in charge of product design and development, and I can already see many problems in that area. We'll see what happens."

"That's so crazy." Coop's voice brightened. "So, how do you like Portland? We're having a terrible heat wave here–walking outside is like going into a steam room. Ugh."

"I'd heard bad things about Portland weather, but summertime is fantastic. Mornings start out cool, then it warms up throughout the day. Zero humidity. The people here are ridiculously friendly. They say hello and thank you in retail shops–it's a little weird. So far, I'm liking it." She was afraid to bring up the subject, since she hadn't heard word from Coop, but she said with trepidation, "Any news about your promotion to partner?"

"I didn't get it." *Again? How much more of this can Coop take?* "Again."

"Oh, Coop. I'm so sorry. Maybe it's time to switch firms. Or do something on your own even." She did her best to cheer up her friend and get him to think about a change.

They chatted awhile until Coop had to sign off. While her new job was all-consuming, Vivien felt a pang of isolation. After only one week she yearned for her usual activities with Coop and her Smasher friends. She repositioned her laptop to get ready for her Skype call with Andi, Grace, and Sofia. Most of all she missed hanging out with Clay. But she just needed to get through this weekend and he'd be visiting the following weekend.

For now, she needed to get up to speed on this business she was trying to turn around and win her team's support.

CHAPTER 9: GETTING THE FIRST GET

Vivien's first weekend alone in Portland was packed with activity. She lined up a Realtor and checked out a number of condos. She dined by herself and noted that everywhere she ate, people knew each other and greeted each other warmly. The small-town feel had a charm to it. By the end of the weekend, Vivien found a promising penthouse in a Pearl District building called the Gregory, a new, modern, well-constructed building.

Now that the press release about her joining Smart Sports had come out, she received email introductions from friends back home who knew people in town. Vivien felt like there was a whole network of friends in Portland just waiting to be discovered. That alleviated her feelings of loneliness.

*

In her first Monday morning staff meeting with her leadership team, she tried to pinpoint the priorities to address. "Where are the biggest problem areas?"

"Everywhere" was their answer. However, no one knew where to start. People worked hard and put in long hours, so why weren't problems getting solved? Lots of activity, but little progress.

Vivien knew they needed focus and discipline. "Team, I'd like to set some ground rules for how we'll operate moving forward to be more productive. First, let's plan and conduct meetings effectively: meetings will start on time, we'll have a meeting objective and agenda, and we'll wrap up with next steps–who is responsible for what and when each task will be completed. If there isn't a good reason to meet, then don't." The immediate impact of this rule was fewer, more productive meetings and clarity on next steps so things actually got done. "The second rule: I want to eliminate face time. Spending more time at work is not going to be rewarded; results will." Instead of people stretching out their work day to give the appearance of working harder, they should go spend some time with their families or work out. "The third rule is called Team Together, Team Apart." Vivien had read about it in a business book and liked it. "It means that when we are discussing an issue as a team we need to hash out all differing opinions. But once a decision is made and we leave the room, everyone must support the decision." Her intent was to gain the advantage of speed. These were simple management concepts that would help her team work together better and achieve more.

Before concluding, Vivien reminded the team, "Remember, tomorrow we're having a special deep-dive meeting on product, so come prepared for a rich discussion."

While everyone exited, Angela, her head of marketing, hung back. "Vivien, we have to make a decision about renewing our sponsorship of the Women's Ironman triathlon series. Here's a sheet with the key facts."

Vivien let out a low whistle. "Whoa, this is one pricey sponsorship. It's like sixty percent of our entire marketing budget. Is it really worth it, Angela?"

Angela said, "Unclear. It is expensive, but it's high-profile." She wrinkled her nose. "Although I don't really think it's helping us reach our customer. We've had this contract renewal request since before you arrived, Vivien, and we need to let them know in the next two days. Can you let me know what you want to do?"

"Sure, will do."

∗

Vivien was heading back to her office when she bumped into the CMO, Steele Hamilton.

"Hey, Steele, can I get your opinion on a marketing issue?"

His eyes brightened. "Of course, Vivien. What kind of advice do you need?"

"I was looking at the cost of our sponsorship of the Women's Ironman. I have two questions for you–does it seem expensive to you? And do you think it's worth it?"

He looked at the floor for a second and then looked at Vivien. "I'd say yes to the first question and probably not to the second question."

"Great, thanks a lot, Steele," Vivien said, "that's just what I needed to know." She smiled. *See, guys like Steele really do want to help me out...I just need to ask.*

Back in her office she rang up Angela and gave her the go-ahead to cancel the triathlon sponsorship.

∗

Pandy had reserved the largest conference room in the apparel building for this meeting, a special session on product. She walked into the room with her boss, who was carrying a large box, while Pandy juggled two smaller ones.

Pandy set her boxes on the table. "What are these for?"

"A little test for the team." Vivien opened the first box. "Just hang those on the grid wall, would you, please?" She pointed to the black metal grid wall.

While Pandy started hanging, Vivien dumped the second box onto the table.

In surprise Pandy said, "There's, like, two dozen shorts there."

"Thirty." Vivien spread them in random order across the expansive table. "I've been doing some homework...I tried on every product, especially the ones with the highest return rates. Have you tried some of these styles, Pandy?"

She answered honestly, "I have. Maybe it's my body type or something, but the tops seem to ride up on me and the bottoms just don't fit me."

"Interesting." Vivien smiled. "I think you'll find today's session quite enlightening."

Next, Vivien hung the clothes from the third box on the grid wall along the left side of the room. Pandy had no idea what Vivien was going to take the team through, but her curiosity was piqued. *Hmm, Vivien sure has a different way of approaching things.*

✳

Vivien had pored over every report, every sales number, every marketing update–all critical data points to understand this business. And the results were discouraging.

When her nine direct reports plus Cat McClintock walked in, they eyed the numerous shorts scattered across the table.

"Okay, team," Vivien said. "Here is a challenge for you. I'd like you to identify the size of each of the shorts on the table–without looking at the tags. The person who can identify all the sizes correctly wins this iPod Shuffle. Okay, go."

As soon as she held up the prize, the team's energy perked up. They progressed down the table, calling out the size of each short. "Small. Extra large. Large. Extra small. Medium. Large. Small. Medium. Extra large. Extra small…"

Vivien stood back with a little gleam in her eye.

Charl was in agreement with the responses, smiling confidently.

"All right," she said, "are those your final answers?"

All nodded.

"Well, here's a secret. See all these shorts on the table? They are all medium size, all of them. See how much variability there is? Some of these barely fit on my head and others I could fit two people into. No wonder we're getting such high returns. If a woman buys one pair of Smart Sports shorts in medium, and then buys another pair later, there's a ninety-nine percent chance they won't fit. That's why our online returns are astronomical." She paused, letting this sink in. Everyone looked stupefied. Except for Charl. And Rebecca. Their faces held stoic expressions. "Why is this happening?"

Rebecca, in a monotone, said, "I'm sure they were designed correctly, so it's probably a production issue with the factory."

"That's possible, but I think there's a bigger issue. Why are we not using standardized sizing specifications?"

Rebecca said, "You'd have to ask Cat. That's the way we've been doing it for a long time." She shrugged. Cat sipped her giant smoothie and shrugged. A silent echo.

"So we don't know why we're doing something that doesn't make sense. Moving forward, we need to determine the optimal sizing specs and use those. Just to satisfy my own curiosity I'd like to sit in on the next few fit sessions with you, Cat, and the rest of the team, to better understand what our process is for fitting garments."

Rebecca nodded, looking worried. The rest of the leadership team seemed to approve. "Vivien, I am in total agreement," Rebecca said, "and I think these changes are long overdue. I've been in this role for over four years, and this is something I've felt was important, but with all the other priorities we weren't able to get to it. My apologies, Madame President."

Wow. Rebecca may not have been skilled at her job, but she was a fantastic politician.

"Let me just set the record straight." Vivien braced her hands on the table. "I'm not asking for apologies. We're looking at the business with fresh eyes, and I just need us to identify what the issues are and fix them. I did a little homework over the weekend and measured some of our products versus competitors like Nike, Adidas, Under

Armour, Champion, and Lululemon. Our pants are quite a bit off in length and in the construction of the gusset."

One of the guys said, "Huh? What's a gusset?"

How could a guy in the apparel business not know the word *gusset*? "The crotch," Vivien replied. "It's not constructed properly–extra fabric bulges out, which is not a pretty sight."

She flipped through her notes. "Our sizing on tops is quite a bit smaller than the average. Our bust measurement, sleeve length, and cross-shoulder measures are all about three to four inches smaller than industry average. I made up this spreadsheet, which shows how far off the average spec we are on tops and bottoms." She gave the sheets to Pandy, who handed them out. "Of course I'm sure you and your team will want to do some more detailed analysis, but this is a good starting point."

"Ooh, this is great, Vivien," Rebecca cooed. "I love it. Of course Cat and I will have to dive into the details to really understand it properly." Tinkle, tinkle–Rebecca wrote down some note in her pink notebook with her Hello Kitty pen, red nails gripping it tightly.

"Yes, we'll look at the details," Cat said.

"Great. When can I expect an updated set of sizing specs? Sometime in the next two weeks?" Vivien countered.

Rebecca hedged. "We have an extremely heavy workload, so I don't know about that. Our product calendar is already tight, and we have so many time pressures."

Clasping her hands together, Vivien said, "Let me make this simple for you. If we don't turn out product that fits, we will not sell anything. Or we'll sell it and the customer will return it–just as they have been doing. What other projects do you feel take priority over fixing the fit?"

Rebecca was silent with pursed lips. For the first time, she opened her black Moleskine notebook and made some notes. The silence was accompanied by the ominous tinkling of Hello Kitty's bell.

"Then we'll put all extra projects on the back burner and get this solved. Agreed?"

Without looking at her boss, Cat nodded. A first. Wow, was Vivien making progress?

"Vivien, I think Rebecca and her team can figure out what their priorities are. They have a lot on their plate right now," Charl said.

Why was he so protective of Rebecca when she was not firing on all cylinders? That warranted investigation.

Vivien turned to the team. "What is the one major way that consumers interact with a brand?"

J. J. said, "Through product?"

"Exactly. Something we need to be clear on is that fixing the product is our number one priority. If our product doesn't fit, people won't wear it. If our design or quality is poor, it doesn't matter what we do with the branding, customer service, operations, or sales. We must fix product first and then work on the rest. I hope I am making myself perfectly clear."

"Absolutely, I'm in total agreement, Vivien," Rebecca replied.

For someone who was supposedly an expert in product design and development, these fit issues seemed like a huge oversight. How did Rebecca even get this job in the first place? Politics? Connections? Both?

"I thought our number one priority was to turn around this business," Charl scoffed.

"That's precisely what we're doing here, Charl." Vivien made eye contact, with the intent of getting him to back down.

She checked the next item on her notes. "Okay, team, I looked at the twenty products with the highest consumer return rates or the lowest sales. I've hung them up here on the left. Let's talk about why these products are having such a challenge."

Vivien waited while her team perused the products on the wall–a mix of pants, tops, and jackets in a myriad of colors.

"Well, a lot of these pants are black or gray and the tops are green or pale yellow. Is color an issue?" asked Sam.

"Color could be an issue. In terms of pants, for bottoms the bestselling color is black, and most of the pants we offer are in black, so that explains why we have some black pants here. But in the case of these pants, color isn't the issue. For pants that are red, navy blue, and pale green I do think color was the issue."

Rebecca said, "Other than some pop colors in bottoms, I don't think overall that color is an issue. I personally oversee all the final decisions about product color." Hah. Now she sounded defensive.

"No, color's not an issue." Echo, echo, from Cat.

Vivien pressed on. "Let's take a look at tops. Some colors are really tough for anyone to wear–namely, pale greens, mustardy yellows, and pale beiges. We offer a very cool color palette and perhaps not enough of a range of colors that work on different skin tones. Seems like a clear miss. Any guesses as to what the other issues are?"

"Fit?" asked Meredith from merchandising.

"We have fit issues. Our pants inseam is about three inches longer than industry norm. Not sure why. Maybe we're planning on selling only to customers with really long legs."

Some of the guys chuckled. Cat's face reddened. This was her area.

"I noticed our waistbands are tight and tend to grab around the midsection, causing a muffin top. Now, no woman, especially one in good shape, wants to wear pants that give her a muffin top. Okay, let's move to jackets. We have a running jacket here that has a hood, drawstrings, and metal aglets. No real runner would buy this product. Who can tell me why?"

People gave her blank looks.

"Of the people who are designing running product, how many runners do we have?"

Rebecca had the temerity to say, "As a matter of fact, I was an NCAA track champion in college."

More than a few people rolled their eyes. They could not have known the real story about little Becky Roche and her true track record. Why would Rebecca make a statement about her running expertise when she was responsible for the mistakes on the running jacket?

"Here are my observations as a fellow runner," Vivien said. "First, most runners wear a hat when it's cold. They don't wear hooded jackets because a swaying hood is annoying when running. Second, drawstrings with metal aglets are a problem. When you're running, the aglets will fly up and hit you in the face. A real runner would not expect this type of trim on a running product...they'd look at this product and we'd lose all credibility as an authentic sports brand."

People nodded and scribbled notes. Rebecca wrote in her black book.

"Let's move on to the training products, the products designed for use in the gym. What are the issues here?"

"Not enough metal?" Sam joked.

Vivien smiled. "Let me ask you, when people are training what are their most common movements?" She remained silent for what seemed an eternity.

Finally, J. J. volunteered, "When I go to the gym I'm mostly lifting weights, so I would say the most common movement is raising your arms."

"Yes, thank you, J. J. In every training top I tried, except tank tops, it was impossible to lift my arms without the entire garment riding up. That, my friends, is a problem." Vivien gave a little wink to Pandy. "Also, quite a few of the Training tops are very low cut, which makes it awkward when you're bending over a weight bench." She noticed that Cat was furiously scribbling notes. Good sign. "Okay, let's move on to the newest line, the yoga product. These three styles all had high returns." Vivien came to three yoga tops, all low cut with embellishments like twisted fabric or bows on the back. "What's common across them?"

"If you ask me, the front kind of dips down a bit. And there's extra design stuff on the back of every one," commented Sam.

"Great observation, Sam," Vivien replied. "You hit the nail on the head. Again, the cut on these tops is too low in the front. When you are bending over for downward dog, all your treasures will be on display."

Rebecca typically wore a low-cut top to work. Her personal style was most likely driving this design detail.

"Personally," Vivien continued, "I think women would like to show some modesty, so the cut is too low for many people. Also, there are fabric details on the back of all these that bulge. That's an issue because if you are doing anything on your back you're going to feel those obstructions."

"At least we have our Stride Track pant, our bestseller," Charl chimed in. "We're really proud of the Stride Track pant, and that's one style that doesn't need tinkering with."

Vivien blinked. How convenient for Charl to change the subject to the only product that seemed to be working. "All right, let's take a look at the Stride Track pant. I also took a look at our product successes. I brought along some of those top styles, which we'll get to in a minute. But something that's unusual about this Stride Track pant is its external drawstring. Why might women not like that?"

"Unless you have a shirt tucked in, the drawstring gives you a tummy bulge. My wife told me that," J. J. offered.

"That's right. We are selling body-hugging products to women who work out and want to look great. Why are we intentionally adding a design feature that gives women a tummy bulge? That doesn't make sense." Vivien looked around, and everyone was nodding. "Now, it may seem like I'm coming down hard on product design and development, but as I said before, a customer's lasting impression of a brand comes from their interaction with our product. If we're selling product for a healthy, athletic woman and our product makes her look worse, she will not buy from us again. That's part of the reason our repeat purchase rate is so low. If we step back and look at all the product, is there anything else you notice, in general?"

The team concentrated hard on the question, but Vivien didn't have any takers.

"A lot of the women's styles are simply copies of our bestselling men's styles. We need to move away from this 'shrink it and pink it' strategy and start designing things specifically for a woman's body and how she moves."

"You may not understand this, Vivien, but we've been aligning with the Men's Apparel product so it ties together on the retail floor," Charl said.

"That might make sense if it was merchandised together, but in all the sporting goods stores I've ever seen, men's apparel is separate from women's."

Charl looked momentarily stupefied, as if he was realizing this obvious fact for the first time.

Shifting her focus, Vivien pulled some sheets from a folder. "Okay, team, last assignment. On the right side of the room we have about forty bestselling apparel products from our competitors, and I've covered up the branding on each garment. Identify which brand each item belongs to." Vivien tossed the sheets across the table. They fluttered down onto the bed of shorts. "Here are some stickers with different brand names on them. Go ahead and put them on the products that belong to those brands. Go."

The team could easily identify the Nike, Adidas, Under Armour, and Lululemon products. Shrewdly, Vivien had mixed in product from C9, Champion's budget brand in Target; Puma; a private label; and Smart Sports apparel. Most people on the team were not able to clearly distinguish their own company's product.

"This is interesting. Why is it so hard to pick out the Smart Sports product from competitors?" Vivien asked.

"It just doesn't stand out. This is a pretty depressing statement to make, but our product can easily be mistaken for a budget brand or private label." This admission came from the IT guy, of all people.

Rebecca had a pinched look of chagrin on her face and made some notes in the black notebook. She was clearly not accustomed to having her team's work questioned in front of the leadership. She let out an audible sigh.

"In other words, we need to create a more distinctive aesthetic, is that what you're saying?" Vivien asked.

"Absolutely."

"No doubt about it."

This was good. She was actually making headway. She removed the tape covering the garment logos. "Now, what do you notice about the product branding?"

"Well, one thing that is working is that our logo is much bigger than our competitors', so that's an advantage." Charl should've kept silent. He was a slow learner, and stubborn.

"A larger logo is an advantage. Why do you say that?" she asked.

"It's hard to miss, so it's great that people can actually see it."

Having the former leader of the division in this meeting was awkward enough, but even Vivien was beginning to feel embarrassed for the guy. Maybe he'd lucked into the job merely because people liked him so much.

"I beg to differ. Unlike the male consumer, who has no problem—heck, he loves wearing a huge logo emblazoned across his chest—the female consumer is more subtle and prefers branding that isn't overt. Just think of designer products. Prada has the little red strip, Christian Louboutin has the red soles on his shoes. Women want brand identification but don't want to look like a billboard. There are creative, more tasteful ways we can execute our branding."

Angela in marketing was nodding vigorously. "I agree, Vivien. For years we've just followed the same product branding as Men's

Apparel, and that doesn't work for our female customer. I think our woman is more sophisticated and turned off by giant, garish logos." Angela shot a concerned look in Charl's direction, as if worried about repercussions.

So...logo size was a battle that had already been fought.

"Let's move to the last topic, our product offering. Are we designing the right number of styles? And what are we known for?"

After quite a bit of discussion, the team concluded that their focus had been simply on churning out new stuff, without thinking about what the consumer really wanted. As a result, the number of new styles introduced per season was out of control. That was impacting the workload on the product design and development team. Also they were also not anniversarying–repeating styles that were authentic hits. That was a miss.

No one could really say what the brand was known for.

"What do we want to be known for?" Vivien asked. "What do we want our pinnacle product to be? A lot of our product line is really high end technical apparel. We have seven different styles of triathlon suits. That seems like a lot. Who's the consumer we're going after, and do we have a good sense of the activities she's doing?"

"That's an easy answer," Charl said. "Our consumer is the hard-core athlete–the woman who's doing triathlons and working out nonstop. That's why we need that many tri-suits. Our woman is cut, with very low body fat percentage. She's got visible six-pack abs."

He could not have been more off-base. The direction he must have been giving the team was a big problem, because he didn't really understand their core consumer.

"Yes, and about eighty percent of our customers are built just like Charlize Theron, right?" Vivien's quip elicited a laugh. Pandy had mentioned how obsessed Charl was with Ms. Theron, a confessed "huge, huge fan." "How many of the women in this room are Smart Sports apparel consumers?"

With the exception of Cat McClintock, every women in the room, including Vivien, raised her hand. "All right, now how many of us are sporting six-pack abs? Come on, don't be shy." Even the women with the hard bodies didn't raise their hands. "Most companies don't have a good enough handle on their customer. We need to challenge our assumptions. Have we sized the market and defined our consumer target segment specifically? Have we built a profile of our consumer? Do we understand what she likes, dislikes, thinks, does, and feels? Gus, what insights can you provide?"

Up until that moment, Gus had been completely mute. When the team was talking about all the problems with product and fit, he'd had a smirk on his face. Now his face grew ashen. "Precisely what kind of insights are you looking for, Vivien?" When he spoke, his thin, oatmeal-colored lips barely parted, which made him look like he was permanently gritting his teeth.

"The useful kind, Gus. For one, who is our current core consumer and is that the same as our target consumer? What types of activities does she do and how often? What's important to her–fit, color, price, fabric, functionality, comfort, design? What does she think about our brand?"

"We have extensive consumer analyses, which I've compiled based on trends pulled from our database. The statistics may be difficult for you to understand, but I can explain them to you offline." Gus smiled smugly and glanced over at Charl, who nodded. "For example, we know our customer is active and spends about five hundred fifty to twelve hundred dollars per year on activewear."

That didn't actually answer any of her questions. Gus seemed to be putting up a screen that he was smarter than everyone and only he could interpret the data. And her not understanding statistics? Insolent. "Five hundred fifty to twelve hundred dollars per year is a pretty broad range. What's the average annual spend?"

"I can get that for you, Vivien. I don't know if the rest of the team is interested. It's pretty complicated stuff."

"Gus, an average isn't complicated, and I expect you to know that number off the top of your head. Do we have any consumer research on our target customer segment?"

"Those of us who have been in this business for a while have a good gut feel for our consumer, Vivien, so why waste money on unnecessary research?" Charl replied.

Another swipe at her relative inexperience. "Hmm. Let me ask you–how many of our customers are doing triathlons? How many are they doing per year? If you think about it, there's a tricky thing about the market for tri-suits. People don't train in tri-suits, they only use them for race day. You'd have to be doing a ton of triathlons to need more than one tri-suit per year. That means the sales rate is pretty low. I'd be curious to know what the inventory turns are on our tri-suits. Meredith?"

Meredith from merchandising said, matter-of-factly, "They're our slowest-turning item. Bottom performer."

Vivien caught the glint of satisfaction in Meredith's eyes. She could only surmise that this was an issue of contention between merchandising and Charl.

"I'm not even going to ask how much inventory we're sitting on in terms of tri-suits." Vivien paused. She could have skewered Charl and Gus further but held back. This discussion only confirmed her decision to cancel the triathlon sponsorship. "We need to understand who our customer is now and who we want our target customer to be. We cannot make this business a success unless we have total clarity on the consumer." She picked up her pen and made some notes. Charl didn't understand the customer, and Gus the consumer insights expert was only good at guessing about the consumer. Shooting from the hip. Vivien preferred to get facts and then unleash creativity to solve problems.

But first they had to all be on the same page.

She dropped her pen. "Here is your homework for tonight. I would like each of you to think about the top three questions you have about our consumer, then email your questions to Gus by tomorrow by ten a.m. Gus, I want you to consolidate and compile the questions and answer them with the data we have. At our next Monday morning staff meeting, we'll set aside some time to review those questions and see where we have knowledge gaps. We will most likely need to conduct some consumer research to get our questions answered. And, Gus, if you'd like my recommendation on a statistical analysis approach and cross-tabulation techniques for doing the segmentation, I'm happy to provide my point of view."

Gus's eyes widened and beads of sweat appeared on his upper lip.

"Team, we need facts here, not just feelings. To reiterate, we are the smallest business at Smart Sports and we're losing money, and unprofitable businesses don't survive. But if we put the right plan in place and work hard we can turn things around. I'm counting on you and together I believe we can succeed. We need to do a few things exceptionally well: focus on the right areas, execute brilliantly, and be accountable." Vivien gave them all a big smile. "Team, I appreciate our robust discussion on product today. As we turn this business around we'll be looking at every aspect of how we conduct our business, so stay tuned."

Someone let out a whistle.

After a long pause, J. J. said, "Jeez, Vivien, some of us have been working in this industry for a long time and for Smart Sports since nearly the beginning. I was probably your biggest skeptic, because you came from outside the industry. But, I have to say...you quickly identified major issues we just weren't seeing. Frankly, this is embarrassing."

"Yeah, this was incredibly insightful."

"Really awesome."

Others chimed in.

Charl remained silent.

Vivien felt a surge of adrenaline. Could she count this as a small victory? Sports training had taught her the value of humility. "Thanks, guys. J. J., there's no need to be embarrassed. We have a lot of great expertise on this team. It is not my intent to make people feel bad about the business. Sometimes when people are so close to a business it's difficult to step back and see the issues. That's what makes coming in with a fresh pair of eyes critical to turning the business around."

Vivien was proud of her skill in identifying problems at lightning speed and then coming up with ingenious solutions. That was what she had built her reputation upon. "Let's be honest here. We have a lot to fix. I believe in giving people the bandwidth they deserve to do their jobs, meet goals, and make decisions. But remember that I will hold you accountable for the decisions you make. I expect you to collaborate with your teammates, and I will also be there to guide you in making the best decisions for the business."

Heads nodded.

All right, that's it for today. Thank you for approaching this meeting with an open mind. We had some good discussions, and we were honest about our challenges. The first step to fixing our problems is recognizing that we have them."

Vivien stacked her notes together and discussed a few details with Pandy, who packed up the clothes. Cat hesitated for a moment. Vivien got the sense she wanted to say something, but when Rebecca summoned her, Cat went trailing behind her boss. It might be interesting to peel Cat away from her boss for a direct conversation.

Charl chatted with a couple of people as they were gathering their belongings, but it was evident he was hanging back to speak with Vivien. While Pandy packed up the clothes at one end of the large room, it was just the two of them left at the other end. Charl came over and stood close. "Vivien, since you're still so new at this, I thought I'd offer a helpful hint."

What possible hint could he give? "Oh, what's that, Charl?" she asked, half amused. She stood up to face him.

"One thing I pride myself on is that people really enjoy working for me. I take the time to make sure they're feeling good about things and that they're happy."

Vivien just looked at him. Was he trying to help, or did he not realize that he no longer called the shots?

"I think it's important for you to be careful about people. You introduced a lot of new ideas and approaches here, and you really shouldn't do too much of that. You have to be careful not to overwhelm the team or confuse them or make them feel bad."

She stepped back. "Feel bad?"

"Yeah, like the way you talked to Gus. I think you were too hard on him. It wouldn't hurt to try and make people feel good about what they're doing. Praise them. I always handle my team a certain way and they're used to that."

"Thanks, Charl. I always treat people with kindness unless there's an issue. As you know, it's my team now, so I'll interact with people in the way I see fit. Any problem with that?"

Charl's head jerked back a few inches, as if he had been slapped. Had he expected her to say, *Sure, Charl, I'll do exactly as you say. I'm sorry?* Vivien had a reputation for treating people well, and they enjoyed working with her. People at Smart Sports called Charl a "great guy," but did that mean he was capable of leading a division? Funny thing, she never heard a successful woman executive being called "a great gal." In the sports industry, was a pleasant personality the main requirement for a man to succeed?

After an awkward few moments, Charl said, "See you later," grabbed his things, and left.

By the time Vivien returned to her office in the executive building, a few of her team members were waiting outside her door.

Uh-oh. Were they there to complain about the meeting? Did

Charl's comments actually reflect what the team felt?

She smiled and said, "Hi, guys, what can I help you with?" A knot formed in her stomach.

"Vivien, I just wanted to say–" J. J. stammered. "We just wanted to say…a couple of comments about that meeting."

Vivien held her breath.

"That meeting was the most insightful we've ever had. Really great. You've got a creative and effective approach to showing us our problems–big issues we've never considered before. Personally, I'm floored at how quickly you've learned this business."

Sam from operations and the finance guy nodded vigorously.

Vivien relaxed. "We have a lot to do, and I'm still learning, but your feedback means a great deal to me. I appreciate it, guys, thanks." She held their gaze for a moment and gave J. J. a friendly pat on the shoulder.

The men walked out of her office, but after a few seconds J. J. poked his head back in. "Vivien, do you have a few minutes?"

"Sure, what's on your mind, J. J.?"

He stepped in and closed the door. "I thought I should mention… in the past Rebecca hasn't necessarily been open to input about product design and development. She manages her team tightly and doesn't take a lot of feedback from other areas. Her comments today seemed like she was open-minded, actually more than I've heard in the past, but she has had a history of being adamant that product is her domain and she is the queen. I just think that's an area that could use…how shall I say this…your strong leadership."

"Okay, J. J., thanks for the tip. I'll keep that in mind." That was a truly valuable nugget of information. Fixing the product was likely to be more challenging than she'd anticipated.

As J. J. walked out, the Smart brothers were on their way in. "Hey, J. J., how's it going?" Malcolm asked.

"We just had the best damn business meeting ever. Vivien blew us away with her insights–and after only two weeks on the job! I had my doubts about bringing in someone from outside the industry, but I think we've got a great leader who's going to turn things around."

"That's exactly why we hired her." Malcolm grinned.

Malcolm and Alex made good on their promise of barbecue, inviting her and Clay over to Malcolm's house for dinner on Saturday night.

"We also need you to get ready for the SBR," Alex said.

"The what?"

"Sorry, the Strategic Business Review."

Malcolm sat in one of her side chairs. "It's basically a quarterly meeting with the board of directors. Each president gives a presentation to the board."

"Recap the business strategy, results, issues, and next steps." Alex leaned in her doorway. "The SBR is coming up in about a month, and we wanted to make sure you had it in your sights."

"Thanks, I appreciate that." She made a note.

"One more thing," Malcolm said. "We're planning a market trip to Asia. We and the four presidents will visit factories, look at market developments, and do some team building."

"Okay. When?"

"Right after the SBR. We'll take the corporate jet for a ten-day trip covering a few cities in China, Korea, Japan, and Hong Kong."

After the Smart brothers left her office, Vivien stared at her calendar. Basically she had one month to lay the groundwork for fixing the business before she'd be out of reach on all this travel. The trip sounded exciting and she loved traveling to that part of the world. But a month wasn't enough time, so she'd have to hunker down.

*

Pandy parked the hand truck outside Vivien's office and stuck her head in. "Where do you want me to put this product, Vivien? I found an empty closet at the end of the hall and I can store it there if you like."

Vivien nodded. "That would be great, Pandy. I like how you're always thinking a few steps ahead. And thank you for all your help with the meeting."

"That was really fascinating, thanks for letting me sit in. Now I understand now why the product never fit me quite right," she said.

"Well, Pandy," Vivien laughed, "that puts you a few steps ahead of some of the folks on the team!"

That made Pandy giggle. This was the first time a boss had made her feel like an integral part of the team and made her feel valued. She replied, "You know, Vivien, having a woman run this business is totally unusual. I honestly believe you're going to make a difference. And I overheard Malcolm and Alex talking about the SBR–don't worry, I'll help you get ready for it."

*

Intent on learning why the fit of the product was so poor, Vivien made good on her promise to attend some fit sessions. Approaching it casually, Vivien said, "Rebecca, you don't mind if I join the next fit session, do you? I'm curious to see how it works."

"Of course, Vivien. You're the president of the business, you can do anything you want." Rebecca's obsequious habit of always reminding Vivien of her title was grating. "I'd love for you to come."

Vivien asked Pandy to free up some time so she could attend the next fit session. Before she embarked on her Asia tour Vivien wanted to get a clear sense of exactly what Rebecca was doing.

On the day of the fit session, when Vivien walked into the room, she noticed something right away about the team's mood. People looked tense. Really tense. Instead of sitting at the conference table, Vivien took a chair against the wall to be less conspicuous so she could observe better.

Rebecca breezed in. "Oh my gosh, I have to show you guys the cutest jacket I got from Banana, take a look. Don't you just love it?" Rebecca mostly talked at her team during the meeting while also doing emails on her smartphone.

As they were getting into product discussions, a pretty, slender girl–Rebecca's newest hire–came in carrying a black lacquered tray with a small white ceramic cup of espresso on a saucer. She placed it carefully in front of Rebecca. This struck Vivien as strangely incongruous with what she knew of the Smart Sports culture, which was quite informal (and self-serve). Rebecca spoke animatedly about some product updates to the fall line, and midsentence she picked up the espresso cup and sipped it.

She narrowed her eyes, turned sharply to the coffee girl, and said in a menacingly low voice, "Cassandra, I've told you before I want my drink boiling hot. This espresso…it's too cold." With that, she tossed the entire contents into the trash can and violently threw the cup back onto the tray. "Bring me another," Rebecca commanded.

Vivien was shocked by the vulgar behavior and took the opportunity to lighten the mood. "Whoa, Rebecca, don't ask me to bring you soup!"

The team giggled and Rebecca spun around, suddenly remembering her boss was observing her. She waited a beat and then joined the others with a shrill, staccato laugh. Then Rebecca turned to the coffee girl and added sweetly, "Thanks, Cassie, you're the best. And please tell Amanda we're ready for her." Cassie asked Vivien if she wanted anything and Vivien politely declined. The room fell uncomfortably silent. Amanda, the very tall and muscular fit model, entered the room, and Rebecca proceeded to gloss over some "updates" to the product she was wearing. The rest of the team was notably silent.

"Hold on a minute," Vivien said, raising her hand. "Why are we adding a big bow to the bottom of that jacket?"

"We need some touches of style, don't we?" Rebecca said,

shrugging her shoulders.

"With a hip-length jacket that bow will be right under the wearer's bum when they're sitting down. Won't that be annoying?" Vivien noticed that heads were nodding in agreement.

"No, I don't think so." Rebecca scrunched up her face.

"Hi, Amanda, would you do me a favor? Can you sit down in that jacket, please?" Vivien said, and Aileen stood up so the fit model could use her chair. "How does it feel to you?"

Amanda said, "Honestly, I can feel the bow a little." She glanced over at Rebecca and added, "But it's not too bad."

"I'm confused, Vivien," Rebecca said. "Are you questioning my taste level?"

Vivien dropped her pen into her notebook. "No, I'm questioning the function of the jacket. I'm all for adding style details, but not at the cost of making the product unwearable. Let's lose the bow, Rebecca."

"Okay, duly noted." Rebecca's red nails gripped her tinkling Hello Kitty pen and made some notes in her pink Moleskine notebook.

The next style was a yoga tank with "updated" straps that were much narrower than the original version.

"See, we made the tank look sleeker," Rebecca explained.

"With the straps so narrow, won't the wearer's bra straps be exposed?"

Rebecca gave a little laugh. "I guess it's possible. But that's okay. The trend now is to have your bra straps showing."

Vivien leaned forward, unconvinced. "Based on the consumer feedback I've read on our website, the reason why women like this style so much–besides the fit and cut–is that the straps are just wide enough to cover their bra straps. If that's a feature the customer likes, why would we eliminate it?"

"Vivien, this is a yoga tank. The wearer is going to be moving around, so no matter what we do her bra straps will show."

"Rebecca, you're saying it's not possible to design a tank top that covers up bra straps? Like we've done before? Like our competitors do?" Vivien crossed her arms.

Rebecca was starting to get testy and it was beginning to show. Defiantly, she said, "No, that's not possible." And she stared at Cat to drum up support. Cat was munching on graham crackers.

Cat echoed, "Not, possible," between bites.

You've got to be kidding me, Cat. Do you ever have an independent thought? Vivien was irked by Rebecca's obstinacy. Despite all this she wanted to be careful about not coming down too harshly on Rebecca in front of her whole team–it was not her practice to humiliate people. She made a mental note to speak with her in private about the yoga tank design.

Rebecca appeared to dismiss Vivien's comments and said, "Let's move on to the next style, the updated Training Tee. Isn't it just the cutest? We've made it sexier by dropping the neckline and changing up the fabric weight."

Vivien tried to hide her dismay, but the neckline was so low it looked more suitable for going clubbing. The fabric was so thin, it was see-through. "Do you think the neckline is a bit too low? Remember, our customer is going to be working out in that top and bending over a weight bench to lift weights and stuff. We don't want it to be too revealing. That fabric also looks extremely thin–is our customer going to feel like she's getting her money's worth?"

Rebecca pursed her lips. "Well, you'll be happy to know that the lighter-weight fabric reduces our cost, so we'll make more money on this style. Anyway, the trend now is to wear a colorful sports bra underneath your workout shirt, so you want it to show through."

Where could Rebecca possibly be getting her news on the latest fashion "trends"?

Vivien spoke calmly. "See-through tops might be fine for a fashion company or an eighteen-year-old customer, but let's remember, we are a performance apparel company–the product has to function.

We need to keep in mind the modesty factor and ask, will our target consumer be comfortable in this garment?"

Sitting upon her throne as the queen of product, Rebecca was probably accustomed to just giving orders. It occurred to Vivien that the two of them really had just started working together, and so far things weren't going so well.

Rebecca persisted. "We have to give the customer something new and different."

Vivien stood her ground. "Actually, I'd say we need to give the consumer something new and *better*. And we need to be wise about choosing where to offer newness. The Training Tee has been our bestselling top—I'm concerned that we're making changes to it the customer won't appreciate."

Aileen spoke up. "I agree. At the end of the day the product has to be saleable, and with these changes I think we are putting sales at risk."

Astonishingly, Cat echoed, "That's true, the product has to be saleable. We worked hard on it and don't want to jeopardize the business."

Rebecca shot a glance at Aileen and made dagger eyes at Cat. She took a deep breath. "All right, Vivien. You're the president, so what you say goes."

"Thanks, Rebecca. It's not necessarily what I want that's critical, it's what the consumer wants. Let's keep that in mind when we're making these decisions. We have to understand what customers like about a style and then continue in that vein—or what isn't working and improve it. So let's confirm we're not making the proposed changes to the Training Tee, correct?"

"Of course, Madame President, we will not change it." Rebecca mustered a saccharine smile, but her eyes held an odd expression.

Next for review was a special capsule collection. "Super exciting," Rebecca said breathlessly. "I collaborated on this with renowned fashion designer Flora Jensen."

There were two bodysuits, a dress, a jumpsuit, leggings, and a top with an asymmetric hem...all flesh colored. Huh?

"Is that a sample fabric or the actual color of the garments?" Vivien asked fearfully.

"Oh yes, this is the color. It's a bit high concept but the idea is 'natural form.'" It was hard to believe but Rebecca looked proud of the collection.

Vivien took a breath. "Um, do you think this will resonate with the consumer?"

Pandy came into the conference room. "Vivien, the Smart brothers need to see you right away."

Vivien left the fit session confident that her input had helped get things back on track. Besides, she felt there was enough time to correct any mistakes. With the lead time on developing product, the consumer wouldn't be seeing these items on the retail floor for about a year.

*

When Vivien entered the Smart brothers' conference room she sensed a bad vibe. Steele Hamilton sat there looking grim.

Alex tugged on his right earlobe. "Vivien, have a seat. Can you tell us what's going on with the Women's Ironman sponsorship?"

Vivien said, "Sure, I looked at it with my head of marketing as it was up for renewal. It was a huge portion of our marketing spend and unclear that it resonated with our target customer."

"Steele informed us that you canceled the sponsorship a couple of days ago...please tell us that isn't true," Alex said.

A knot was tightening in Vivien's stomach. "Yes, Alex, I did cancel it. They needed a response right away. I conferred with Steele before making a decision. He said it wasn't worth the money. Remember that, Steele?"

Steele raised his eyebrows. "Yeah, Vivien, I do remember. You asked me if I thought the sponsorship was expensive and if it was worth it. But you didn't ask me if you should cancel it—if you had I would have said absolutely not."

Great, thanks for the help, Steele.

"I'm not sure I understand. Did I do something wrong?"

Malcolm sighed. "Vivien, you couldn't have known this, but these sponsorships are extremely hard to come by—we waited six years for that sponsorship opportunity to open up and we were hoping to protect it."

"Oh. Well, I can call them back and tell them we changed our mind," Vivien offered.

"Not possible. I heard this afternoon that Nike swooped in and signed on as sponsor at a higher price tag," Steele said.

Vivien's stomach churned...her second week into the job and she had already made a huge rookie blunder. "I see. I'm really sorry about that."

"Let's just chalk it up as a lesson learned," Malcolm said, glancing at Alex.

Trying to turn around the situation, Vivien offered, "We do have other creative marketing ideas. One is a program called One Thousand Everyday Athletes aimed at our target consumer. We've never spoken to the women's market before."

"Sounds promising." Alex looked up at his assistant, Marla, who was standing at the door.

"Justin Stewart is here," she said.

Steele jumped up, barely able to contain his excitement. "We're trying to grow the tennis category and hoping to sign Justin Stewart." He rushed out to greet the athlete.

She couldn't believe they were considering signing the guy, especially after the recent US Open incident. Just because you disagree with the call of an African-American line judge, you don't resort to using racial slurs. Vivien had zero respect for him.

Smiling broadly, Justin entered the room. He was tall and thin, with long lean muscles and a head of uncontrollable curly hair.

Malcolm and Alex gave him a warm welcome and introduced Vivien.

"Hey, Vivien," Justin said somewhat dismissively, and offered a limp hand.

"Nice to meet you, Justin." She shook his hand firmly.

"Vivien is our newest president of Women's Apparel," Malcolm said.

Justin's eyes lit up. "Oh? Cool."

"Well, I'll let you guys get to it," Vivien said, making her exit. As she walked out she heard Steele dive into his "grand plan" for Justin as a Smart Sports athlete.

PART THREE

CHAPTER 10: TOGETHER
FOR THE FIRST TIME

Vivien sat and listened as Pandy reviewed her packed schedule for the following week.

"Tell Charl to clear his schedule for the latter part of next week." Vivien checked her watch. Clay's plane should have landed by now. She was so excited to see him, her pent-up energy came through her pen, which she was tapping rapidly on the desk.

"What should I tell him it's about?" Pandy asked.

She looked at her watch again. "Just say…details will be coming."

"Okay, boss. Maybe you should get going. I'm sure you can't wait to see Clay."

"Great idea, Pandy. The Realtor is picking him up from the airport and we're meeting at the condo. I have to be there by five p.m."

"You've been working so hard, why not get an early start to the weekend? Have some fun."

"Thanks, Pandy, you have a good weekend, too."

Vivien grabbed her purse and stuffed her laptop into her computer bag. She dashed out the door to the parking garage. Taking a moment to check her reflection in the rearview mirror, she gunned the engine and headed to the Pearl District.

＊

When she arrived at the Gregory condo building she called the Realtor on her cell and was buzzed up. Breathless, she swung open the door to the condo. She saw her fiancé's tall silhouette against the window. Clay was engaged in animated conversation, but when he heard the door open he whipped around. He rushed toward Vivien, dipped her, and planted a huge smooch on her lips.

"Oh, this is like a scene from *Casablanca*," the Realtor gushed, and smiled.

"I missed you so much, honey!" Vivien squeezed his arm.

"Me too, babe. By the way, these are for you, Vivi." With a flourish Clay whipped out a bouquet of flowers he'd stashed behind the door. So sweet.

"What a beautiful reunion." The Realtor paused. "I was just showing the place to Clay." She ran down the key stats: new construction, southwest-corner penthouse condo, 2,800 square feet, open floor plan with a wraparound terrace. The condo had two bedrooms, two and a half baths, a huge laundry room, and an office. The most distinguishing feature was the wall of windows curving gracefully along with the lines of the art-deco inspired building.

"Check out the size of this kitchen," said Vivien.

Clay laughed. "That granite island alone is bigger than the entire kitchen in your old place. This condo is amazing."

"Isn't it? Who knew you could live in a place this big? You can practically ride a bicycle in here." Vivien had been spent too much time in too many cramped NYC apartments. Not Clay, however. His parents had purchased his four-bedroom, four-and-a-half-bathroom apartment for him as a B-school graduation gift.

"Let's do it, Vivi," Clay said, and nodded.

The Realtor shot Vivien a puzzled look.

Hesitating for a moment, Vivien said, "Clay, um…I already bought it."

He stepped back in shock. "What? I thought we were just looking at it tonight. You're saying it's a done deal?"

The Realtor tried to help. "There were several other offers so we had to act quickly. Vivien made an offer and they accepted it. I know it's a surprise, but it is a fabulous condo. I'm sure you'll both love it."

"I'm sorry, Clay," Vivien said, "I had to act fast so we wouldn't lose it." She tried to cuddle up to him but he withdrew. "Anyway, I bought it with my own money, so it's not like you got roped into a bad investment," she said, trying to make a joke.

Judging from Clay's stony reaction he was still in shock.

*

Back at the hip boutique hotel they dropped off Clay's bags and freshened up. They always dressed for dinner and continued the tradition that night in Portland. Clay looked handsome in his light blue French-cuff shirt, dark slacks, and black sport coat. "I thought we'd have a drink at a popular watering hole before dinner," Vivien said. She dabbed on some lip gloss and was ready to go, but Clay sat on the corner of the cream-colored sofa, which contrasted with the cerulean walls.

"Vivi, I can't believe you bought that place without having me see it first."

She protested, "But I explained that there were competitive bids. I had to move fast."

Clay shook his head. "You do realize that when people are married they make decisions together, right? This kind of decision is supposed to be made jointly."

But I used my money to buy it. Vivien didn't fully appreciate why Clay was so upset. After all, he would only be spending occasional weekends there. Still, she figured she should apologize. "Honey, I'm sorry, I really am. But I knew you'd love the place. You do, don't you?"

"That's beside the point. But it is a great condo, babe."

"Can we reset and have a happy evening? I'm so excited you're here."

He shook his head and chuckled. "All right, all right. I'm looking forward to spending time with my beautiful girl."

"Those cuff links are quite smart, are they new?"

Looking proud of his acquisition, Clay said, "Yes, they're Paul Smith. I liked them so much I bought two pair."

Typical Clay. It still made Vivien chuckle to see his immense closet filled with duplicates of almost every item.

When they walked into the bar, a group of Smart Sports employees were enjoying happy hour and waved to Vivien. "Looks like you've made friends already," Clay said.

"Those are people from Smart Sports. You'll see, honey, Portland is a pretty small town, but really nice and friendly." Now that she was buying a piece of property she needed to sell Clay on spending time there.

They enjoyed a glass of champagne and reveled in each other's company, then left for dinner. The owner of the modern Vietnamese-fusion restaurant, Silk, greeted them warmly. "Oh, hi, aren't you Vivien Lee, the new president at Smart Sports? I saw your picture in the *Oregonian*. Nice to meet you."

Clay shot Vivien a glance. When they were seated he said wryly, "This is a big change from New York...seems like everyone recognizes you."

"Mmm-hmm." She placed her napkin on her lap.

"You're going to have to watch what you do and what you say...and who you're with." He winked.

They were digging into their appetizers when Vivien realized the table to their right was a group from Nike–she could tell by the head-to-toe swooshes and snippets of conversation. And the table to their left was an Adidas group. She whispered to Clay they were surrounded by competitors.

"How can you tell who works for what company?"

Vivien set her chopsticks down. "I figured it out. If someone's wearing a certain brand of shoes, that doesn't mean they're an employee. But if they're wearing that same brand of apparel, it's a good bet they work at the company. If they have an accessory–like a watch, hat, or backpack–it's one hundred percent."

What that meant was Vivien would not have the freedom to talk about work or coworkers when they were out in public. She and Clay agreed to make up some code names for key people when they got back to the privacy of their hotel. In the meantime they had plenty to catch up on, like their wedding plans. Clay reached across the table and entwined his warm hand with hers.

After a while their talk turned to work and Clay drew back. He swirled the wine in his glass. "Vivi, are you sure this is what you want to do? I mean, moving to a small town and working in a tough industry just to sell workout stuff? Is this really your destiny?"

"I think so, Clay."

"It's just"–he shrugged–"you could have any job you want back in New York. What makes this so special?"

Vivien bit her lip. "I can't explain it fully, honey. I wanted to take a risk, try a new challenge. And while you think of it as 'workout stuff' I find the sports business and this company exciting and inspiring. Okay?"

Clay shook his head. "Okay, if it's what you want, babe."

✳

They spent a delicious, lazy Saturday morning in bed enjoying room service and reading the paper. Later, as they ambled around downtown Portland, Vivien got a call that the condo owner could close in a week, and she couldn't wait to move into her new place. As she and Clay strolled around Pioneer Courthouse Square, Vivien imagined life as a married couple, perhaps in Portland. They stopped for coffee before heading over to Powell's Books.

Clay winked. "I have to admit, one great thing about Portland is they know how to make a damn good cup of coffee."

That evening they made the short drive to Malcolm Smart's home in the Portland hills. His house was tasteful and spacious but not over-the-top. The large old home had been fully modernized, with floor-to-ceiling windows in the great room. Dense trees surrounded the property, making it feel like it was in the middle of a forest. Family photos and exotic mementos were strewn around the home, giving it a warm feel.

Malcolm and Alex introduced their wives and Vivien introduced Clay.

Sheri, Malcolm's wife, offered the couple some wine. "I'm not on call tonight, so I can relax and have some vino—yahoo," she joked.

"You're a doctor? What kind of medicine do you practice?" Clay asked.

"Pediatric surgery at OHSU. I just love it."

"Wow, you must be even smarter than Malcolm," Vivien said, half joking.

"Ain't that the truth." Malcolm joined his wife on the sofa and draped his arm around her. "Hon, you think the girls are staying out of trouble tonight?" Their twin teenage daughters were out at a movie. Sheri smiled and shrugged.

Tina, Alex's wife, set a tray of assorted cheeses, fruit, and crackers on the coffee table. "This okay here, Sheri?"

"Perfect, thanks." Sheri handed Tina a glass of wine.

Tina sat across from Vivien and Clay. "It's great to meet you both. Clay, I hear you're an investment banker?"

"Yes, I've been working for the same firm since graduating from HBS. Investing is our family business so I guess it's in my blood."

Tina squinted. "Oh, yours is the Finch Investments family?"

"The very same." Clay smiled. "After my dad passed away about seven years ago my mom took over the business. Definitely a take-charge kind of woman."

That was an understatement.

Vivien said, "I understand you're a professor, Tina. What do you teach?"

"I was a finance prof at Stanford and commuted for a bit, but when we started having kids that was not tenable. Now I work with VC firms advising startups." Tina gave a worried glance out onto the terrace, where smoke was billowing from the barbecue grill. Alex caught her look and waved a mitted hand. "Don't burn down your brother's house, dear!" she called out.

What struck Vivien was how down-to-earth they all were. She was hungry and the savory barbecue smoke that wafted into the house was enticing. Vivien cut a sliver of cheese and popped it in her mouth with a cracker. Then she took her first sip of Oregon Pinot Noir. The dark raspberry color belied the richness and complexity of the flavor–it was fruit forward, acidic, and earthy with a smooth, spicy finish. "This wine's incredible. Did you try it, Clay?" He nodded enthusiastically.

"Domaine Serene, one of my favorites," Malcolm said, showing them the label. "So, Clay, did you play basketball growing up? You've certainly got the height."

Clay laughed. "At first I was pretty hopeless. Maybe because I had a major growth spurt and was so uncoordinated. I tried out for JV basketball and even though I was the tallest kid in school I still got cut. Came home crying and my mom said, 'Clayton, we're going to fix this.'"

"What did your mom do?" Sheri asked.

"She hired a former NBA coach to work with me and a recently retired NBA player to show me some moves and improve my technique," Clay explained. "I was the best-trained kid around. The next time I tried out I got a spot on the team."

Malcolm smiled. "Nice. We'll have to hook you up with our latest basketball shoes. Just have Vivien email your size.".

"Grub's up in a few minutes," Alex called from outside.

Finally everyone moved over to the large dining table in the great room. The meal of steak, mashed potatoes, and grilled asparagus was delicious. After a while the talk turned to Smart Sports.

"You know you're our trailblazer, Vivien." Malcolm looked serious. "We're hoping you'll be a great role model and pave the way for other talented women."

"No pressure," Alex teased.

Sheri chimed in, "Don't worry, Vivien, you'll do great."

"I'll try my best and then some," Vivien said, and bit into an asparagus stalk. Still embarrassed about her sponsorship mistake, she hoped the Smarts had forgotten about it already.

Malcolm put down his fork. "We think if you can be successful here, then we can entice more outside talent to join. While we have pockets of talent, we need to upgrade our executive team."

"Oh, where are your gaps?" Clay asked so Vivien didn't have to.

"Our executives over in footwear are both strong–Duncan and Tim. Duncan knows the business cold but needs to develop his people better. Tim's an all-around fantastic footwear guy. In apparel we have Vivien, so things are looking up." Malcolm winked. "Johnny O's a capable guy but needs to put in more effort and execute better. In finance we're good. Marketing, IT, HR, and operations are all weak spots. Our head of HR is great, but he's looking at retirement and our head of recruiting doesn't have the skills to take his place." So that's how the brothers viewed Zac Archer. Interesting.

Alex explained, "Over the past eight years we've had explosive growth. Who would've thought when we started this that we'd already be in third place behind Nike and Adidas. It's just that the talent side of Smart Sports hasn't caught up with the business side."

Malcolm swallowed a bite of steak. "We don't have a lot of bench strength because we don't have enough leaders who are great at developing people. That's one of my priorities for the next year. It's going to be critical now that we're about to be a public company and everyone is watching everything we do."

✳

Sprawling on the bed in their hotel room, Vivien showed an uncustomary moment of doubt. She stared up at the George Nelson pendant lamp hanging from the ceiling. "Oh, Clay, if I don't succeed at this it's going to impact everyone who comes after me...or maybe the opportunities will end with me. I don't want to let people down. Can I really do this job?"

Clay gathered her up in his arms. "Hey, this is a ton of change for you, babe, and it's scary. But you're going to do great. I believe in you–so much that I'm going to be spending a lot of time in Portland, against my mother's advice!" He smiled.

The comment caught Vivien off guard. "What, your mom doesn't think I can cut it? Or she's afraid I'm taking her precious son too far away?"

"Oh, no, that's not it..."

"She never seemed too thrilled about our engagement, Clay. Maybe she regrets that you didn't propose to Elizabeth Atwood. Then she could brag to all her friends about how her daughter-in-law is on a morning news show."

Wasn't being in charge of an investment company enough to satisfy his mother's ample ego? Did she feel it necessary to control every aspect of her son's life?

Sitting up, Clay stammered, "Babe, I was, uh, just making a silly comment. Come on, forget it. What mother wouldn't want her son to be married to a fantastic woman like you?"

She noticed he hadn't addressed her concern directly.

"Anyway, Malcolm and Alex are strong, upstanding leaders who are rooting for you, and they've got your back. Can't ask for a better setup."

Forgetting about Clay's mom for a moment, Vivien said, "That's true. Having their support is key." Also key would be keeping it.

"I know it's not going to be easy, Vivi, but I know you. You're one of a kind. And I'm confident that you've got this. You've got this, babe."

✳

On the Smart Sports campus, it was too easy for Charl to take refuge. He was obviously avoiding Vivien. If she wanted time with him, she'd have to get him off-site. She put a plan in motion.

She kicked off her weekly staff meeting by revisiting next steps from their last meeting. "Gus, you were asked to bring the answers to everyone's questions about the consumer."

All he had was several pieces of paper covered in chicken scratch but he was haughty as ever. "Frankly, this analysis is a bit too complex for most of you to understand."

Vivien forced a smile. "I've worked with some extremely bright people, and a great skill of theirs was the ability to take complex analyses and distill them into simple truths about the consumer. That's what I'm expecting from you, Gus." She might need to make an example of Gus.

"Let's move on," Vivien said. "Distribution. The majority of our business comes from wholesale. We can learn a lot from the retailers who are unhappy with our product, so I set up meetings with accounts where business was going well, and also accounts that kicked us out."

An issue she had discussed with J. J. was that over the past year Smart Sports apparel had gotten kicked out of some retail accounts due to many product problems.

"But, uh, Vivien," Meredith informed her, "Smart Sports executives typically don't visit accounts, especially ones we no longer do business with."

"Mmm-hmm. That's exactly why we're going to do it. It's a great opportunity to learn." Vivien pressed on. "Charl and I are going to travel to selected accounts for a few days and J. J. will join us for the last day of meetings."

More than one raised eyebrow was directed her way, including Charl's, which she duly ignored. You could learn a lot about someone by traveling with them. This would be a good way to break through with Charl and get him on board...or figure out if he needed to be axed.

Before she left, Vivien pulled Gus aside and looked him in the eye. "Gus, I'm going to make this extremely simple for you." She handed him one sheet of paper. "Here are ten basic questions I want answered about our consumer when I return from my trip. If you need me to explain anything, call my cell. Otherwise I'll expect to see completed, high-quality work from you. I need to feel confident you're capable of doing this job well for you to continue as the head of consumer insights. Do you understand my expectations?"

Looking petrified, he just nodded silently.

✻

And so, during Vivien's third week with Smart Sports she and Charl embarked on a road trip. She had no idea what she'd be walking into with these accounts and was a little uneasy. Some of the retail accounts knew who Charl was, and so as not to embarrass him, Vivien simply said they were working together to improve the business and wanted to hear the good, the bad, and the ugly from their customers.

Their first stop was a large sporting goods account that Charl, who had come up through sales, knew well. He spent fifteen minutes on idle chitchat with the store owner about various people they knew—blah, blah, blah.

Finally, Vivien broke in. "Tell me, who do you think is making the best sports apparel out there and why?"

The store owner stroked his beard and named his top three picks.

"Can you tell me what's working or not with Smart Sports' product, marketing, and execution, or any areas of concern?"

He looked hesitant, as if he was weighing if he should speak freely in front of Charl.

"Oh, come on," Vivien prodded. "This is a good learning experience for us. Feel free to tell us all the problems–we're interested to learn what we can do better. That's why we made this trip to see you. For example, we've heard rumblings that fit has been an issue; is that something you've seen?" When Vivien made this admission, it opened the floodgates and they got a lot of great, albeit exceedingly negative, feedback.

They visited four accounts that day–two current and two former– and by day's end even Vivien was worn down. Her back ached and her fingers were sore from taking notes about the myriad issues. Listening to all the complaints even from current customers was tough. The Women's Apparel team had their work cut out for them.

As they pulled into the parking lot of their hotel, Vivien threw a bone. "Hey, Charl, that was a tiring but productive day. How about grabbing some dinner together in the hotel restaurant?"

"I'm beat. Think I'll just order room service," Charl replied.

Vivien ate on her own. Exiting the restaurant, she heard a familiar voice.

"Yeah, Dunk, I need to play nice and get through this trip. It's tough, but I have to suck it up for now." Charl was sitting at the bar talking on his mobile phone. He finished his conversation and dug into his dinner, chatting up the female bartender and watching the ballgame on TV. Understandably he did not want to spend time with his new boss.

Vivien emailed Charl that night, inviting him for a run in the morning, but he declined. Despite being a "great guy" he wasn't making it easy for her.

Could she work effectively with Charl? Would keeping him on the team be too disruptive? Might be wiser to cut him loose, but firing him might generate harmful political ripples.

Following a busy morning, their afternoon appointment was with a retailer who was notorious for being demanding and ornery. "This is not going to be a picnic," Charl said with a look of dread on his face.

Vivien started to sense that the real reason Charl was so distant was that he was highly uncomfortable in this situation. He made a comment that brought it all home: "I've run Women's Apparel for years, but this is the first time I've visited all these accounts."

They were meeting with Stan, founder of the Sporting Life, a chain of nine large-format sports stores. They entered the clean and well-merchandised store and asked for the owner. Stan, a beefy guy with a football player's stance, greeted them curtly. "Look, I don't have time to waste. I've got a business to run, and frankly, your products and service have been crap." Vivien noticed the sales staff was hopping, attending to every detail. "Our dealings with Smart Sports Women's Apparel have been terrible." He planted his feet wide, hands on his hips. "This is the first time anyone from corporate has come to see us. I don't plan on doing business with you in the future, so I only agreed to take this meeting to tell you all the things you're doing wrong. You got fifteen minutes of my time and that's it."

Charl was, for once, stunned into silence. His cheeks turned bright pink.

Vivien kept her voice steady. "Stan, that's exactly what we want to hear. I understand we've screwed up in the past, and one of the reasons we came to see you is to apologize in person. We are truly sorry about all our mistakes. We want to improve and your perspective will be really valuable–you have a reputation for straight talk. I promise to respect your time. Whenever you need to cut the meeting off, just say so."

Within minutes, Stan relaxed, opening up and giving candid feedback.

Charl shot a look of admiration Vivien's way.

When Stan complained about some of the products, Vivien said, "Can you show me? Let's compare them to competitors' products that you feel are superior."

Stan went to the stockroom and brought up a tattered old box of Smart Sports product. "This stuff is unsalable. I couldn't get rid of it even marked down by seventy percent. Because of the deal I signed with you guys, I'm stuck with this inventory." Stan exhaled, disgusted.

"What would make you happy, Stan? To get rid of this stuff?" Vivien said. "Well, I'm going to take it off your hands. Just this once I'll buy back all the old inventory at the price you paid for it. How does that sound?"

He flashed her a satisfied grin and sent someone to grab the other boxes of aged inventory. "That's great, Vivien, thank you. Now, can I tell you about our account servicing problems?"

He went on for awhile, and Vivien asked plenty of questions.

"Okay, Vivien," Stan said, "I have to admit we're having challenges with some other brands of women's apparel in our stores. I'm going to give you a little test."

Vivien smiled, her curiosity piqued.

Charl just shrank into the background.

Stand lined up some tops. "Here are six styles, Vivien. Take a look at them. I'd like to know if you think these are selling or not and why."

She loved a challenge. "Okay, Stan, here's my take." Vivien tossed shirts right and left. "Selling, not selling, not selling, selling well, selling, not selling."

"Wow," he replied. "That's exactly right. How did you know how these styles are performing?"

"Easy." Vivien picked up the "selling well" top. "Your top-selling style is well designed and constructed and has nice visual interest as well as a reasonable price point. The darker color blocking on the sides gives it a slimming effect on the body, which appeals to women." She set it back down. "As for the other styles–here you have a relaxed body but really tight cap sleeves, which doesn't make sense for the customer who might purchase this style." She traded it for another. "Here you have a graphic pattern that draws attention to a woman's midsection–never a good thing." She continued providing insights, and Stan smiled and took notes. "I also noticed you don't have a full-length mirror anywhere near the women's section. Now, that's a miss, Stan. Women want to see what the clothes will look like on them before they head to the fitting room."

As they wrapped up, Vivien said, "Stan, thank you, this was incredibly helpful. We're definitely going to fix the problems you've shared with us today and turn our business around. I have an ask, though. I'd like to come back to you in six months' time and show you what we've done to address all the issues. At that time I hope you'll place a full order with us."

Stan laughed heartily. "I like your confidence and your style, Vivien. You have a great sense of what works. I would definitely be open to having you come back, and if I like what I see I'll consider buying it. But there are a lot of things you'll have to fix first, and I think you guys have your work cut out for you."

"Fair enough," Vivien replied. "We just want a chance to show you the changes we've made based on your feedback, that's all. Thanks, Stan, we greatly appreciate your time." She handed him a business card.

Stan looked at it, eyes wide. "Oh. You're the new Smart Sports president? Why didn't you say so? I would have offered you guys some coffee."

In the end Stan had spent nearly two hours talking with them, and now even Charl seemed energized by the opportunity.

They walked back to their rental car and Charl let out a huge sigh, running his hands through his wavy black hair. "Wow, tough meeting! But it ended up going way better than I expected. You really won him over, Vivien."

"Thanks, Charl, I thought it was a good learning experience."

"Sure was. That was the first time I've heard some of those comments, although I had an inkling about a few of the problems. It was good to visit these accounts and hear their feedback."

"Charl, I know this can't be easy for you, and I appreciate your being open to working together, regardless of who has whatever title now."

"Titles aren't that important to me. My feeling is we're all equals at Smart Sports. I'm just looking to do work I can be proud of and contribute to our team. It's all about the team." Charl's feel-good words raised a red flag. Experience had taught her that anyone who said they didn't care about titles was, in fact, consumed by them.

Though she liked to think she was making progress with him, Vivien wasn't convinced Charl could be that genuine about being "all about the team" after suffering such a humiliating demotion. Was he just great at playing politics and saying what he thought she wanted to hear, or was he really coming around?

Charl liked to say that he had done work he was proud of, yet Vivien wondered what work he was referring to, since the business had been tanking for some time.

He flashed a smile. "Coming to these accounts was a good call, Vivien. I wish I had done this a long time ago."

The sincerity of Charl's compliment touched her. "I heard from one of Stan's sales associates that there's a great Mexican place a few blocks away. Want to check it out for lunch?" In fact, before they'd embarked on their trip Vivien had asked Pandy to find out Charl's favorite foods and locate some good local restaurants.

A couple of hearty beef, black bean, and jack cheese enchiladas later, Charl seemed to be on board. They even joked around a bit and Vivien was starting to see Charl's appeal. He was attractive, polite, and came across as humble. Maybe that was why people liked him.

Charl could be a good businessperson, and Vivien wanted to make him feel like a critical part of the turnaround team.

Between sips of her water, Vivien tried to get more intel about the business. "Look, Charl, you have skills that are key to executing our new vision. I know if we work together we can make it a success."

"Thanks, Vivien. I know I've made some missteps–it was my first time leading a business." Charl wiped some lunch remnants off his face.

"Oh? What did you do before Smart Sports?"

"I was in a sales role at Reebok. Met Zac Archer at an industry event and he recruited me to the company, with Dunk's support." Yet another connection. How did Charl know Duncan?

On the third and final day of the trip, J. J. joined them. When they stopped at Starbucks in between account visits, Charl recounted the previous day's meeting with Stan and how masterfully Vivien had handled it.

She tried to hide her smile when J. J. shot her a look of pure incredulity.

After Charl excused himself to use the restroom, J. J. asked, "Any progress with Gus?"

"Not so much." For someone who wasn't doing his job, she couldn't understand why he was so smug. She'd left Gus a message earlier in the week asking him to send any completed work by email, and so far she hadn't received a thing. "But I did get a killer recipe for a bacon cheesecake from his blog."

Vivien allowed herself to enjoy a hearty laugh with J. J. It felt good to loosen up a bit.

"Gus has been in that job for a long, long time," J. J. said. "He's one of the people at Smart Sports I call the Untouchables. Those are the folks who, no matter what they do, still hang onto their jobs. Gus went to U of O with Johnny O and they're buds, so he thinks he's entitled to keep his job without actually having to do his job. It's been pretty frustrating for the rest of us. I can't remember when he actually produced anything useful. On top of that Gus is dating Charl's little sister."

Vivien's eyes widened.

J. J. shrugged. "Oh, it's a tangled web we weave."

That explained it. Gus thought he was safe with Johnny O's protection. And dating his former boss's sister only increased his level of confidence. "Gus may be an intelligent guy, but I need intelligent people who want to excel at their jobs and can deliver the goods. I'll be curious to see what he's got done when we get back." She leaned across the table. "By the way, what's the connection between Duncan and Charl?"

"They go way back. Went to high school together in Ohio–Charl was the equipment manager for Duncan's varsity tennis team. I guess Duncan was someone Charl always admired, so when he got his chance he followed him to Smart Sports."

This was a labyrinth of intricate personal connections the likes of which Vivien had never seen in a company. "Is this typical?"

Draining his coffee cup, J. J. replied, "Welcome to the sports industry, Vivien."

CHAPTER 11: COUNTDOWN TO THE FIRST SHOWDOWN

Vivien laid the groundwork for getting rid of Gus by giving the Smart brothers a heads-up on the issues with him. They gave her carte blanche to do what she deemed necessary.

She also conferred with the head of HR, Ron Billings, about the situation. He was a smart and pragmatic HR professional, one of the best she'd ever encountered.

"What about severance?" she asked.

He shook his head. "When someone's doing a crappy job they shouldn't be rewarded."

Vivien agreed.

Ron cleared the path for the inevitable by working the political channels–namely Johnny O and Zac–to prevent anyone from interfering.

In her short tenure Vivien had heard many complaints that Gus never did any real work and spent the bulk of his time at the office writing his bacon recipe blog. Vivien could not afford to keep someone on the leadership team who was not pulling their weight. She had to cut the fat.

She stopped by his office to check on his progress, but Gus was not around. She checked the conference rooms, the cafeteria, the gym and playing fields–he had mysteriously vanished. She nicknamed him Houdini.

Finally she got Pandy to call Gus into her office to sit down and review his work.

"Well, I don't have it," he said petulantly. "My computer is broken."

"I see. So for the past week you've had no computer and couldn't do any work?"

"Pretty much."

"Did you call IT and ask for a loaner laptop? They're available."

"I asked IT to fix it, but I thought it'd be better to wait to work on my own laptop."

"What have you been doing with your time, Gus?"

"Well…I was working from home."

"Gus, I don't get a sense of urgency from you. I asked you to do something concrete with a specific deadline, yet you didn't act with alacrity." Vivien was doing her best not to show how annoyed she was, but her hands gripped her Aeron chair. "Do you have *anything* to show me?"

Gus's fingers trembled as he pulled out a thin manila folder containing a few charts with notes written on them. The axes were mislabeled, among other errors–Vivien had seen higher-quality work from first-year analysts at SCP.

"What are these charts are telling us, Gus?"

What followed was a painful volley of Vivien asking simple questions and Gus mumbling incoherent responses that were inconsistent with what the data showed.

Finally Vivien sighed. "Gus, let me share my observations. You don't seem passionate about your job or about understanding our consumer. You're the head of consumer insights but are unable to answer basic consumer questions, and so far I haven't seen you produce any work of note. You're a member of our leadership team, and I don't see you setting a good example or working collaboratively with others. You spend more time at work writing your bacon blog. Why should I keep you on my team?"

For the first time Gus's eyes widened in fear, and his mouth was agape. In an instant he recovered and said smugly, "What, are you gonna fire me or something?" There was a glint in his eyes and a smirk on his face.

"Hang on a sec." Vivien left him in her office while she got Ron Billings from HR. Ron knew Gus's reputation all too well and had already amassed a number of written complaints, along with the IT department's tracking of Gus's Internet usage and time spent searching and posting bacon recipes while at work.

Gus glanced up from his smartphone as Vivien and Ron walked in. Firing someone was never easy.

"Gus, I don't doubt that you are an intelligent, capable person. But we need people who are passionate about doing the work. I'm sorry, but there just isn't a place for you on this team."

As much as Gus deserved it, Vivien still felt bad for him. She and Ron delivered the news that Gus was being terminated for poor performance immediately. Ron escorted him back to his office to gather his things.

When the rest of the team saw Gus, red faced, packing his things in a box, it sent shockwaves through the apparel building. No one had imagined Vivien would get rid of an Untouchable.

Just like Houdini, Gus vanished, never to be heard from again.

*

In order to get the business on track, Vivien had to do some serious multitasking, and fast. First, she had to stop the bleeding so it wasn't losing money. At the same time she had to build a compelling future vision. A key step in building the future was to conduct a strategic war game, a competitive simulation game. In the war game, four teams would compete for industry dominance over the next three to five years.

To mix things up, Vivien included her leadership team plus participants from other businesses–people who could think strategically and creatively. Tim Kelley and Doug Hawke showed up ready to play, as well as Albert Chu, Duncan's strategic planning analyst, and Colin Murphy, Johnny O's analyst. The game allowed teams to make four big strategic moves, like an acquisition, and they had to present their move to all the other teams and the judges. It was played over two days, and Vivien was pleased to see the level of intensity of the teams. The winning team would be the company who had captured more market share, created more brand equity, and had superior financial results versus their competitors. From the war game Vivien and her team would distill the top ten insights, which would inform their go-forward business strategy.

At the end of the game Vivien conducted a debrief to get feedback.

Tim stated, "This was the most forward-looking technique for building a strategy I've ever seen. We've always developed our strategy looking in the rearview mirror; I realize now how ineffective that is." He rubbed his chin thoughtfully.

"This was totally awesome," Albert chimed in.

Doug Hawke put it most eloquently. "Those old approaches we've been using? Not worth a crap. This is by far the best way to build a winning strategy, period." Vivien couldn't have asked for a better endorsement.

*

The following Monday at the executive staff meeting, Vivien was feeling proud of all the progress made in the prior week. And Smart Sports had successfully launched their IPO, so the mood of the executives in the room was jubilant.

Suddenly Johnny O stormed in and in front of everyone said, "Vivien, have you single-handedly changed Smart Sports' customer policies?"

Confused, she replied, "No, I don't think so, Johnny O."

"Well, I just got a call from the Sporting Life account and Stan said you agreed to take back all aged inventory at cost. Is that right?"

Vivien reddened. "Yes, I agreed to do that, but only for Women's

Apparel."

He fumed. "Well he was asking what I was going to do for him. What, so now we're all expected to take back useless inventory from retailers because of you? You can't just go out there and do whatever you want, Vivien. You're setting a bad precedent for the other divisions."

Alex Smart interjected "I'm sure Vivien made it clear that it was a one-time exception. You did, didn't you?" He looked hopeful.

She nodded.

"Even though the divisions are run separately, Vivien, we're still one company. I'm sure you had the best intentions, but moving forward just keep us all apprised if you agree to something out of the ordinary. Okay?" Malcolm said gently.

Jeez, another mistake? And Charl was standing right there...why didn't he warn me?

*

Still smarting from the exchange with Johnny O, at the multidivisional meeting that afternoon Vivien was a bit gun-shy and continued to follow Duncan's advice on keeping silent.

Afterward in the restroom Vivien overheard two of the female meeting participants from other divisions.

"It's great to have a woman in a senior role, but I wonder if Vivien really understands the sports business. Did you notice she didn't say one word the entire meeting? I couldn't believe she was so meek. And it was the same thing the last meeting, too."

"Yeah, that surprises me. Especially after seeing her at the company meeting, where she came across as very confident and smart. Hopefully she'll contribute more next time or I'm afraid people will think she's not up to the job. As a senior woman that everyone's watching she's gotta speak up."

Another low point and another lesson for Vivien. While Duncan had given her some helpful hints, what worked for other executives might not work for her. She'd have to pick and choose. After all, she was under the microscope more than any other executive at Smart Sports.

∗

The Strategic Business Review was fast approaching, and the Smart brothers were both traveling. It would be Vivien's first big presentation at Smart Sports and she wanted to be prepared. She emailed Alex, who gave her a short list of items to cover with not much elaboration. She didn't want to bother the co-CEOs further. Tim was in Thailand setting up a new footwear factory and wouldn't be back until the night before the meeting. And her trusty assistant, Pandy, was out with strep throat.

One evening in late August, as Vivien was headed back to her office she passed by Duncan's office and saw Dunk and Johnny O shooting the breeze.

Not only in mannerisms, but in style of dress, these two were nearly clones. Duncan favored dark-washed jeans and a dark V-neck T-shirt with the sleeves shortened to show off his biceps. Johnny O had a similar getup minus the sleeve alterations. When either was making a point, he would state his case and lean back, clasp his hands behind his head, and flex his biceps. Duncan sometimes modified the choreography by first running his hands through his hair before the bicep flex. It was a testosterone fueled display that signaled, *Hey, check out my muscles. Who dares disagree with me when I'm sporting these guns?*

That evening when Vivien walked in, Duncan and Johnny O were mirroring each other in the bicep-flex pose, looking like two proud peacocks admiring each other's display.

She almost laughed out loud. "Hi, guys, I had a question about the SBR."

"Well hallo, Vivien, come in. How can we help you?" Duncan lowered his arms and sat forward.

"I was wondering what I need to prepare for the SBR. Alex sent me a list of a few items to cover but not much direction. Is the meeting pretty formal–like do I need to put together a PowerPoint deck–or is it more off the cuff? What's the most important information to cover and how does the board like to see it?"

Johnny O and Duncan exchanged a look.

"Aw, Vivien, nothing to worry about," Johnny O said. "It's not too complicated. The board just wants to hear how the business is doing and what your plans are. You can decide how much detail to get into."

"Right, yeah," Duncan chimed in. "Not to worry, Vivien." He paused. She noticed his pupils contract and his left jaw muscle twitch. Interesting tic. "Three reasons: One, you're so new. Since you're only five weeks into the job, they're not expecting anything big. Two, this is your first SBR, so they can't bloody well expect you to prepare a full review. And, three, they usually leave less time on the agenda for the smaller businesses, so if you just share your general impressions of the Women's Apparel business that should suffice."

Oh no. Was he one of those Pyramid Principle devotees, who always broke down problems into three points, then three subpoints, and so on?

"Frankly I've been so swamped with getting up to speed, I haven't put much thought into this, so it's a relief I don't need to do much prep work. Given that the SBR is coming up in just a few days, I figured I should check with you guys on what they expect since no one else is around."

"Honestly, if you just talk about what you've learnt, that'll be more than they're expecting, Vivien," Duncan said. "Oh, look at the time. I'd better get home or my partner will be cross with me."

On the West Coast everyone seemed to call their significant other their "partner." This was confusing, because back in New York only her gay friends used the term *partner*. Here she had to assume that any time someone used the word *partner* it meant "spouse."

"Okay, so basically just talk about the business highlights and keep it pretty low-key? No presentation or slides? I just want to keep with the regular program."

"Yeah, if you just give some casual comments, that ought to do the trick, right, Dunk?" Johnny O replied.

"Sounds about right. And don't forget, you should talk more about what you've done versus your team."

"Thanks, guys, that's helpful. Well, have a good night."

"Right then, Vivien. If you have any more questions, feel free to ask." Duncan gave a charming smile. "I'm sure you'll make quite the impact."

She went back to her office to take the top fifteen insights from her strategic war game and translate them into an actionable business strategy. Her goal was to get that done before heading home for the evening. Since the SBR was only a few days away, she was relieved that she wouldn't have to pull any all-nighters to get ready. If all they expected was informal comments, she'd be able to cover that just fine.

*

Duncan pumped his fists and waited for Vivien to walk down the hall before he and Johnny O started laughing.

Catching his breath, Johnny O said, "How do you think she's going to do at the SBR?"

Duncan replied, "Probably as good as old Idiot–I mean, Elliott."

Elliott was an outside executive who'd been brought in to run Women's Footwear prior to Tim Kelley. A nice enough guy, but fairly clueless, and that made him an easy mark. Dunk and Johnny O had told Elliott that for the SBR every executive was dressing in a paisley theme, and they even pulled out a paisley shirt to show him. Elliott showed up to his first SBR with paisley corduroy pants and a paisley vest over a collared shirt, probably thinking he looked good. Of course there were no other traces of paisley in the room. The board squinted at Elliott's horrific choice of attire.

"Aw, man, this is going to be fun," Johnny O said.

Duncan leaned back in his bicep-flex pose, secure in the knowledge that he was the heir apparent at Smart Sports. Nothing and no one was going to get in his way.

CHAPTER 12: THE FIRST SIGNS OF TROUBLE

The night before the big SBR meeting, Vivien worked late and was spent. Stress showed up in the form of two giant knots in her shoulders. She dialed Clay's number, hoping for some words of support. Unfortunately, with the time difference in New York, he had long since gone to bed. She had burned the candle at both ends and her strength, and patience, had run down like melted wax.

"Honey, it's my first big meeting with the board tomorrow. I was hoping to get a moment of your precious time and a little support. Guess you forgot about me and went to bed. Thanks a bunch."

*

As Vivien made her way to the boardroom, Malcolm came rushing down the hallway. Instead of his usual casual attire, Malcolm wore dress slacks, a button-down shirt, and a suit jacket. Vivien sighed with relief that she had dressed up a little, wearing black pants and a printed silk tunic top. "Vivien, I'm glad I caught you. Alex and I just flew in from Europe last night. He showed me the email he sent you about what to prepare, and I'm afraid he didn't give you enough specifics. Things have been a bit chaotic lately–we realized late last night that we did not prep you sufficiently for the SBR. I really apologize for that. Were you able to get some pointers from some of the other executives?"

"Yes, I asked Duncan and Johnny O what was expected, and they said it was a pretty casual meeting and that I didn't need to prepare a formal presentation."

Malcolm furrowed his brow. "That's not the advice I would have given. Sorry, Vivien. I'll have a word with those guys. If you can talk about the highlights of the business and your plans to move it forward, that should be fine. You may want to mention the key aspects of your ninety-day plan. I'll prep the board so they know you're just starting your sixth week–I'll manage their expectations." He hesitated for a moment.

Does Malcolm think I'm not up for this challenge? With the mistakes I've made so far does he regret hiring me for this role?

"Thanks, Malcolm. I think I'll be fine. I planned something a little unusual, and I should be able to cover the information you want me to."

They walked into the boardroom together and Vivien was startled to find one of the most formal meeting settings she'd ever seen. A giant oval conference table with a hollow center took up most of the room. On one side sat the board of directors, each in a massive leather chair, with two seats in the middle reserved–as evidenced by printed name cards–for Alex and Malcolm Smart. In front of each seat, a slim microphone stuck up out of the table.

On the other side of the table were assigned seats for all the Smart Sports presidents. Duncan would have the seat closest to the presentation screen, then Tim Kelley, then Johnny O, and lastly Vivien. The boardroom smelled like a combination of leather, new carpet, and men's cologne.

Malcolm introduced Vivien to each of the six board members, who were all wearing suits and ties, and she shook everyone's hand. Every member of the board was an older white male, including a familiar face–Doug Hawke. She'd had no idea he was on the board. Tim came in and gave Vivien a hug, then made his way around to greet the board members and the Smarts, giving them a quick rundown on the Thailand factory.

As Vivien sat and prepared for the meeting, she reached for her phone to put it on silent and saw a text from Clay.

Babe, you're going to be awesome today. Knock 'em dead! Love you.

She was lucky to have such a supportive fiancé. She'd have to apologize later for her voice mail bomb.

Duncan and Johnny O came in. Duncan had topped his usual garb of dark V-neck T-shirt and jeans with a slim-fitting sport coat that accentuated his physique. His magnetic charm seemed to work magic in the room full of guys. He made his way around, shaking hands and he even stopped to greet Vivien, putting a hand on her shoulder. "You look lovely, Vivien."

The chairman of the board, Otto Eckbrecht Utz came around to their side of the table and gave Duncan a big bear hug.

Vivien gaped.

Tim sidled up to her and whispered, "Didn't you know? Otto is Duncan's father-in-law."

Was there no one in this town who wasn't related, school chums, dating someone else's sibling, or married to someone's offspring? "That's pretty cozy."

"You have no idea." He rolled his eyes.

The Smart brothers called the meeting to order, and an agenda was projected on the screen. Each president had one hour to review their business, including fifteen minutes of Q & A. After all the presentations, the Smart brothers and the board would provide feedback to each president.

Duncan kicked things off by walking around and handing out bound copies of his thick presentation as Alex's assistant brought his PowerPoint presentation up on the screen. When he handed Vivien her copy, she took it in both hands, feeling the weight of it. "Yeah, this feels like a pretty casual presentation, Dunk."

He glanced down at her, flashed an impish grin, and shrugged.

That said volumes about him. Making her look bad was a game to him–a source of amusement. No matter how the meeting turned out for Vivien, he didn't expect her to hold a grudge.

Duncan, as was common to the industry, kicked off his presentation with an "adrenaline video," a series of high-energy shots of athletes in motion wearing Smart Sports footwear, all accompanied by a heart-pumping soundtrack. As the video played, he leaned back in his chair doing his famous bicep flex.

He cleared his throat and started to give his presentation from his seat, which Vivien found odd, but as she listened, she learned that Duncan was a skillful speaker. He had great stage presence and with his ersatz English accent and mellifluous tone she found herself being drawn in.

Duncan led with his three most important points about the Men's Footwear business. Vivien had to admit, he was a solid presenter with a smooth delivery. She wondered if just being a great presenter was a guarantee of career success in the sports industry.

Duncan reviewed where the business had come in for the last quarter and what the next quarter and full fiscal year looked like. The bulk of his presentation was spent on his strategy for Smart Sports Men's Footwear, highlighting new products and the performance of the current line, then finishing by showing videos of upcoming commercials.

When he opened it up to the Q & A there were a couple of softball questions. It was pretty clear Duncan was used to sailing through his presentations effortlessly. "Right then, if there aren't any more questions, it looks like I am done." He relaxed back in his chair and flexed his biceps yet again.

"I have a question, Duncan," Vivien piped up.

He sat forward and gave her a slight look of exasperation. Maybe it wasn't common for presidents to ask questions of each other.

"I'm curious–why you are cutting the Phantom shoe?"

"It's not a good shoe. The Phantom shoe has sold less than any other shoe in our line, so it doesn't make sense to keep it."

"It could represent a bigger opportunity than you think," Vivien said.

"I've been responsible for fourteen major footwear launches and as someone who's been in the business for about twenty-five years, I don't agree with you, Vivien. You don't have experience in this industry, so we couldn't possibly expect you to grasp the business. But anyone who knows anything about footwear knows it's time to kill this style for three reasons: One, this is a style that's run its course. Two, I and our consumers don't think the Phantom shoe is that cool. Three, the sales numbers don't support keeping this shoe around. It might not be evident that it's the right decision, but you'll learn these things over time." He gave a smug smile as he ran both hands through his movie-star hair and leaned back into the bicep-flex pose. He even gave his biceps an additional squeeze for impact.

"News flash, Duncan. Biceps aren't brains," Vivien shot back. That elicited a lot of laughs.

Duncan went along with the others and laughed somewhat, then self-consciously lowered his arms.

Maybe that zinger wasn't the nicest, but Vivien was unusually ticked by his dismissive attitude and his attempt to make her look bad at her first SBR. "Would you mind putting slide thirty-four back up on the screen?" Vivien asked sweetly. He complied. "I'm new to this business, Dunk, and maybe I'm interpreting this chart differently, but according to what you have on this slide, it looks like the Phantom shoe is in significantly fewer points of distribution than your bestselling shoe. And it looks like out-of-stocks are the highest for this style."

"That sounds about right. So what?" Duncan raised an eyebrow.

"If you look at shoe sales by retail door, I think you'll see that the Phantom shoe is in fact your top-selling style. That the out-of-stocks are so high for this style means that more people want to buy them and you may not be providing enough inventory to retailers. See what I mean?"

Duncan's right hand went to the back of his neck and rubbed it for a moment or two. "Uh, hang on a sec. Let me have a gander at this."

Alex chimed in, "You know, Duncan, I think we should be looking at this style the way Vivien is describing to get a true sense of its potential. Let's be careful not to make a hasty decision here to kill a great shoe."

Vivien pressed on. "What might be happening is that people are coming to a retailer looking to buy the Phantom shoe and when they can't find it they end up purchasing another Smart Sports style of footwear. So you may be getting additional sales lift of other styles as a result of the Phantom's scarcity. You could run the risk of losing that store traffic if you decided to cut this style completely out of the line, because then you don't have a magnet drawing them to the store."

There was a lull as the co-CEO's, members of the board, and Duncan worked through the numbers on the chart, furiously punching buttons on their calculators. Finally, in his thick German accent, Otto Utz said, "This woman is absolutely right. Duncan, this is your business, you should know this. Vivien is new to the company, yet she understands the business even better than you. We would be crazy to kill this shoe. We should be distributing it more widely, *ja*?"

Duncan's face reddened at being chastised by his father-in-law, especially in front of others. He nodded and simply said, "*Ja*," his hand rubbing the back of his neck. That was the end of his presentation. He leaned forward in his chair, head bowed. Then he looked up ever so slightly and shot Vivien a sideways look. Oddly enough, it was a look of confidence.

That was okay with her. Vivien wasn't afraid of a little competition and she'd brought her A-game today.

During the morning break, Vivien pulled Tim aside. "What's up with Duncan giving his presentation sitting down?"

Tim sipped his coffee. "We usually give presentations sitting down, so we have all our material in front of us, in case there are any questions or challenges from the board. There are too many financials, market-share numbers, and other stats...it's too much to memorize."

Vivien was accustomed to giving presentations standing, because one of the best ways to control a room and focus people's attention was to be physically in front of them. She decided she would not do her presentation like everyone else. As a woman who took up less real estate than the guys, she would get lost behind the giant boardroom table. More importantly, she knew she could give a more energetic presentation if she did it her own way.

Now she just had to figure out a natural way to make a transition.

Tim Kelley went through his review of Women's Footwear and did a fantastic presentation. The board was particularly blown away with his lightweight running shoe line and some of the innovative products he previewed. No dummy, Tim had a sample pair of the lightweight running shoes for each member of the board.

Then Johnny O teed up the apparel business, presenting the results of the Men's Apparel segment. He demonstrated both competence and confidence.

Finally it was Vivien's turn in the spotlight to cover Women's Apparel. Her heart pounded in her chest. *Please let this go well.*

The first thing she did was to get everyone on their feet. "As you know, the Women's Apparel division sells product for running, training, yoga, swimming, triathlons, team sports, and outdoor activities. The yoga category happens to be our fastest-growing segment. So in that vein, I'd like to ask everyone here to try a few yoga poses."

Alex laughed, "Seriously, Vivien, you want us to do yoga? This is not going to be pretty."

"That's all right, Alex. You're all athletic guys so this should be a piece of cake." She knew that throwing them a sideways compliment would compel them to try something new. "I'll run through three poses, and I'd like you to think about what your body is doing while we do them. The first one is Warrior Pose–let me demonstrate." Vivien showed the men exactly how to do the pose. "I chose Warrior Pose because our business has been challenged and, as you know, has never been profitable. We're engaged in a battle to turn the business around." She scanned the roomful of guys all in lunges with arms outstretched. "Good job, everyone. Now, let's move on to Side Angle Pose. To get where the business needs to be, we really need to stretch ourselves and reach for bigger goals than we have in the past, which is why I chose Side Angle Pose." Everyone had their feet spread apart and torso bent to the side with the top arm reaching over. "Lastly, Eagle Pose looks like this–find your balance and ease into it. Nice job." This one was a bit more challenging as the men had to balance on one bent leg with the other leg wrapped around it, arms bent in front and intertwined. "The eagle is one of the most majestic creatures in nature, and like the eagle we plan to inject a newfound pride into our team and soar above the competition." Looking at all the guys trying to keep their balance and do the poses was amusing, but she appreciated they were game to try. Duncan did not seem flexible at all. Funny. Probably too much weight-lifting and not enough stretching.

"All right, thank you. You can take a break and sit down." Vivien smiled. "Now that you're all yoga experts, what's the thing that you most need from a garment when you're doing yoga?"

"Comfort."

"Something stretchy."

"Freedom."

"Something that holds in my stomach."

"Absolutely, you need to feel comfortable in the fit and the fabric; it has to allow for freedom of movement, and it also has to be wicking."

"What is 'wicking'?" Otto asked. Typical guy, no clue about apparel.

"It has to move sweat away from the body. Believe me, when you're doing an hour-long yoga class, you can really work up a sweat."

She talked about how their current women's apparel was not

designed to suit the specific movement needs of yoga, let alone other sports, and this was something she would change. "Next up, I have a little surprise for you guys. We're going to have a little fashion show." She signaled Pandy, who was waiting by the door and swung it open. Sports models walked in as pulsating music came through the sound system. Having a parade of attractive, fit young women was an easy way to capture the attention of every man in the room. Each model wore the same top but a different pair of black shorts.

"I'm just starting my sixth week here, but something that has surprised me is how much product duplication we have. Can anyone guess how many pairs of black shorts we have in our line annually?"

A couple of the guys called out guesses.

"Twenty."

"Forty-five."

"Good guesses; we'll get back to that in a minute. For now each model is wearing a different pair of black shorts and also holding that style in her hands. I'm going to ask each model to place the extra shorts on this table here. Now let's move on to the business details."

As Vivien was speaking the models came in and piled up the black shorts.

Alex's assistant, Marla, raised her hand. "Um, Vivien, I didn't get a presentation from you."

Duncan and Johnny O smiled like Cheshire cats.

"Oh, sorry about that, Marla. Here it is." Vivien handed her a flash drive.

Marla plugged it in and launched the presentation.

Up came a video that spoke specifically to women's sports and active women's pursuits. Instead of doing an adrenaline video with pumping music, Vivien had pieced together a thoughtful film that spoke to the emotion of sport, set to a subtle violin music. It struck right at the heart, and Vivien swore she saw tears welling up in some guys' eyes. She moved on to a short, slick PowerPoint presentation complete with the financials of the business in the last fiscal year, this quarter, and the next quarter, as well as the full fiscal year projection. She demonstrated her command of the numbers by calling their attention to the healthy IMUs, or initial markups; mediocre gross margins; and terrible maintained margins.

"My concern on the P & L is that certain elements of operating expense are out of whack..." She identified the problems. Lastly, instead of showing slide after mind-numbing slide of graphics detailing her strategy, she had one slide.

Smart Sports Women's Apparel Winning Formula: 3E x I = P.

"This, gentlemen," Vivien said, "is our winning formula. It represents our business strategy and what we will be focusing on for the next few years. Let me break down the equation for you. Three E stands for the three elements we need to do a superior job at: 'essence,' bringing clarity to what our business stands for and how we compete; 'execution,' optimizing across our product offering, fit, and aesthetic; and 'emotion,' injecting emotion into our brand that resonates with our consumer.

"So those are three critical elements. The *I* stands for 'innovation.' Simply put, we need to inject innovation into every aspect of our business. The last part of the equation is *P*. Any guesses as to what that stands for?"

"Pretty clothing?" Johnny O piped up.

No one laughed.

"The *P* is for 'performance.' We all know this business is losing money, and I don't like being in charge of a money-losing business. My goal as president is to make it profitable as quickly as possible and get the business on track in terms of performance. This is my team's focus and objective."

The members of the board smiled.

"Now let's get back to our black shorts." She turned to the Mount Everest of apparel the models had piled up. Shorts were sliding off the table. "As you can see, we have a *lot* of black shorts. It may surprise you to learn that we annually make eighty seven styles of black shorts. That seems like a *lot* of shorts to me. We're wasting resources designing, developing, and manufacturing too many similar styles. Part of what I am doing is rationalizing the product offering in Women's Apparel. I want to manage our product portfolio like a stock portfolio. Keep a consistent number of styles in the line, and as we find a better-performing style, we simply drop one of the worse-performing styles."

"My god, Vivien," Otto said, "this is brilliant! I can't believe how quickly you've mastered your business. You're bringing lots of great new thinking. I can't wait to see where you take this business."

The other board members nodded enthusiastically.

"Outstanding, Vivien," Alex said. "Truly an impressive job. I have no idea how you managed to get up to speed this quickly."

"Thank you, but I don't want to get ahead of myself. I still have a lot to learn. But I think we're now on the right track. Oh, I almost forgot–here's a copy of my presentation for everyone. I didn't want to kill more trees and make you carry more paper." She handed a flash drive to each of the board members, who thanked her for not making them travel back with another book.

She glanced at Duncan, who sat with his hands tightly clasped in front of him and his head down, jaw tightened. Perhaps he was learning that driving Vivien out was not going to be an easy task.

The meeting concluded with each board member giving feedback to each president. The greatest number of compliments was given to Vivien. Not that she was keeping score. But her colleagues probably were.

Malcolm grinned. "Vivien, you've just made company history. You're the first person ever to get the board to do yoga! Your understanding of the business is amazing, and the strategy you've laid out is exactly what we need. Phenomenal job!"

At this point in the meeting, Duncan and Johnny O had to be

scratching their heads. How on earth did Vivien know what to prepare and how did she do it so quickly? The last time they'd "advised" her about the meeting was only three days ago.

✳

Otto Eckbrecht Utz snapped his briefcase shut and laughed softly. He had been a board member of Smart Sports for over ten years, but this particular SBR meeting was a doozy. It was the first time a woman had ever given a presentation to the board and the first time he'd seen anyone dissect a business so insightfully and in such an entertaining manner. Up until that day Otto had presumed only someone with years of experience in the sports industry could be successful and get up to speed so quickly.

Humph, this Vivien Lee will be certainly interesting to watch.

Otto saw Duncan give him a slightly hurt look, so he walked around the conference table to have a word. Putting his hand on Duncan's shoulder, he said, "Duncan, I hope you were not offended by my comments about the Phantom shoe. I know you understand your business better than anyone, but everyone has a slipup from time to time. No big deal. Are we okay?"

Duncan managed a smile and said, "Sure, Dad, we're okay. No issue here."

Slapping him on the back, Otto said in his deep, German-accented voice, "Good boy. See you on the tennis court tomorrow afternoon. Who knows, maybe this time I will beat you. Ha ha!"

✳

That evening when Vivien arrived home, the first thing she did was call her fiancé.

"How did everything go, babe?" Clay didn't even mention her voice mail bomb.

"Better than I imagined! But first I want to apologize, honey. I've been totally stressed out about the SBR for the past few days; I guess that came across in my message. I'm so sorry."

"Don't worry about it, Vivi. I know you're under a lot of pressure."

"I had to scramble like crazy to get ready for the meeting."

"That doesn't sound like you–you're always on top of things. What happened?"

Vivien told Clay about asking for advice from Duncan and Johnny O on preparing for the SBR. And how they steered her wrong.

"How did you figure out these guys were trying to dupe you?"

"Dumb luck. The night I spoke with Dunk and Johnny O, I was starving and ready to head home. I happened to walk past the copy room and saw Albert and Colin, the two strat planning analysts, running around in a panic. I asked them if they needed help.

"Albert and Colin were in a flurry of activity trying to copy and bind two sets of presentations. Albert handed me an eighty page presentation. The cover read, 'Smart Sports Quarterly SBR Presentation, Men's Footwear, Duncan Doric.'"

"Whoa," Clay said, "after Duncan told you it was just an informal, off-the-cuff thing?"

"Exactly," Vivien muttered. "The decks they were binding were copies of Duncan and Johnny O's presentations for the SBR. Colin asked who was helping me. I told him, 'No one. I don't have a strat planning analyst yet. And I didn't think I'd even need a presentation.' He got a worried look on his face. He said if I didn't prepare a formal presentation for the SBR, it would be a company first...and not in a good way. I realized I needed a deck."

There was ire in Clay's voice. "Great, so Dunk and Johnny O have been working on their presentations for a month and you only had days."

"Yup. And to make matters worse Pandy's been out with strep throat, so I've been on my own. I asked the analysts for copies of each deck on the QT, so I could study up on what they were presenting.

Albert even offered to help me build in some cool PowerPoint slide transitions."

"Sweet, but geeky." Clay chuckled.

That evening Vivien had kept her cool. She figured out how to give a creative, compelling SBR presentation, while cutting out unnecessary time and labor. Hence her decision to put her presentation on flash drives, skipping the step of printing and binding. Vivien had emailed Pandy that night and asked her to recruit a dozen athletic women from the company for the day of the SBR. They would serve as her models for the fashion show.

"Sounds like it all went brilliantly, babe. I'm proud of you. Especially for pulling something like that off at the last minute."

"Aw, thanks, honey."

Clay hesitated. "Vivi, you know, there's nothing wrong with asking for help. It's not a show of weakness. Remember, you're new there and still learning." A gentle nudge to get her to adjust course.

"You're right, Clay, I should have. I've always been terrible about that…letting my pride get in the way. Next time I'll be more proactive about getting detailed direction from Malcolm and Alex. Or I'll try harder to track down Tim Kelley for his advice."

"What about your ghost mentor, Doug Hawke? Isn't he supposed to be helping you?"

"I'm such a dope. I didn't even know Doug was on the board, so it didn't occur to me to go to him." She rolled her eyes at her own mistake. "I was lucky this time, but I won't be caught flat-footed again."

Only six weeks into the job, she was already swimming in dangerous political waters. She would need to stay on high alert to keep afloat.

"Miss you, babe." Clay's voice softened. "Can't wait to see you next weekend. And Coop, too!" Clay and Coop were flying out to help Vivien get her new furniture set up in the condo and get the place unpacked. Coop's favorite hobby was home décor.

"I really miss just being able to have dinner with you or spend time together during the week," Vivien said. "Guess I'll have to make do with seeing you on the occasional weekend."

"We'll make the most of our weekends together," Clay said. "By the way, Mother offered to help with our wedding planning since you're trying to do everything remotely. But, no big deal, you can think about it. Good night, babe."

With all the work pressures consuming her Vivien could have used a little help on the wedding front, but she wasn't sure if getting Clay's overbearing mother involved was the answer. She wasn't even convinced that his mom wanted her as a daughter-in-law.

Vivien sighed and sorted through her stack of mail, coming to an envelope from her father. Inside was a single piece of paper with a crisp fifty dollar bill enclosed. The paper had a pizza drawn on it and written across the top was, "Vivi, don't forget to take time out for a pizza party! Love, Dad." Just like he did when she was in college. She laughed for the first time in ages.

*

At her regular Monday morning staff meeting, Vivien saw suppressed smiles on the faces of her leadership team. She looked at them quizzically.

Meredith blurted, "Is it true you made the board of directors do yoga at the SBR on Friday?"

"As a matter of fact, that is true." Vivien chuckled, recalling the sight.

Peals of laughter spread across the room.

"I would've paid good money to see that," Meredith said.

"Must have been a hoot." Rebecca's eyes widened and she traced her cheekbone with a long red nail.

"Well, congratulations are in order, Vivien. I heard your presentation was one of the best at the SBR–ever." J. J. gave her a nod of respect. "Apparently the fashion show was also a big hit."

Even Charl mimicked a tip of the hat to her.

Vivien debriefed her team on her SBR presentation and then got down to strategy.

"I want to share our winning formula, 3E x I = P." The team was eager for more as she explained her ideas.

"This all sounds great," Charl said. "But how do we make it work? Where do we even start?"

"We build a detailed execution plan. The plan will include key actions, timing, milestones, metrics, and accountabilities. Here's how it will all work..." Vivien sketched out notes on the whiteboard and stepped back. Something clicked and her team got it.

For the first time the Women's Apparel division would have a vision, a strategy, and a roadmap on how to get there. Finally, the team was excited about what they could accomplish together. Even Rebecca and Charl looked enthusiastic. Now all they needed to do was execute.

*

A couple days later, knowing that Rebecca Roche was taking a few days off for a trip, Vivien made her move. Right before lunchtime, she walked over to the apparel building and stopped by Cat McClintock's office.

"Hi, Cat, how's it going?" Vivien stuck her head in the door. Cat whirled around in her chair. She kicked her bottom desk drawer shut, but not before Vivien saw the half-eaten bag of Oreos. Sitting on her desk was an orange.

"Oh, hello, Vivien. Things are fine, just fine." She looked a little unsettled.

"Have you had lunch yet?" Vivien said. "If not, I thought I could treat you and we could talk a bit."

"Lunch? Oh, I was just going to have this orange."

"Come on, Cat, you need more sustenance than that!"

Hesitating a bit, Cat said, "All right." She scooped up her brand-new Louis Vuitton bag. Vivien had to say that Cat was always well dressed and well accessorized.

As they strolled over to the commissary, Vivien tried to learn more about her head of product development. "Since we're working for a sports company, Cat, I'm just curious, are you passionate about any particular sport?"

"Yes. Figure skating."

"Really? Like Olympic figure skating?"

Cat nodded enthusiastically and shyly said, "In fact, a long time ago I used to be a figure skater. Did skating competitions, the whole nine yards."

Whoa, what happened to her?

"You're probably thinking, *What happened to her?*, right?" Cat stated.

Catching herself, Vivien said, "Um, do you still enjoy skating?"

Over lunch Vivien learned that Cat was born and raised in Idaho–a small, skinny kid who showed skating prowess at a young age. An Olympic skating coach saw her skate and convinced her parents to let him coach her. He put Cat together with a skating partner, a boy who was a year older.

"Skating with Tommy was like a dream and we were a pair for three years. We meshed together so well as skaters and got along great off the ice. Even talked about getting married when we got older. And, oh, how I loved all the gorgeous, sparkly costumes." Cat stopped eating her chicken salad and her gaze floated up. "We were winning competition after competition, and even went to nationals. That's where it all went wrong."

Vivien munched on her turkey sandwich. "What happened at nationals?"

"We were practicing a lift and Tommy dropped me, which was very unusual. He said he was just tired and needed to lie down for a bit. After twenty minutes, I went to check on him, and he–he was dead."

Vivien's face grew ashen and she set down her food. "My gosh, what happened?"

"They said it was a congenital heart defect, usually undetectable." Cat's eyes still reflected her sorrow. "That was the end of skating for me. My parents and coach pushed me to skate with a new partner, but I just couldn't do it without Tommy."

Vivien reached across the table and put her hand on Cat's. "I'm so sorry, Cat. What a terrible thing to deal with at such a young age." How could anyone cope with such a loss? Vivien couldn't imagine having Clay suddenly and tragically ripped out of her life.

Cat continued, "Anyway, in college I majored in fashion. I took a job for an apparel company in Los Angeles, but the fast-paced city life wasn't for me. And I had a terrible boss. She was an Asian lady."

Aha. So that was partly why Cat was so cagey around Vivien.

"Well, you may have noticed I am also Asian." Vivien winked. "But don't worry, Cat. People have always enjoyed working with me, and I treat people well..." She realized that firing Gus might be a cause for Cat's concern. "So long as they perform. How about if we start with a clean slate?"

"Okay." Cat gave a little laugh that sounded relieved. "Anyway, a few years later I got connected with Rebecca. She was heading up product at Coldwater Creek in Sandpoint, Idaho, and brought me on board. She really took an interest in me and helped me...even convinced me to become a redhead! When Rebecca took the job at Smart Sports she recruited me to come along."

The tidbit helped Vivien understand their strong connection. "You hold a critical role on the team, Cat. We know product fit has long been an issue, and it's one that I believe we can solve together. I'd like to work with you and Rebecca on getting this thing licked. How does that sound?"

"I'm excited about what we can do. Of course I don't want to be responsible for product that doesn't fit well, so I'm open to trying new approaches." Cat gave a her an enthusiastic smile.

Those were exactly the words Vivien wanted to hear. All she had to do now was get Rebecca Roche to come around.

"By the way, where is Rebecca?" Vivien asked.

Cat shrugged. "Oh, I thought you knew. Rebecca and Charl are attending the ESPN's Women + Sports Summit in Boulder, Colorado."

What? That was an important industry event that Vivien, as the leader of Women's Apparel, should have been attending. So Rebecca and Charl had gone on the sly and didn't bother to tell her.

*

Vivien sat back in her chair. She looked at the gorgeous river view outside her office window and exhaled. That had been one tough week to get through.

Before packing up her things for the day, she fired up her laptop for her weekly Skype call with her Ceiling Smasher friends. She wanted to catch them up on her week and to hear how everyone was doing. By the time Andi, Sofia, and Grace had had their first glass of wine the friends had caught up on the most important happenings. In Sofia's apartment they huddled around her oversized computer monitor and Vivien saw their horrified expressions as she told them about the trickery involved in the whole SBR incident. Her friends were elated to hear how Vivien came out on top.

When they asked Vivien about her team, she shared her frustration with her insubordinate head of product design and development, Rebecca Roche.

Sofia pointed out a painful truth. "The problem is Rebecca doesn't think of you as her boss. With Charl still in the picture to defend her she feels she has the license to do whatever she wants."

Sighing, Vivien said, "Yeah, you're probably right, Sofi. I don't think Rebecca has the skills for the job, but I just fired my consumer insights guy. I can't fire another key team member so quickly or it will create a wave of panic."

Grace laughed, "You're supposed to be turning around that entire business and you're worried about making waves?"

Vivien groaned. "I'm making progress, but at the same time I've already made some big mistakes. I'm a human Ping-Pong ball–I'm up, I'm down, up, down. Plus I've never had to deal with this level of corporate politics."

"Doesn't sound like some guys are even giving you a chance. Bunch of jerks," Andi said.

"Hey, I have to try to fit in with these people. Get them to like me, or at least trust me."

Sofia made a comment that was tough to hear. "Listen, Vivien, I have no doubt you'll win over your team. But no matter what you do to befriend others, you may never be accepted by the guys at your level. You're always going to be a threat. You're challenging the way things have been done–that makes you a revolutionary. No one wants a revolutionary. It scares people."

Andi guessed correctly that the typical guy working in the sports industry was a former jock or athlete wannabe, probably not the sharpest knife in the drawer, and one who traded on relationships. "When it comes down to it, guys like that gravitate toward predictability. Predictability is safe; it's good."

"Vivi, you need to launch a strategic campaign," Grace said, "to solidify your position and make it clear you belong there. Try and separate these guys and befriend them. See if you can get a few guys in your camp so Duncan doesn't hold all the cards."

The Smashers celebrated Vivien's success so far but also wanted to help her navigate the murky waters ahead.

Back in New York, Sofia was getting ready to give a big speech the following week and was all nerves, for some odd reason. Andi's broken foot had healed and she was headed to a team-building off-site in Bermuda. Grace was doing some research on her branding book.

"Oh, look at the time. We better head out, girls," Sofia said. "Sorry, Vivi, but I managed to snag a table at Zentropy tonight." Zentropy was a hot new restaurant Vivien wanted to try.

Waving good-bye, Grace said, "Are you coming to our Ceiling Smashers dinner this month, Vivi? I'm sure everyone would love to see you."

She sighed, "I'd love to and you guys know it's rare for me to miss one of our bimonthly dinners. But I'll be in Asia for work and can't make it. Say hi to everyone for me!"

As Vivien signed off and shut her laptop, she realized how much she missed her friends. Sure, Clay and Coop were arriving that evening, but during the week she felt completely alone. She resolved to solidify more friendships in Portland, and especially at Smart Sports.

CHAPTER 13: FASTEN YOUR SEAT BELTS

Vivien stepped outside her new condo building into a waiting limo to head off for the tour of key Asian markets. A dry, warm breeze whipped Vivien's long silky hair about when she exited the car. She was the first to arrive at the private airport, and while her bags were put away, she enjoyed a hot cup of gourmet coffee and a chocolate croissant in the lounge. Tim Kelley arrived next and they had a few minutes to recap the SBR meeting. Vivien shared her experience with Duncan and Johnny O's "no prep required" advice.

"Those guys…" Tim shook his head. "Hey, V, I should warn you." Did he just give her a new nickname? That was all right with her…V stood for "victory." And getting a nickname was a sign of acceptance.

"There's always some hazing on these trips, especially for the 'new guy,' which is you. So if we go out for drinks, don't drink anything that you haven't seen poured directly by a bartender. Dunk and Johnny O have been known to slip something in people's drinks, and believe me, it's not a pretty sight. They may get a big laugh out of it, but you'll feel like you've been hit by an eighteen-wheeler. The last guy they did that to missed nearly three days of the trip because he was puking his guts out in his hotel room." Tim sat back in the large leather chair.

"Jeez. Thanks for the heads-up, Tim."

"Also, I should let you know there's a specific way to board the jet, not dictated by the Smart brothers–in fact, I think Dunk was the originator. We wait for everyone to get here, then walk out to the tarmac together. The Smart brothers usually get on the plane first–they like to sit in the back. Then the president running the biggest business–which is Duncan–gets on and picks his seat, and so on down the line."

It struck Vivien as comical that even boarding a jet was fraught with politics and the potential to make a mistake. Since she was running the smallest business she'd have the last pick of the seats, but that was okay.

"I was wondering," Vivien said, "how did Duncan end up being the son-in-law of the chairman of the board?"

Tim stirred some cream into his coffee. "Ooh, that's an interesting one. Basically, a case of being in the right place at the right time." Tim leaned in close. "When he was at Nike, one of the senior execs threw a holiday party and Otto happened to be there with his daughter, WNBA center Giovanna Utz. The moment Duncan saw her he was on missile lock and pursued her like crazy. Never mind the fact that he was already engaged."

"Lovely." Vivien raised an eyebrow.

"He ended up proposing to Giovanna, then breaking things off with his first fiancée."

"Ouch."

"Yeah. Around that time, Otto joined the Smart Sports board. When the Smart brothers needed a president to grow the Men's Footwear business, Otto suggested they hire Duncan. Everyone in this industry knows the plum jobs are gotten through connections." So it was that easy.

Duncan got his fairy-tale ending–he was married to an attractive woman with the added cool factor of being a professional athlete, and he'd landed a coveted role. Having an influential father-in-law was an even bigger bonus.

"Something else I've been wondering about," Vivien said. "Under Duncan's signature line in his emails it says, 'Leader of fourteen major footwear launches.' Is that somehow significant?"

Tim smirked. "Actually, it's not a ton of launches given his years in the industry, and if you count his successful launches it's even less impressive. It's all fluff, really."

Within the next fifteen minutes the rest of the guys arrived. Duncan appeared last, according to his customary habit, and gave a hearty greeting.

Soon the copilot, clad in khakis and a golf shirt, came to collect them. "Is everyone ready to board?"

The five men and Vivien walked out to the tarmac. She hung back a little, since she would be the last to board. However, as they reached the jet, Malcolm stopped. "Vivien, please"–he gestured up the stairs– "after you."

Vivien smiled at him and ignored the glare from Duncan. The flight attendant from Vivien's first plane ride greeted her warmly. She made her way to the back of the plane and picked a nice comfortable seat facing toward where the Smart brothers would sit. It would be a long flight, and she could get some quality time with the co-CEOs.

✳

In Beijing they visited sports retail stores and had a private banquet at the palace of a former prince. Each executive had two servers, one for food and the other for beverages.

"Between the time difference and the jet lag I'm not sure if I should be eating dinner or breakfast," Malcolm quipped, and yawned.

But they were famished and the aromas wafting up from the heaping plates were mouthwatering. Vivien was well aware they were being treated in a way that few native Chinese people would ever be lucky enough to experience.

On day two they landed in Shanghai for meetings and more retail visits. A couple of Mercedes limos picked them up from the tarmac and whisked them to the Four Seasons hotel, where they were greeted by name and escorted directly to their rooms. Each executive was accompanied by a team of hotel employees: one to handle check-in from the comfort of their room, one to serve chilled water with cucumber, and one to unpack their luggage.

With some free time before dinner, Vivien took a brisk walk to explore one of the city's new, luxurious shopping malls, where she found not one but two huge Louis Vuitton stores and two Prada stores. After a quick spin around the shops, Vivien left the mall and crossed the street. She was nearly hit by a man on a bicycle transporting eight cages of live squawking chickens. He deftly swerved around her, leaving a shower of dust and chicken feathers dancing in midair. What a jolt to go from the pristine interior of the ritzy mall to the loud, furiously busy, and crowded streets. The air felt like a heavy fog seeping into her lungs and depositing particulate matter.

The Smart brothers had scheduled a low key dinner at the hotel restaurant, and then Malcolm recommended turning in early. "We have to leave before dawn to drive out to the factory in Guangzhou."

Morning arrived too soon. Still rubbing their weary eyes, the executives journeyed to a major footwear factory in Guangzhou. The driver of their minivan spoke in halting English but conveyed that the factory didn't get many VIP visitors.

"Who was the last VIP to visit?" Vivien expected it was an executive from a competitor.

The driver gave a toothy smile, revealing some gaps. "Oh, very exciting! Michael Jordan. He come last year. Closed all highway to traffic so he could come very fast."

Vivien laughed, "Wow, that must have been fantastic." The most famous athlete in the world was a tough act to follow. To the factory workers, a visit from Smart Sports executives was probably a big yawn.

"You work for Smart Sports?" the driver asked her.

"Yes, I do."

"You a secretary?" Vivien realized the driver was just trying to be friendly. In rural China they probably never saw a female executive, especially an Asian one.

"No." She smiled. "Not a secretary."

"Oh. I ask because you very pretty like secretary."

Vivien accepted the compliment. "Thank you. You see those three guys in the back? Each of us runs a business at Smart Sports." Vivien turned to see Duncan, Johnny O, and Tim tittering. She gave them a mock look of annoyance.

"She is one of our presidents," Malcolm said. "Very smart and successful."

"Oh, I see. Big job. Very exciting!" The driver's eyes widened. "First time to meet lady president!"

"Not as exciting as Michael Jordan, though, right?" Vivien joked.

She looked out the window and saw a river the oddest shade of greenish brown, choked with pollutants. They pulled up to a massive complex that housed thirteen factories, all making footwear for competitors like Nike, Adidas, Asics, Under Armour, and Saucony. Security was tight, and there was no communication between factories in order to alleviate fears that designs would leak across to competitors.

The Smart Sports factory manager ran out to greet them, along with their head engineer. After introductions and the customary posing for photos, their tour began. First they visited the room where midsoles were manufactured.

"What's this?" Johnny O picked up a piece of white material from a bin.

"That's the midsole, the part of the shoe sandwiched between the upper and the outsole," Duncan explained. "Most midsoles are made out of EVA, or ethylene vinyl acetate." He pointed to a valve on a large machine. "Here EVA is pumped through and air injected into the material under pressure, forming a closed-cell foam."

Vivien and Johnny O poked their heads in a little closer to take a look.

"The midsole is the most critical part of the shoe, because it determines the amount of stability and cushioning the shoe will provide." Duncan seemed to enjoy giving his lecture. "Every footwear company creates their own secret recipe for the midsole, and we guard ours jealously."

During their morning runs, Vivien had gone to school on footwear, asking Tim all sorts of questions. That had prepared her well for the factory tour. Having a science degree didn't hurt either.

The plant engineer was explaining to Duncan and Tim a problem they were struggling to solve. There was too much variability in the quality of the midsoles produced.

"What's the expansion rate of the EVA?" Vivien asked.

The engineer looked shocked. "You are a footwear manufacturing engineer?" he asked.

"No, why?"

"Oh, I–I am confused," he stammered. "I thought you must be an engineer because no one from headquarters has asked a question like that."

"I'm wondering if you can control the density of the polymer going in and create a vacuum in the expansion phase, adjusting for the expansion rate of EVA. That would determine the amount of air that ends up in the foam and should make the quality of output more consistent. You've probably thought of that already, though."

"No, we haven't, and that's a great idea. I will do some calculations and see how we can achieve that." The engineer gave Vivien a grateful bow.

Tim nodded. "Great thinking, V."

The Smart brothers just smiled, while Duncan appeared surprised and Johnny O looked as if Vivien and the engineer were speaking in Mandarin.

Around lunchtime the team was ushered into the main conference room, where the plant manager greeted them and said they had a special treat for lunch. The Americans figured it would be some kind of Chinese banquet, and their stomachs were growling. Because of the early start they hadn't had time for breakfast. Vivien had brought some emergency protein bars for the trip and inhaled one on the drive over, but that was hours ago and she was famished.

The managers from each manufacturing line stood along the wall to pay their respects to their visitors. With some fanfare, the plant manager had the lunch ladies wheel in carts and present the special meal–Kentucky Fried Chicken with a side of white rice and a mix of unidentifiable vegetables. Apparently the Chinese workers thought all Americans craved KFC.

Vivien said, "This looks delicious, thank you." She tucked into the chicken.

Alex and Malcolm followed suit and graciously thanked the plant manager for the special lunch. Duncan and Johnny O exchanged puerile looks.

The executives quickly finished eating and continued their tour, arriving at the portion of the factory that made the rubber outsoles. Men sat on wooden stools cutting up small pieces of rubber for multicolored outsoles. They jammed the pieces into a large metal mold resembling a giant waffle iron, then closed the top of the mold and stuck the entire contraption in a giant shoe-making oven. After the oven melted the rubber, workers wearing heat-resistant gloves pulled out the mold and pried out the singular piece of rubber that was now an outsole.

"Wow, I can't believe all the steps involved in just making the outsole," Vivien said.

"It's very labor intensive," Tim agreed. "But labor's cheap here, so that's why it's done this way."

"Isn't it possible to use injection molding? You'd get better consistency and higher output."

"Sure, but..." Alex rubbed his fingers together to represent money. "The cost of changing out these lines would be high, and labor is cheap. It's actually more economical to just throw more people onto the production line."

"I understand. But what happens when labor costs go up?" Vivien asked.

"That won't happen," Duncan scoffed. "Three reasons why we do it this way, Vivien. First, all the footwear companies produce in China, where labor is cheap. Two, it would be close to impossible to set up this kind of manufacturing facility elsewhere. And three, we're giving these factories so much business they want us to keep producing here. Realistically, I can't see labor prices ever going up. That's just not a concern."

"Maybe, but it can't hurt to have a backup plan in case labor costs creep up. If that happens it will definitely impact the manufacturing process."

Tim seemed to mull over what she was saying, while Duncan just shrugged. "That's such a remote possibility. Really."

The uppers of the shoes were produced, appropriately, on the upper floor of the factory. A sea of women sat at sewing machines and stitched together fabric components. To let his visitors have some fun, and to show them how difficult it was to make a quality shoe, the plant manager invited each president to sit at a sewing machine and piece together just two components of the upper.

Duncan went first. His hand-eye coordination was not the greatest. Frustrated, he tossed out his first attempt and insisted on having another go, with the same disastrous results.

None of the guys could figure it out. Their stitching was off course or uneven, because they tried to force the material through the machine and they slammed down the foot pedal as if they were driving a NASCAR vehicle. The area manager tossed their work into the scrap bin.

Vivien asked a seamstress for some tips. Through some sign language and broken English, she learned that she needed to let the leather pull itself through the sewing machine, going slowly and not forcing it. When her turn came, she approached it delicately, pulsing the foot pedal as the workers did, so she could maneuver the leather better. The area manager inspected Vivien's work and gave her a thumbs-up as he placed her upper into the production pile–which meant it would be used for an actual pair of shoes. A small win.

Duncan punched Johnny O in the arm. "Too bad, Johnny O, yours was ree-jected."

"What, I'm supposed to feel bad that I can't do a woman's job? Not!"

The guys chuckled until Malcolm glared at them.

The plant tour moved on to a line of people stretching the uppers over a wooden mold and trimming off the excess to get them ready for assembly. A machine took the outsoles and glued them to the midsoles, spitting out bottoms ready for their uppers. Then came the labor intensive process of attaching the uppers to the shoe bottoms and wiping the excess glue with what looked like a Popsicle stick. The strong chemical smell of the glue invaded Vivien's nostrils and strangled her lungs. How could these factory workers sit all day inhaling those vapors? It was a tough job in a miserable environment and she felt for them.

*

Their next stop was an apparel factory. The guys, except for Johnny O, seemed less interested in that, but Vivien was in her element and conversed in detail with the factory manager about quality control, technical pattern making, and production issues. Vivien explained what she was trying to do with the product line and how it would impact their business, and in the process she enlisted his support to ensure critical things happened.

They came to the area of the factory where layers of fabric were laid out in stacks across large tables and markers for the pattern pieces were placed on top. The fabric was cut with a special tool to carve out the pattern pieces. She noticed that there was ample room around the markers, which would lead to excess fabric. Waste. Suddenly, she had an epiphany and motioned for the factory manager to come closer. "Look, here we have a lot of space between the markers. Can we turn this scrap material into headbands or hair ties? We need to offer some accessories, and that would just be free money for us."

The apparel factory manager gave a broad smile. "Yes, wonderful idea! We can surely do that. The way the pattern pieces are set up we can't get them any closer, so using the excess fabric makes a lot of sense."

Malcolm said, "That's genius. Let's do it." He and Alex gave a thumbs-up.

Meanwhile, Johnny O was wandering around and goofing off with Duncan, not paying attention to what was going on in the factory. For someone who was responsible for Men's Apparel he didn't seem terribly concerned about the production side of things.

Vivien felt the visit was time well spent. From her previous experience she knew that building face to face relationships with factory managers was key to success. If a production or quality issue arose, she'd be able to call him directly and sort things out. That could be worth gold.

CHAPTER 14: JUST ONE OF THE GUYS

The next stop was a brief visit to Hong Kong to focus on product innovation. The team flew in that morning and went directly to the Smart Sports Product Innovation Center, which had been in the works for eighteen months. After a long day, they went to dinner at a fancy restaurant overlooking the harbor and sampled some of Hong Kong's best cuisine. Bellies full, they departed the restaurant sapped; this trip and the jet lag were wearing them down.

"When we get back to the hotel, I'm going to check out the rooftop Jacuzzi and give these dogs a rest." Malcolm gestured to his aching feet. "Who's up for it?"

The rest of the team agreed to meet up on the roof in fifteen minutes. Being athletic and having done lots of water sports, Vivien was comfortable in a bathing suit. What she wasn't comfortable with was seeing the guys she worked with in skimpy swimsuits. Fortunately, none of the guys sported a banana hammock–they all wore the same style of baggy board shorts.

Alex, Malcolm, and Tim, all being avid runners, had similar builds– slender but fit with great muscle definition. The Smart brothers were older but they clearly kept in exceptional shape. Duncan was in fairly good shape, with mostly upper-body muscle and relatively skimpy legs. It turned out that under the baggy T-shirts and jeans, Johnny O had a bit of a soft belly and sported some ink on his pumped-up arms–a barbed-wire tattoo snaked around his right bicep, and the names of his kids adorned his left arm. In Portland having a tattoo or a few was a commonplace fashion statement.

As they relaxed in the Jacuzzi, the mood became jovial.

SHAZ KAHNG

Vivien realized this was the first time a female executive had come along on one of these road trips. "Okay, guys," she said, "what was your most memorable sports moment?"

The Smart brothers and Johnny O all picked a moment in professional sports that was particularly meaningful to them.

Duncan thought a bit. "One summer in London I was earning extra money doing construction work. I was sweating it out with the other workers, most of whom came from a blue-collar background. I noticed the time and had to dash. Made an excuse about meeting my sick aunt, but really a friend's uncle had box seats at Wimbledon and I had to clean up and get to the stadium. I sat there in my blazer and ascot watching the match, praying my construction mates wouldn't spot me on TV. I'd have been mortified to be seen sipping champagne in a box seat."

Tim shared a humorous and self effacing tale.

Everyone enjoyed the warm, burbling water.

Duncan turned to grab his drink from the side. Partially hidden under his wavy silver-blond mane was a tattoo on the back of his neck, a coat of arms featuring a column and a banner with some Latin writing. Although his neck was a map of weathered wrinkles and the green ink was faded in spots, Vivien could make out the words *Vires Sub Pressurā*.

Johnny O caught her studying Duncan's tattoo. "Okay, Miss Smarty Pants, why don't you tell us what that means?"

"It's Latin for 'Keep back two hundred feet,'" she quipped, and the guys laughed. "My Latin's a bit rusty, but I think that translates to 'Strength Under Pressure.'"

"Quite right. Well done, V." It was the first time Duncan had called her by her new nickname, and he didn't sound at all sarcastic. Were they making progress?

"Oh, I get it, it's a Doric column, like your surname. So 'Strength Under Pressure' is for the column and for the Doric family. Clever

196

motto, Dunk. Is it your family's crest?"

"Well, er, not exactly. I had it designed specially for the Doric name. What do you think?"

The Doric column portion of the tattoo was directly over Duncan's spine. Vivien found it odd to see a guy in his late forties sporting a tattoo with a fake coat of arms, and the placement of the tattoo was peculiar. Didn't most people get tattoos where they could look at them and remember why they got the ink in the first place? Duncan could never see his own tattoo, so it was clearly done for the benefit of others. But exactly what was he trying to show? Was he trying to make himself seem special? "It's pretty cool."

Duncan smiled, and for the first time it looked genuine.

"What was your scariest sports moment ever?" asked Malcolm. "V, how about you?"

"That's an easy one, although it may not technically be considered a sport. I was on a scuba diving trip with some school friends in the Coral Sea. We were doing a shark feeding dive and descended to the bottom, where three huge steel cages sat. My dive buddy Brooks and I got into our cage along with the dive master, and we noticed there was a huge opening in the cage about three feet square. We looked at each other like, 'What's up with that?' and shrugged, figuring the dive-boat operators must do this all the time. The guys on the boat chummed the water with chunks of bloody tuna. Within seconds the place was swarming with over fifty sharks–blacktip, silvertip, whitetip, and some others. A chain was dropped into the water with a float on top and with lines of large whole fish dangling and oozing blood. When you hear the phrase 'feeding frenzy,' that's exactly what it was. The sharks went nuts, tearing at the bloody flesh on the line. Sound travels well in water, so the creepiest part was that you could hear low growls as the sharks fought each other to devour the bait–and you could clearly hear the sound of bones getting crunched in the sharks' teeth."

"Man, that's intense," Tim said.

"It was, but that's not even the scariest part. I was taking some underwater photos when suddenly my dive buddy grabs my shoulder. I turn to Brooks, and his back is pressed against the cage wall and he's pointing up. There's a shark *inside* the cage with us. About six feet long. The dive master jumps on the back of the shark, grabbing its pectoral fins and pushing the shark's nose into the latch on the cage door, trying to unlock it. Finally the dive master realizes that's not working so he releases the shark, which by now is even more agitated. The shark shoots to the top of the cage, turns, and dives right at me. Looking up I realize, *Hey, that shark is in the attack position just like we saw on the predive training video!* It torpedoes toward me and all I can see is teeth...rows and rows of sharp, jagged teeth. I'm like, *Oh shit!* and I duck. The shark swims over me toward Brooks, who also ducks. By that time the dive master has unlocked the door, so we get behind the animal and shove it through the door and slam it shut. Brooks makes a gesture like he's wiping off his brow. Once we get back on board, Brooks rips off his mask and yells, 'Vivi, I wet my wet suit!'"

The men roared with laughter.

"So I can safely say that was my scariest sports moment."

"Mind-blowing story!" Alex said.

"Incredible, V," Tim echoed. "I'm not even going to compete with that one."

Duncan and Johnny O exchanged furtive glances.

What she viewed as a casual, fun moment sharing an experience meant something entirely different to them. They saw this situation—heck, the entire trip—as a competitive arena where points were won or lost. Having the Smart brothers in the audience only raised the stakes. Even the sewing exercise at the footwear factory was a contest among the guys.

Being an athlete, Vivien loved competition, not because she felt she had to beat someone else, but because she enjoyed a challenge. So far on this trip Vivien seemed to have the most points on the board, and that probably didn't sit well with Dunk and Johnny O. Sensing an awkward lull, Vivien said good night, and the Smart brothers and Tim got up to leave as well.

As she walked away she heard Duncan's cell phone ring and Dunk say, "Charl, what's up, bud?" She hadn't heard a peep from Charl the entire time, and he was calling Duncan?

Vivien looked back and saw Duncan and Johnny O in the Jacuzzi with their heads close together as Duncan spoke intently on his phone. His right hand rubbed the back of his neck–his tell for when he was feeling stressed.

*

Next stop: Tokyo, where the group wandered around the Ginza shopping district before dinner. Vivien sauntered into the Prada store, a stunning modern building with amazing visual execution inside; spinning skirts twirled around on poles suspended from the ceiling like exotic birds. When she was wrapping up her store tour, she saw Duncan at a counter making a purchase.

"Aw, Dunk, you don't have to get anything for me, really."

Duncan's pupils contracted and his left jaw muscle twitched. What did that weird tick mean?

He half smiled. "Oh, just getting some inspiration samples to take back to the footwear team. I really like these materials." He was buying two women's wallets–one made of a silvery leather with a honeycomb print and the other a floral embossed leather. Duncan used his Smart Sports corporate credit card to make the purchase.

"Pretty snazzy wallets," Vivien replied.

The team regrouped at a highly regarded but little-known gem of a restaurant specializing in *robatayaki*–varieties of grilled meats, seafood, and vegetables cooked over an open fire. In this type of restaurant the diners sat around the *robata* grill pointing to whatever they wanted. The chef would cook it and hand it to the patron on a wooden platter with an extremely long handle. The precisely sliced and seasoned food was the freshest and highest quality, accompanied by plenty of Japanese beer and sake.

After dinner the Smart brothers returned to the hotel to prepare for their meeting the following night with Starbucks founder Howard Schultz, to discuss issues with expanding in Asia. As Malcolm and Alex headed out, Tim's cell phone rang–his spouse was calling from the States, so he stepped outside the noisy restaurant to take the call and say hi to his kids.

Vivien took the opportunity to use the restroom. As she stood up, she caught Duncan and Johnny O giving each other a big smile and nudging each other. She attributed this exchange to their simply having a good time.

When she returned to their table, Duncan handed her a full glass of a cloudy drink and said, "Here, V, we ordered a round of this special unfiltered sake to toast you, our newest member. Three parts to the toast: One, we're glad you're on our team and are one of the guys. Two, even though we all like Charl, we're also looking forward to working with you. Three, it's been fun having you on this trip. So cheers to you!"

"Aw, thanks, guys." Vivien clinked glasses with them. Their smiles and kind words suggested that maybe they were beginning to accept her.

Duncan had an odd smile. "Oh, here comes Timmy. Hey, man, here's one for you." The four of them toasted again and Duncan started loosening up, telling an amusing story from his Nike days involving Phil Knight, some Japanese visitors, and a nutria. Vivien had only once seen Oregon's native nutria–basically a gigantic black rat with a long orange tail, like a subway rat on steroids. Totally freaked her out.

She was taking in Duncan's story, and within a matter of minutes she was hit by a wave of nausea. More like a tsunami. She felt weirdly dizzy and needed to get out of that place before she tossed her cookies.

Trembling, she stood. "I gotta get back to the hotel and call Clay." Johnny O insisted that they walk her out and get her a cab.

Seconds ticked by excruciatingly slowly as Vivien had to wait for them to pay the drinks bill, listen to them decide which bar to hit next, and finally walk outside. Beads of sweat populated her brow and soaked the back of her blouse.

A taxi sat just yards away. With increasingly unsteady legs, Vivien leapt in, saying a hasty good-bye. By the sour metallic tinge at the back of her tongue, she knew she would be ill in a matter of minutes. No way she was going to vomit in front of Duncan and Johnny O. "Cerulean Tower Hotel, *kudasai!*" Vivien said to the driver in Japanese, and he sped off. The second they rounded the corner and were out of sight of the guys, she lowered the window, leaned her head out, and threw up. Twice.

The cab driver didn't flinch or even look back at her. Maybe late-night passengers who imbibed too much often vomited in cabs. This was strange, though. Vivien hadn't had that much to drink. Her head was pounding and she felt another wave of nausea building.

The taxi pulled up in front of her hotel, and she threw the driver a wad of cash, giving him a generous tip and mumbling an apology in Japanese. She dashed into the elevator, smashed the button for her floor, and made it to her room just in time to get sick again. At least this time she was in the comfort of her hotel room. Her stomach convulsed, and for a brief moment she thought an alien creature might burst out of her belly.

As she lay on her back on the bathroom floor, drenched in sweat, she tried to think about what she could have eaten that would make her so violently ill so quickly.

Too late, she recalled Tim's warning about the drinks. Bingo. That's why she felt so awful.

Fumbling through her suitcase, she found the pouch of emergency medicines she always brought on trips. A bout of stomach flu had taught her to always carry an antiemetic. Hopefully, it would work on this, too. She found it and quickly popped a tiny Gravol pill with as much water as she could stomach, then immediately crawled into bed. She set her alarm, and that's the last thing she remembered.

*

When Vivien awoke the next morning her throat was parched, her head was aching, and she was annoyed. She had been in the business world for over a decade and never suffered this kind of treatment. Why were Duncan and Johnny O ganging up on her and, worse, playing dirty? Was Charl in on it? He'd spoken with the guys the previous night. Were they scheming together?

Best to brush it off. If she whined about it to the Smart brothers, that would only make her look weak. The guys who were hazed before her had certainly taken it without complaint.

She knew the other execs would probably be working out at the hotel fitness center, and she needed to make an appearance. Even though a crew of jackhammers was walloping away inside her head, she jumped up, got into her workout clothes, and rushed down to the gym.

To build a relationship with this dastardly duo, she'd have to divide and conquer–approach them separately and try to win over each one individually.

Despite her shattered state, she spent a few minutes on the treadmill, splashed her face and shirt with water, and grabbed a towel. Her display was timed perfectly. She left the gym just as the guys were coming in.

"Holy shit, V, have you worked out already?" Johnny O said, staring.

"Yeah, had a good night's sleep so I decided to get in an early workout. Man, that was some sake bomb you guys gave me last night. Remind me never to drink unfiltered anything again–ha, ha! See you guys at breakfast in about an hour."

Duncan squinted as if she were some sort of hologram playing a Jedi mind trick on him.

A long, warm shower rehydrated Vivien. She knew a little trick–a shower was a good cure for a hangover, even a drug-induced one. By the time the guys arrived at breakfast, Vivien had already downed a ginger ale–ginger reduced the electrical activity in the stomach and was a good elixir–and was feeling significantly better. She ordered scrambled eggs and wheat toast, and caught Dunk raising an eyebrow at Johnny O.

*

The purpose of the Japan visit was to research retail concepts. The Smart Sports Japan team was excited to host the corporate leadership and greeted them formally in the hotel lobby. Vivien quickly forgot her physical ailments, fascinated by the ideas in the Japanese market. At a used-clothing exchange, an entire wall was covered with an intricate network of bamboo cages containing chipmunks. Vivien wasn't sure what they were going for, but it was interesting.

"Our concept stores back in the States aren't meeting expectations," Alex said, "so let's use this opportunity to pick up some new ideas we can apply. Figure out how to engage our customer better."

It was a whirlwind day packed with lots to see, and at the end they had a couple of beers with the Japan team. Vivien never let her glass out of her sight.

She and the others headed back to their hotel while the Smarts went off for their dinner with Howard Schultz.

It was Tim's turn not to feel well, although it was probably just a cold. As they walked into the hotel Vivien's phone rang. It was Rebecca.

Vivien got a quick and not-particularly-content-filled update. As she was ending the conversation, Rebecca asked if Duncan was around.

"Sure, he's standing right here. Do you want to speak to him?"

"Oh, no, forget about it," Rebecca said, and they ended their call.

Ten seconds later Duncan's cell phone rang. He answered it and walked off.

Tim put his hand to his forehead. "V, I'm going to order room service and hit the sack early, try to shake off this cold."

"Sure, Timmy. Feel better. Call me if you need anything."

Tim walked off, so with Duncan standing outside still chatting on the phone, Vivien asked Johnny O, "Any plans for tonight? Would you and Duncan like to get dinner with me?"

"Um, I think everyone's just doing their own thing tonight. No group plans. See you in the morning, V."

Vivien was fine with that. Frankly, she was looking forward to some solitude. She had been careful about not eating too much that day, and by now she was fully recovered and starving. She asked the concierge about a recommendation for a tasty, casual place within walking distance, and he suggested a restaurant specializing in *tonkatsu*.

She made the quick walk to the restaurant and was seated at a small table facing the window with her back toward the door. Her table was next to an opaque rice paper partition.

Her *tonkatsu* arrived in good time. The deep-fried, breaded pork was sliced into strips, a perfect golden-brown color, crispy outside, and juicy and steaming hot inside. The meat and tangy dipping sauce combined with the simple rice and cabbage sides made for a hearty meal. Vivien savored every bite.

Soon she heard people being seated on the other side of the rice paper partition. Although she couldn't see them, she recognized Duncan and Johnny O's voices. Apparently the concierge recommended this place liberally.

For a moment, she considered letting the guys know she was there, but if they didn't include her in their plans, it meant they didn't want to spend time with her. It would be awkward for everyone if she came around the partition and surprised them.

She would just eat her meal quickly and quietly and get out of there without being seen. But it was impossible to ignore what was being said at the next table.

"So, how long do you think this Lee character is going to last?" Johnny O asked.

Vivien Lee couldn't believe the first thing out of his mouth involved her. What were these guys, gossiping schoolgirls?

"Lee who?" Duncan scoffed, and they both laughed. "I'll be damned, though, she made a miraculous recovery from last night. That is one tough cookie. Are you sure you put enough of the stuff in her drink?"

"Yeah, I used the same amount as always and then some. Good idea about the unfiltered sake–much harder to see the powder. But, seriously, how long do you give her?"

"She won't last the year. She doesn't realize she's playing in the big leagues now. Who gives a damn how clever she is or how much the Smart brothers like her? We can't just let some outsider come in here and make us look bad. It's all about relationships in this industry, and she's got none. Vivien's already stumbled, and Charl is just waiting for her to make even bigger mistakes so he can jump back in and take the reins. Everyone likes Charl, so they'd support him. Less than a year, and she'll give up and leave."

Why were these guys so against her? She'd just moved cross-country for this job. She was definitely staying put, no matter what these bozos thought.

"Did you get a load of the questions she was asking at the footwear factory and the suggestions she was making to the engineer? That's not even her business, who does she think she is? She should stick to apparel." Johnny O sounded indignant.

"I wouldn't get my knickers in a twist about her. Obviously the Smart brothers wanted to bring in a little diversity–she's a woman and a minority; that counts double. When it doesn't work out, at least they can say they tried. Same thing happened at Nike…folks from the outside would barely last a year. No one will care about another new person leaving, and she won't be with Smart Sports long enough to have an impact. But, man, it bugs me how people think she's so great. And did you get a load of that shark tale? No one wants to hear her little stories."

Vivien felt the sting of Duncan's remark. She felt like shouting over the partition, *Hey, I was asked to tell that story.*

The restaurant lighting cast Duncan's shadow against the rice paper. Vivien noted his stooped, question-mark posture. It was such a strong visual image of what she had on her mind. Would it ever be possible to work with this guy, win him over, or even trust him?

It was evident that Duncan was highly competitive and jealous of Vivien, and the things she was doing as a matter of course were making him feel insecure. Before she showed up, Duncan was the golden god, the guy everyone wanted to be like.

"Yeah, you're right, Dunk," Johnny O said. "Anyway, with your years in the industry, and all the people who are loyal to you, there's no way some outsider could challenge you."

"You watch," Duncan said. "Someday, I'm going to be a captain of this industry…even Phil Knight will look small-time compared to me!"

She could imagine the glint of naked ambition in Duncan's eye.

"I'm down with that, bro. So what was the other thing you wanted to talk about? You looked kind of freaked out when you got off the phone, man."

Through the rice paper partition Vivien could see Duncan's hand coming up to rub the back of his neck, a signal she knew meant he felt stressed out.

*

Duncan took a huge swig of beer, still reeling from his phone conversation. It would be good to talk things out with his friend. "I'm freaking out big-time, Johnny O."

"Why? What's going on, man?"

"You know how Giovanna's been traveling for the WNBA game schedule and promotional activities? Well, I've had this little flirtation on the side for a while."

"Dawg. Mind if I ask with who?"

A bit sheepishly, Duncan said, "You remember the pretty blonde in Women's Apparel, Rebecca Roche? I met her years ago when she was interviewing for a job at Nike. When I got to Smart Sports she contacted me looking for a job, so I got her in. She was so grateful for my help, man, inviting me out for lunch, drinks...Anyway, we've always been on friendly terms, and she was sending some strong signals that she wanted to hook up. So, we've had an occasional shag when my wife's been out of town. Portland can be a bit of a snoozefest, and I needed something to entertain me."

"Um, okay, I don't see any problem with that."

Duncan rubbed the back of his neck. "There wasn't a problem. It was just a harmless bit of fun. But Rebecca called me this evening. Turns out she's pregnant. That's what the call was about."

"No way! You sure it's yours, man?"

"Rebecca is absolutely certain the kid's mine. I've got a mind to have her do a DNA test when the time comes. Bloody hell, man, this has turned out to be a nightmare, especially since she wants to keep the baby. To tell you the truth I'm completely panicking right now."

*

Vivien sat frozen in place, afraid to even breathe in case the guys heard her. In the past few minutes she had gotten a huge data dump, including an indicator of Duncan's true character–that he was cheating on his unsuspecting wife. Wasn't Giovanna the prize he'd pursued so arduously? His actions made zero sense. Vivien also realized that she'd have to find a temporary replacement to head up product design and development while Rebecca was on maternity leave.

She finished her meal. Despite an overwhelming urge to stay and hear more, she felt she had to discreetly hightail it out of there before the guys spotted her. She silently signaled for the check while Duncan and Johnny O yammered on. Vivien paid her check and hastened out of the restaurant, unnoticed by her colleagues.

*

Duncan could see the concern in his friend's eyes and it touched him.

"That is rough, Dunk. Is there a chance Giovanna could find out?"

God, what a nightmare. That could never, ever happen. It would be his ruin.

"No way, dude. I've been very clear with Rebecca all along that there's no way I'd leave my wife, and this news simply cannot get out. We'd both lose our jobs. I must protect my stellar reputation at all costs. We'll figure out a way to deal with it. Maybe she'd be okay with telling people the father is someone else."

"Like who?"

Duncan gave a sly smile. "I dunno, want to volunteer for the job, Johnny O?"

"Whoa, wait a minute." Johnny O put his hands up. "You know I've got your back, Dunk. I'll figure out a way to help you. But we'll have to come up with a plan that doesn't involve my wife wanting to murder me. Don't worry, we'll sort it out."

Duncan exhaled for a long time. His personal life was a complete mess. He had to figure a way out of this. "Thanks, man. Who knows, maybe Rebecca can quickly find a boyfriend and sucker him into believing he's the father. The big letdown is that Giovanna and I have been trying to have kids for a while–spent a bloody fortune on fertility treatments. A total no-go. Meanwhile I have this harmless little flirtation and the girl gets pregnant!"

"It'll all work out, man."

"You're lucky, Johnny O, you've already got your kid situation sorted."

"My kids are the best. I am lucky," Johnny O said with a sentimental look in his eyes.

"Yeah, yeah. I mean, it's not the greatest situation but at least I'll have a kid that will carry on the Doric genes. Maybe it'll be a boy."

"That'd be cool."

"Wonder what we'll call him. I've always been partial to the name Damian..."

*

On Friday morning the six executives boarded their corporate jet for the flight home. The Smart brothers shared the highlights of their meeting with Howard Schultz and discussed some insights from the trip they could apply to Smart Sports retail stores.

After what seemed an eternity, the plane touched down in Portland.

As the executive team stood bleary eyed in the private terminal waiting for their bags, they said their good-byes. The Smart brothers gave a friendly hug to each executive and to each other, and everyone else followed suit.

Vivien made her way around to hug each person, but when she came to Duncan he hung back. She initiated a motion toward him, but he stiffly bumped one shoulder with her in an ersatz embrace. It was the most awkward hug Vivien had ever experienced.

After all the traveling and time spent together she was exasperated that Duncan still kept her at arm's length. Vivien had always been skilled at winning people over. And she'd never even mentioned the sake poisoning incident. Shouldn't he give her some points for that? She just had to figure a way to crack that Duncan nut.

*

That sunny weekend, still jet-lagged, Vivien dragged herself and Doug Hawke to a practice round at the Reserve golf club in advance of her big game on Monday.

"I don't think Steele Hamilton is too happy about me playing against Mackey Keeyes."

Doug, in his usual manner, said, "The little guy's going to have to suck it up."

Steele had tried his darnedest to cancel the golf match, imploring Alex and Malcolm not to risk embarrassing one of their sponsored athletes.

"Mackey dug his own grave by making those comments at the company meeting. He's agreed to play, so this *is* happening, Steele," Alex had said sharply.

"Not only is it happening, but we're joining them for the round!" Malcolm chimed in.

Steele pouted. "It's a lose-lose situation." He wasn't a golfer and was therefore excluded.

"It'll be fine." Alex's tone told Steele to drop the topic.

*

As scheduled, the golf showdown took place on Monday morning. The semiprivate club had agreed to delay foursomes for ninety minutes after their tee-off time, giving the Smart Sports execs and Mackey ample time to play their round. Vivien would be playing against a professional athlete along with the co-CEO's of the company...no pressure.

When Vivien arrived at the Reserve she spotted all three guys on the practice range hitting balls. The Smart brothers looked like decent golfers, but Mackey was a different story. He was doing what many male golfers did: using his muscles to power through his swing. Experienced golfers knew that relaxing and swinging smoothly actually got you more distance and consistency.

She greeted the Smart brothers and waved to Mackey, who waved back and wiped some sweat from his brow.

"He's been practicing for nearly two hours," Malcolm shared in a low voice.

"Yeah, but sadly that's not going to help him," quipped Alex.

"Mackey looks worried," Malcolm observed.

"With a swing like that, he should be worried. Although, I haven't seen you hit a ball yet, V." Alex winked.

Vivien went ahead and hit some practice balls, running through her clubs in her usual routine. First she loosened up with her seven iron. Then the five iron. Then her fairway woods. Then her driver. Lastly, she hit with her pitching and sand wedges. Fifteen minutes later, when she felt warmed up, she proceeded to the putting green. This was something many golfers neglected to do, but putting was where strokes were lost, so Vivien always practiced putting to get a feel for the greens.

Although she preferred to walk the course, Vivien thought it better for relationship building to share a golf cart with Mackey. Alex and Malcolm shared another cart. The foursome loaded their golf bags onto their carts and pulled up to the first tee, a straightforward par-four hole.

The Smart brothers teed off first to relieve some of the tension, playing from the white tees. Both had decent drives, although Alex's went left and Malcolm's went right. Mackey stepped up to the tee. He was a gifted athlete and extremely tall. But he had the most awkward golf swing Vivien had ever seen. His backswing started out fine, but he had a hitchy downswing and crouched as he swung through. There was a vertical drop of two to three feet between his backswing and downswing.

Mackey duffed his first drive. The ball rolled about fifteen yards. Vivien said, "Take a mulligan if you like. No big deal."

The athlete gave a thankful nod and tried again. He repeated his strange swing but this time got the ball airborne. He sliced the ball way right and it landed about 115 yards out.

"Vivien, you gonna play from the ladies' tees?" Mackey said. After a terrible shot like that, he actually dared to trash-talk?

"You mean the forward tees, Mackey? No, I'll play from the same tees as you guys."

Vivien put her ball on the tee and allowed herself a quick practice swing. She lined up and took a deep breath to relax. She swung the driver smoothly and connected with the ball well. It was the longest drive of the four. Straight. Middle of the fairway. What a relief.

Malcolm whistled. "Nice ball, V."

Mackey furrowed his brow. They advanced down the fairway, albeit at different paces, and then onto the green.

Vivien drained an eight-foot putt.

Alex, the official scorekeeper, said, "Nice par, V! Mackey, should I put you down for a double bogey?"

"Uh, it was actually a triple," he replied grumpily but honestly.

There was not much small talk and Mackey was stone-faced. Maybe he was starting to regret the whole thing. Was Steele's instinct to cancel this game right? Arriving at the second tee, they could see it was a tricky dogleg right with a ravine cutting across the fairway and then uphill to an elevated green. Not easy.

The Smart brothers hit their balls and then Vivien hit. Mackey sighed and bent down to tee up his ball.

"Listen, Mackey, we don't have to make this a competition or even keep score. Let's just relax and have fun. But later, maybe you can do something nice, as a conciliatory gesture to the women of Smart Sports."

For the first time a wide grin broke across Mackey's face. "What,

Vivien, you quittin' already?" he taunted her.

"Me? Quit? No way, man."

"Okay, then. I knew what I signed up for, so let's just keep going. We can still make it fun." The athlete seemed to be relaxing a little.

"All right, Mackey, bring it."

"Watch out. And watch this, V." He drew his club back and swung it so hard it made an audible whoosh as it sliced through the air. The ball remained on the tee, untouched.

"Mackey, I know you're a great athlete and you seem like a good person. But, man, you have got one ugly-ass swing!" Vivien said. The Smart brothers' eyes widened. Silence. "What? You just said to make this fun," she joked.

Mackey busted out laughing. The basketball player responded, "You better get used to my ugly-ass swing, 'cause you're gonna be seeing it all day!"

The ice was broken. Now the four of them could enjoy some good conversation and their game. Again, Mackey sliced the ball.

Riding in their cart, Vivien said, "May I offer you a little tip, Mackey?"

He turned toward her with a skeptical look but he nodded.

"You know how you've perfected the release angle on your fadeaway jumper? Well, the same idea applies here. I noticed your club face isn't square to the ball as you're swinging through– that's why you're slicing it." Vivien demonstrated using a ball and her palm as the club face. "If you roll your wrists over as you make contact you'll close up the club face more and that'll straighten out your shot."

Mackey chuckled. "We're supposed to be competing, V, yet you're helping me out? That's cool." He bumped fists with her.

At the end of the round, Vivien was officially declared the winner over nachos and beer. A favorable outcome was that she'd gotten to know Mackey and the Smart brothers even better.

A man of his word, Mackey Keeyes had a present waiting on the desk of every female Smart Sports employee later that week: a bottle of champagne and a sleeve of golf balls with Mackey's smiling face on each ball, and printed underneath, "Ladies, go ahead. Hit me."

On Vivien's desk was a brand-new pair of limited-edition, Smart Sports basketball shoes signed by Mackey in a gorgeous, ornate glass case. When Duncan and Steele stopped by her office to take a look at her treasure, Dunk pointed and said, "I want those." Steele just glared.

PART FOUR

CHAPTER 15: KEEPING UPBEAT IN THE DOWNPOUR

For the past two months, Portland had lived up to its reputation as one of the rainiest places on the planet. The gorgeous summer weather had come to an abrupt end in mid-September with an ominous gray day that ushered in the rains. Cascading sheets of precipitation came pummeling down from the skies for an uninterrupted streak of forty-five days.

When Clay came out to visit they had to stay holed up in her warm, cozy condo, venturing out in the blustery, wet weather only for food or coffee. His reaction to the deluge was that they should start building an ark. The dreary weather only made Clay more hesitant to visit.

Rather than losing out on time with her fiancé, Vivien traveled back to New York most weekends that fall. She was getting used to Portland but welcomed the chance to spend time with her dad, Clay, Coop, and her Smasher friends.

The first week of November, Vivien stepped outside the Smart Sports executive building and her eyes felt a stabbing pain. What was happening?

The rains had stopped suddenly for an afternoon, and the sun peeked out, assaulting Vivien's eyes, which teared up from the bright light. She felt like one of those rodents that burrow deep underground and never actually see daylight, eventually losing their sight.

Her team was starting to gel, and things would only improve once her intractable head of product design and development went on maternity leave. Vivien was secretly counting down.

Rebecca was savvy enough to at least give the appearance of listening to her new boss, supporting the new direction, and working more effectively with her teammates. Still, Rebecca repeatedly showed an ego outsized for her talent, and a stubborn streak. The two of them had clashed over Vivien's decision not to produce the capsule collection codesigned by Flora Jensen. Rebecca came back with "better" ideas: a skinny denim workout pant, or "jegging"; a cropped jacket that exposed a woman's butt; a youth-inspired collection of expensive hoodies; and a white yoga pant. Rebecca's aesthetic sensibility was in question as she continued to choose product colors that were her favorites–sweatshirt gray, pale yellow, mint green–even though they hadn't performed well. Rebecca often made illogical remarks and demonstrated an aching desire to always be "right."

J. J. once commented, "Rebecca inhabits her own little world. Sometimes her communication is so irrational it's like you're speaking to someone stuck in a circular reference. I always say, a little Rebecca goes a long way!"

*

Vivien was just steps away from Rebecca's office when she heard Rebecca and Cat talking with Aileen. Rebecca said, "Ooh, these sketches are fantastic, Aileen. I just love them and appreciate all your hard work. This is sooo awesome!"

Aileen walked out smiling and clutching her large sketchbook, not noticing Vivien, who stood off to the side. Just as Vivien was about to knock on the door, she heard Rebecca say in a low voice, "There's no way we're making this collection. Aileen's ideas are just too far off the mark. You agree with me, Cat, don't you?"

"Totally, too far off the mark," echoed Cat. "Anyway, the construction would be challenging. I really love your idea about doing a resort collection. Now, that's exciting."

Vivien knocked, walked in, and greeted both women. Their heads were close together, and with their haughty expressions they looked like sorority girls blackballing a candidate. Cat sipped a smoothie, while Rebecca's long red nails encircled a cup of latte.

"I just saw Aileen walking down the hall. She looked pretty happy. How did the follow-up from the design review meeting go?"

"Oh, unfortunately, not so well. As we all agreed in design review, we need to add another collection to the spring line. I asked Aileen to come up with some ideas but she just didn't deliver," Rebecca stated flatly.

"Didn't deliver at all."

Come on, Cat, show some original thought.

"That's surprising. Aileen is a talented designer–she's designed some of our bestselling products. What was the issue?" Vivien asked.

"Aileen came up with a premium yoga collection and some swimwear. That's just not what I'm looking for."

"Our customers practice yoga frequently and we need to focus on delivering performance product at a slightly higher price point. Why wouldn't we do an interesting yoga offering? And swimwear has great margins."

"I happen to have a fantastic idea for a collection that I just love. Since everyone goes on vacation that time of year, we're going to do a resort collection! It will be a capsule collection of linen product. A super-cute jacket, some capris, palazzo pants, a drapey dress, and cute shorts. It's going to be adorable!"

Cat chimed in, "Adorable!"

"Wait a minute, linen? Let's keep in mind we're a performance company making activewear. Why would our customer buy linen product from us?"

"Vivien," Rebecca said snippily, "linen *is* a performance fabric."

She had a pretty good bullshit meter, and this one was off the scale. Vivien's skepticism must have shown on her face.

"Please," Rebecca said, "just let us show you the samples that are being made, and you'll see how great the collection is. I promise, this will make total sense for our product line. As you know I have many years of expertise in product, and I just need a little freedom to experiment here. Also, Charl saw a sneak peek of the designs and was super supportive."

Rebecca was strangely overconfident in her abilities, her instincts about what consumers wanted, and her taste level–the three areas critical to success.

Choosing linen over much-needed performance material didn't strike Vivien as the right decision, especially if Charl supported it. Vivien would have to shoot it down. But she had challenged the team to think more creatively, so she felt she should give Rebecca a chance.

"Rebecca, I don't think linen is the right way to go for our consumer, but I'll hold off on a final decision until I see the samples. Cat, I need to touch base with Rebecca on some other issues. Would you mind giving us some privacy?"

"Sure, no problem." Cat clutched her smoothie and hoisted her frame up from Rebecca's conference table.

"Cat, just a sec," Rebecca called out. "Here's the money for my latte. Thanks, sweetie." She pulled a crisp five dollar bill from her silver leather Prada wallet, which had a honeycomb design.

Cat collected it and shuffled out the door.

"Rebecca, there's something I don't understand. Aileen walked out of your office smiling–that isn't the expression of someone who's just been told her designs 'didn't deliver.' What message did you as her boss convey to her?"

Rebecca gave her a sideways look and gripped her notebook tightly. "I'm not sure what you mean."

In a slightly stern voice, Vivien said, "Did you let Aileen know what you really thought of her designs and whether or not we'd use them? If not, she walked out of here thinking she hit the ball out of the park and will be crushed when her work never gets produced. Wouldn't it be better to tell her, in a diplomatic way, what your honest reaction really was?"

She said slowly, "Oh, I see what you're saying. I'll try and do things differently in the future." Rebecca pulled out her black notebook and jotted a few notes with the tinkling Hello Kitty pen. After a minute she gazed up at Vivien with a sincere look and almost whispered, "Thanks for coming over here, Vivien. There are actually two serious issues I want to discuss."

"Okay, Rebecca, I'm listening."

The two issues did not surprise Vivien at all.

"First, I'm concerned about the level of morale on my team. It's very low." The statement, combined with her worried expression, was almost comical. Just minutes ago Vivien had witnessed how terribly she treated people. "Turnover on my team is so high, it makes things so difficult for me," Rebecca said.

In fact employee turnover on Rebecca's team was the highest in Women's Apparel, if not the entire company. "Why do you think it's so high?"

"There's only one reason: burnout. The team's working too hard. Our workload is too high."

"Yes, I've seen the team working late. Often." Vivien had walked the halls of the apparel building late in the evening and knew the designers and developers were overloaded. She did, however, notice that Rebecca always left her office promptly at five p.m.

"I've spoken to HR to get some ideas, and Zac suggested I institute a Friday team lunch." Rebecca pouted. "But people haven't been showing up!"

Vivien threw out a bunch of suggestions that Rebecca could try. She eagerly captured those ideas in her pink notebook. Not that it was of major import, but Vivien was trying to figure out which notes made it into the pink notebook vs. the black one.

"I'm particularly concerned about my team's low morale given the next piece of news...I'm pregnant! Super exciting, I know. However, due to some complications, my doctor recommended I go on medical leave right away." Rebecca summoned sad eyes as she looked up at Vivien and apologized for leaving her in the lurch. "I only pray that morale doesn't drop further while I'm gone."

Vivien had already started to formulate a plan for Rebecca's maternity leave, but this was a godsend. Now she could accelerate things.

Vivien responded graciously and feigned surprise. "Congratulations! I wish you and your partner the best. Of course, your health and the health of the baby are of the utmost importance. Your partner must be excited about the news." Vivien couldn't resist.

"Well, yes, it was a surprise since Fred and I haven't been together that long—you do know Fred Andrews from finance?"

So that was Rebecca's cover. She must have convinced Fred the baby was his. The poor schlub didn't have a clue. Curious that a numbers guy hadn't worked out the math regarding Rebecca's due date—or maybe he was just too trusting.

"Do you have anyone to take my place in the interim, Vivien?"

Of course she did, but Vivien couldn't let on that she'd been planning for this. "Well, Rebecca, this is a lot of news you've shared with me. But given the need for speed, the only solution is for me to step in for the time being and oversee product design and development."

"Oh, you'd do that for me? I can't thank you enough!" Rebecca beamed.

Vivien knew the business needed stronger direction and better leadership, and taking on this role would allow her to get under the hood and fix things. It was a stroke of luck that Vivien would have the freedom to run this portion of the business exactly as she envisioned. She could supplement any skill gaps with a product design freelancer. The two women quickly sketched out plans for the handoff and for making an announcement to the team. The meeting concluded with both feeling pleased.

Rebecca would start her medical leave in two weeks, and her due date was in May. With her maternity leave and the extra vacation time she was tacking on, Rebecca wouldn't return until three months after having her baby–sometime around August. That gave Vivien ample time to get the design team on track.

＊

Vivien had yet to fill the position of strategic planning director. It wasn't for lack of trying. Zac Archer was responsible for helping her fill the role, but the few candidates he'd presented were subpar, and he was sluggish in sourcing new candidates. He seemed to butt into all aspects of her business, yet the one time she actually needed him, it was a nonstarter.

Working his connections, he had gotten himself into a *GQ* photo shoot about men with the best jobs in the sports industry. Clearly he had priorities that took precedence over work.

＊

In November, at First Thursday, the monthly event in Portland's Pearl District where art galleries stayed open late and served cocktails, Vivien perused the work of an abstract artist with some Portland friends.

Someone called out, "TC, is that you?"

It was none other than a beaming Scott Abelman.

"Scott, what a surprise!" Vivien said. "Last time I saw you was back at SCP. Great to see you." She gave him a hug. Scott was a smart, clean-cut, and energetic MBA grad from Columbia University and one of Vivien's favorite people from her old firm.

"Oh man, am I happy to see you, TC. I heard you joined Smart Sports, how's it going?"

"So far so good, some ups, some downs. How about you, what

are you up to?"

Scott rubbed his forehead. "Remember back at SCP when I wanted to take a job in industry and you said I should go for it?"

"Yes, you joined Target as I recall."

He smiled. "I did. But after four winters freezing my butt off in Minneapolis, I decided to accept a job in strategic planning at Nike."

Vivien gave him a look of approval. "Nice. Are you enjoying it?"

"Truthfully, not so much. I've been there for a year." Scott's normally happy face shifted to a look of despair. "It's been miserable, in fact. I was supposed to be reporting to a woman with a great reputation named Julia St. James."

"Yeah, I've heard the name. She's supposed to be a bright woman and a strong leader."

Vivien had recently heard an anecdote about Julia St. James–she didn't know if the specifics were true, but it was certainly entertaining. Years ago, Julia was meeting with Nike's senior leaders (including her ex-fiancé) and presenting innovative ideas to grow the footwear business. Her ideas were well-received by the executives…except for her ex-fiancé. Afterward her ex wrote an email to Julia and copied everyone else from the meeting where he criticized her ideas as "a bit dodgy" and "daft." Julia sent an email back (copying everyone) reading, "Thanks for the thoughtful feedback. I'll be sure to give your comments the consideration they deserve." Then she added, "PS: Fuck you." Evidently all the other guys found the email hilarious and it increased their respect for her–they gave her ideas the green light. An added benefit was that it made her ex-fiancé, Duncan Doric, look like a complete jerk.

Scott's mood grew serious. "In between the time I accepted the job and when I started work, Julia was tapped to run the international footwear business as general manager, necessitating a move to the Netherlands. So HR assigned me to work with a woman named Gabby Oxendine, who runs the US women's running apparel business, as a co-strat planning manager with another person."

"That doesn't sound too bad, Scott."

He shrugged. "I figured that if a woman could make it to the senior ranks in this male-dominated industry," Scott said, "she must be smart, talented, and a great leader–like you or Julia St. James. Unfortunately, my experience with Gabby has been a disaster, and working with her so-called team has been the most painful experience of my career. What kills me is the business is tanking and I could help so much more, but they've basically made me a glorified PowerPoint jockey."

What? How could someone leading a business not appreciate Scott's intelligence, initiative, and ideas? He was a hard worker and someone who got on well with others. The situation on Gabby's team must have been terrible if Scott couldn't make a go of it.

His cheeks reddened. "The politics involved are just unreal. It's a corporate prison and I'm like a POW being tortured every single day." Scott frowned and, stressed out, rubbed his forehead red. "I even tried transferring to another business unit, but Gabby blocked me. I have nowhere to go but out, because there's no way I can stay at Nike. At this point I'm ready to quit without another job lined up."

"I'm sorry to hear that, Scott. Sounds awful." Vivien put her hand on his shoulder. "But I may just have a solution for you."

"Really?" His eyes lit up.

"Yes, I'm looking for a strategic planning director. Why don't you come work for me? It's a much better title and you'll have a terrific boss." Vivien winked.

Scott jumped up in excitement, sloshing wine out of his glass. "Oh my gosh, TC. That would be so awesome! Sign me up." He knelt down to wipe up the floor.

"All right, but I'm going to need to lay some groundwork first." She'd have to play the internal politics.

She coached Scott to quickly write an effusive letter to Zac Archer. "Be sure to throw in a comment about a Lamborghini, that's his passion."

Meanwhile, Vivien enlisted Ron Billings' help to accelerate her search. She told him it had been dragging on and that she'd love to get someone who'd worked for both a competitor and also a premier retailer, like Zara or Target. She timed the conversation with Ron so that by the time he went to speak to Zac, Scott's résumé was already sitting in Zac's inbox. As Zac waved the résumé, he claimed he had "discovered" the perfect fit for the job. He didn't even seem to notice SCP on Scott's work experience.

✳

"Fantastic morning, isn't it?" Scott showed up early for his first day of work, his usual bright, eager self. He even brought Vivien's favorite drink from Starbucks. "I can't thank you enough for this opportunity, TC. I'm so incredibly grateful."

"Welcome, Scott, it'll be great having you on the team," Vivien said, "and thanks for the coffee, that was very thoughtful." She shut her office door and sat across from him. "Listen, you know the level of politics involved in this industry, right?"

He nodded with a wide-eyed look.

"I think we need to err on the side of caution, here, Scott." Vivien leaned in. "I'd like for you to be my eyes and ears. That means it would be better if people didn't know we worked together before." Not long ago Vivien might not have exercised this much political savvy–perhaps she was finally learning the ropes.

Scott agreed it would be wise to approach Smart Sports with more caution. It was a different company with a distinct culture, but it was still in the sports industry. "Sure, TC," he said, "that makes total sense."

"Thanks, Scott. But that also means you can't call me TC." Vivien chuckled. "You'll have to stick with calling me Vivien. Can you remember that?"

Scott gave her a goofy grin. "No problem, *Vivien*."

When Scott was introduced to his colleagues and asked about his work experience, he named only Nike and Target as former employers.

✳

One evening Vivien was in Duncan's office to chat. He was digging around for an article he wanted to show her in which he was interviewed about Smart Sports' latest footwear launch. While she waited she glanced at his oversized computer monitor. Duncan was composing a scathing email to the Smart brothers outlining numerous complaints about Klaas, backed up by others, and suggesting he be replaced with someone more "team oriented."

Vivien felt that the poor guy was being treated unfairly. Klaas was a smart person and a great CFO, even if he was a bit socially awkward. That night she called Klaas to warn him.

"Klaas, it's Vivien. I need to tell you something."

Sounding surprised to be called in the evening, Klaas replied, "What's the matter, V?"

"Duncan is campaigning to get you fired. He's got his buddies supporting his case. I don't think you have a lot of time, so you need to get ahead of this."

The Dutchman was silent. Blindsided. With a tone of desperation, he said, "My gosh. What can I do? V, please, tell me how to save my job. I don't want to leave Smart Sports."

He was begging her for help.

Vivien tried to calm him down. "You can handle this, Klaas. Here's what I suggest. Touch base with Malcolm and Alex first thing in the morning and subtly remind them of your instrumental role in planning the company's IPO. Mention the importance for a public company of having continuity and the ability to manage Wall Street's expectations. There's no way they'd change you out at this critical point." She also gave him a few pointers on to how to handle Duncan better.

"Thank you so much, V. I can't tell you how much I appreciate this. I will do exactly as you recommend."

By the time Alex and Malcolm received Duncan's email complaint, the situation had been handled and the threat of Klaas's losing his job neutralized.

Thank you for watching my back, V," the Dutchman said, exhaling in relief. "You know you can always count on me to do the same for you in the future, okeydoke?"

*

On a Friday afternoon, as usual, Vivien fired up her laptop for her weekly Skype call with her Ceiling Smasher friends. So far, they'd only missed one Friday call. That was because Andi, Sofia, and Grace had surprised her with a visit to Portland in October. Thrilled to spend time with her Smasher friends, Vivien had shown them all around her new city. Their tour of the Smart Sports campus was particularly impressive to her friends. "A sports paradise," Andi called it, then added, "Too bad it's so damn soggy." Vivien tried to convince her girlfriends that Portland was a nice place to live. But with the daily heavy rain, they weren't buying it.

"Are you kidding?" Andi peered straight into the computer camera. "My clothes still have water stains from that trip. And what's up with Portlandians not using umbrellas? That's just weird."

"Okay, I have to admit, it's not great weather-wise." In the short time that Vivien had lived there she'd had to convert all her footwear to waterproof shoes and boots. Also, Vivien was forced to switch to a ballpoint pen so the ink wouldn't run when her notebooks got wet.

Grace piped up, "Vivi, it was so great to see you and your condo was fabulous. But all that rain. How do you manage it?"

Vivien gestured toward her office. "Well, most of the time I'm in meetings. The only time I get outside is to grab lunch or go to the fitness center. You're right, though, this is the wettest place I've ever lived."

Sofia was silent on the topic. She probably didn't have anything positive to add. From the looks of it, Vivien's Smasher friends weren't eager to journey there again anytime soon. They spent some time getting caught up on the happenings in everyone's lives. Again, Vivien noticed that Sofia was fairly quiet, and it worried her.

"Well, I'll be coming home to New York for Thanksgiving with my dad and Clay, so I'll see you guys then. And I have a trip to Boston in early December, so I'll be back for our next Ceiling Smashers dinner. Truthfully, I'm looking forward to escaping this weather for a bit."

"Great," Grace said. "We can't wait to see you."

Before signing off Sofia said, "Vivi, can you give me a call over the weekend? I wanted to get your opinion on a sticky work situation."

Vivien promised to call her friend and breathed a sigh of relief.

✳

The next morning Vivien dialed Sofia's cell number. "Hey, Sofi, what's going on with work?"

Sofia paused. "Actually, I made that up as an excuse to talk to you privately."

"Oh? What's up?"

"I'm not sure how to tell you this, Vivi, but the headline is I saw Clay having drinks with another woman at Cipriani. I was on my way out and they were sitting at the bar. I didn't say hello to him or anything. Who knows, it could have been totally innocent..." Sofia trailed off.

Vivien felt her stomach tighten up but tried her best to sound casual. "Oh, it was probably someone from work. Did you happen to recognize her?"

"Yes. It was Elizabeth Atwood, the morning news show host. She's Clay's ex, isn't she?"

Her heart skipped a beat. What did this mean? Vivien managed a little laugh. "Oh, that. Yeah, they still keep in touch. Clay mentioned something about getting together with Elizabeth. Don't worry about it, Sofi, after all Clay is engaged to me and everything's perfect."

"Oh, so you knew about it? That's a relief. I wasn't sure what to think, Vivi. Okay, well, enjoy your Saturday and we'll talk soon."

Vivien hung up feeling uneasy. This was news to her, but maybe it didn't mean anything. She'd just bring it up with Clay–there had to be a reasonable explanation.

*

A critical task that Vivien and her team had set out to do was to learn more about their consumer. After she'd fired Gus, the consumer insights lead role was wide open. Vivien was quick to fill the job with a talented executive whom she had worked with in NY. Sue Callaway was happy to return to the Pacific Northwest, where she was raised.

The first area of focus for Sue was to conduct ethnographic research on their target consumer. Vivien wanted to know more about their consumer's life. What drove them? What did they care about? What did they do for work, for fun? What did they wear when working out and why? What was important to them in choosing activewear? All great questions, and Sue designed and led the study.

It would take three weeks, but the Women's Apparel leadership team would spend time with twenty active women across the US–some Smart Sports customers, some not. Of course, the twenty women would not know which company the team worked for.

First stop: Boston. Vivien, along with Sue, J. J., Charl, and Cat, visited the home of Jessica, a mother of two who ran four marathons a year. To begin with, they sat around Jessica's dining table talking about her exercise regimen and what drove her to do marathons. Then they went upstairs to her bedroom, where she opened her closet and dresser drawers. Tossing garments in piles onto the bed, Jessica explained which were her favorite workout pieces and why.

Charl picked up a top and could barely contain his smile. "Why,

Jessica, I see you have a Smart Sports training top. How do you like it?"

Squinting at it, Jessica said, "Oh, that. I got it as a gift. Frankly, I never even knew Smart Sports made clothing, but it didn't fit me at all. Hmm, I thought I threw that out."

Tossing it back onto the pile, Charl looked down and remained silent.

The next part of their visit was to go with Jessica for a workout. When they arrived at the gym the team asked Jessica to work out as she normally would. Sue noticed that Jessica had a jacket tied around her waist the entire time. She nudged Vivien and they exchanged looks. After her workout, when Jessica was stretching, they had a chance to ask some questions.

"Jessica, were you concerned about getting cold?" Vivien said.

"Oh no, they keep the gym at a pretty good temperature."

Charl whispered, "Maybe she's using the jacket for the pockets."

Vivien shook her head. "No, she put her keys and her phone on the treadmill shelf, along with her water bottle."

"Then why the jacket, Jessica?" Sue asked. "I noticed that it kept riding around when you were running on the treadmill. Did that bother you at all?"

Jessica shook her head. "Yeah, that was super annoying."

"Then why the jacket?" Sue repeated gently.

She hesitated, then admitted, "Well, I wear it to cover my bum."

An aha moment. There was a modesty factor, even among very fit women.

Vivien seized upon an idea. "Cat, perhaps we could design and develop run capris with a skirt attached. What do you think?"

J. J. couldn't contain his enthusiasm. "That would be awesome!"

"Yes, awesome," Cat echoed.

Surprisingly, there was even a vote of confidence from Charl: "This was a really useful way to learn about our consumer, Vivien. Nice job."

All of the additional consumer interactions were videotaped, and from the hours of footage, Sue did an excellent job of distilling what they learned down to seven key truths about their consumer. Those seven truths would drive product design, marketing strategy, tone of voice, and retail execution.

＊

Vivien prided herself on her ability to manage up. Every two weeks she provided a biweekly "flash report" to the Smart Brothers covering her accomplishments, next steps, and challenges.

"Your flash report is great, V," Alex said. "It's a quick way to keep on top of what's happening in your business. I find it highly informative."

Malcolm nodded. "It proved helpful when I got a call from Flora Jensen, who wasn't pleased about her capsule collection getting cut. I was able to explain that her designs were a bit too 'fashion forward,' as you put it, V. And I agreed with you about skin-tone garments being a total nonstarter." Malcolm picked up the piece of paper. "I really like this tool. Alex, I think we should ask the other presidents to do a weekly flash report. It will be quite valuable."

Vivien smiled, then frowned a little.

"Is something bothering you, Vivien?" Malcolm asked.

"I'm glad you like the tool. But if you ask the other presidents to use it, can you not mention that it came from me?"

Malcolm raised an eyebrow. "Sure you're not being too humble, V? It's okay to get credit for your ideas."

Vivien took a breath. "I'm still trying to fit in with the other guys, so maybe being called out for this isn't necessary." Then she joked, "Anyway, I have so many great ideas, I don't need to get credit for every one!"

Alex laughed. "Okay, we'll say we got the idea from a female B-school professor. Sound good?"

Vivien nodded.

It was nearing the end of the year, the time when the Smart brothers asked each president to lay out their annual goals.

Alex handed her a one-pager. "Here's an example so you can understand what we're looking for, V." The name of the person who'd written it was hidden.

Vivien perused it and read it aloud, "'Goal number one, grow revenues and market share. Goal two, deliver superior gross margins and EBITDA. Goal three, create an improved product development process. Goal four, be a better coach to my team.'" It all made sense. "And 'Goal five, act with integrity.'" She chuckled.

Malcolm gave her a curious look.

"Sorry," she said, "the last one sounds strange to have as an annual goal. It's like, 'Okay, this year I'm going to act with integrity. But next year? Forget about it!'"

Malcolm laughed and rubbed his left forearm with his right hand, something Vivien noticed he did when he didn't like something (as opposed to Alex, who tugged on his right earlobe). "I thought that was kind of odd, as well."

"To me, a good leader is someone who acts with integrity all the time, not just one particular year. Integrity should be a core value, not an annual goal," she explained.

"We couldn't agree with you more," Alex said. "We've been looking at updating our company core values to: creativity, courage, integrity, and teamwork. What do you think, V?"

"I like those. Simple, clear, and something the people at Smart Sports can rally around. How about including performance?"

"Yes, excellent. Let's add that one," Alex replied enthusiastically. He scribbled it down in his notebook. "So, besides what you've been covering in your flash report, how are things going in Women's Apparel?"

"I'm feeling pretty good about things. We've accomplished a lot and the team is collaborating well. As you know, I'm overseeing product design and development with Rebecca out, so we're working on a more strategic and consumer-focused product offering that will use the team's time more effectively. And we're going to overhaul our sizing specs so the fit will be much improved. That's the plan for next week."

Malcolm clasped his hands together. "I know I speak for Alex, too, when I say we're in disbelief at how much progress you've made. And in such a short time." He gave her a friendly slap on the shoulder.

"I know I've made some mistakes, but I'm learning quickly and trying my best."

"We don't expect perfection," Malcolm said. "As Vince Lombardi said, 'Perfection is not attainable. But if we chase perfection we can catch excellence.' You're doing an amazing job so far, V. Just keep on doing what you're doing."

It was a relief to have the Smart brothers' full support.

＊

Later that afternoon, Vivien was walking by Johnny O's office and overheard Duncan complaining that based on feedback from the Smart brothers, he'd have to redo his annual goals.

"Bloody hell," he grumbled.

CHAPTER 16: HO-HO, HUH?

To no one's surprise, except Cat's, Vivien killed the linen line. The samples came back and looked awful, not to mention it was a bad business idea.

Aileen proved to be a standout performer and Vivien wanted to make a positive example of her. Obviously her talent had been a source of concern for Rebecca, who wanted to be the one with all the big ideas. That explained the tension between the women.

"Aileen, I'd like to share some news. I'm promoting you."

Her jaw dropped. "Seriously? Oh my gosh!" Aileen practically jumped up and down.

"Also, I'm giving you the green light on your premium yoga collection. I'd like you to expand it even further by adding some layering pieces. Can you come back to me in a few days with some designs?"

"I'll have my sketches on your desk tomorrow morning," Aileen said.

"I'm glad you're excited, Aileen. Please don't stay up all night sketching; in a couple of days is fine." Vivien was aware of how hard Aileen was already working. "I think you're really talented and have contributed a lot. I'm going to expect even more from you as a senior designer." She smiled.

"Wow, Vivien, this is the best meeting I've ever had!" It had probably been years since anyone had given Aileen the recognition she deserved.

"You've earned the promotion and it will be announced next week. I do have a special, top secret project I'd like you to work on, along with the materials team. It's on a fast track for the Olympics. Let's touch base tomorrow so I can brief you on it, okay?"

"I'm so excited, Vivien. What else can I do for you?"

"Just keep on doing what you're doing," Vivien said, borrowing Malcolm's phrase.

Aileen pranced out of Vivien's office and nearly crashed into Cat.

"Oh, hi, Aileen. Are we still meeting later to review the design for the run capris with the skirt?"

"Absolutely, Cat. Can't wait!"

"Come on in, Cat," Vivien called out. A big believer in cultivating talent, Vivien was looking to create opportunities for some deserving people on the team. "I wanted to show you something interesting. Here, take a look."

Cat sat down and set her smoothie aside as Vivien pulled out a gigantic portfolio and opened it. They flipped through the pages together. Inside were tech packs—instructions for a manufacturer on how to construct a garment—and computer-generated patterns for garments.

"These are great," Cat murmured. "So many interesting ideas here, and I like the execution of the patterns. Who did these?"

"Lacey."

"Lacey? Lacey, the administrative assistant? I don't understand..."

"Well, Cat. I was talking to Lacey the other day, and it turns out she has a degree in technical pattern making, so I asked to see her portfolio." Vivien placed her hands onto the huge book. "She took the admin job just to get her foot in the door at Smart Sports. But I think we could put her talent to better use. What do you think?"

"Yes, we could definitely benefit from having a technical pattern maker on my development team. I have an opening for a product development specialist. Think she'd be interested?"

"I think so. Why don't you go ahead and talk to her about it, Cat? Tell her we chatted."

Cat reported back that it took Lacey less than two seconds to say yes. "You know, Vivien, it's great to see a leader who seeks out talent and gives people a chance."

＊

Vivien's desire to heed her father's advice "Be great and be good" and to help the Smart Sports people who asked her for career advice had to be balanced against the political ramifications. While her focus was on turning around the Women's Apparel business, she empathized with the people seeking help and couldn't turn her back on them.

Jeff, one of the guys from the Men's Footwear team–Duncan hired mostly men–complained bitterly to Vivien, "Duncan was the consummate salesman. He courted me heavily and brought me on board. Promised he'd help develop my career with Smart Sports. I uprooted my entire family and moved here from Boston."

"And how's it going, Jeff?" Vivien asked.

He frowned and his eyes darkened. "I've been working with Duncan for three years now. Do you know how many phone conversations we've had in that time? Zero. Do you know how often he responds to my emails? Never. I'm in exactly the same job I was when I was hired. But, of course, when Duncan wants something he'll email me at midnight and expect a response immediately. Or he'll 'request' something from me requiring lots of time and effort and expect me to get it to him the next day," Jeff harrumphed.

This sounded familiar. It seemed more than a few people regretted their decision to ever work with Duncan. In fact, a lot of his team members were coming to her and asking how to get on her team. She advised them as best she could, all the while trying to keep her good deeds under the radar.

*

On her way to the gym that day someone shouted, "Hey, V, what kind of Kool-Aid are you handing out in Women's Apparel?" It was Ron Billings calling out from down the walkway. He ran to catch her, splashing through a large puddle along the way. He shook the water off his pant leg.

"What are you talking about, Ron?" Vivien slowed her pace, steadying her umbrella.

"In the past month I've had a number of people asking about transferring onto your team. That's a first at Smart Sports–people wanting to transfer to the smallest business unit. Now, that says something about how people view you as a leader." He grinned and gave her a little punch of approval in the arm.

"Really?" Vivien smiled back. Maybe, just maybe, she was making headway.

*

As she navigated the company's politics better, Vivien had developed a strong ally in an unlikely person: Johnny O. Since they both ran apparel businesses for Smart Sports, Vivien reckoned they could team up on certain things and it would help both their divisions. At the last Ceiling Smashers dinner her friends had helped her figure out how to pick the guys off one by one, and Vivien put that plan in motion.

"Hey, Johnny O. Got a minute?" Vivien stood at the entrance to his office.

He looked up from his computer. "Sure, V, come on in. What's on your mind?"

"Saving money."

Johnny O's ears perked up. "I like the sound of that."

"We each spend a lot of money researching new fabrics and trims every year. What if we created a combined materials library to share any new materials we find? That would save developers time and allow us to stretch our research dollars further."

"Say, that's not a bad idea." He rubbed his shaved head. "Maybe we could even share our research priorities so, for example, we're both not looking for a fabric that doesn't hold odors."

"That would be great. If you're on board with this I'll get one of my developers to team up with one of yours to organize it. There's a big, vacant storage area on the second floor that would be perfect."

"Cool, sounds like a plan." Johnny O gave her a thumbs-up.

"I'm also working on something that might interest you. We're creating innovation platforms to develop new apparel capabilities that will set our product apart from competitors'. One area my materials team is focusing on is smart fabrics. We've figured a way to weave in fibers that give a garment some unique properties." She handed him a page outlining the new fabric details and then plopped into one of his overstuffed chairs. "It's still in development, but would you be interested in using it?"

He blinked and stood up. Moving closer, he said, "This is an incredible idea. You come up with these great ideas and just give them away? For free?"

It was as if his mind-set was that they should be competing. "If we collaborate and make all of Smart Sports apparel more successful, we both benefit. Right?"

Johnny O shook his head and laughed. "You really surprise me, V." He took a knee as if he were speaking to his football coach and hesitated. "I think…you know, you're just a good person…and good to work with."

"Why, thanks, Johnny O." Vivien punched his shoulder playfully.

"The only catch is that being a good person isn't going to necessarily help you succeed in this industry."

"Well, I can't change who I am, so we'll just have to see how things pan out."

Vivien's respect for Johnny O had grown recently. In observing how he interacted with his team, she could tell he was a skilled people person and an effective manager. Despite his sometimes goofy demeanor, he'd demonstrated that he really did care about people and the business.

*

A week later, Johnny O came by her office with an unusual request.

"Hey, V, you free Thursday evening? My product development team and I want to invite you and your team out for beers. Kind of a thank-you for sharing your ideas. Can you make it?" This was a milestone, because socializing outside of work really meant something in this industry.

"Sure thing. Sounds like fun."

From then on, Vivien made a point of stopping by Johnny O's office a few times a week to shoot the breeze and build on their relationship.

*

She often ran into her peers at the fitness complex. One day between weight-lifting sets, breathing hard but in a jolly mood, Duncan boasted to her about his grilling skills. "Giovanna and I would love to have you and your fiancé over to our house for dinner sometime. I can grill you my world-famous salmon steaks."

Could this mean the tide was turning, that Duncan was finally warming to her? Maybe because she had won Johnny O's approval, he was clearing the path with Duncan?

Many important decisions were made based on casual discussions at the fitness complex or in the locker room. She learned it was almost as important to be at the gym as it was to attend key meetings. Cleverly, she would work out at the end of the day, after an important meeting had taken place. Accidentally "bumping into" someone at the gym was the best way to get intel on what a person really thought about decisions from the meeting. Vivien made certain that Pandy blocked time on her calendar for workouts on those days. She was starting to learn the subtle art of how to influence others...and it felt good to have some friendships developing.

✳

On a chilly Monday morning in December, Alex stormed into the regular executive staff meeting looking furious. Of the twin brothers, Alex was the more hot tempered. He pounded a fist on the table and his eyes darkened. "Someone is stealing our ideas." Everyone looked at him. "We've got intellectual property and possibly HR violations at the factory in China that makes most of our footwear. It looks like some of our proprietary designs may have been compromised."

Tim frowned and shook his head, looking visibly agitated. Duncan let fly a string of expletives.

Malcolm rubbed his left forearm. "Tim, Ron, we'll to fly to China tomorrow to address these problems in person. This factory either had a security breach or has leaked our newest footwear designs to our competitors. It disturbs me to hear the employees who were the whistleblowers have been mistreated. It'll take at least a week to sort out."

"Dunk, we think it's best for you to hang back here," Alex said, "since we have our biggest accounts coming in. You'll be in charge of next week's executive staff meeting."

Steele said, "Can you guys keep me updated on the situation, so I can cover any PR issues?"

The team wrapped up the rest of the meeting as usual and made sure they discussed anything critical since the Smart brothers would be tough to reach for the next week.

*

Vivien's focus for that week was to work closely with the entire product design and development team to fix a number of underlying problems.

On her way to the apparel building, Vivien heard someone come up behind her.

"How's it going, V?" J. J. asked. "Have you fixed all the product by now?" He nudged her playfully.

"Working on it," sighed Vivien. "I had asked Rebecca to complete a number of tasks before she left–like revising sizing specs–and none of them got done. This is my chance to get things jump-started."

"Well, I'm sure you'll whip that team into shape." They walked into the building together and J. J. gave a wave as he ran off to his meeting.

*

At the first fit session Vivien attended, she could see that the fit model they were using (who was a friend of Rebecca's) was all wrong. Their consumer research showed their core consumer was a fit woman, size six to eight, and slightly taller than average–about five foot six. Amanda, the fit model, was the same height as Vivien at five foot ten, and extremely muscular, with broad shoulders and bulging quadriceps.

"If we fit our garments on that model and expect them to work on our target consumer…that's just not going to happen," Vivien had said in private to Rebecca and Cat. "Find another fit model who's closer to our consumer's body type."

Rebecca hadn't gotten around to it, but Cat had made some good suggestions. The day that Vivien took over the product area, she and Cat had hired a new fit model.

Today's meeting was about getting the size and fit of their products right and coming up with some new ideas. Vivien kicked things off.

"Okay, guys, I asked you to buy some competitors' products. What have you got for me?"

The team had done their homework. Products were grouped by type and put in piles on the large conference room table.

Cat stood up, looking pleased. She had come prepared. "Vivien, we have all our competitors' bestselling products. Short-sleeve workout tops here. Yoga pants over here. Jackets there, etc."

Vivien nodded. "Good."

"We took key measurements of competitors' products and compared them to ours. This chart shows how different ours are..." Cat passed a stack of handouts around. "Is Molly ready?" she asked Lacey.

Molly, their new fit model, came into the room wearing the bestselling Smart Sports yoga outfit. The team oohed and aahed about how great the product looked.

Vivien made no comment on the fit but said, "Molly, I brought along a yoga mat. Would you mind doing a downward dog in that outfit? Actually, let's see an entire sun salutation, please."

Molly rolled out the mat and complied. An avid yogini, she could do all the poses Vivien asked for and then some. It was immediately obvious that the inseam on the pants was too long and the leg opening too wide–the pant legs were falling back on themselves whenever she was inverted. The wide leg openings also caused Molly to catch her foot inside the pant leg and nearly trip.

This was their bestselling yoga pant, and it had this many issues?

When Molly lay on the mat, she had to adjust her body, since a decorative bow on the back of the tank dug into her. She tried on the competitors' products, all of which fit and functioned better.

Next up was a training outfit. Vivien said, "I brought some dumbbells, so, Molly, would you please do some weight-lifting moves?" Molly could not move her arms freely in their bestselling training tee due to the design and construction of the sleeves.

"Team, what do you see here?"

When Molly raised her arms up, the entire shirt moved up, which it was not supposed to do. When she bent over to do rows, it was clear that the length of the training tee was too short and the neckline too low.

Lacey, the newest addition to the team, surprised everyone. She grabbed some scissors off the table and went up to Molly. "Hold still." She cut slits in the fabric. "These are not articulated armholes–that's why she can't move freely. If we move the seam placement to here and add a touch more fabric here we can fix it."

Way to go, Lacey. Vivien loved her bias for action and problem-solving approach.

The run legging had a zipper that cut into the model's ankles. The cycling and triathlon products had similar issues. When Molly tried on competitors' products and went through the same series of movements they did not witness the same problems.

Finally, the team grasped the exact issues with each of their products.

"Oh my god," Aileen blurted, "these are our bestselling items, and every single one of them has a problem. We've gotta fix these."

Cat raised her hand. "You know, it just occurred to me, our fit process is very static–our fit model just stands there on a platform."

"Yes," Vivien said. "Unfortunately, that's not how activewear product is worn. That's why I asked Molly to do the activities that we're designing the product for."

"Maybe we ought to change our fitting process, so Molly is moving around in the product. Then we can tell if it'll work or not."

Thank you, Cat, for saying something meaningful.

It was like a light had been turned on. Cat grabbed a marker and wrote notes on the flip chart as teammates shouted out ideas for how to change the fit process. Before long, they had five movements required in fitting garments for each type of sport. The team also noted what competitors did well. For example, there were some common features among running products: bright colors, so the garments were visible; 360-degree reflectivity for safety; and hidden storage pockets for keys, money, or lip balm. The next step was to convert the ideas on the flip charts into standards for the design and fit process.

Around noontime, Pandy had catering wheel in a couple of carts of sandwiches, wraps, salads, and fruit. Instead of grabbing their food and clearing out for the lunch break as usual, the team stayed in the room, continuing an animated discussion of the product.

Vivien sat back and watched the interaction–the team was really collaborating, except for Cat, who had a look of concern on her face.

"Everything okay, Cat?" Vivien asked. She noticed that Cat was attempting to eat healthy but always made the wrong choices. She chose an egg salad and a tuna salad sandwich, both loaded with mayo. And she had her ever-present giant smoothie. Did she have a clue how much sugar was in that thing? Might be a good idea to bring in a nutritionist to talk to the team.

Cat said in a low voice, "Shouldn't we make sure Rebecca is okay with all these changes? You know, get her blessing?"

Vivien tried to reassure her. "We're changing so many things about our business so quickly, Cat. We have to move forward or we'll never make progress. I'll bring Rebecca up to speed when the time comes. Don't worry about it, this is my call."

After lunch the focus was on innovation. Vivien kicked things off. "The last piece of homework was for you to bring in an example, outside of the sports industry, of a great design or functional detail in apparel. Let's see what you've got."

Each team member did a show-and-tell of the product they'd brought and how a certain idea could be applied to Smart Sports apparel. The positive energy in the room was palpable.

"These are great examples so far," she commended her team. Vivien brought in a favorite swing coat that had an intricate fold-over collar that could be buttoned up to wrap around the neck. "I love this origami-type collar because it's so stylish and unique, but it's also functional. We could put a collar like this on one of our knit jackets so it could be worn open before class and then after yoga, when you're chilled, you can close it up so it keeps your neck warm."

Aileen immediately reached for the jacket to study it.

Cat went next. She had brought an expensive designer sweater made of a beige cashmere that was drapey and had a long train in the back, which was a detail that Cat just loved.

Vivien tried to remain open-minded, but she could not see how a train would be relevant for their product. She focused on the drapey silhouette. "We might do a 'to and from' drapey wrap that could be worn after yoga class."

Out of that portion of the meeting they had well over two dozen ideas on which they would experiment. Vivien encouraged the design team to continue to do this exercise at their weekly meetings. "Now, team, we've just come up with a lot of exciting ideas for you to work on. I know you are already working hard and staying late, and I'm not looking to add to your workload. In fact, I would like for us to work smarter by focusing on fewer things. Therefore, I've asked Meredith from merchandising to share something we've been working on. We've developed a new strategy for our product offering that will be better for our business and make better use of this team's talent."

Meredith came in and said hi, then plugged in her laptop, and a PowerPoint presentation came up on the screen. "Here are some key facts that Vivien and I wanted to share with you."

A chart showed that the number of styles from Women's Apparel had increased over 30 percent season to season. Another graph showed their bestselling products had the highest out-of-stocks. The last graph showed that margins had been on a straight-line decline for the past few years.

Vivien said, "This analysis shows we're making a lot more stuff every year. But we're not making enough of the best stuff to satisfy demand. And despite all our hard work, we aren't making money. The big conclusion? More stuff doesn't mean better business. We need to make fewer, better things that sell well. And that means a more manageable workload for you."

Heads nodded all around.

Meredith walked them through the new product portfolio she and Vivien had created. "There are three parts to the pyramid. The base, the largest portion, is called Core Styles–hit products we'll keep in the line and available year-round. These are our most popular items, so having them in stock will stabilize revenue and drive business growth. This portion of the pyramid"– she gestured to the base of the pyramid–"represents over fifty percent of our styles. Once we tweak these Core Styles so they're perfect, they only need to be updated every couple of years."

Moving up, the next portion of the pyramid was called Seasonal Styles. "These are either seasonal or on-trend products that reflect the latest fashion," Meredith said. "These will need to be designed from scratch each season and will represent about thirty-five percent of our line."

She pointed to the peak of the chart. "The top of the pyramid is Headliners, which are the coolest, most innovative products that we can build storytelling around. These create interest and drive the marketing message but are not going to be a huge portion of the revenue at only fifteen percent. That limits our risk."

"The most critical point for you to absorb," Vivien said, "is that once the Core Styles are done correctly, the bulk of your time will be spent working on the exciting new products in the Seasonal Styles and Headliners categories. That will allow you to use your time more wisely."

Meredith turned the meeting back over to Vivien to discuss the sheer number of styles being designed. "What is the largest account we have right now?" Vivien asked.

The team threw out some answers.

"Dick's Sporting Goods?"

"The Sports Authority?"

"REI?"

"Nordstrom?"

"Yes, it is Nordstrom. And in those stores what's the maximum amount of product we can fit on the retail floor?"

Again, the team threw out some responses.

"Even in our Smart Sports stores, what's the maximum product we can fit?"

Vivien went to the whiteboard and sketched out a box representing the sales floor and a number of hanging racks for apparel. She looked at the maximum capacity of each fixture and worked through some numbers, coming up with a single number that she wrote on top and circled in red. "So, this is the maximum number of styles we could conceivably fit in our largest retail account. How does this compare with the actual number of styles we're producing per account?" She wrote another number on the whiteboard and circled that in blue. "Note the difference."

It was a simple and logical approach, but the team had never been exposed to it before. In fact, they were horrified to realize how much time and effort they were wasting.

"Do you wonder why you're working so many hours on so many designs, yet despite all that there's no business result? We're overdesigning by four times the number of styles we need." Vivien snapped the cap back on the marker. "That's a lot of product that never even makes it to the sales floor. Wasted effort. I don't want to waste your time or burn the midnight oil unnecessarily. Yes, we want to work hard and have some extra designs we can choose from, so there will be select cases where we'll do double development of ideas, but we need to focus on doing work that will move the business forward."

There were more than a few "Oh my god!"s from the team.

"Here's our product strategy moving forward. Now you know what you are expected to design and develop and how much to create: about one-quarter of the styles you've been working on. This should make life a lot easier for you guys," Vivien concluded.

The team nearly cheered in unison.

"This makes total sense!" Aileen said. "Finally, a clear road map for what we need to do. Plus we get to work on the really cool things and take time to be more thoughtful about our designs. I feel like I finally know what to focus on now. This is awesome!"

Even Cat echoed, "This is awesome. One of the most productive meetings we've had in a long time...she paused. "But will Rebecca have a chance to weigh in on this?" She'd totally missed the point that her boss's boss was where the buck stopped.

Vivien felt compelled to make it clear. "Listen, team, what we don't want to do here is change course every few months. I will get Rebecca on board with the work we've done. Let me be crystal clear. *This* is our path forward for the foreseeable future. This is what we are implementing to turn around our business. Do you understand?"

Heads nodded most vigorously, except Cat's. She held a slightly skeptical expression but nodded anyway when her eyes met Vivien's.

*

For the remainder of the week Vivien worked with the team on aesthetics, quality, functionality, and innovation. She included the merchandising team so they could make adjustments to their pricing and classification strategies, and avoid the earlier problem of making eighty seven different styles of black shorts.

Spirits were high and she wanted to keep the momentum going. After the Friday team lunch, she asked, "Do you guys like these weekly team lunches? Do you want to keep them going?"

Nearly everyone said just having lunch together was not what they wanted. Vivien found it amusing that all of the previous group activities planned by Rebecca had revolved around food.

"Okay, what could we do to keep your morale up? Something active? What would you like?"

"Yoga would be fun," Lacey said. A few other product developers agreed.

Some designers talked about doing a team run or power walk. What everyone agreed upon was a Team Power Lunch on Tuesdays and Thursdays, where Tuesdays would be a team run or power walk along the Willamette River and Thursdays would be a free yoga class.

This was a good investment of time. It was important for her team to actually do the activities their consumers did.

After the last working session, Aileen sought out a private moment with Vivien. "This was the best, clearest direction the team has ever gotten. We're excited to get moving on these efforts. You've really been a tremendous leader, Vivien."

Vivien closed the conference room door. "Can you tell me–confidentially–about the team's morale?"

"Oh god," Aileen flopped into a chair. "In the past, direction on priorities only came from Rebecca, and things changed constantly. She'd ask for a certain design and then when she was shown the product she would no longer want it. We ended up spinning and spinning, spitting out work that was never used."

Vivien sat next to her and waited.

"We were working longer hours and not getting anywhere. Did you know Rebecca was not trained as a designer?"

"I had heard that, yes."

"Can I be honest?"

"Please do. I assure you this is confidential."

"She fancies herself to have design talent and often changes our sketches, which results in fit or construction problems, and later, when these come to light, she blames someone else. We're not given clear direction, not listened to, overworked, and then blamed for mistakes she makes. Then, to be expected to attend a team lunch where we have to listen to Rebecca talk about herself the whole time–it's too much to take."

Low morale? It was easy to understand why. Vivien had learned from Cat's team that her management style was one of command, control, and blaming others for problems. It seemed like Rebecca and Cat had trained at the same people-management school. Yet Vivien felt low morale was one of the easier problems to fix, and she intended to do just that. And perhaps, with a little coaching, she could nurture better people skills in Cat.

✳

Vivien's first executive staff meeting without the Smart brothers took on a decidedly different, more testosterone-laden, tone. Hearing some commotion as she approached the conference room, Vivien walked in and saw Duncan holding court. He was showing photos on his computer from a recent skiing trip. "This one's called Shit Chute because you jump off the ledge and start flying down at thirty miles an hour–most people shit their pants before they reach the bottom!" He let out a guffaw, and the other guys laughed loudly in manly unison.

Steele slapped Duncan on the back. "Man, that is awesome!"

Vivien said good morning to her peers and sat down.

Zac Archer from HR was sitting in for Ron, most likely at Duncan's request. Zac's sense of self-importance was even more inflated since his *GQ* magazine spread. He'd brought the magazine in to show everyone, especially the photo of him wearing flat-front pants and a slim-fitting T-shirt. The pièce de résistance was that he was leaning over and kissing…his Lamborghini.

Klaas pointed. "Uh, Zac, you are kissing an *automobile*?"

Vivien quipped, "Why yes, Klaas. Didn't you know Zac is an autosexual?"

The guys whooped it up on that one.

Usually, the small talk revolved around the weekend box office. Instead, Johnny O said, "My wife absolutely loved the redecorating job Giovanna did in your home. Living across the street from you where she can see it anytime doesn't help. Your wife just cost me another fifty grand!"

Even Klaas, who had worked hard to patch up relations with Dunk, said something about how his wife had enjoyed meeting the other wives.

Zac stopped texting and put down his phone. "Great wine, delicious food–Charl and I probably made a big dent in your wine cellar. I'll have to get the name of your caterer."

Steele piped up, "Great party, Dunk, total class act."

Duncan glanced briefly and uneasily at Vivien and swiftly brushed off the compliments. "We, uh, just kind of threw things together."

Vivien swallowed hard. So Duncan had thrown a Christmas party over the weekend and included all the key executives, even Charl, plus wives...minus Vivien. She had a thick skin, but she wasn't unfeeling. This experience hurt her in an unfamiliar way. Why would they exclude her? Wasn't she part of the team? She'd thought they were starting to bond and become her friends. She took a few deep breaths to settle herself, maintaining her calm, unflappable exterior.

Within minutes her wounded feelings were replaced with anger and her cheeks burned. How could these guys be that callous, to talk about the party in front of her? Didn't they realize that she was the only person who didn't attend? Could people really be that heartless?"

Even in the male-dominated consulting industry she'd always felt tight with her colleagues, treated just like one of the guys. But in the super-macho sports industry this was still foreign.

Vivien said casually, "Sounds like everyone had a good weekend. Shall we get started? I'm sure we all have a lot to get done today." She'd had a relaxing weekend on her own and gotten a lot done with

Clay away in London for work again. Would she really have wanted to spend time hanging out with these jerks? Not so much. She recalled a pseudo-Latin saying from Coop: *Illegitimi non carborundum*–"Don't let the bastards grind you down."

She did, however, find it curious that Duncan had held his party while the Smart brothers were out of town. Vivien filed away this experience, hoping it would help her understand the MO of these guys better.

After the meeting, while Vivien was walking away briskly to have a quick touch-base on financials with Klaas, someone called her name. Duncan.

He ran to catch up with her and sheepishly explained that over the weekend he and his wife, Giovanna, had a last-minute "smallish cocktail party–just a few friends."

A *catered* last-minute party? Right.

"So I gathered," Vivien replied dispassionately. "Glad you had a good weekend, Dunk."

"Thanks ever so much. Uh, did you have a nice weekend, V?" His hand went up to rub the back of his neck. Feeling a bit tense, she observed.

"Great. Saw some friends. Worked on wedding plans. Very relaxing."

"Oh? That's good...good."

Was this his form of an apology? If so, it was pretty pathetic.

Duncan stammered, "G-Giovanna and I must have you and Clay over for dinner sometime."

By now Vivien had learned this was a common phrase some Portlandians would say, never intending to make good on the offer. So different from New York, where if people said they wanted to host you they really meant it. No phony invitations. To poke him a little, Vivien replied, "I'd love that, Dunk. How about next Saturday when Clay is here?"

"Uh, right. Let me check with Giovanna and I'll get back to you. Brilliant." They parted, and Vivien knew it would never happen.

She walked into the CFO's office and sat down across from Klaas, exhaling a long breath.

"Is there some kind of problem here, Vivien?" the Dutchman asked in a monotone.

"Oh, nothing, just had a chat with Duncan on the way here."

Klaas, never one to show any emotion, said, "I noticed you did not attend Duncan's party over the weekend."

"That's right, Klaas. I did not attend Duncan's party because I was not *invited* to the party."

Now, a typical response to this revelation might be, "Oh really?" or "That's too bad," or "Gee, why wouldn't Duncan want you to come to his party? You're so great!"

Instead, Klaas tried to offer up an explanation: "Well, perhaps Duncan did not invite you to the party because he does not like you." So blunt. No sugarcoating.

Vivien sat there with a scowl and said, "Ouch."

In a feeble attempt to assuage her, he added, "That's okay, Vivien, not to worry. A lot of people don't like Duncan either, probably more than those who don't like you."

Hmm, a slap in the face and a backhanded compliment at the same time. Klaas was a master at that. "Honestly, I don't even know what to do with that, Klaas." She shook her head. "Let's just go through the numbers."

Klaas was a smart man who had somehow not yet learned the lesson that sometimes it's better to just keep your mouth shut.

∗

By midday her head was pounding, so Vivien was looking forward to the trial Team Power Lunch–a run/power walk. On her way out of the executive building she ran into Steele, who smiled sweetly. "Hey, V, I missed you at Duncan's party. Wish you could've made it."

What, was he trying to play dumb or alleviate his guilt? Steele was always in the know, so he must have realized that Duncan hadn't invited her.

"Yup, too bad," she replied.

Steele's shtick was to come across as a friend to all, but Vivien knew exactly where his allegiance lay. He reminded her of a mischievous little elf, and she didn't trust him one iota.

Vivien was eager to get some exercise and clear her head. Her team knew this was a voluntary activity and they should only participate if they wanted to, so she wasn't sure how many people would show up. She figured the first time out she might get a handful of folks and they'd have to decide about continuing the Power Lunches. When she arrived at the meeting spot she was surprised that it wasn't just the product design and development team who'd shown up. It was pretty much her entire Women's Apparel team. Apparently the rest of the team had heard about it and wanted to participate. This was a great outcome. Even the weather cooperated and they got a break from the constant drizzle.

But when Vivien scanned across her team and noticed what people were wearing, she felt sick. Her people wore Nike, Adidas, Champion, Under Armour, Lululemon, and even some Reebok apparel. Reebok, for god's sake! Who wore Reebok *apparel*?

"Hey, guys, why am I the only person wearing our brand?"

She heard a few lame excuses. It had not dawned on them that they should support their own business, their own company, and their own brand.

"How do you think this looks? People will say, 'There goes the Smart Sports Women's Apparel team. Great, they're exercising together. Oh look, they're wearing Nike. They're wearing Lululemon. Champion. Under Armour. If the people who are designing, making, and selling Smart Sports women's apparel won't even wear it, then it must not be any good. Why should I buy it?' Do you understand? If anyone should take pride in our label, we should. I know we need to fix a lot of things with the product, and we will. But moving forward I'd really like for you to make an attempt to wear our product, all right?"

Her team nodded but looked a little taken aback at the intensity of her tone.

"Look, guys, I'm sorry I snapped at you. I've had a rough morning. But we have to show that we believe in ourselves–otherwise no one else will."

To her surprise, Charl stepped up and said, "Listen to what Vivien is saying, guys. It's just like if you're a Ducks fan you'd never be caught wearing a Beavers jersey. Right?"

Those were the University of Oregon and Oregon State teams, but she kept forgetting which was which.

But the team got Charl's explanation, and Vivien shot him a grateful look. "Team, it's simple," she said. "The more we wear our own product, the more we'll know how to make it better. Okay? Let's go."

The team split into a running group and a power walking group. Vivien started off with the running group and realized that it would be good for her to mix it up so she could interact with different team members, so she made a mental note to do the power walk next time. Charl picked the power walking group, maybe so he would avoid any small talk that might tip off his boss that he was at Duncan's party.

The more the team interacted during the Team Power Lunches, the more they seemed to communicate and even enjoy working together. Ideas popped up from different team members on what they could improve about the product. People were actually in sync.

Many other Smart Sports employees wanted to join in, too. Vivien and her team added a boot camp workout on Mondays and Wednesdays and opened that up to the whole company.

Everyone seemed to be relishing the team workouts, so Vivien was blindsided one day when Zac Archer showed up early at the meeting point for the Tuesday run/power walk.

"V, might I have a moment of your time?"

"Sure."

"So, how do you like living in the Gregory building?" It turned out he also lived in the Pearl District, in a nearby building called the Henry. "I should break out my binoculars, I can probably see into your condo," he semi-joked. Then his manner turned overly solemn. "Vivien, I'm a bit concerned about what I'm hearing from your team."

She had no clue what he was talking about.

"I'm getting reports that you're forcing your team members to exercise." His extra-serious face caused Vivien to burst out laughing.

"Let me get this straight, Zac. This is a sports company and you're concerned about people working out? Anyway, how am I supposedly making people exercise against their will?"

Zac explained he'd gotten some complaints, though he couldn't divulge names, that people felt forced to participate. He had also heard that she was criticizing what people were wearing.

"Isn't it well accepted that it's verboten to wear footwear from a competitor's brand? Everyone knows that when Nike was wooing Shaquille O'Neal and he showed up on their campus wearing Reebok shoes, that was the kiss of death–they never signed him. Why should apparel be any different?"

Vivien wondered if the complaints were coming from Cat. She hadn't participated in a single Power Lunch. Rather than focusing on a healthy lifestyle, Cat's main hobby was acquiring the latest fashion handbag and coordinating shoes. By contrast, another overweight woman on the team had taken an entirely different approach, eager for the opportunity to get back in shape and was now training for a triathlon.

Zac said, "My advice is to cancel the Power Lunches and just let people work out on their own if they want to."

Vivien didn't waver. "How about this, Zac. You wait here, and when the team shows up you can see for yourself how happy or unhappy they seem about this activity. I've made it clear this is completely voluntary, but let me know if it doesn't look that way to you. If people look as miserable about it as you suspect, then I'll consider canceling the Power Lunches." She wondered why Zac, who was in charge of recruiting, was even meddling in this matter. He was the human equivalent of a fruit fly swarm whose only reason for existence was to buzz around and annoy people.

Sunshine glanced off his greased-back hair while Zac stood there with arms crossed, watching and waiting. Within minutes the Women's Apparel team members came bounding out of the building laughing, joking, and looking pumped up. A few said hi to Zac and encouraged him to come along.

"It's a lot of fun and a great way to break up the day. Come on, join us!"

They all chatted excitedly, clearly eager to be there. Charl walked up to Zac, clasped his hand, and drew him in for a man hug.

Vivien watched the two friends talking. Charl swept his hands in front of his body to show he was clad head to toe in Smart Sports product. It had completely slipped her mind these two characters were so close. Had Charl complained about the Power Lunches? Had he made comments divulging Vivien's wish to have her team wear their own brand? Why would he defend her viewpoint to the team, then go behind her back and complain to HR? Witnessing their interaction, Vivien was reminded yet again that politics were inescapable. She'd need to cultivate a broader network of allies, but figuring out whom to trust was key.

The team was antsy to start and called out to Charl to join them. Since reality wasn't delivering on what Zac had expected to see, he just shrugged and waved at Vivien as if to say, *Oh, never mind*, then ambled away.

After an invigorating power walk, Vivien swung by the commissary, still in her workout gear, to grab lunch. On her way in she ran smack into Cat, clutching a large smoothie and a salad. "Hi, Cat, how are you?" Vivien was a little cagey. She still didn't know who'd ratted her out to Zac.

"Oh, hi, Vivien. Are you coming back from the Team Power Lunch?"

"In fact, I am. You know, Cat, we'd love it if you want to join in sometime. But no pressure."

"Well, I can't. And there's a good reason."

"What's that?"

"I know I'm carrying around a few extra pounds, and I've been trying to eat right. I'd like to start exercising again and spend time with the team."

Vivien waited to hear the problem.

"But, well...Smart Sports doesn't make women's apparel in my size. So I can't wear our brand." That was the truth; the company's apparel, like most brands in the industry, only went up to size ten.

So simple to fix.

"Cat, why didn't you just come and talk to me about it? I'm sure we can work something out. Perhaps you can wear whatever workout pants you want—but maybe cover up the logo with electrical tape—and if you don't mind wearing a men's top I can get one from Johnny O."

"Really?" Cat's face lit up. "That could work."

"All right, when you're ready we can even do the power walk together. How does that sound?"

"Great, Vivien. I appreciate that. Just remember I walk a lot slower than you."

"No problem. And I'd like your help in solving a business problem. I think we need to extend our size range so more women can wear our product, say take the upper end of the size range up to a size twelve or fourteen. We can start on that next week, okay?"

"That sounds perfect."

Cat had an unusual little spring in her step as she walked away.

CHAPTER 17: HAPPY, HAPPY, HAPPY

Vivien put her hand to her forehead. She was burning up and feeling terrible, distracted from the conversation with Scott Abelman and her division CFO. They were mapping out the strategic and financial plans for the next five years for Women's Apparel and the outlook for growth was phenomenal.

"Uh, are you okay, Vivien?" Scott asked. "You don't look so great."

She'd had noticeably lower energy in the last few days, and that morning she'd woken up with chills and could feel the growing pressure of congestion. "I've had better days, Scott."

Pandy tapped on the door and brought in some chicken soup and crackers for her boss. "Thought you might need this, V."

"Oh, Pandy, you're an angel, thank you." Vivien sniffled. She rarely got sick.

They wrapped up their meeting and even after having the soup, Vivien still felt ill as she tried catching up on emails.

"Maybe you better call it a day, boss." Pandy stood at her door.

Wearily, Vivien looked up. "No argument here, Pandy. Would you please cancel the rest of my meetings? I'm going home to hopefully sleep this off."

✴

The next day Vivien still felt lousy, so she changed her key meetings to conference calls and arranged for a checkup.

Malcolm's wife, Sheri, had recommended a doctor to her. "You will not find a better diagnostician than Anjali Patel."

As she checked her over, Dr. Patel said, "It could just be the flu or some sort of bug. After all, this is the season. But let me run a couple of tests to be sure, Vivien."

She returned to her condo. Never one for rest she did the laundry and tidied up. She texted Clay, who was in Geneva all week for a banking conference. Vivien only lay down when Clay texted back to remind her to take it easy. Her schedule at work was always so packed, it was a welcome respite to have a day off, even if she was sick.

✳

A couple of days later Vivien was wrapping up a meeting in the conference room with J. J. and Charl about expanding their retail accounts when Pandy said she had an important phone call waiting.

Vivien walked briskly back to her office and snatched up the phone.

"Hi, Vivien, it's Anjali Patel. How are you feeling?"

She was surprised to hear the doctor's voice. "Oh, hi, Dr. Patel. I'm feeling a lot better, thanks. Guess it was just some sort of bug."

"Actually, Vivien, it was something else entirely."

The doctor shared the results of the tests.

"Excuse me, Dr. Patel, would you repeat that, please?" Vivien said. "I'm not sure I heard you correctly."

"You are pregnant, Vivien. The test came back positive. Congratulations! It looks like you're about eight to ten weeks along."

Vivien and Clay had discussed having a family, but they hadn't planned on having kids this soon. After all, they were still in the midst of planning their July wedding.

"Wow," was the only response Vivien could muster.

"I'm delighted for you. I'd like to recommend an OBGYN named Laurel Harding–she's an excellent doctor with a wonderful bedside manner. I'll have my assistant email Dr. Harding's contact information to you. I recommend that you make an appointment for next week so the doctor can start monitoring your pregnancy. All right?"

"Okay, thank you, Dr. Patel."

They spent a few more minutes going over what to expect and precautions she should take, such as avoiding alcohol. Given that Vivien was an exceptionally healthy, athletic woman, Dr. Patel expected her to have a smooth pregnancy.

Vivien set the phone down gently. It was hard to fathom she had a life growing inside her body, a baby Finch. She could hardly wait to share the news with Clay.

But first, she had to get through the rest of the day and then attend the Smart Sports Awards ceremony. All senior executives were expected to show up to this annual event.

In fact, Malcolm came by to remind Vivien about it. "Each January the entire company gathers to recognize the individuals who made the biggest impact on the business the previous year. A number of prizes are awarded, but most coveted is the Smart Sports Award for MVP, Most Valuable Player. All employees vote on the rightful recipient of the honor."

Pandy had already told Vivien that typically the designer who came up with the most successful footwear product that year was the recipient, so the announcement of the MVP winner was somewhat anticlimactic.

On that Friday at three o'clock p.m., all employees started heading to the Stadium for the ceremony. Bending over to put some papers into her computer bag, Vivien felt queasy all of a sudden and had to sit back down.

*

Pandy was putting on a fresh coat of bright pink lipstick when Malcolm stopped by.

"Hi there, Pandy. Can you and your boss use my services as a bodyguard to accompany you to the ceremony?" Malcolm winked.

"Sure thing, that would be great, Malcolm. Let me go get Vivien."

She got up and went to the door of Vivien's office and saw her boss hunched over the trash bin vomiting. "Holy crap, V, are you okay?" Pandy started toward her.

Vivien's complexion was a pasty shade of gray and she waved her away. "Uh, that egg salad sandwich I ate for lunch must have been bad. I'm just going to tie up this trash bag and head home."

Pandy furrowed her brow. "Need help getting to your car?"

Vivien shook her head no.

"Okay, I'll let Malcolm know you're ill and can't make it. I hope you feel better, Vivien. It's been a rough week for you, get some rest."

Pandy closed the door behind her quickly so Malcolm wouldn't see Vivien in such a state and explained the situation. Looking disappointed, he said, "Oh, what a shame. I hope she's all right."

Shrugging, Pandy said, "Guess you'll only need to escort me, Malcolm."

She took his arm and they strolled down the hallway. Pandy felt terrible for her boss but also a bit giddy. *Not too shabby, arriving at the awards ceremony on the arm of the co-CEO.*

*

A millisecond after Clay answered his phone Vivien blurted, "Clay, I've got some news."

Expecting to hear something work related, Clay said, "What, you discovered a revolutionary new material for your Smart Sports apparel line?" Funny, that actually was something she was working on. "Or something really life changing, you came up with a new sports bra design?" A little condescension in his voice. All right, she wasn't curing cancer, but her work was important to her.

Impatiently Vivien said, "No, nothing to do with work, Clay."

"Uh, what is it, babe?"

She noticed a tinge of concern in his usually confident manner. Vivien had never brought up the topic of his having drinks with Elizabeth Atwood, hoping her fiancé would explain it at some point.

Was that what was worrying him?

"Clay, you know how we talked about having a family?"

He let out a chuckle. "Yes, of course I remember. And I've enjoyed all our practice."

"I know we're both overachievers and like to be ahead of schedule and…well, we're ahead of schedule. I'm pregnant, Clay." There was a pause. Would he be elated, terrified, unhappy?

There was a crashing sound on the other end, but she heard Clay let out a huge whoop of joy. "Sorry, babe, I got so excited I dropped the phone. That's awesome! And a little crazy. God, I'm just thrilled to be having a child with you, Vivi."

What a relief that he shared her excitement. Pure happiness.

"I think it must've happened over Thanksgiving. There were a couple of days when I forgot to take my pill."

"Wow, this is huge. Huge. So when did the doctor say you're due?"

Vivien paused. "That's the kicker. I know we were planning on having our wedding in July, but I'm due in late August. I'm not too keen on walking down the aisle and having my water break then and there."

That elicited a belly laugh from Clay. "Don't worry, babe, we'll push the wedding back to whenever. Remember, we're going to have our wedding pictures for the rest of our lives, so I'm guessing you don't want to have our ceremony when you're eight or nine months pregnant and a chubster. Don't worry, we'll figure it out."

"Okay, sounds good." She paused. "I know you might want to share the news with your family and friends, honey, but I'd rather wait until the doctor says I'm in the clear. Is that all right?"

"Sure, Vivi. I'm so happy about our baby. I know it's a little earlier than we expected, but this is a wonderful surprise. Let's not be anything but positive about it."

Despite her queasiness a serene feeling came over Vivien. She was engaged to the man she loved and they were expecting a child together.

"So, how are we going to do this, Clay? Raise a baby with you in New York and me out here?" Her shoulders started to tighten up just thinking about the logistics facing them.

"Hmm, well this certainly changes things. I can talk to my firm about transferring me to the San Francisco office, maybe work out an arrangement so I can commute from Portland a few days a week. I'll talk to my boss tomorrow about it. Okay, babe?"

Vivien said, "And what about your mom? Isn't she going to be unhappy that you'll be on the West Coast?"

"Don't worry about my mom, I'll deal with her. Who knows, maybe she'll be so thrilled about having a grandchild she won't give my location a second thought."

Her tension started to ease up. Maybe this wouldn't be that difficult. "Oh, Clay, that would be great! I really appreciate your willingness to move. I miss you so much and having you here would be perfect."

Clay said matter-of-factly, "It's not that big a deal. I own my apartment so I'll just keep it the way it is and move some of my clothes out there. We'll need a place to stay when we visit New York anyway, and eventually we'll move back here."

✳

Feeling elated about her pregnancy, Vivien was less apt to let some of the political battles get her down. Even when it came to Steele Hamilton.

"Ever since that triathlon sponsorship fiasco I'm learning to trust Steele less and less. And I don't agree with how he's spending the marketing budget," Vivien said as she leaned back in the leather chair in Doug Hawke's office.

Doug scrunched up his face. "I never supported his Justin Stewart strategy–blowing eighteen million dollars on one athlete contract. I liked your One Thousand Everyday Athletes women's campaign idea. Too bad you couldn't get it funded."

"Thanks, Doug, but clearly Steele didn't get behind it. It bugs me that while Justin Stewart may be a great tennis player, he's such a jerk. I think it tarnishes our brand to have the Smart Sports logo on that guy."

"Frankly, Justin's not the right brand representative for us, but Steele was relentless in socializing the idea with Malcolm and Alex. That's why he got his way and they signed him."

While asking for help was difficult for her, Vivien was getting into the habit of bouncing questions and ideas off of Doug during their weekly meetings. Maybe she could avoid any more big blunders.

*

Vivien walked by Johnny O's office on a blustery day in March and he called out, "Hey, V, can you come here a sec? Got something to show you." He was holding a tennis hat custom-made for Justin. In front of him were two charts—one showing the tennis player's current measurements and the original chart done back in September. Johnny O pointed to the new chart. "Have you seen Justin lately? He looks like the Incredible Hulk."

She'd seen the athlete, who now had the V-shaped physique of a bodybuilder and had packed on about thirty-five pounds of muscle. "Yeah, I saw him in the commissary earlier today with his new coach and Steele," Vivien said. "I had to do a double take, nearly didn't recognize him. He looks pretty jacked up, man."

"You think he's juicing?" Johnny O used the sports lingo for steroids. "He told me it was protein powder and a new weight-lifting regimen."

"Hmm, I don't know...let's see." Vivien scowled and leaned over the charts. "The circumference of his head is almost two inches larger than it was about six months ago. I don't know of any 'protein powder' that grows your head like that, do you?" She wondered if this was part of Steele's "grand plan."

Johnny O shook his head. "Yeah, I guess it could be HGH...or something. But you're right, it sure looks like he's doping."

Yet, whatever Steele was recommending to the athlete seemed to be working. In recent months Justin Stewart had been the victor in two big tournaments, upsetting the favorites. Steele had developed an irritating habit of holding up two fingers every time he talked about his prized athlete to signify the two wins.

CHAPTER 18: LET THE GAMES BEGIN

The Smart Sports Games were just getting under way on a cool April day and the sun peeked out as if on cue. The games happened annually and consisted of a series of agility, speed, and strength contests. There were two competing teams, the Red Team and the Blue Team. People representing each of the divisions were assigned randomly to either the Red or Blue Team. And the contests were not revealed until the opening ceremony, preventing anyone from gaining an advantage by practicing for them. The purpose of the Smart Sports Games was to build team spirit, have fun, and get the competitive juices flowing–for some participants that last objective was the main focus.

That morning, when Vivien put on her workout clothes, everything was conspicuously tight, especially around the midsection. She was over four months into her pregnancy and feeling good. With her tall, slender frame and drapey clothing choices she had been able to successfully hide her weight gain so far.

At the executive staff meeting, just as Vivien bit into a chocolate croissant she was the recipient of a comment no woman wishes to hear.

"Better watch those pastries, V, looks like you're putting on a few pounds there." Klaas nudged her and motioned to her tummy bulge.

She looked down. It was official; she had her first muffin top.

Upon receiving her withering stare Klaas added, "But, hey, you still look great."

The rest of the guys sat in amused silence as they witnessed the exchange.

Resignedly, Vivien turned to everyone and said, "Guys, I'm not just getting fat...I'm pregnant."

"Oh," Klaas said. "Wonderful!"

"Congrats, V."

"Great news."

"Best wishes to you and Clay."

Each of the guys came over to give her a hug. Malcolm whispered, "You're going to be an awesome mom." She returned his smile.

Vivien said to her peers, "I'm trying to figure out how to handle my team when I'm on maternity leave, so I'd appreciate it if you guys could keep my pregnancy a secret for now."

Her doctor had given her the all clear to participate in the Smart Sports Games but cautioned her on certain types of activities to avoid. So, that day as the executives discussed the games, Vivien explained what types of activities she'd have to sit out.

*

The beautiful campus on the banks of the Willamette River was adorned with extravagant decorations and banners hailing the Smart Sports Games. That morning, the entire company showed up for the opening ceremony. Teams wore their respective red or blue uniforms from head to toe–or as they would say at Smart Sports, "from toe to head," since footwear was their heritage. The executives were also split up between the two teams. Steele was the emcee for the games, which conveniently meant he didn't have to participate in any of the events. He was a slick guy who always managed to work the system to his advantage.

In keeping with her relaxed style, Vivien approached the Smart Sports Games casually and with a sense of fun. That wouldn't last long.

Johnny O sidled up to her. "As soon as they announce the events and who is assigned to do what, let's huddle on how to maximize our Red Team points, okay?" She must've looked surprised because he said, "Dunk's been working with a trainer for months so he can win as many events as possible."

"Seriously?" Vivien raised her eyebrows. "No one knows what the events are, so how could someone prepare for them?"

Johnny O explained, "Duncan based his training off events from the previous games."

The executives were split up onto the two teams: the Red Team consisted of Malcolm, Johnny O, Tim, and Vivien. The Blue executives were Alex, Duncan, Klaas, and the CIO, Norm. Ron Billings was benched because he didn't want to risk reinjuring his hip.

Steele kicked off the opening ceremony by asking the Smart brothers to say a few words. Then they brought out their guest athlete–Mackey Keeyes. That year Mackey had led his team to the NBA playoffs, which were starting in two weeks. The crowd roared in excitement to see Mackey and he bounded out onto the platform and regaled the crowd with a short, funny story.

"Hey, where's my friend, Vivien?" he called out. She waved and they both smiled as he said, "I want to see you bring it today, V! I'll be rooting for you."

Steele scowled momentarily at this interaction–he was supposed to be the one the athletes befriended. He guarded his relationships with Smart Sports athletes jealously. The flags flapped in the wind as Steele stepped up front wearing a lavaliere microphone. With a flourish, he revealed the events.

"We'll have five events for these Smart Sports Games–a vertical jump contest, a two-hundred-meter sprint, a dexterity drill, a footwork speed and balance drill, and a visual acuity contest. Each event has a certain point value, as you can see on this chart." Steele pointed to a huge sign that was being uncovered. "Each team will have only certain team members assigned to each event. The team with the highest point value at the end of the games will be the victor."

Steele said, "First event, the vertical jump, which is really high-tech. The contestant will stand here on this electronic platform and from a crouching position must jump as high as they can with one arm extended straight up." Steele pointed upward. "The electronic eye here will track the exact height of the jump, while the electronic platform will record hang time. A combination of height and hang time gives you your score for this contest. All right, let the games begin!"

A bullhorn sounded and officials herded the Red and Blue Teams to the first station, where assignments for who would be doing which events were announced. As Vivien made her way to the vertical jump platform someone grasped her arm. Klaas was wearing his Blue Team uniform and a worried expression.

He whispered sheepishly, "Vivien, I know we're on competing teams, but I have a big favor to ask you. Even though I'm very tall, I've always been so terrible at jumping–that's why I never played basketball. I saw that they have us competing against each other–can you please try not to jump higher than I do? It would be embarrassing to get beaten by a woman, even though you are a very athletic woman."

Their interchange tickled Vivien, who teased her friend. "Klaas, you're asking me to throw this one? You've got, what, about eight inches on me!"

His pale blue eyes telegraphed real fear.

"Okay, Klaas, why don't you go first–you'll probably do better than you think. But if you do terribly, I'll see what I can do to help you out."

The Dutchman gave her a huge smile of relief and a firm pat on the shoulder as he called out his thanks and ran back to his team. When it was his turn to jump, Vivien realized Klaas was not being at all modest; he was indeed a pitiful jumper despite being close to six feet six inches tall. He looked dejected as they announced his dismal score and shot a hopeful glance at Vivien. She might have difficulty jumping lower than Klaas and making it look believable, so she aimed to jump almost as high but reduce her hang time. That way Klaas wouldn't look too bad and she'd still be contributing points to the Red Team.

At the start of the games Vivien had noticed people laughing and smiling, but as people competed in the first event the mood shifted to intense concentration. This was, after all, a sports company full of former jocks looking to relive their glory days.

*

Steele moved everyone on to the next event, the race. "Second event, the two-hundred-meter sprint, which is simple and straightforward."

Vivien was running in the first heat with a mix of Red and Blue Team members. Walking onto the track, Vivien looked to the lane next to her.

She smiled and said, "Have a good race, Dunk."

Duncan nodded blankly and seemed preoccupied with retying his shoelaces. Of course he was under pressure–he was the president of Men's Footwear and this was a footrace. People expected him to perform well. He stood up and rubbed the back of his neck, stressed out.

Running was her forte, but Vivien was used to longer distances. She'd have to judge how fast to go out and how much kick to leave for the end of the race. Not only was she out of practice, but with the extra pregnancy pounds, she wasn't feeling too light on her feet.

They got in their starting blocks and the gun sounded. All Vivien could hear was a blur of background noise and the sound of her own breathing. She advanced rapidly to the tape, neck and neck with Duncan, who was in the lead. They crossed the finish line together. A final heat would determine the winner. Again Vivien was in the lane next to Duncan. She figured by now the others were getting tired, so if she had a fast start she might be able to maintain a lead through the finish.

The gun sounded and Vivien shot out of the blocks, taking a sizable lead. She had to keep up pace to win and did just that. The employee crowd cheered and Steele, who called the race, announced her as the winner.

He said over his microphone, "I'd say V pretty much smoked everyone." Steele couldn't resist a little needling as he guffawed, "Hey, Dunk, you just got your ass kicked…and by a pregnant woman, no less."

Immediately, Vivien shot a laser-beam glare at Steele. It took the CMO a minute to realize his error–he had just leaked her big news when they'd agreed not thirty minutes earlier to keep it secret. Oops. Steele gave Vivien a feeble smile and shrugged apologetically. She noticed Duncan walk over to Steele and grasp his arm–apparently Duncan didn't take well to being teased in front of everyone.

J. J., Aileen, Scott, Charl, and others from Vivien's division rushed over to congratulate her on the baby news and then hustled back to their teams. She glanced at Duncan, who clutched his back and limped over to the first aid tent, complaining loudly that he'd tweaked a muscle. Easier to claim an injury than admit he was beaten fair and square.

*

Steele announced the third event. "This is the dexterity drill. You will stand at this cone in the center of a diamond shape, with a cone in front, back, and on each side spaced twelve feet away. Each of the cones has a flag sticking out of it. At the whistle you need to sprint forward and grab the flag and return to the center, placing the flag in the stand. Then sprint right and return, then left and return, and back and return. Points are awarded based on speed and placing all four flags in the holder. A point is deducted if you miss or drop a flag. This should be fun."

Teams huddled together to see which teammates should do the dexterity drill. When the whistle blew everyone cheered hard for their teammates.

✳

The fourth event was the footwork speed and balance drill. The contestant had to stand at the center of a large rectangular electronic platform. When lights lit up on a corner of the rectangle the person had to move both feet quickly to that light and then back to the center of the platform. This contest was particularly entertaining to watch as it was set to music.

Steele gave a wicked smile. "When someone is doing the drill accurately, the machine automatically accelerates the drill, requiring the contestant to move faster and faster."

Vivien sat out the third and fourth events–the footwork speed and balance drill was especially hilarious to watch with the accompanying music. It was surprising how many athletes in the company had no sense of rhythm.

✳

The last event was a visual acuity contest, which pitted one contestant against another, with both facing a large white screen. A scorer was assigned to each contestant and they took alternating turns. A series of twelve numbers flashed briefly on the screen and the contestant had five seconds to recite them back correctly. Points were awarded for speed and accuracy.

Red Team members competed against the Blue Team over a number of elimination rounds, until there were only two final team members competing for the championship title.

This event was custom-made for Vivien as she had almost a photographic memory for numbers. She was matched up against Alex, and even though he was a sharp guy with a head for figures, he missed on quickness. People watched in awe as Vivien hammered out the twelve flashing digits exactly as they'd appeared, fast and accurate. A bit nerdy, but it elicited some hushed praise from the crowd.

At the end of the games Steele made the announcement. "Coming in with the highest total point value is...the Red Team! The Red Team is the victor for this year's Smart Sports Games."

✳

Vivien was having her regular Friday afternoon video call with Andi, Grace, and Sofia. Andi shared a hilarious story about her last day on the job and what ensued. Sofia was meeting her boyfriend Jasper's family that weekend and was uncharacteristically nervous. Grace had shifted gears on her business book and decided to write what she was calling The Ceiling Smasher's Guide to Career Success, a book with helpful tips for women navigating their careers. Her three Smasher friends were thrilled about it. Grace had also met an intriguing man whose identity she was keeping under wraps for the time being. By now Vivien and Clay had shared the news of her pregnancy with family and friends, so the word was out. Her Smasher friends had been keeping up to date on her pregnancy and making sure Vivien was in good health.

Vivien admitted, "I'm definitely moving more slowly these days with the baby weight, and getting tired more easily. But other than that I'm doing great." She told them all about the Smart Sports Games and about Steele's announcing her pregnancy to the entire company.

Grace snorted, "Didn't I tell you that little guy was a weasel? I'd like to punch the freckles right off his face."

The other women giggled.

"Seriously, Vivi, watch out," Grace warned. "You've got more than a few people at Smart Sports who are threatened by you, and it sounds like Zac and Steele have you in their gun sights now."

Frowning, Vivien said, "I've made a few friends here, too, you know."

"Of course you have, sweetie," Grace said. "But don't forget, you're not one of them–you're an outsider. What's to stop these guys from ganging up on you again?"

Vivien was feeling decidedly less secure in her position with Grace laying out all the facts. She sighed, "I don't know how I can protect myself one hundred percent. Fortunately, I've got strong support from the Smart brothers and from my ghost mentor, Doug, who sits on the board—they've got my back. But you're right, I do need to watch the politics more carefully moving forward."

The Ceiling Smashers spent some more time catching up and then finished their call. Vivien got a message from Coop saying he was having some issues at work he wanted to discuss over the weekend.

It was the end of a mentally exhausting and physically demanding week, and Vivien was just looking forward to spending time with Clay, who was making the trek to Portland for the weekend.

*

Everything was going so smoothly with the product team, Vivien didn't give a second thought to the eventual return of Rebecca Roche. In mid-May Rebecca gave birth to a baby boy she named Damian. From the deluge of baby photos Rebecca emailed to the team it was evident who the father was—the baby had the signature dimpled chin and hawkish nose of Duncan Doric. The similarity was so obvious. Vivien chuckled when she saw Duncan was growing a goatee—was that an attempt to mask his chin dimple? She had to wonder if the redheaded Fred Andrews, current boyfriend of Rebecca, noticed that his "son" did not have a speck of red hair or resemble him in the least.

CHAPTER 19: THE SUNDAY PUNCH

Vivien and Clay were enjoying a barbecue at a friend's home over the July Fourth weekend. They joked with their friends and basked in the abundant sunshine, while the savory scent of cooking meat filled the air. Clay sipped a glass of rosé and chatted about his recent relocation to his firm's San Francisco office, while Vivien stood up to get a glass of lemonade. Her belly was bigger and she was moving more slowly these days; she was about seven weeks away from her due date. Vivien grabbed her beverage and returned to her seat on the patio. After a few seconds, she jumped up.

"Oh, something must have spilled on the seat." She looked down and the back of her sundress was drenched with water.

"I'm so sorry, Vivien, let me get you a towel," the hostess said, scurrying into the house.

She thought nothing of it until they were driving home.

"Babe, are you all right? You have a funny look on your face," Clay asked.

"I've been feeling some cramping for the last fifteen minutes or so."

Alarmed, her fiancé gently put his hand on her tummy. "Do you think you could be going into labor, Vivi?"

"I'm not due for another seven weeks, so this would be pretty early. Maybe I should just go home and rest."

"Actually, just to be safe I think I ought to take you to the hospital. Okay? We've got your overnight bag in the trunk anyway." Clay maneuvered the car in the direction of the hospital and called their doctor to meet them there.

*

It turned out to be a prudent move, as the wetness on her seat didn't come from a spill–it was from her water breaking. That night, after several hours of difficult labor, Dr. Harding opted to perform an emergency C-section and Vivien gave birth to a baby girl.

Clay kissed her, their eyes wide in wonder as their baby was placed in her arms. Even in the harsh lights of the operating room, the tiny human was as radiant as an angel.

"She's so beautiful," Clay said in a hushed voice.

"And so tiny," Vivien said, still in a fog from the procedure. Her daughter wrapped her delicate little hand around her mother's finger. "Dr. Harding, is she normal size?"

The doctor moved closer to examine the baby. "Well, Vivien, she's about seven weeks premature, so low birth weight is common. She's slightly under four pounds."

Vivien thought, *This is an entire human being and she weighs so little.*

Dr. Harding said, "Her breathing seems a bit labored. That is not atypical, but I'd like to get her into the NICU as soon as possible. We should boost her oxygen level in an incubator, just to be on the safe side."

They looked on helplessly as the nurse whisked away their baby. Clay accompanied her into a private room, and while Vivien rested he called her dad and his mother with the happy news. They named the baby Lily. Clay sent out a short email to their friends and relatives to announce her birth.

*

The next morning, the pain emanating from her midsection disappeared the moment Vivien saw baby Lily in the NICU. The nurses maneuvered Vivien's wheelchair into a corner and proceeded to show her and Clay how to hold and feed their baby using a bottle of formula so small it looked like a child's toy. The couple was oohing and ahhing over their daughter when Dr. Harding stopped by to check in.

"Vivien, we can discharge you tomorrow. You'll probably be more comfortable recuperating at home anyway," Dr. Harding said with a kind smile. "But we'd like to keep Lily here a bit longer to monitor her blood oxygen level and make sure she's stable. You and Clay can come visit her at any time; the NICU is open twenty-four hours to you."

"Okay." Vivien nodded. She was wiped out from the pain from the surgery as well as the excitement of their tiny new arrival. The hospital was noisy and the endless parade of nurses entering her room to monitor things made it impossible to rest.

The following day, although it felt distressing to leave the hospital without their baby, Clay drove Vivien home in the afternoon and made sure she was resting peacefully in their bed. That evening, he brought her a tray with a light supper of scrambled eggs and toast, which Vivien devoured. It was still quite painful to move around, but she gingerly got up to brush her teeth and wash her face and then returned to their warm, comfortable bed.

Clay lay down next to her and whispered, "We'd better get some rest while we can, babe. We won't be getting much real sleep once we bring Lily home." He kissed her. Vivien was worn down from the pain of the C-section. Not realizing how exhausted she was, she fell fast asleep in minutes.

✳

When Vivien and Clay arrived at the NICU the next morning, there was a big commotion. A team of nurses was running down the hall wheeling baby Lily in her incubator.

Chasing after them, Clay cried, "Hey, that's my daughter. What's happening?"

The nurse turned and said, "She's having a problem with her

breathing. Let us take care of the situation and we'll send Dr. Harding to talk to you."

Adrenaline shot through Vivien's veins and fear gripped her chest, making it difficult to breathe. She moved cautiously to a chair and eased herself down.

Clay knelt in front of her and took her hands. "I'm sure Lily will be fine, babe. Let's just sit here and wait for the doctor." His calm voice and demeanor eased her dread, although she could see in his expression he was worried.

An hour later the couple was preoccupied looking at the precious photos of baby Lily on Clay's smartphone when Dr. Harding appeared. "Vivien, Clay, would you come with me, please?" She avoided eye contact as she led them to a private examination room. The doctor waited patiently as Vivien was still moving slowly.

"What's happening?" Vivien asked anxiously.

"Please, let's sit down." The doctor looked ashen and drew in a deep breath. "I'm afraid I have some terrible news. Lily has passed away."

Was she really hearing those words? In shock, the couple clung to each other tightly, while the doctor explained.

"Your daughter was so small because of a rare disorder called intrauterine growth restriction. The baby's growth in the womb did not happen as normal, and her lungs did not fully develop…that was why Lily had trouble breathing. I'm sorry to say that for babies born with such severe issues, survival is next to impossible."

Vivien felt as if someone had ripped a hole in her heart, and it left her gasping. She and Clay sobbed openly. Seventy-two hours ago they were proud first-time parents. Now their happiness was shattered, their dreams for Lily's future demolished.

"I'm so sorry," Dr. Harding said, and hugged them both. "There's nothing anyone could have done. This is such a rare occurrence. I know that's of little comfort to you now."

They asked to see their baby to say good-bye. Vivien could not stop the flood of tears as she held Lily's tiny, pale hands in hers and kissed her cheek. After a heart-wrenching parting, they left the hospital not with their adored baby, but with paperwork on arranging her burial.

As Clay helped her gently into the car, he wiped away a tear and said, "I don't know what to say, Vivi."

Wearily, she shook her head and reflected in silence. In sports they would call this a Sunday punch: an unexpected knockout–a blow so devastating you cannot even imagine it.

*

The week that followed was a blur. Although it was agonizing, Clay handled all the communication, sharing the shocking news with their families and friends and colleagues. He dismantled the crib and hid away in the back bedroom closet all the paraphernalia–diaper cakes, stuffed animals, nursery decorations, blankets–that everyone had sent for baby Lily. Vivien was recovering from the physical toll of the C-section, but she couldn't imagine ever recovering from the emotional trauma. Her body would always bear the scar of having a child with nothing to show for it.

Clay's mom sent a big basket of fruit with a note that read, "Vivien dear, I hope you are recovering well. I am simply devastated about the loss of my grandchild." Her loss? What about Vivien's loss? That was so typical of Clay's mother–always thinking of herself first.

Vivien's dad was on the first flight out and spent the week taking care of his daughter and cooking all her favorite childhood meals, which was more comforting than she could describe. Clay rented all of Hugh Jackman's films to take Vivien's mind off of things. Meanwhile Coop and her Ceiling Smasher friends offered to come out and help but were sensitive to the fact that their dear friend probably needed some space.

Vivien felt raw and, for the first time, started to prepare herself for the possibility they might have a childless marriage. In bed and scared to broach the subject with Clay, she blinked back tears. Looking into her fiancé's crystal-blue eyes, she said, "Clay, what if we can't..." It was harder for her to speak the words than she'd expected. "We may not be able to have children, Clay. It might just be the two of us. Do you think we can be happy with just the two of us?"

Clay cupped her face gently in his hands. "Babe, we have each other and that's plenty for me. I love you; you're my girl."

*

After two weeks off, Vivien returned to work. Her typically professional assistant, Pandy, burst into uncontrollable sobs when her boss walked into the office. Just keep it together, Vivien had to tell herself. When Malcolm Smart saw her he was silent but gave her a strong, supportive hug. Judging by the uncomfortable looks she got from people on campus, everyone knew about Lily's birth and sudden death. People were kind and tried to act normally, not even bringing up the topic except to ask if she was doing all right. No one seemed to know what to say.

One afternoon J. J. stopped by her office. "Okay, V, I'm whisking you away."

"Away where, J. J.?"

"The team has a little surprise for you. Just follow my car and you'll see."

They drove separately to a restaurant in the Pearl District and parked. When J. J. escorted Vivien inside she saw her team was throwing her a surprise cocktail party in a private room. So thoughtful. Vivien mingled with everyone, and they did their best to lighten the mood.

"How are you feeling, Vivien?" Rebecca Roche asked, back from her extended maternity leave.

Oh, I completely forgot she was due back. Before this incident Vivien had intended to sit down with Rebecca when she got back to update her and ensure a smooth transition.

"I'm doing all right, thank you, Rebecca, and welcome back."

"It's only my third day back and I'm getting caught up on things. Wow, you sure changed a lot in the product area during my absence." Rebecca sounded rattled.

Pandy had the good sense to come over and whisk Vivien away from Rebecca.

Vivien felt she needed to say something to her team, so finally she stood in front of them. They immediately drew to a hush.

"First of all, I want to thank you for your kindness. I can't tell you how much this surprise party means to me–it was really sweet of you guys. Second, I want to talk to you about where I'm at. Losing Lily is the most devastating thing that's ever happened to me and Clay, but we're coping. I've had many sleepless nights. Truthfully, I'm probably not as focused on the business as I should be. It's been tough…"

Vivien scanned the room and noticed out of the corner of her eye that Rebecca was holding up her smartphone and aiming it straight at her. *Is she* recording *me?* Vivien wondered briefly, but was so caught up in the moment it didn't register fully.

"So, I apologize if I may not be as on top of things as usual. You might need to remind me of certain discussions or repeat information to me, and I hope you'll be patient with me over the coming weeks. Third, I have a request…please don't let this tragedy define me. This is one part of my life, but there is much more to me as a person. We have so much ahead of us that we need to accomplish together, and I don't want your pity, but I do need your support. The best thing we can do is to focus on the future. Thank you for your thoughtfulness; I appreciate it more than you know. Cheers to all of you."

J. J. pulled her aside for a quiet word. "Vivien, I understand some of what you're going through. My wife and I struggled with having a family and she had two miscarriages, which was really rough. I want you to know that we're behind you and will do whatever we can to help. And for the record, I know you'll be a fantastic mom someday."

She smiled gratefully. "Thanks, J. J., that means a lot to me."

Rebecca swooped back in like a vulture spying fresh roadkill and intruded on their conversation. "So, do you think you're ready for tomorrow?"

"Well, I'm going to have to be ready. Hopefully I won't embarrass myself or burst into tears." Vivien half-laughed. "Anyway, I'm not planning on sharing any information about my personal situation."

Scott came up and put his arm around her shoulder. "Don't worry, V, you're gonna be great!"

Rebecca looked distracted but cooed, "Oh yes, Vivien, I'm sure you'll be perfect...as always." A trace of contempt.

As she talked to other members of her team, Vivien noticed Rebecca and Charl conspiring in a corner.

*

Pandy tried to act as if everything were normal the next day, but it was a big day. Not only had Vivien made the Wall Street Journal's "50 Women to Watch" list that year, but she was one of five women who'd been selected for an in-depth profile. That meant a WSJ reporter was coming to campus to interview her.

She knew Vivien wasn't one who craved the spotlight, but Malcolm had prodded her to do the interview. "This is your opportunity to encourage other women to strive for the upper echelons, especially in male-dominated industries."

Pandy had overheard the whole conversation from her cubicle.

Vivien must still be reeling from losing her baby and recovering from the painful surgery. I'll need to do my best to make sure she has a calm morning and is prepared, Pandy thought. Vivien was wrapping up a call when Pandy popped her head in to let her know the reporter was in the lobby. The two of them made their way downstairs. As they walked into the lobby, Pandy sucked in a quick breath and instinctively grabbed her boss's arm.

It was a jolt to see the *WSJ* reporter sitting there–a very pregnant journalist named Kay Wyskowski. *Oh god, now this? Poor V.*

✳

Vivien was adept at compartmentalizing–separating her own situation from the task at hand and setting her emotions aside–and this was one time when she'd need to deploy that skill. She took a deep breath and steeled herself. She'd get through this. Vivien winked at her assistant, as if to say, It's okay, and moved forward to greet the journalist. After introductions were made, Pandy offered to get the women some tea from the commissary.

Vivien and Kay took the elevator to the fourth floor. Down the long hallway, she spotted Rebecca and Charl exiting her office. *Odd; what could they be doing in there?* Once inside, they sat at Vivien's conference table and Vivien glanced at her computer screen to make sure it was locked. Everything appeared normal.

Kay had a list of questions to get through, then they got deep into conversation about how Vivien was turning around the Women's Apparel division and the challenges of working in the sports industry.

Just then Vivien noticed a miniature Smart Sports shoe box sitting on the conference table. Her curiosity got the best of her and she pulled the box closer as she spoke. When she peeked inside the box, her heart stopped. It was a pair of tiny white sneakers with pale yellow embroidery across the toes. The shoes had obviously been designed for Lily. That this "gift" had been left in her office for her to discover was a stiletto right through her heart. She had to stifle a gasp. Vivien had a sickening realization–Rebecca and Charl were trying to sabotage her interview and throw her off.

The reporter gave her a curious look.

Vivien pressed on with their discussion. "Kay, one of the problems with our business was we were just selling stuff. What people choose to put on their body is so personal and emotional. We realized we needed to inject the art of storytelling and tell a story that would resonate with our consumers. Taking a fresh approach to our marketing and advertising has helped us accomplish that."

"How can you tell a compelling story in such a telegraphic vehicle, like an ad?"

"It's not easy, but here's an example. Take this pair of shoes. Cute sneakers, right? But what happens when you inject emotion and meaning? What impact can that have?" Vivien searched her memory for the right anecdote. "Ernest Hemingway and some writer friends once challenged each other to a contest—who could write the best story using the fewest words. Most of the writers took paragraphs to tell their stories. Hemingway did it in six words. 'For sale: baby shoes, never worn.' Powerful story. Rips your heart out. A story like that makes you look at the product differently, right? Storytelling and emotion were what this brand was missing. And it is what's helped us in connecting with our consumer."

The reporter said, "Wow, that's impressive."

Kay was especially tickled when Vivien said, "By the way, these shoes are a gift for your little one." Peeking into the box, Kay saw a pair of adorable baby sneakers.

When Kay asked Vivien about the challenges of working as a senior female leader in the sports industry, she spoke about some of the difficulties, but chose to keep the tone upbeat. When their interview wrapped up, Kay gratefully clutched the shoe box and Pandy escorted her back downstairs.

*

After the interview ended and she'd had a moment to reflect on what transpired, Vivien was shaking with anger.

She left a sticky note on Pandy's computer screen: "Went for a workout."

As she was changing, her mind raced. Her relationship with Rebecca was tenuous at best, but she couldn't believe she'd resort to such despicable tactics. Even worse, Vivien had put so much effort into cultivating her relationship with Charl. And now he'd turned on her to join forces with Rebecca? That stung.

Vivien punched the heavy bag so hard it was swayed violently on its chain. One of the trainers passing by noticed it and stuck his head in the door. "Way to go, Vivien. You're kicking that heavy bag's ass!"

"Just getting started!" she bellowed.

In the days that followed, Vivien learned that Tim Kelley had had the baby sneakers made as a gift for her and had shown them to her leadership team. But when he heard the terrible news he put them aside. Somehow the shoes had gone missing from his office.

The incident hurt her more than she would admit, but the best thing was to move on and act as if it had never happened. Why give Rebecca and Charl the satisfaction of knowing they'd gotten to her?

When her leadership team asked about the *WSJ* interview, she simply replied, "I think it went fine. You'll have to read the article and let me know what you think."

She formulated a plan for how to deal with Rebecca and Charl and began laying the groundwork with Ron. She just had to wait for the timing to work out.

As Andi had told her, "You can't work with people you don't trust."

＊

"Sweetie, what you need is a few days in the warm sunshine of Puerto Rico with your dear old friend," Coop told her.

Vivien held her cell phone to her ear and sat down on a bench overlooking the Willamette River. It was a sunny day and Vivien was taking a break outside to have a quiet conversation.

"That sounds wonderful, Coop, you know I'd love to. Maybe we can plan a long weekend together."

"How are things going at work, Vivi? Oh, how did the *WSJ* interview go?"

She still felt a stab of pain when she thought about Rebecca and Charl's treachery. Vivien shared with Coop the whole saga about the baby shoes.

"For the love of god," Coop huffed, "that woman is a psycho witch from hell. How malicious can a person be? As a new mother, you'd think she'd have some compassion! That's despicable."

Vivien grimaced. "I agree. She's a nightmare."

"How can you work with such awful people?"

"You know, Coop, I've always prided myself on my ability to work with just about anyone," Vivien said, "but even I can't envision the possibility of developing a positive relationship with Rebecca or Charl. Unfortunately, I'm stuck with them for now. Have to make the best of it."

Coop sounded solemn. "You know it will probably only get worse, don't you?"

"You think? Now that Rebecca's given birth to Duncan's only son she thinks her future here is secure no matter what she does. When I took on this role I was just focusing on doing a great job, but I now realize the more important thing to do is to play the game better."

"The whole situation sounds dangerous, Vivi."

"You're telling me. I need to figure what to do, and fast."

✳

A week passed, and with renewed verve about the business, Vivien shared an idea with her leadership team she'd been kicking around for a while.

"Our category is all about movement, yet it occurred to me all our descriptions of our product online are accompanied by static photos. It would be exciting to do some videos highlighting our key products and have the designers who worked on those products explain the inspiration, product details, and function. We can show a model exercising in the product."

The team was launching the fall season with new products that Vivien had fast-tracked. An innovative running jacket with 360-degree LED piping was a great candidate for one of the videos. Another new product was a yoga pant with a unique crossover waistband that didn't give the dreaded muffin top yet stayed in place during vigorous exercise.

The last product Vivien wanted to feature was a reversible hiking jacket that had thermal properties on one side and cooling properties when turned inside out.

"Oh, that's the one Aileen told me about," said Angela, the marketing director. Turning to the others, she relayed the story. "The jacket's design was inspired when Aileen was hiking up Mount Hood with her family and their two dogs–a yellow Lab and a black Lab. She noticed the yellow Lab handled the heat of the climb better, but the black Lab handled the cold winds at the peak better. That got her thinking about the jacket–brilliant!"

Scott piped up, "We could have someone interview Aileen on the video so she can share that story. I think we could also do more in terms of leveraging social media to get our brand name out there."

Heads nodded.

Angela scribbled some notes down. "The videos sound like a great idea and a chance to show not only the product, but the thought behind them. I think this could be really cool."

"Great, can you work with Rebecca to script out the videos, get the designers prepped, and prepare to shoot them?" Vivien said. "I was thinking we could call the videos *The Story Behind the Style* and feature them prominently on our website."

"Love it," Angela said. "I'll work with Rebecca and share our ideas with you before we shoot the videos."

"Sounds good." Vivien nodded. "If you guys can do the groundwork we can review everything and get them produced."

*

These days Rebecca was all smiles as she proudly displayed photo after photo of her son, Damian. She also showed off her latest trophy–an emerald engagement ring from Fred. Rebecca had her hands full these days, but she paid unfailing attention to keeping her platinum-blond bob in precise condition, the ends coming to the dagger points that framed her face.

As insurance against any more bad product decisions, Vivien had indicated she'd stay more involved in design and development. That might not have sat well with Rebecca, but she appeared cooperative, all the while taking copious notes in her thin black notebook, her Hello Kitty pen tinkling ominously. By now, Vivien had deduced that Rebecca was recording actual work notes in her pink notebook and reserving the black notebook to keep track of complaints about Vivien, probably to share with HR and Duncan. These days Rebecca was writing noticeably more often in the black notebook, but Vivien didn't care. She was hoping to be rid of her soon. The torture of working with Rebecca was a low point for Vivien.

A bright spot for Vivien was Cat McClintock. She'd made huge strides while Rebecca was gone and had kept it up–not only was she taking more ownership of her work and managing her development team better, but in the last five months she'd dropped thirty pounds. She was working out regularly and, with the help of the nutritionist Vivien hired, finally eating properly. Recently, Cat came into her office and said triumphantly, "I want to show you something, Vivien. I can now fit into our product!" Cat showed off her head to toe Smart Sports outfit and the women high-fived each other.

PART FIVE

CHAPTER 20: FASTER, HIGHER, STRONGER

The Summer Olympics, the most vaunted of sporting events, were about to begin. While the Olympic stage was typically the place for industry competitors to introduce their newest footwear, for the first time a special Smart Sports apparel product would be unveiled that August.

A darling of the US Olympic team and a Smart Sports-sponsored athlete, Waverly Brown was a sixteen-year-old track and field phenom. She was a sprinter who specialized in the two-hundred-meter and four-hundred-meter races. While Waverly was a strong contender, other, more experienced runners were expected to prevail. "I came here to win," she told the press, "and if I leave here without a gold medal I will have failed myself." Mature beyond her years, Waverly was humble but hungry. The media hype surrounding her was frenzied and about to get even more amped up. When Waverly showed up for her first event, the four hundred meter, she wore a Smart Sports Electrify track skin–a black suit with fiery red wings imprinted on the back.

The racers lined up in their starting blocks. The gunshot sounded and the race began. Waverly's track skin was programmed to respond to the athlete's body heat and create a chromatic effect. As her long brown ponytail flew out in the wind behind her, Waverly shot ahead of the field. She crossed the finish line well ahead of her competitors. As she did, her track skin instantaneously morphed into a white suit with gold wings. The crowd of spectators roared. The sports commentators went wild. A million bursts of camera flashes filled the stadium with triumphant light.

"Incredible!" the commentator shouted. "That Smart Sports Electrify track skin is simply amazing. Have you ever seen something like that before? Have you? And the color change is especially fitting since Waverly Brown has taken the gold medal."

✳

Back at Smart Sports headquarters, Vivien was standing there watching the race unfold on the television in her office when Pandy burst in.

"V, there's a reporter from *Sports Illustrated* on the line who wants to talk to you about the Electrify track skin. Can I put him through?" Pandy was practically exploding with excitement.

"Sure thing, Pandy. Thanks." Vivien sat down and picked up the phone.

The reporter, Tom, introduced himself and dove into gathering the details of how the product was developed.

"When I first arrived at Smart Sports my materials research team showed me a technical fabric they were tinkering with, one with an unusual property–its revolutionary microfibers conducted electrical current and could morph along with the wearer, depending on how the garment was programmed. I was blown away. It was also lightweight yet opaque, fast drying, and had a luxuriously soft, silky feel."

"How long did it take to go from cool fabric to new product?" She could hear the staccato sound of the reporter typing his notes on his keyboard.

Vivien smiled. "Fastest development in Smart Sports history. With the support of the Smart brothers, my team worked at breakneck speed with a high-tech apparel manufacturer to go from fabric and sketches to physical product in a quarter of the normal timeframe. We wanted to launch the Electrify track skin on the world's greatest sports stage."

Tom whistled. "Wow, great story. You've got a visually stunning piece of sports equipment the likes of which have never been seen before. Congratulations, Vivien. I'd like to send a photographer out there to get a picture of you, would that be all right?"

"Thanks, Tom, but if you want a picture I'd like it to be of the entire team that worked on the track skin—it's their hard work that made this possible."

"Sure thing." The reporter hung up.

Vivien reclined in her chair, satisfied that she had succeeded in putting Smart Sports Women's Apparel squarely on the map.

Just then her smartphone buzzed. A text from Malcolm who was attending the Olympics with Alex: *Awesome job, V! Well done.*

Vivien responded, *Thanks. I'll pass that along to my hardworking team. Here's another surprise: for the first time in history our division will post a quarterly profit...two years ahead of schedule.* ;-)

Malcolm sent two smiley-face emoticons back with two words: *You rock!*

It was Vivien's gold-medal moment.

A year into her reign as president, Vivien and her team had achieved a rare trifecta: the business was profitable for the first time, it was the fastest-growing division in the company, and despite having a limited marketing budget it was getting the most positive buzz. Waverly Brown's four-hundred-meter win was the most photographed Olympic moment of the games, and the number of media impressions that Smart Sports got from it was priceless.

*

Clay had a bottle of champagne on ice and popped it open when Vivien arrived home from work. He kept replaying Waverly Brown's race, which he'd recorded on their DVR. "Babe, that was spectacular! Check out the crowd's reaction. Cheers to a phenomenal job!" He handed her a champagne flute.

"Thanks, honey. I'm really pleased with how the past year has gone," Vivien said and sighed. "And it flew by so fast. We've made so many changes and are really turning things around."

"That's awesome but no surprise. I knew you could do it." Clay put his arms around her and kissed her. "Who knew sports clothing–I mean sports apparel–could be so exciting? I'm proud of you, babe."

"And we've even made the business profitable, way ahead of schedule. Hard to believe we've come so far."

His eyes widened. "Alex and Malcolm must be thrilled."

"Yeah." She smiled.

Clay cast his eyes down. "Listen, babe, I got a call from my boss today and there's an important, high-profile deal he'd like me to work on."

"Oh, that's great, honey. Congratulations. When do you start?"

"Well, there's the catch. He wants me to get started on it next week, but it means I'll have to work out of the New York office again. But we'd be together on weekends, babe; we'll make it work. Okay?"

Her fiancé had been so patient and accommodating throughout the pregnancy and the aftermath. He deserved a chance to shine in his career. Anyway, she had some major business trips planned for the fall. "Sure, Clay, go for it."

*

A few days after the Olympic Games ended, the new Women's Apparel fall line launched in stores. This was the last product that Rebecca had touched prior to taking her maternity leave.

Vivien was visiting a retail account with J. J. and the moment they saw the Training Tee, their number-one seller, she knew something was wrong. Although Vivien had personally reviewed the product at final line review, what had ended up in stores was not what she'd approved.

"Goddamn it!" Vivien slammed her hand on the hood of her car. J. J.'s eye's widened–he had never seen his boss angry. She got into her car and said, "J. J., I've got to go deal with this issue."

Back on campus, Vivien charged through the apparel building, fists clenched, in search of Rebecca. She rapidly rounded a corner, nearly knocking over Aileen.

She demanded, "Aileen, what happened to the fall product, namely the Training Tee?" Vivien was never that abrupt and Aileen looked startled. She glanced around furtively and pulled Vivien into an empty office.

"The product you approved was not the product that got produced," Aileen said.

"I can see that. Why is that?"

Aileen was trembling. "I'm so sorry I didn't say anything to you earlier, but I was really scared. Remember the first fit session you attended where you told Rebecca not to make the changes she wanted to? And she said, 'All right, Vivien. You're the president, so what you say goes.'?"

Vivien crossed her arms and nodded.

Her designer continued, "Well, the minute you walked out of the room, Rebecca turned to us and said, 'Listen up, people. I'm in charge of product, not Vivien. I don't care if she is the president, *I* make the product decisions. We are moving ahead with the changes I want. If you have a problem with that, then you're history. And if you breathe a word of this to anyone outside of this room, I'll make sure you never work in this industry again.'"

Vivien let out a puff of air in disgust.

"I know I should have warned you"—Aileen's hands were trembling—"but I was sure Rebecca would find out it was me. I was terrified of losing my job. My husband had just gotten laid off and our daughter was starting treatment for diabetes—I couldn't afford to lose our health care. I kept my mouth shut even though I knew it was wrong and just prayed Rebecca wouldn't mess up the product too much. I'm terribly sorry, Vivien. You've given me so many fantastic opportunities and I know I've let you down."

Vivien plopped into a chair, feeling suddenly drained. "This is really disturbing, Aileen. And disappointing. I appreciate your honesty, but next time I need to be able to count on you. You've got to tell me these things before it's too late…now there's nothing we can do." Vivien ran her hands through her hair. "That product Rebecca changed is not going to sell and it will negatively impact our business–that's not okay. I understand your fears and I won't let Rebecca know that we talked. But in the future if you come to me with an issue like this, I will protect you. Don't ever let fear get in the way of doing the right thing. Okay?"

Aileen nodded.

*

Stopping by Cat's office to delve into the situation further, Vivien got some more answers. She learned that Rebecca Roche had done something so diabolical her name should have been Rebecca Machiavelli.

Cat said sheepishly, "Rebecca gave us specific instructions on what to show you. Rather than showing you the actual fall product samples at final line review, for the styles Rebecca 'updated' she told us to pull out old samples. That was what you saw. It was to make things appear as if Rebecca hadn't changed a thing. I'm really sorry, Vivien, I know the modified product is in stores now and it's too late to do anything. I'm so ashamed of what I did."

Instead of Vivien letting her anger get the better of her, she decided to cool off a bit before speaking with Rebecca. She swung by the commissary for some green tea and to formulate a plan. Her eyes scanned the room and rested on a booth in the back corner, where Rebecca sat with Duncan. They were talking, heads close together.

Vivien walked straight up to the pair. They reacted as if they'd just been caught together in a seedy motel room by a paparazzo. Coolly she said, "Rebecca, I'd like to see you in my office in ten minutes."

"Oh. Is something the matter, Vivien?" Rebecca mustered an innocent look.

Vivien's eyes flashed. "I think you know exactly what I want to discuss."

Rebecca nodded hesitantly and said meekly, "Um, okay, I'll be there soon." She must have known the showdown was coming. Did she believe Vivien wouldn't discover the duplicity?

*

"Would you like the door open or closed, boss?" Rebecca asked sweetly as she walked in.

"Closed." Vivien's curt response seemed to make Rebecca even more nervous and she bit one of her red dagger nails. "Explain to me what happened to the fall product, Rebecca."

"I'm not sure I understand what you're talking about. I think the product looks great and I'm sooooo excited about it."

"We agreed in the fit session way back when not to make any changes to certain styles. At final line review the samples you arranged to have shown to me were not the actual samples from the fall line. From what I can see, you went ahead and changed those products without my approval." Vivien sat forward in her chair, her fingers intertwined tightly. "Not only does that product look terrible, but you deceived me. That is unacceptable."

Rebecca looked like a petulant child being scolded by a schoolteacher.

Vivien was on a roll. "We're supposed to be a team, Rebecca, and I can't have someone on my team who behaves dishonestly." Her manner was still calm, but her voice was firm. She was fuming.

For the first time Rebecca looked scared, her eyes wide. "Well I, uh," she stammered, "*I'm* responsible for product...and I was just trying to make it better. I wasn't trying to do anything wrong or disrespect you in any way." She shrugged, palms up. "Maybe Cat and the development team misunderstood what I wanted and they made the wrong changes while I was out on maternity leave; I really don't know what happened."

So now she was throwing her buddy Cat under the bus to save herself?

"If, as you say, *you* are responsible for product, then how could someone make a change that you didn't know about, Rebecca? I find that hard to swallow."

Instantly, tears welled up in Rebecca's eyes. "Um, maybe I just wanted to prove to you I could make good product decisions on my own. I only wanted to help our business, Vivien." Big teardrops rolled down her cheeks.

This performance had probably worked on her previous, male bosses but had no effect on Vivien. Indifferently, she pushed a box of tissues toward Rebecca and leaned back. "Rebecca, you acted irresponsibly and put our business at risk. The products you changed will lose money for sure. I need to be able to trust those I work with and I don't trust you. I'm not even sure if it's possible for us to continue working together."

Rebecca wailed, "I didn't mean to do anything wrong, Vivien. What's going to happen to me?"

"I'm going to speak to HR about what happened. And I'm going to have to think about your situation and figure out what to do. Starting now, I will approve any and all product changes. Got it?"

A dark look came across Rebecca's face and she nodded. "Got it." She solemnly took some notes in her black Moleskine notebook. In the awkward silence that followed, her tinkling Hello Kitty pen was the only sound in the room. Rebecca switched gears, turning on the charm. "Vivien, all I can do is apologize sincerely–it was simply a misunderstanding on my part. Remember you said we needed to make the product better? That's what I was trying to do. I respect you and know I can learn a lot from you. There are so few women in this business, and we sisters need to stick together."

Sisters? Her comment made Vivien cringe.

"You're such an amazing leader and I want to continue to be on your team. I hope we can get things back on track."

"We'll see." Vivien stood up to indicate their discussion was finished.

Head down, Rebecca shuffled out.

Just then her phone rang. It was Johnny O asking Vivien to join a discussion in his office with his head designer. They wanted to incorporate the technology from the Electrify line into their men's product offering and had a deadline to meet.

As Vivien walked past Duncan's office she could make out Rebecca's profile through the frosted glass wall. She was sitting there, dabbing tears from her eyes and speaking animatedly. Although Vivien could guess what Rebecca was saying to Duncan, she had to marvel that this woman had wasted no time seeking political protection. Knowing the game, Vivien needed to be the first one to get to HR. As she walked, she fired off a quick email to Ron informing him of a major issue with Rebecca that she needed to discuss with him. She said she'd stop by his office within the hour.

After she finished her discussion with Johnny O and his team, Vivien went directly to Ron's office. She told him about Rebecca's grand deception, as well as the threats she made to her team, and the potential negative impact to the business. Ron listened with a sympathetic ear.

"That's deplorable, V. How would you like to handle this situation?"

"I'd like to fire her, Ron. She doesn't have the talent or skills for the job. She has zero instinct about product. Even worse, she thinks she's great at what she does–arrogance plus ignorance is a dangerous combination." As Vivien sat back in the chair she recalled the baby shoe incident, about which she'd told no one at the company. "Rebecca is dishonest and treats her people terribly. Why would I want her on my team?"

Ron scratched his neck and let out a long sigh. "I understand, it's not a good situation." Judging by the pained look on his face, he didn't want to say what was coming next. "But Rebecca cannot be fired. There's an unusual circumstance with her."

Vivien shot him a look of surprise. "Such as...?"

He shifted uncomfortably. "V, this conversation stays in the room, okay? Duncan asked to speak urgently with me and the Smart brothers just a short time ago. He admitted he and Rebecca have been having a 'dalliance.' Apparently Rebecca told him she'd had difficulty acclimating to your leadership style. She feels there's a level of competitiveness between the two of you."

Competitiveness? What a joke. And after Rebecca was yammering on about sisters sticking together? Vivien remembered a story Coop had told her about the opera singer Maria Callas. Someone asked her if she considered another singer her competition. Maria Callas said, "Competition? How can she compete with me when she cannot do what I can do?" At this moment Vivien was tempted to say the same thing about Rebecca, but she held her tongue and gave Ron a skeptical look.

He continued, "Hey, I'm just relaying what I heard. Anyway, Rebecca is afraid of losing her job and she's desperate to stay at the company. And, well..."

What could Ron possibly have to say next?

"Duncan believes that if we were to fire Rebecca, she would sue the company and maybe Duncan, too, for sexual harassment. Given that we're a public company now, news like this would be devastating." Ron shook his head. "As you'd expect, Alex and Malcolm were livid. They told Duncan, 'Keep your job and lose the girl, or keep the girl and lose your job.' Duncan chose the job. In all the years I've known the Smart brothers, I've never seen them that angry or disgusted."

Good for the Smart brothers; Vivien always knew they were honorable people. Jeez, if they found out Rebecca had given birth to Duncan's son, their heads would explode. The thought of spilling the beans crossed her mind, but many lives would be ruined as a result, and that wasn't something Vivien felt right about doing.

"Given the situation, we've agreed not to terminate her for now."

Vivien threw her hands up. "So, I'm stuck with someone who can't do the job and is impossible to work with, just because she's been sleeping with an executive?"

Ron shook his head. "In a word, yes."

"If I can't fire her, then can I change her out? Transfer Rebecca to another division?"

"That's a possibility, Vivien. Listen, you're a skilled leader and an excellent people person, I've seen you win over some very tough people. Could you take a shot at coaching Rebecca and see if you can bring her around?"

Vivien shook her head. "Ron, I honestly can't see anything changing. Rebecca's like a cancer I just need to cut out of the team's body. We've got to figure something out, please."

"Ugh, this whole thing is such a goddamn mess." He rubbed his forehead in stress.

So Rebecca Roche had officially become one of the Untouchables.

✳

When their fall product arrived in stores, Vivien started receiving phone calls from her customers…the calls she was dreading.

"Vivien, what happened to the product? It was looking great, but now the quality has dropped back to where it was a few years ago."

"Some of these styles look terrible."

"My customers are not going to buy this stuff."

Vivien had called it and irate retailers groused about specific products–the exact ones that Rebecca had changed. Negative consumer reviews started popping up online, with many complaints about the Training Tee.

"This used to be my go-to workout top. Now the fabric is tissue thin and cheap looking, but the price is the same. Huh?"

"What happened to the Training Tee? The neckline is too low cut, it's terrible."

Even her cleaning lady, who hailed from Mexico and spoke mostly Spanish, was able to communicate her dissatisfaction in no uncertain terms. "Ms. Vivien, the Smart Sports top–why it is see-through? The quality, it's no good!"

Vivien couldn't change the product at this point, but she was able to stop production on anything that wasn't made yet and return it to its original specifications. She responded to consumer complaints by personally contacting the most irate consumers and apologizing, offering to replace the product. That surprised many people, who wrote about their experience on social media, and it helped Vivien rebuild some goodwill. She also made sure to share all the negative consumer and retailer feedback with her team, including Rebecca.

Turning her nose up at the news, Rebecca said, "I guess it was too sophisticated for the consumer–they just didn't get it."

Vivien took her complaints to Ron. "Rebecca's arrogance and disregard for the consumer, as well as her inability to own up to her mistakes, are infuriating. Something has to give, Ron–this situation can't last much longer."

*

As Vivien was conducting her Monday morning staff meeting with her leadership team, two masked men burst into the room and placed a pillowcase over her head.

"Sorry, guys," one of them said, "we're borrowing your boss for the next hour."

Peeking from under the pillowcase, Vivien could see they were sporting Smart Sports footwear, so she relaxed. Some kind of gag. She played along.

"J. J., take over for me, would you?" Not to make it too easy on her abductors, she said, "Listen, guys, I'm a second-degree black belt in Tae Kwon Do. If necessary I'll break out some of my moves."

One of the guys put his arm on hers and whispered, "Don't worry, V, everything's okay. This will be fun. And whatever you do, please don't hurt me." The voice of Johnny O.

She was put into a car and driven a short distance. Judging by the bumpy terrain, she guessed she was on the Broadway Bridge. The blast of wind that hit her as she got out of the car was a little alarming. She was slowly led down a walkway, and then her hood was suddenly whipped off. In front of her stood the Smart brothers, Duncan, Steele, Klaas, and her two captors, Tim and Johnny O, grinning goofily.

"What's all this about?" she asked.

"A little initiation ceremony, V." Alex grinned. "You survived your first year with Smart Sports; let's see if you can survive this."

With that, a Smart Sports trainer whom she knew came from behind and fastened a harness around her ankles. She stood at the edge of the metal bridge looking down…she was expected to bungee-jump off the Broadway Bridge?

Her colleagues looked at her, half-smiling.

Vivien glanced down to make sure her ankle straps were secure. She yelled, "Kowabunga!" and threw herself off the bridge.

Johnny O shouted, "Holy shit, I can't believe she just went for it!"

In the few seconds it took to hit the bottom of the bungee cord, Vivien prayed that the trainer who'd calculated the length of the cord had judged her weight correctly. Her head spun as they yanked her back up, cracked open the champagne, and passed glasses all around.

"Forgive the frat-boy prank," Malcolm said, smiling. "We just wanted to wish you a happy and memorable one-year anniversary with Smart Sports!" All the guys raised their glasses.

"Thanks, guys, I appreciate the thought." She laughed. "But next year a Hallmark card will do just fine."

CHAPTER 21: BENEATH THE SEA

Rather than have their year-end planning session confined to a hotel conference room for days, the Smart brothers took a different approach. They flew their entire executive leadership team to Sydney, Australia, to see the market, spend a couple of days working on their annual strategic plan, and then as a treat take a scuba diving trip in the Great Barrier Reef. Their intent was to build team spirit and to celebrate another year of spectacular growth.

On the flight over Alex reviewed the quarterly sales numbers. "V, can you explain why some of the fall Women's Apparel sales numbers fell short of expectations?"

"Yes. Because we made some bad product decisions, Alex."

He frowned a bit. "My wife was a big fan of the Training Tee and was disappointed in this season's product–she said the shirt was see-through. What happened?"

Time to activate her plan. "Some products didn't just fall short, they were a disaster. I take full responsibility for the results and have made changes to ensure this doesn't happen again."

Duncan looked up and listened.

Vivien continued. "I've learned two important things, Alex: first, I need to step in and make all major product decisions and second, I have a person in charge of product who lacks the proper skills and instincts. We need to make a change there…it's something Ron and I have already discussed."

She glanced over at Ron, who said, "It's been clear for some time that we need to make a change. We're working on it."

Conversation concluded, Vivien made her way back to her seat.

Duncan grabbed her arm a little too tightly and hissed loud enough for others to hear, "I can't believe how you threw Rebecca under the bus like that, V. You make it sound like she's responsible for all the product problems. That's not on."

"Since your focus is footwear and not apparel, Dunk, I don't expect you to be familiar with all the facts, so let me lay things out for you." Vivien shook off his grip and leaned over him, aware that everyone was watching and listening. "Rebecca made decisions and took action on product without my knowledge. Not only did she make changes to product that we agreed not to make, but she deliberately misled me by having the wrong samples shown to me at final product review. I didn't learn about her deception until it was too late and the product was already in the market. Rebecca's actions jeopardized our sales and negatively impacted our business. Those are the facts." She spread her hands out in front of her as if she were a gourmet chef presenting a dish.

Duncan scowled and said loudly, "Well, I think Rebecca is a gifted product person and I, for one, believe wholeheartedly in her talents."

Vivien had to check herself from saying, *And what talents might you be referring to, Dunk?* How could he have a clue about Rebecca's proficiency in apparel design? She said, "I have a great idea. If you have such a high opinion of Rebecca's skill, then why don't you put her on your team, Dunk? I'd be happy to transfer her over to you."

Both Smart brothers shot Duncan a look, unmistakable in its meaning: *Do not go there.* Undaunted, Duncan turned to his buddy. "Johnny O, there's gotta be room on your Men's Apparel team for a talent like Rebecca. Isn't there?"

Surprised by Duncan's request, Johnny O stiffened up in his seat. He may not have been confident about Rebecca's product skills, but this industry was all about relationships and Johnny O couldn't leave his buddy hanging. "Uh, sure, I can find a spot for her."

Slam dunk. This exchange had gone better than Vivien anticipated.

Perhaps she was learning to play the game after all. The matter was settled then and there, with Ron set to put Rebecca's transfer in motion when they returned to Portland. Vivien let out a big sigh–she had finally gotten out from under the boulder dragging down her division. Even Duncan seemed content with the outcome. Unable to contain his amusement, Tim flashed Vivien a smile and a nod to say, *Well played*. Now all she had to do was get rid of Charl and her team would be right where she wanted it.

*

The brilliant Australian sun shone brightly, blinding Vivien's tired eyes. The executive team had wrapped up their Sydney tour and were waiting to board the corporate jet bound for Port Douglas. Back in Portland, the October weather was dreary and overcast, while on this side of the globe a glorious spring day was starting.

As a gift for those new to scuba diving, Alex and Malcolm paid for their lessons and open water certification. Duncan, Johnny O, and Steele had completed their coursework back home and would do their final certification dives on this trip. The team was to rendezvous with the live-aboard dive boat in Port Douglas, just off the coast of the Great Barrier Reef.

No stranger to diving trips, Vivien thought live-aboards were the way to go. The executives boarded the luxury boat, called the *WaveMaker*, which was 125 feet long and equipped with catamaran stabilizers to ensure a smooth ride. They were greeted on the deck by the crew members, standing at attention in their crisp dress whites.

Passengers were offered a glass of champagne and a chance to relax, while porters took the luggage down to their preassigned cabins. The efficient porters also unpacked the guests' dive gear on the back deck. The divers wouldn't have to lug a single piece of equipment or haul their own air tanks on this trip.

The chef served scrumptious appetizers and the guests relaxed during the cocktail hour. Besides the Smart Sports executives, the other guests introduced themselves.

"Hi, I'm Greg and this is my wife, Sandy. We're from Tampa. I'm a contractor, but my passion is underwater photography. Hoping to get some good shots." Judging by his Nikonos camera and digital video camera, Greg took his hobby seriously.

The second set of dive buddies shook hands all around. "Greetings, I'm Marc-Antoine and this is my son Julien. We are from Montreal." All the divers were fairly experienced–with the exception of Duncan, Johnny O, and Steele–and eager to start their diving adventure.

Lynette, the captain, welcomed the guests. She introduced the crew members, explained the amenities the ship had to offer, and talked about the diving schedule. The three dive masters gave a safety briefing and reinforced that the predive briefing was mandatory for every diver. Finally, the guests went down to their cabins to change for dinner. For the rest of the four-day trip, they'd be wearing only swimsuits, wet suits, shorts, and T-shirts, and no shoes.

The powerful engines roared to life as the dive boat commenced its overnight steam out to the open ocean. Once their gourmet dinner was finished, many of the guests retired, weary from their long travel. Klaas and Vivien hung out in the main cabin to play a game of Scrabble, which she won handily.

Looking up from his magazine, Duncan said, "V, are you ready to take on a worthy opponent?" He seemed to have gotten over her remarks about Rebecca on the trip over.

"Sure, Dunk. Bring it."

Matt, one of the dive masters, sauntered over, chatting cheerfully and previewing some of the dives. His green eyes twinkled, fringed by eyelashes so lush they seemed too dainty for someone so masculine. Tattoos snaked up both his arms. "Gee, Matt, you seem to know a ton about marine life. Can't wait to dive with you," Vivien said.

Klaas was feeling jet-lagged and decided to turn in. Toward the end of her Scrabble game with Duncan, Vivien went to get a sparkling water from the refrigerator outside on the deck, asking Duncan and Matt if they wanted anything. When she returned, Matt was gone and the two of them finished up their game. The few times she'd played against Duncan on the corporate jet, Vivien had been the victor, but tonight Duncan prevailed. His thin lips bared all of his teeth and he gloated about his upset win.

"Congratulations, Dunk," Vivien said, "let's see if you can repeat it sometime."

Vivien climbed the stairs to the lido deck to take in the magnificent view. The stars glittered over the vast, dark ocean—it was so peaceful a sight, and she was lost in her reverie when she was startled by a voice that came out of nowhere.

"You know, we're going to see a lot of sharks out there, but I'd watch out for that shark of a friend you've got."

Vivien spun around and saw a dark figure reclining on a chaise lounge. Matt.

"Oh, hi. You're talking about Duncan? He's not my friend exactly, we just work together." She leaned against the railing. "Why should I watch out for him?"

"I saw him do something crafty. When you went to get a drink, I was organizing the log books. My back was turned on Duncan, but I could see his reflection in the window. Not only did he look at your letters, but he exchanged his. The bloke's a wicked cheater!" Matt's Brisbane accent made the word sound like "cheetah."

Cheetah or snake? Vivien laughed, "Can't say I'm surprised. Duncan's one of those guys who has to win, no matter what."

*

It took the gentle rocking of the boat and the muted, metallic ping of scuba tanks knocking against each other to remind Vivien where she was when she awoke. Blinking, she looked around at her well-appointed cabin. A delicious aroma drifted in, and she opened her cabin door to find a mug of steaming coffee and a biscuit. She devoured the biscuit and sipped her coffee, trying to wake up. In the small bathroom she splashed cool water on her face, then changed into her swimsuit and a T-shirt and headed upstairs.

After a light breakfast of cereal and toast, the bell clanged, signaling the dive briefing was about to start. Everyone assembled out on the deck.

"Divers, gather round," said Matt, who was leading the dive. On a whiteboard he drew an elaborate sketch of the dive site, showing different depth levels and comical drawings of "critters" they could expect to see. He wore an exceptionally tiny bathing suit and Vivien had to avoid staring. Fit, muscular, and darkly tanned, Matt stood confidently in front of the divers. He explained how to do the dive to ensure they were within safe limits. "We don't want any of you lot getting the bends. We'll be doing four dives throughout the day and then a night dive. The first dive of the day will be your deepest. So, remember to keep an eye on your max depth." Matt indicated that the other two dive masters would be watching them closely.

"Our first dive is a wall dive down to a maximum depth of thirty-five meters, or for those of you not on the metric system, one hundred fifteen feet. This area is called Dart Reef and the dive site is called, aptly, the Wall. I'm assuming you've all done deep dives?" Matt looked around and saw everyone except for Duncan, Steele, and Johnny O nodding their heads. "Okay, you fellas stick close to me, we'll be doing your certification dives at a shallower depth. The rest of you should be good. Descend off the anchor line, stick close to your buddy, and watch your air-pressure gauge and bottom time. When your air tank hits seven hundred psi, give me the signal and start your ascent. You should arrive on the surface with no less than five hundred psi in your tanks, and we monitor this closely and record it on this clipboard." Matt made eye contact with each diver on this point.

As Matt answered questions about the dive, Duncan and Johnny O leaned back in their familiar bicep-flex pose, scrutinizing the physiques of the other guys on the boat. Vivien felt their eyes rest upon her, clad in her bikini, and she was glad she had lost most of the baby weight. The divers were itching to get into the water, so Matt closed with one final piece of advice: "Remember, life's a beach and then you dive!"

Pairs of dive buddies bolted to their stations to suit up. Alex and Malcolm buddied up, Vivien and Tim would be dive buddies, and Klaas was with Ron. Steele was assigned to one of the dive masters, so that left Duncan and Johnny O as the last pair of buddies. They had a few minutes to get on their wet suits and don their equipment: lead weight belt, buoyancy control device, scuba tank and regulator, dive computer, compass, dive knife, mask, snorkel, and fins. Vivien strapped her titanium dive knife onto the inside of her left calf.

Eyeballing it, Steele said, "Hey, V, what's the knife for?"

"Protection against sharks," she replied.

"Really? That little piece of metal can fend off a huge shark?" His eyes widened.

"Sure. When you see a shark coming, you take the knife and cut your buddy, then swim away. You don't have to swim faster than the shark, just faster than your buddy." Vivien winked at Tim, who stifled a laugh. Meanwhile Steele gulped in horror.

*

Upon completing the usual safety checks, the pairs of dive buddies descended the steps off the back of the boat and splashed into the sapphire sea. Vivien stepped off the platform in a giant stride entry, careful to hold her regulator and mask in place. Tim followed. The water was about 82 degrees Fahrenheit but felt cool compared to the tropical air. She sensed a fleeting chill as water seeped rapidly into her wet suit, forming a thin layer that would warm up to her body temperature and keep her comfortable throughout the dive.

The waves tossed them around like corks bobbing on the surface of the sea. Vivien set the bezel on her dive watch to mark the start of her dive as a backup, and she checked that the water had activated her dive computer. She glanced at the rest of the guys. Greg and Sandy had already descended, as had the Canadian father and son. Klaas and Ron were on the move. A dive master was patiently showing Steele how to read his dive computer. Johnny O looked on as Duncan fumbled with his mask, trying to get the strap over his thick movie-star hair without mussing it.

Vivien signaled to Tim that she was ready to descend. They swam to the anchor line and dropped down, entering into a peaceful world of aquatic wonderment. She spiraled slowly, looking up through clear blue sea and listening to the glub-glubbing of air bubbles floating by. She pinched her nose and expanded her jaw to equalize the pressure in her ears.

Visibility was fantastic at over two hundred feet and the marine life was abundant. A huge pack of yellowtail snappers darted around Vivien's legs, sniffing for bits of food. They were pesky little fish, like the NYC subway rats of the sea. The multicolored parrotfish and varieties of butterfly fish were too numerous to count. The coral was healthy, vibrant, and gigantic. Suspended nearby, a great grouper with oversized lips regarded her eerily.

Further down the wall, Vivien spotted three white tip reef sharks lurking. It was a diver's paradise and the time flew by. Malcolm was nearby and she made the diver's signal for "beautiful," and he nodded.

Back on deck the dive crew helped Vivien remove her equipment. She took a warm rinse in the deck shower, and then a crew member wrapped a heated towel around her shoulders, a delicious sensation. Tim was enjoying the luxurious treatment, judging by his huge grin. Hungry again, Vivien ordered up a cooked breakfast with eggs over easy, crispy bacon, and hash browns. Whatever calories she burned from the diving activities, she might make up for with all the mouthwatering food.

The rest of the day was interspersed with incredible diving, savory meals, a short nap, and some light reading before their night dive and then dinner. A scuba safety rule was no alcohol before a dive, so dining after their night dive allowed them to enjoy a glass of wine. The executives intermingled with the other divers, recounting what they'd seen and trading anecdotes.

Duncan challenged Vivien to another game of Scrabble. Matt observed close by with an amused look on his face. This time Vivien stayed put and won the game, as usual. Duncan grumbled about being unlucky and getting bad letters.

"Don't worry, Dunk, you won fair and square last time, so there's no reason you can't win again. Right?"

He was silent, but his pupils contracted and his left jaw muscle twitched. Vivien noted the reaction and it triggered her memory. She had seen it before...when she was new to the company and asked Duncan how to prepare for the SBR. And a few other times. Must have been Duncan's "tell" indicating he was lying or afraid. Good to know.

CHAPTER 22: IN DEEP WATER

On the last day of their scuba trip sunlight danced on the surface of the clear azure sea, making the water playfully inviting. Rays of light speared the liquid blue, fracturing into thousands of shimmering slivers. Vivien drew in a breath of clean, salty sea air. Visibility was so good from the boat that she could see deep into the ocean and make out the coral formations below. As with many of the dives on this trip, this was a wall dive and they expected to see a lot of pelagics.

Matt said, "I'm not making any promises here, but the last boat to dive at this site radioed that a tiger shark was in the area, so maybe we'll get lucky."

For all the other dives Vivien had buddied up with Tim. But this time a change was requested.

One of the dive masters said, "Vivien, Tim, this is going to be a challenging dive, and you guys are both very experienced. Would you mind splitting up and each of you diving with one of the less experienced divers?"

She hesitated, but then they both agreed. The dive master buddied Vivien up with Duncan and Tim with Johnny O. Duncan was appreciative, but Vivien felt uneasy. A diver essentially puts their life into the hands of their dive buddy, and she wasn't at all sure about giving that kind of responsibility to Duncan. Her gut was telling her to sit this one out. But in her hundreds of dives she'd never come close to seeing a tiger shark; despite her reservations about Duncan, Vivien just couldn't pass up this chance.

The eyes of all the divers lit up with anticipation and they suited up with more alacrity. Greg asked Sandy to hand him his digital video camera once he got into the water.

Duncan, as a novice diver, fumbled a bit and moved slowly. Vivien was getting impatient to get into the water–she hated to be the last one in.

"Come on, Dunk," she pleaded. "There's going to be some cool stuff on this dive. We don't want to miss the tiger shark, do we?"

"Uh, right. Of course not," Duncan replied unconvincingly. His right hand went up and rubbed the back of his neck. He was stressed out, and he wasn't the only one.

Finally, they were ready and stood at the platform, waiting to make their giant stride entry. Six or seven reef sharks swam close to the surface near the dive platform. Interesting the sharks showed no fear of the humans, and why would they? Vivien signaled she was going to go.

Once under the water the two started getting more comfortable diving together. Vivien spotted two giant loggerhead turtles and a huge school of great barracuda with rows of jagged, pointy teeth and stern gazes. The barracuda huddled together, like a bunch of New Yorkers waiting to board the number two train to Wall Street. She pointed out the marine life to Duncan, who nodded excitedly. She was tracking a huge puffer fish when a sharp metallic clang pierced the water. Vivien turned to see Matt, about forty feet away, banging his tank with his dive knife to get everyone's attention.

What was the hullabaloo? Typically, a dive master signaled in this way when there was something unusual or interesting to see. Or something dangerous. Matt put his hand in profile against his forehead to signal a shark and spread four fingers alongside his abdomen…the unmistakable diver's signal for a tiger shark.

Vivien felt a rush of exhilaration. She turned toward Duncan and saw a strange look on his face…confusion? She tapped his arm and signaled him to come closer.

On her underwater slate she wrote, "Tiger shark nearby." His eyes grew wide and he nodded in comprehension. Vivien wiped her slate clean.

She strained her eyes to make out the tiger shark in the distance but saw nothing. Sharks attacked from below, so she carefully scanned the waters beneath them. Nothing. Again, the clanging sound from Matt. This time he made a signal instructing everyone to get against the wall. Most of the divers were near Matt and clustered around him. His face revealed an emotion Vivien had not seen in him before: alarm.

Then something peculiar happened. Fishes of different species and sizes started whizzing past them, as if on overdrive, all moving in the same direction. A huge school of fish whipped around Vivien and Duncan, who were still out in the open water, making a surgical split and then reforming once they passed the divers, clearly in a hurry to get somewhere–or away from something. In all her diving experience, Vivien had never seen that happen. She felt a knot in her gut and knew they had to get to the wall. And fast.

Vivien quickly spotted a shallow opening in the wall and motioned to Duncan to swim toward it. He took off in that direction, jerking his head around in a desperate attempt to see what was coming. Vivien followed, keeping her eyes trained on the depths below.

Duncan was fifteen feet ahead of her when he abruptly stopped and turned. He flailed his arms madly and swam backward into the indent in the wall. When she got closer, she saw his pin-dot pupils and twitching jaw muscle. Duncan was sucking hard on his regulator. Vivien instinctively checked his air supply to make sure he had enough air.

She signaled, *Are you okay? Slow down your breathing.*

Duncan was frozen. He didn't move at all. Was he having a panic attack?

He grabbed her slate; scrawled, "*SARK!*"; and pointed below. Apparently proper spelling under pressure was not one of Duncan's advertised skills.

Out of the blue, a Cadillac drove past–at least something the size of a Cadillac. Vivien recognized in a split second the eighteen-foot tiger shark speeding past them. He was massive. Magnificent and terrifying at the same time. As Vivien watched the shark, Duncan pulled her in front of him with a swift jerk, so she was facing outward.

Oh, that's nice, she thought, *he's concerned about my safety.* She began to feel uncomfortable, though, as Duncan clamped onto her buoyancy control vest so tightly she couldn't move at all. *Jeez, I must be blocking his view of the shark.*

She peered into the murky depths, hoping to catch another glimpse of the automobile-sized pelagic. She wasn't disappointed. A grayish blob sped into focus. From above, the shark's broad head had a squarish look to it. This time it came close enough for Vivien to see distinctive side markings, those brownish tiger-like stripes. Below its belly the claspers indicated it was a male. The creature moved so swiftly and gracefully, she had to marvel at its majestic presence and sheer size–it was wider across than her first studio apartment in Manhattan.

Duncan gripped her. Vivien didn't like being held so forcefully. She squirmed to get him to loosen up.

Without warning, the gray Cadillac shot up from below, its mouth agape. As the beast drew rapidly near, Vivien felt herself being pushed outward toward the oncoming death machine. What the hell was Duncan doing? She whooshed through the water like a rag doll. The force of being pushed forward caused her legs to swing out from under her. Her fins shot out toward the open water within reach of the shark's massive jaws.

Vivien felt a sickening tug on her leg. She expected to see a dark cloud of her blood tingeing the seawater; at that depth the color red would appear black in the available light. They say when a shark shears off a limb it's so swift the victim can barely feel it.

She waited a second and looked down with trepidation. The shark had bitten off a large chunk of her right fin, leaving a perfect half-moon set of jagged tooth marks. She began to feel something she rarely felt: fear. And found it was possible to sweat underwater.

She struggled to get Duncan to let her go. She tried to bat his arms away, but his fingers were locked tightly around her BCD vest.

Through her regulator she yelled sharply, "Let go! Let go!"

Duncan was using her as a human shield.

Her heart pumped like mad. She concentrated on keeping her breath even and not using up all her air. In a few seconds the tiger shark would be back to finish its afternoon snack–her. As she twisted violently to escape Duncan's grasp, her elbow came into abrupt contact with his jaw. He released one hand to put it to his jaw but kept the other firmly affixed to Vivien's vest.

Only one way out. Vivien unclipped the straps on her buoyancy control vest and wriggled free. She turned to face Duncan. Planting one foot on the wall and the other squarely in Duncan's stomach, she wrenched her dive gear free from his grasp. Heart racing, she spun around in a split second. Just in time to face the oncoming shark.

It zoomed toward her with a powerful flick of its tail fin. As the shark opened its huge mouth, all she could see was rows of razor-sharp, serrated teeth–a cornucopia of jagged teeth, an orthodontist's dream. The shark lunged forward, jaws snapping out to capture its prey.

Vivien held her dive unit in front of her. The shark closed in. She thrust out the tank and banged the shark smack in the nose. Stunned, the tiger shark retreated to collect itself. Only the sound of her breathing and the pounding of her heart filled her ears.

The carnivorous Cadillac turned and came at her again. This time when she pushed out the tank its teeth closed around it. It was clear the shark did not enjoy the taste of metal. It looked disappointed and lingered for a moment, then tilted its head back, putting its teeth away. The tiger shark eyed Vivien as if to say, *I'll give you this one*, and shot off into the darkness below.

Watching the shark disappear, she let out a long stream of air bubbles. Then she checked her air gauge and donned her BCD and tank. Out of sheer habit she looked toward her dive buddy to check if he was okay, forgetting for an instant that the jerk had tried serving her with a garnish to a giant shark with a huge appetite.

Matt, who had been keeping all the other divers together and out of the shark's way, rushed over to check if Vivien was okay. He also reached out and shook Duncan to see if he was all right. Seeing he was fine, Matt gave him a swift slap upside his head as if to say, *What were you thinking, man?* Then Matt signaled to everyone to get back to the boat.

Greg, the guy from Florida, was gesticulating feverishly to Vivien that he had recorded the events on his underwater digital video camera. Malcolm swam up to Vivien and signaled to see if she was okay. He shook his head in disgust.

They reached the ocean surface and Duncan, in his haste to climb back on board, shoved Vivien aside in the water. His elbow slammed the side of her head. Then she lost it. Reaching out swiftly, she grabbed him by the scuba mask dangling around his neck and pulled him back into the water with a mighty splash.

"Hey, buddy," Vivien said, "here's a little memento for you." She cocked her fist back and threw a jab smack at Duncan's eye.

Even Steele, normally one of Duncan's posse, let out a guffaw. "That's gonna leave a mark."

With trembling limbs Vivien climbed back aboard the boat, expressionless on the outside, but inside her emotions swirled. By rote, she removed her dive gear and then walked to a remote section of the deck to sit down. The crew tried to act as if everything were normal. She felt all eyes upon her as she struggled to make sense of what just happened.

Back on board, the rest of the divers regarded her with awe and respectfully gave Vivien a few moments to collect herself. It was a high-voltage silence and the air crackled with electricity.

"My god, V, are you okay?" a voice asked, sounding strangely far away, like the words were bubbling up through tapioca pudding. It was Tim, looking agitated.

Despite the warm climate, Vivien shivered uncontrollably. Water dripped off her hair into discrete puddles at her feet. Fixing her gaze on the painted white deck, she mustered all her strength to sound calm. "Yes, thanks, Timmy. I'm fine. Just need a minute."

Matt came over and placed a heated towel around her trembling shoulders. The sensation had a profound comforting effect.

Vivien exhaled slowly. The catastrophe was the result of her ignoring her gut. She had read the gut instinct is actually your unconscious mind processing information and helping you make correct judgments. She hadn't listened to her gut…and as a result she'd almost died. What the heck had just happened?

"Vivien, I'm here if you need anything, all right?" Matt said in a gentle voice.

"Okay, thanks," she said, voice low and steady.

Malcolm Smart sat next to her and put his arm around her shoulder. "That was the most courageous thing I've ever witnessed. You have no fear, Vivien."

Alex, Klaas, and Ron came over and tenderly nudged her into the main cabin. "Let's go inside, V, and get you a cold one."

As Malcolm and the others led Vivien away, she looked back to see Duncan sitting hunched in the corner staring at the floor. He was drooped over in that familiar question-mark posture, his hands clasped together. Just visible was the faded tattoo on his wet neck, glistening with its now-ironic motto, *Strength Under Pressure*.

*

Inside the main cabin, the rest of the divers soon surrounded Vivien. Greg slapped her heartily on the back, applauding her courage and quick thinking. Sandy handed her a small plate of cheese and crackers. "Eat something, dear."

Down to a person, everyone expressed shock at what they had seen, even Johnny O.

Alone outside, Duncan remained hunched over, looking utterly humiliated. Vivien noticed that everyone avoided gawking at him, as if he were a human solar eclipse.

Vivien downed a can of VB beer, and Tim handed her a second one.

Greg plugged his camera into the TV, displaying everything that had happened. There was an uncomfortable silence when Duncan pushed Vivien out into the mouth of the oncoming shark. Seeing it from that perspective was more terrifying than the actual ordeal had felt.

Ron said drily, "Yep, I'd say that qualifies as an HR violation."

Duncan had entered the cabin unnoticed and stood at the back of the room.

Vivien finished her beer, chatted briefly with the other divers, and finally excused herself to take a nap. What she really wanted was a few minutes alone. Of all her possible worries about working in the cutthroat, male-dominated sports industry, having a coworker feed her to an attacking shark had never been a remote concern.

Lying on her bed, she heard voices just outside her window. Duncan and Johnny O sat on the side of the boat, their backs leaning against the glass.

"That was some crazy shit down there, Dunk. Scary stuff, huh?" Johnny O seemed supportive but also wary. Probably counting his blessings they weren't buddied up that last dive.

"Dunno what happened, man. I just panicked and sort of blanked out. Didn't even realize what I was doing," Duncan babbled, his hand absentmindedly rubbing the back of his neck. The other hand held an ice pack to his burgeoning black eye.

"Well, one thing's for sure, man. You owe V a big friggin' apology." Johnny O was looking out for her. That was encouraging.

"You're right, Johnny O, quite right," Duncan said.

✳

A short while later there was a soft knock at her door. She opened it to see Duncan with his head hanging down.

"Uh, can I come in, V? I just wanted to say a few things." He stepped inside her cabin and sat down on her bed. "One, I've never seen a shark up close and that was the scariest thing in my life. Two, I panicked and didn't have control over my actions. And three, I'm just sorry and terribly embarrassed about it all. I feel like a complete wanker. Honestly, I didn't know what I was doing!"

Saving your butt? Vivien kept her eyes averted.

What happened next was perhaps even more outlandish than what had happened on the dive. Duncan buried his head in his hands and sobbed uncontrollably, like a child who'd just received a terrible scolding. The shock of seeing him cry left Vivien in an awkward stillness as Duncan continued his heaving sobs. She shifted her weight, leaning against the chest of drawers in the tight space of her cabin.

Trying to curtail the weeping, she reassured him. "That's okay, Dunk." She put a hand on his leathery shoulder, which was gritty with dried particles of sea salt. "It's only natural to panic in a situation like that. Fortunately, things turned out all right. Anyway, you certainly made it one of my more memorable dives." She smirked. "Sorry about the black eye."

Duncan gave a weak chuckle and wiped the tears and snot away with the back of his hand. He peered up at her with a grateful look and stood. As he walked out, Vivien quipped, "By the way, Dunk, you owe me a new set of fins when we get home."

He nodded and with a wave retreated slowly to his cabin.

✳

Later that afternoon, Vivien climbed up to the top deck to warm herself in the sun and relax. Malcolm put down his book and came over to sit in the chaise lounge next to hers.

He put his arm on hers and in a hushed tone said, "You all right, V?"

She replied in the affirmative.

"And what about your coworker?" he asked. Funny, Malcolm didn't use the term *colleague* or *buddy* when he referred to Duncan. Perhaps his estimation of the man had declined.

"Duncan came by my cabin and apologized. He was really rattled by the whole experience and said he just panicked. I feel bad for the guy. I guess panic is the natural reaction to that kind of situation."

"Dunno about that. You didn't panic at all." Malcolm shared his observation in a soft voice. "Listen, this may be out of left field, V, but Alex and I are working on a succession plan...to decide who will take the reins at Smart Sports when we retire. We considered Duncan as a possibility, but we've concluded he doesn't have the values we want in a company leader. We need someone who's the right culture fit and has broad skills and business acumen." He leaned closer and clasped his hands. "Vivien, you're a visionary leader who not only gets phenomenal business results but conducts herself with strength, integrity, and humility. Critical qualities we want in a CEO. So, what I'm saying is you're our number one choice. Over the next few years, we'll groom you for the role and ensure you're getting the experiences and exposure to be able to step into the CEO role smoothly. But let's keep this between us for now, okay?" Malcolm smiled.

"Of course, Malcolm," Vivien replied. "I'm honored and also a bit shocked. Wow, what a day–to go from shark bait to CEO!"

Malcolm threw his head back and laughed with abandon. He gave Vivien a squeeze on the shoulder and then got up to get dressed for dinner. There'd be a fancy banquet for their last night on the live-aboard, so guests were expected to spruce up a bit.

✳

Duncan stayed in his cabin during dinner that night, sending a message via Johnny O that he felt ill. The rest of the divers were eager to dine with Vivien, pour her more wine, and recount the events of the day. Vivien was enjoying a much needed buzz after a traumatic experience. The ample wine helped her fall right to sleep that night, despite her taking a few moments to imagine what it would be like to be the CEO of Smart Sports.

Duncan also missed breakfast the next morning, when the guests and crew members were saying their good-byes and trading business cards. Sandy gave her a hug, and Greg pulled Vivien aside. He was obviously trying to be delicate about broaching a subject.

"Greg, is there something you want to ask me?" Vivien finally said. "Just ask."

"I was wondering if you'd be okay with me selling the footage of the shark dive to Discovery Channel. It's an amazing video and the digital detail is incredible. Naturally, I'd give you half of the proceeds. I bet we could get a good price–this is something no one's ever seen."

Vivien hesitated. "You know what, Greg, let me think about it. I know it's an incredible video, but I also want to be sensitive about embarrassing my coworker. Can I get back to you?"

"Sure, sure, here's my card. Just email me and let me know what you decide, no rush," Greg said good-naturedly. "I'll be happy to send you a copy, too."

Vivien laughed. "Oh, yeah, a nice shark video to add to my DVD collection, right between *Sex and the City* and *The Sound of Music*."

Matt came over and gave her a bear hug. "You're amazing, Vivien, and I'm sure I'll be reading all about your future successes. Take care of yourself, all right?"

*

Duncan waited until he heard the voices fade. After the other guests had departed and the van for the Smart Sports executives was loaded up, he finally emerged. He couldn't wait to get off that goddamn boat.

Bloody awful dive trip.

Rubbing the back of his neck, he groaned. Just thinking about yesterday's events and how he'd made a fool of himself stressed him out. Bad enough his buddies had all witnessed it, but even worse that Malcolm and Alex had seen it. Soon he'd be on the corporate jet and could hopefully put all this behind him.

Their long flight home was fairly quiet. Too humiliated to try to make conversation, Duncan donned headphones and pretended to sleep most of the trip and no one bothered him.

Duncan couldn't have been more miserable. In one fell swoop, he'd achieved three things: First, he'd gone from being the shoo-in for CEO of Smart Sports to possibly being knocked out of contention. Second, his godly status had been diminished in the eyes of his buddies. And third, his unspeakable actions had only made Vivien, his archrival, outshine him.

*

A shark of a different sort waited for Vivien when she got back to the office. During her leadership staff meeting she got updates on the progress that had been made while she was away.

"Where are Angela and Rebecca today?" Vivien asked.

Scott gave her an uneasy look. "They're out filming the product videos."

"What? They're shooting already?" The product videos had been

Vivien's idea and she'd expected to be consulted before they were made. But she tried to show patience. "Moved on it faster than I expected. All right, next topic."

After the meeting, Vivien was feeling hungry so she hustled over to the commissary to grab a quick bite. Walking in, she bumped into Aileen, who was munching an apple.

"Hi, Aileen. How are you?"

"Good!" Aileen replied. "Great to have you back, Vivien. How was Australia?"

"It was quite a trip…hey, wait a minute," Vivien said. "Why aren't you at the shoot for the product videos? Your hiking jacket is still one of the featured products, isn't it?"

"Yes, Vivien, one of the videos is about the jacket. Unfortunately, I'm not in it."

"Why not, Aileen?"

"I don't know…you'll have to ask Rebecca. She just told me I wouldn't be needed."

Strange.

The next morning, Vivien stopped by for a chat with her marketing director.

"Hi, Angela, how did the video shoot go yesterday?"

Her look communicated her lack of enthusiasm. "It was okay. Vivien, I actually wanted to talk to you about it. The plan was to discuss our concept with you first, but Rebecca was adamant that we go ahead and shoot to get it on the website in time for product launch. She said you'd be pleased to have all the videos already wrapped up."

"I see. Were there any issues?"

Angela frowned a little. "I know your idea was to have the individual product designers talk about their inspiration for the product, etc."

"Right."

"That was a source of debate. Rebecca thought it would be confusing to have different people talk about the products. So she suggested having only one person in all three videos."

Somehow Vivien knew exactly what was coming next. "And the one person you chose was…?"

"Rebecca. She actually self-selected to be in the video. She did okay, but the shoot took all day because she insisted on getting her hair and makeup redone and changing outfits multiple times." Angela rolled her eyes. "Fortunately, we shot it at the Smart Sports studio, so even though it took three times longer than planned it didn't cost extra."

"I'd like to see the rough cuts of the videos, Angela. Then we can make a decision about using them."

Angela nodded. "Absolutely, Vivien."

How convenient for Rebecca to make the casting decision while Vivien was unreachable. It spoke volumes about Rebecca as a leader that she'd snatched the spotlight, refusing to give credit to the talented designers who'd come up with the great products. No wonder the morale of the team working under Rebecca was always rock bottom.

✳

Later that day, after a product design review wrapped up, Vivien asked Rebecca to stay behind for a chat, and she acted as if she knew nothing.

"So, Rebecca, how did the product videos turn out? The designers must have been excited to highlight their work, especially Aileen."

"Oh, actually…," Rebecca said nervously, "the videos came out great! But, um, Aileen didn't want to do it." Although the two of them were alone in the conference room, Rebecca glanced around cautiously. "None of the designers wanted to be in the videos–something about not wanting to be on the Internet, blah, blah, blah."

"Really? That's surprising." Vivien played along.

"Yeah, they all said no. We were in such a bind, I felt an obligation to step in and be in the videos. I normally shy away from the spotlight, but Angela said I was the best choice, so in the end I did it for the team."

Vivien had to admit, this woman was masterful at deviousness–much more treacherous than the tiger shark.

"That was big of you, Rebecca," Vivien replied, amused.

Rebecca should've kept silent, but she couldn't stop herself.

She framed her hands around her face. "Oh my gosh, Vivien, I was thinking about it. All these people who knew me from way back when are going to see my videos on the Internet! Friends from high school, ex-boyfriends, college roommates, and people I worked with before. They'll all say, 'Wow, look at Rebecca Roche now!'" Her eyes looked skyward as her glossy red nails lightly tapped her cheekbone. Her beaming face belied any trace of the modesty she'd laid claim to only moments ago. Apparently, Rebecca was also okay with everyone's thinking she'd designed the products in the videos. She was talented all right…in self-promotion.

"By the way, Rebecca, there's something I need to discuss with you."

Rebecca squinted her eyes into narrow slits. Did she have a clue what was coming?

"You and I have had some challenges in working together–challenges we haven't been able to get past. I talked to HR and we think the best solution is to transfer you to another team." Vivien maintained a professional demeanor despite her delight.

"Transfer," Rebecca repeated. "Is this some kind of promotion?" Her voice was hopeful.

"It's a lateral move," Vivien said, shaking her head. "You'll be transferred to Men's Apparel effective Monday." She would have preferred this odious woman leave Smart Sports entirely, but at least she had the satisfaction of having a Roche-free team.

Rebecca pressed two red nails to her lips and nodded.

"I'm sure you'll enjoy your new team, Rebecca." Vivien stood up and offered her hand.

After they shook hands, Vivien left. She turned and saw a stunned

Rebecca just sitting there.

＊

At the Women's Apparel quarterly team meeting, Vivien shared her regular updates. By then most of them were aware of Rebecca's transfer; good news traveled quickly.

Vivien stated, "As some of you know, Rebecca will be transferring over to the Men's Apparel team starting next week. Rebecca, thank you for your contributions and we wish you the best."

Around the room there were obvious expressions of unmitigated joy.

It was a Smart Sports tradition for a team to take their boss to lunch when they were leaving the team. Interestingly, no one on her team organized a lunch, so Rebecca's exit was without any fanfare.

Rebecca stood up and smiled. "It's been so great working with you guys, and I'm sure you'll miss me as much as I'll miss you."

Zero reaction.

Rebecca couldn't resist trying to put a positive spin on things. "Anyway, I'm excited about this move and the chance to contribute to another business. And I hope you all find inner peace."

Bizarre closing comment…was she somehow implying she was spiritually superior to everyone? There was an audible sigh of relief when Rebecca left the room.

＊

Rebecca's videos were scrapped and new ones shot with the designers as Vivien had envisioned. Rebecca's chance at fame ended up on the cutting room floor, never to be seen by her legions of ex-boyfriends. Judging by the number of hits to their website the Story Behind the Style videos were a tremendous success.

*

It was time for the annual Christmas lunch celebration for the Women's Apparel team and everyone gathered in the large conference room, laughing and joking. Vivien caught a few snippets of conversation about the business and the mood was exuberant.

Vivien said, "We were able to correct the problems with the fall product, and now we're on track to turn in a record year for the division, I'm really grateful to all of you. You should feel proud."

Smiles lit up the room.

Wow, so different from my first meeting with this team, Vivien reflected.

"Because of your hard work, we will turn in the first full fiscal year of profitability in our division's history. And we've put Women's Apparel on the map. Congratulations, team. Time to celebrate!" She signaled to Pandy.

The conference room doors swung open and a marching band played jubilant music while strutting around the perimeter of the room. Team members laughed and jumped back to get out of the way. When the music stopped the team cheered and applauded.

Pandy wheeled in a cart of champagne bottles and glasses. J. J. and Scott helped her serve drinks all around.

Vivien moved over to the corner of the room, where a stack of boxes were piled up. "Come on, everyone, I've had a special gift made up for each of you."

Each person got a cool laser-cut running jacket, designed by Aileen, with their name embroidered on the front. Once all the jackets were passed out and tried on, Vivien had another surprise.

"Time to head outside to where the buses are waiting. We're going to a Trailblazers game!"

Whoops and hollers were heard as people clamored to get on the buses.

"Now, this is what I call a celebration," J. J. said, clapping his boss on the shoulder. "Thanks, V."

"It's been quite an adventure so far," she laughed.

CHAPTER 23: THE BIG W

At the start of the New Year a pleasant surprise awaited Vivien in a brief meeting with Charl Davis. He first congratulated her on turning around the Women's Apparel business and then broke some news.

"Vivien"–his look turned solemn–"I've really enjoyed working with you, but I've found another opportunity."

Perfect; perhaps Charl wanted to be reunited with his old clique. "Oh, what is it, Charl?"

"I found a spot on Johnny O's team, so I asked HR to transfer me. Hope that's all right."

Charl had never been a big contributor to her team and given his treachery she was glad to lose him.

Vivien shook her head sympathetically. "I understand, Charl, you need to do what's best for you."

She was ecstatic to finally have her team cleaned up, with all the scheming and conniving characters gone. Now Vivien could move ahead with a team of people she respected, trusted, and enjoyed working with. *I owe Johnny O a drink for this.*

✳

Over the past few months, Malcolm and Alex had realized they had to adjust their expansion strategy. The fierce competition in the sporting goods channel meant they were battling with behemoths like Nike, Adidas, and Under Armour who dominated the sales floor.

"We've got to deploy a different strategy and open more Smart Sports branded stores. That will give us control over our retail execution, our profit margin, and our destiny," Alex said to Vivien in one of her touch-base meetings with the Smart brothers.

Vivien nodded. "And we could make twenty more margin points selling our apparel in our own stores."

"The only problem," Malcolm said, "is that you're our only senior executive with vertical retail experience. We know you have a lot on your plate already, V, but we'd need you to lead the retail effort. Are you willing to do that?"

Shrewdly, Vivien knew that a key aspect to running successful retail was to drive traffic, and that was done with apparel. At the Smart Sports branded stores women's apparel would take center stage because women bought more apparel than men and shopped more frequently. That would only increase the importance of her division to the company. "Sure, I'm happy to take it on."

"That's great, V, thanks." Alex smiled, then switched gears. "As you know our succession plan is still a secret, but we've shared our intent to make you CEO with Doug Hawke and with the chairman of the board, Otto Utz. It's a delicate subject with Otto since he's also Duncan's father-in-law, but with this added responsibility I think Otto will see how much value you bring to Smart Sports."

*

Once again it was time for the Smart Sports Awards ceremony. Employees packed the Stadium to learn who'd made the biggest contributions to the company.

The Smart brothers came out onstage to the cheers of the audience. They cued up a highlight reel of the greatest Smart Sports moments over the past year, set to an exhilarating soundtrack. Vivien noted with pride that some Women's Apparel product, like the Electrify line, and magazine headlines about their business were featured in the video. In the middle of the stage the Smart Sports MVP Award sat on a pedestal–a beautiful metal and glass trophy, modeled after the torch that topped the roof of the very building in which they sat.

Alex and Malcolm talked about the company's progress over the past year and how they'd fared as a public company. They shared some entertaining anecdotes and called out individuals who'd made significant contributions. Vivien felt a little wounded when no one on her team was cited, especially after all their hard work and excellent results.

That's okay, there were lots of successes and it's tough to name everyone.

"All right, everyone," Malcolm said, "let's get to the awards."

The audience buzzed with excitement as the Smart brothers started handing out the annual awards. Vivien noticed that many employees had spruced up for the event–some even wore shirts with buttons!

Finally the time came for the last award, and the Smart brothers asked Duncan to come up and present the MVP Award. By the mere fact that Duncan was making the presentation, Vivien, along with many others, figured that the award was going to a footwear designer. Again.

The spotlights shone on Duncan's wavy head of silvery-blond hair, and tiny flecks of light glinted off his glasses. He rubbed his goatee and smiled. In his ersatz British accent, Duncan talked in broad terms about the award recipient, careful not to use any pronouns.

"This person brought many innovations to the product and the business. And they were instrumental in one of the most successful product launches in Smart Sports history, the Electrify apparel line."

That had come out of Vivien's team! Perhaps the award would go to Aileen–how exciting would that be? Duncan continued to describe the recipient's ability to accomplish what many thought was an impossible task and to do it in record time.

"Furthermore," Duncan continued, amping up his accent, "for the first time in Smart Sports history the MVP Award is not going to a product designer, although this person has definitely shown expertise in that area. This year the award goes to…"

He paused for dramatic effect.

"...Vivien Lee. Please join me in congratulating our Smart Sports MVP."

She was immobile, stunned at hearing her own name. Did she just imagine it?

"V, please come up and accept your trophy." Duncan looked out into the crowd.

Vivien felt a few hands pulling her up out of her seat and pushing her down the aisle of the auditorium. It was like being the director of an independent film nominated for a Best Picture Academy Award and then having the shock of Meryl Streep announcing your name.

In a fog, she made her way to the stage. What sounded like a rolling clap of thunder reverberated throughout the Stadium as seats flipped up when the entire company gave her a standing ovation.

Duncan whispered in her ear, "We thought having me present the award would throw you off." He smiled and gave her a slightly awkward hug.

"This is nice, Dunk, but what I really want is salmon steaks at your place." She winked.

In their year and a half of working together, Duncan had yet to make good on his promise. By now it had become a source of amusement for her.

Alex and Malcolm Smart each gave her a heartfelt hug. Malcolm placed the heavy trophy into her hands. He gave her a gentle nudge toward the microphone, encouraging her to say a few words.

Still in a state of shock, Vivien blurted, "Man, am I glad I didn't skip out early!"

The audience laughed.

"I'm at a loss for words, which doesn't happen often." Vivien paused. "This is such an honor. This award validates the fantastic work of my team, and I wholeheartedly share this with them. It's been quite a journey so far, and we've worked hard to get Women's Apparel to where it is today, haven't we, guys?"

They responded with cheers and hollers.

Vivien looked out at the section where her team was sitting and smiled, recalling the heated debates and late nights. "To have our accomplishments recognized by all of you...it's just great. In a company dominated by such incredible footwear, it's meaningful that apparel has a place, too. So thank you. I'd like to invoke the words of Oscar Wilde: 'I have the simplest of tastes. I am always satisfied with the best.' I'm proud to have the best team and be part of Smart Sports, the best company on the planet. Now, let's go kick Nike's ass."

At the burst of applause both Smart brothers smiled broadly. Vivien walked offstage to the sounds of a cheering crowd.

✳

The lobby of the Stadium was beautifully decorated. Food and drink stations with white table cloths and colorful flowers were arranged around the atrium. Tim ran over and gave her a congratulatory hug. Then Johnny O and Steele came over to say well done.

Perhaps most surprising was Charl, who pulled her aside and said, "You know, Vivien, when you came here, I was pretty skeptical. But you've accomplished great things with the business, you really have. Congratulations."

It must have been sobering for him to say that, which made her appreciate it all the more.

"Thank you, Charl, really." She held out her hand and instead he gave her a hug.

She noticed that Charl worked the room masterfully, and people appeared genuinely happy to see him. Within earshot she heard him throw out flattering comments. "Hey, man, you been working out? Check out those guns!" and "You look gorgeous, have you lost weight?" Was that the secret to Charl's reputation as a "great guy," his skill at making people feel good? Had she been a recipient of Charl's artifice?

Did he mean what he'd just said to her?

It did not escape Vivien's attention that Rebecca, who had been on maternity leave during the entire ideation, design, development, and launch of the Electrify apparel line and was now with another division, chattered excitedly. Sharing in the credit, Rebecca squealed, "Oh my gosh, I can't believe we won!" Her comments were directed to Duncan, Fred, and any others who would listen.

As Vivien was observing this, Klaas put his hand on her shoulder. He had a goofy smile.

"Congratulations, V, what a fantastic achievement," Klaas said.

"Thanks, Klaas."

The Dutchman adjusted his wire rimmed glasses and looked worried. "The only hitch is that you now have a big target on your back."

"Huh? Why do you say that?"

"You're the first executive ever to win this award so there are two problems: Number one, whatever your successes, people are going to expect more from you now. Number two, winning this award makes you a threat to the other executives"–Klaas chuckled–"except for me, of course, since I have no shot at ever winning MVP. Sure, Duncan presented the award to you, but how happy is he really? I'd be cautious if I were you, Vivien. But, hey, congratulations on the big W!" He gave her a hearty slap on the back.

By now she knew the Dutchman well enough to know he was genuinely happy for her–and genuinely concerned. Vivien decided not to let Klaas's cautionary words put a damper on the evening, even though his comments held a nugget of truth.

PART SIX

CHAPTER 24: THE CELEBRATION

Smart Sports was sprinting ahead of its competitors and the Smart brothers took every opportunity to thank their employees. On a rare sunny Thursday in February, Alex and Malcolm Smart threw a blowout bash for the entire company.

It was an extravagant, carnival-like atmosphere and the brothers pulled out all the stops. At one end of the campus a rock band played live music under a tent. Nearby, a gigantic barbecue pit was set up, with meat grilled to order. Kegs of beer and snack stations dotted the lawn. There was a slew of carnival games where employees could try to win big prizes, like product autographed by elite athletes. The grand prize was a trip for four to Hawaii on the corporate jet, something any Oregonian would covet during the rainy extended winter.

The most popular attraction was the Dunk Your Boss booth. A senior executive would sit atop a large glass water tank, while an employee hurled baseballs at a target painted on a metal plate. A bull's-eye released the seat platform and plunged the poor executive into the water. It was all meant in good fun, although Alex and Malcolm had made it a point in the executive staff meeting that they expected all the senior executives to take their turn as a potential dunkee.

*

Vivien was working harder than ever and was grateful to her team for all their support. However, she knew she'd have to suffer through the Dunk Your Boss booth and the probability was high she'd get drenched, so she'd planned ahead and brought a full change of clothes.

The Smart brothers interrupted the festivities briefly to welcome everyone and to say thank you. Each brother wore a small, high-tech microphone looped over one ear.

Alex addressed the company. "Since our IPO we've been on a meteoric rise. The big news we want to announce today is that based on industry revenues we are number two, behind Nike!"

A huge cheer reverberated across the crowd. Alex and Malcolm exchanged a few quips, then alluded to a little surprise they would unveil later. There were smiles all around as employees enjoyed the party and reveled in their success as a company. The Smart brothers slipped away.

On the plaza between the Stadium and the Willamette River bank, a large circle was painted on the ground with a square with a large H inside it. Vivien noticed the new addition and wondered what it was. It was hard to see, as it was behind the barbecue pit and smoke obscured the view.

Vivien and Tim joked around with employees as they did a tour of the different game booths. She kept an eye on the Dunk Your Boss booth to see who was currently getting soaked. At one point, an extremely long line snaked around the plaza for the booth. Not too hard to guess who was in the hot seat: Duncan. Tim gave her a nudge and they both chuckled.

Fortunately for Duncan, the company comprised mainly runners, not ball players, so many employees who tried to dunk Duncan were not successful in their three allotted attempts. He did go in the tank a fair number of times, though–more than any other executive. Climbing out of the tank after his last drenching, he wrung the water out of his socks.

"Bloody hell," he snorted, "I should have brought along some goddamn dry clothes!"

Tim was up next in the booth and only got soaked a few times.

Then it was Vivien's turn as the target. She had to laugh at some attempts to hit the target. Aileen threw the baseball so wildly it bounced off one of the other game booths.

"Hey, Aileen, no need to throw that badly on purpose!" Vivien joked.

J. J. was up next. Uh-oh. He had once played AAA baseball. Vivien was still dry at that point, but her number was up.

J. J. called out, "Hey, V, remember that seven thirty a.m. meeting you called last week? Payback!"

He hit the mark on the first try, and Vivien barely had time to take a breath before plummeting into the tank. Coming up for air, she swung her wet hair back and wiped the water from her eyes.

"Nice one, J. J." She scowled at him in jest, climbing back onto the platform.

Out of thin air, the voices of Alex and Malcolm Smart came over the loudspeakers, but they were nowhere to be seen. Heads turned in every direction as the brothers joked about a big surprise. In a few moments, it would become clear...the brothers were hovering above the campus in a sparkling new helicopter adorned with the Smart Sports torch logo. They waved down at the cheering crowd, and Vivien climbed on top of the dunking tank, shielding her eyes from the sun, to get a better view. She got a reprieve from dunking as everyone's eyes followed the Smart brothers.

Alex said, "Hey, everyone. This is our new toy, but also a practical one. We can make quick trips to the airport or the distribution center in it."

Sitting behind him, Malcolm said, "Today we're being flown by Ted, a retired army helicopter pilot."

Ted's gravelly voice crackled like an old recording; he sounded just as a craggy old military guy ought to. Ted flew the helicopter way back down the river and did some fancy maneuvering over the Broadway Bridge, flying low over the river. As he swooped over the campus he described his route.

The helicopter made its final turn to zoom back to campus. Just then a small flock of geese approached from the opposite direction. Ted didn't see the birds until it was too late and let out a yell. One goose crashed through the front windshield. From down on the plaza, Vivien could see the pilot suddenly slump over the controls.

"Ted! Ted!" Alex cried as he grabbed the bird, whose wings fluttered wildly in the cockpit from the air whipping around inside.

The helicopter sputtered and started to move in a slow spiral. Everyone stood frozen in shock, utterly silent, as they watched the horror unfold. Alex tried pushing Ted's body back, but they were spinning out of control and losing altitude quickly. The copter was dancing dangerously close to campus–it looked like they were going to drop right down onto the plaza, crashing on top of the Smart Sports employees.

Malcolm shouted helplessly, "No! Hit the water, hit the water!"

Vivien climbed down from the platform and ran to the edge of the plaza. She was close to where the helicopter might come down, but she had a clear view inside the cabin. Malcolm ripped off his safety harness and lurched forward over the pilot, grabbing the cyclic control stick. At the last second, the helicopter banked sharply left and dove straight into the Willamette river, to the screams of the employees, who could only stand there and watch in panic. The rotors slowed to a stop.

Vivien turned back and pointed at J. J., shouting, "J. J., call 911 and get three ambulances."

Tim had moved next to her.

She grabbed his arm. "Let's go."

Without hesitating, the two of them jumped into the river and swam the short distance to the now partially submerged copter. All three men were unconscious. The cabin was filling rapidly with water. Tim yanked the door open. Vivien wriggled inside to grab Malcolm. Tim unclipped Alex's harness and pulled him and the pilot out of the sinking helicopter.

They swam to the surface. By that time, Duncan and Johnny O had jumped into the water. Vivien passed Malcolm gently along to them, then turned to assist Tim with Alex, whose head was bleeding profusely. Other employees jumped in to help.

Someone laid a bunch of tablecloths on the ground to serve as blankets. Vivien checked Malcolm's vital signs to see that he was breathing and she instructed someone to look after him. The pilot was unresponsive and looked well past the point of resuscitation, but she quickly gave CPR instructions to Johnny O and Dunk to help the pilot. She moved over to Alex and could not detect a pulse or any evidence of breathing.

Panting, she called out, "Tim, help me. I'll do two breaths, then you do fifteen compressions two fingers up from the sternum, here."

Within several minutes the paramedics arrived. Vivien briefed them as they took over.

She stepped back, heart pounding, and stood alongside the other dripping-wet executives.

Doug ran up. "You okay, V? Jeez, you jumped in so quickly."

"I…I just knew we had to help them."

"Damn brave of you," Doug stated.

"Well, I was wet anyway," Vivien said feebly.

"V, you've got balls of steel and a heart of gold." Doug had someone toss him a blanket, which he draped around her shaking shoulders.

Ron joined them, the color drained from his face. Vivien looked around and saw all the employees sitting on the ground in shock, many in tears. She turned to see the Smart brothers being loaded onto the ambulances and the pilot now covered up with a sheet.

Bowing her head a little, Vivien said, "Ron or Doug, maybe one of you should say a few words. Let them know we'll keep them posted on how Alex and Malcolm are doing. Someone should also call their families right away."

"Yes, good thinking, V." Ron nodded. "I'll get in touch with their families. Doug, can you make a brief statement and send people home? It's been a hell of a day. Steele, can you deal with that?" He gestured to the commotion near the ambulances. News vans.

Steele was in his element and he took off running toward the reporters.

Vivien didn't feel like talking to anyone, let alone the media. Ears still ringing from the sickening sounds of the crash, she made her way back to her office to change and then head to the hospital.

✳

Later that evening, when Vivien returned from the hospital, her heart was heavy. Clay had flown in and was waiting at home for his fiancée.

"I saw the news about the accident. Horrible. Are you okay, Vivi?" He wrapped his arms around her in a tight embrace.

"Oh, Clay, it was awful. Malcolm's in terrible shape and Alex is even worse. It doesn't look good."

They sat down on their living room sofa together. Vivien was trembling. "I can't believe what happened. It's crazy how quickly things can turn."

Clay's expression was serious. "I know, babe. Seems like such a short time ago we were at Malcolm's house laughing it up and enjoying their company. God, I sure hope their families are doing okay."

Shaking her head, Vivien said, "I just pray Malcolm and Alex will be all right."

✳

The next morning when she arrived at the Smart Sports campus, there was an emergency meeting for senior executives. When they'd gathered together in the conference room, Ron sat in front of them.

"I'm afraid I have some terrible news." He looked drained.

Vivien's heart dropped into her stomach. *Please don't let the news be too bad.*

"As you saw yesterday the pilot of the helicopter got knocked unconscious by the bird strike, which caused the helicopter to spin out of control. Ted was pronounced dead at the scene. When the aircraft crashed Alex suffered a severe head injury. Last night he had a massive cerebral hemorrhage and..." His voice lowered to a whisper. "We lost Alex early this morning."

Oh dear god. Tears welled up in Vivien's eyes. Alex was so full of vitality, and he'd left behind his dear wife, Tina, and their son and daughter.

Around the table people choked back sobs.

Ron continued unsteadily. "The news about Malcolm isn't promising either–he has a fractured spine, broken ribs, and head trauma that was causing swelling in his brain. To make matters worse, he slipped into a coma shortly after Alex died. We're all praying for him, but no one knows if or when he'll come out of it."

Tim said softly, "This is unbelievable. They were the heart, the soul, and the brains of this company."

Everyone nodded.

Ron said, "We've got to share the news with the employees. I need for you, as leaders, to keep your teams calm and focused. We'll just have to wait and see if Malcolm can pull through."

*

At ten o'clock that morning a company meeting was called, with everyone asked to come to the Stadium. Ron Billings stepped up to the microphone, his posture stooped over as if the weight of all that had happened was too much to bear.

"As many of you have heard, we've lost our dear founder Alex Smart. He passed away early this morning." Ron's voice cracked. "Malcolm is in critical condition and has slipped into a coma. We don't know what will happen with him. We're sending our prayers to their families during this tragic and terrible time." He paused, and it looked as if he might not be able to continue without breaking down.

The audience was silent, except for some muffled sobs.

He took a deep breath. "I have another piece of news to share. The board of directors met early this morning today to discuss a transition plan for who will lead the company while Malcolm is recovering from the accident. To that end, the board decided to go with a leader who has proven himself over the past ten years with Smart Sports."

He paused, looking obviously uncomfortable at having to share the news. Vivien was sitting in the back of auditorium and had already guessed what he was about to say.

"The board has chosen Duncan Doric to lead Smart Sports. Please welcome our interim CEO, Duncan."

Ron looked stage left as a triumphant Duncan strode out waving. For the occasion he wore a black deep-V-neck T-shirt and hoodie with jeans along with Smart Sports footwear. His hair glistened under the stage lights.

Subdued applause sounded. It appeared that people weren't as excited about the announcement as Duncan.

Duncan was smart enough to make it short and sweet. "I'm so honored to have the interim CEO role and hope I can do it justice. We're all praying for Malcolm to make a quick recovery and our hearts go out to Alex's family."

While Vivien wasn't enthusiastic about the announcement, she didn't anticipate any problems with Duncan. She'd been performing so well–how could anything bad happen to her, even if she didn't have the Smart brothers around to protect her?

After the company meeting broke up, Vivien went to congratulate Duncan and then returned to her office. Ron popped his head in the door.

"Do you have a minute, V?"

"Sure, Ron, come on in. What's up?"

"I wanted to let you know this is the end of the road for me."

Vivien leaned against her desk and crossed her arms. "What are you talking about?"

Ron scratched his neck and sat down. "I've worked long and hard to help the Smart brothers build this company, and I've enjoyed every moment working with them. Alex and Malcolm are two of the best people I've ever had the privilege of knowing." His eyes held a look of melancholy.

"I understand; I feel so fortunate to know both of them."

Ron shook his head. "But in dealing with this tragedy, I'm realizing how important it is to spend my remaining time with my family. Who knows what life has in store? So, I'm going to turn in my resignation at the end of the month."

"Gosh, Ron, I'm so sorry to see you go. This is the time when we need a levelheaded executive like you. But I appreciate what you're saying," Vivien said. "Who's going to take your place?"

"I'm going to recommend they bring in an experienced HR professional from the outside. Hopefully Duncan will take my advice." Ron raised an eyebrow. "Anyway, I'll still be knocking around Portland after I leave the company, so if you ever need to talk, give me a shout."

They gave each other a heartfelt hug and then Ron was gone.

CHAPTER 25: THE GAME CHANGE

It didn't take long for Duncan to show how comfortable he was inhabiting his new CEO role, even though it was an interim job. *I must prove to everyone that this is exactly where I belong. This is my destiny.*

On a Monday morning one week after the big announcement, Duncan felt giddy as he drove down the executive row of the Smart Sports parking garage. Having switched out his old Lexus over the weekend, he maneuvered his brand-new black BMW 7 Series into his parking space. He got out and stood admiring his car, wiping away a couple of spots. Just then Vivien pulled into the adjacent parking space.

Duncan boomed, "Oh, hallo, V. Beautiful morning, isn't it?" Now that he had won the CEO job and the threat from Vivien was nullified he could afford to be convivial.

She stepped out of her Audi A7 and eyed Duncan's car. "Looks like you got yourself a fancy new set of wheels, Dunk. Sweet."

He beamed with pride. "And check this out…vanity plates." The license plates read, "DUNK 1."

"Hmm, which model BMW is it? There are no markings on the car. What, did they make a custom model just for you?" she joked.

His eyes lit up and he chuckled. "Oh, no. I made them de-badge my car before I'd drive it off the lot. I told them everything must go but the BMW logo."

"Really?" Vivien said.

"It's not that hard, all that other stuff is put on with a hot-glue gun. Now my car really stands out. I'm so pleased you noticed, V. And it's got a six-liter, V-twelve engine!"

She nodded. "Uh-huh, very nice, Dunk."

✳

With Duncan in charge of the executive staff meetings, he was free to make the changes he desired. Sitting alone at one end of the conference table, he said, "I've decided to modify the order of things. Instead of each of you giving your updates first, I'll lead off."

Duncan started with a long diatribe. There was a lot he wanted to tell the others, so he continued to talk. Loosening up, he leaned back in his chair, giving his biceps an extra squeeze as he spoke. He worked out hard in the gym and enjoyed the envious glances the others gave him.

✳

Despite being enamored with his new level of power, Duncan had enough common sense to play it safe in the hopes that the CEO role would become his permanently. That meant holding off on any major changes. The one change he did make that caused some ripples was to promote Zac Archer to become the interim head of HR, replacing the retiring Ron Billings. Duncan was able to make a case to the board that promoting from within showed confidence in the talent of the team.

✳

Sitting erect at the boardroom table, Otto Utz stared outside and drained his cup of espresso.

Malcolm Smart had lain in a coma for over a month, and by now his family had moved him to a private medical facility with round-the-clock care and physical therapy. His prognosis was cloudy, with doctors wondering if Malcolm would ever return to normal function.

Smart Sports was a public company, and at the news of Alex's death and Malcolm's coma the stock had taken a hit. Investors weren't sure what the future held.

Otto intertwined his fingers, squeezing his hands together. As chairman he had a fiduciary responsibility to ensure the situation was stabilized and the company regained its footing. He'd called a special board meeting that morning to discuss a solution.

It had been a close vote, but a decision had been made. One of the board members had stayed behind after the room cleared to express his concerns: Doug Hawke.

He stated in his sharp New York accent, "Otto, this is bullshit. You and I both know this is not what the Smart brothers wanted." He glared at Otto, his eyes in a squint.

Replying in his thick German accent, Otto tried to calm him. "Doug, listen, the company is in turmoil right now. How can we put someone who is untested into the role of CEO? As smart as she is, Vivien did not grow up in the sports industry. And she has never led a company, let alone a public sports company. She's not CEO-ready."

Doug harrumphed. "Do you realize that Vivien has accomplished things no other executive has? She's probably the most talented executive in the entire sports industry."

Holding his hands up, Otto said, "I don't disagree about her talent. But being a CEO is about more than talent–it's also about safety. It's about knowing what to expect. Doug, you saw that video of Vivien– she admitted she wasn't leading her team well after her baby's death. How can we expect someone recovering from such a tragedy to take charge of this company? We need someone who is focused. We must go with the safe choice, and that is Duncan. For years he has run the biggest and most stable business here. With Duncan we know what to expect. I play tennis with him every weekend, I'm comfortable with him, he's not going to surprise us."

The sarcasm in Doug's voice was clear. "And the fact that he's your son-in-law has nothing to do with it? Come on, Otto, get real. We have a responsibility to do what's best for the company and we owe it to the Smart brothers to respect their wishes. They wanted Vivien as CEO. She took a dog of a business, turned it around in record time, and made some of the best product in the industry."

"That is true, Doug, yes." Otto tilted his head. "But the timing is not right for Alex and Malcolm's succession plan. Even they were thinking a few years out, and we need someone right now. Let's just join hands and support this decision. Making Duncan CEO is a natural next step and I believe it will calm the jitters Wall Street is having about Smart Sports."

Doug stood. "I was there on the day of the accident, Otto. Do you want to know who jumped in the water first and without hesitation to save the Smart brothers? It wasn't your son-in-law. It was Vivien Lee. She's shown courage, integrity, and a natural ability to lead. Everyone else in the company saw the same thing I did. What has Duncan done to deserve the CEO spot?"

"Please, just give Duncan a chance. I know that in time you will see this is the right choice."

"Otto, I think this decision is going to be a bona fide disaster. At least I'm on record as saying I don't agree with it at all."

Doug stormed out of the boardroom, smashing into Pandy and sending her stack of folders flying.

"Damn it. Oh, sorry about that, Pandy," he mumbled as he bent down to help scoop up the papers.

∗

Pandy had been walking by the boardroom door when she heard two voices in heated debate. Once she heard her boss's name mentioned, she decided to camp out and listen. Finally Doug burst out of the room, clearly perturbed, and nearly knocked her over. From what she'd heard and Doug's expression, Pandy could sense the tide was turning…against Vivien.

She hustled back to Vivien's office and knocked on the door.

"Do you have a minute, V?"

"Of course, Pandy, come on in. What's going on?"

Pandy closed the door behind her and sat across from her boss. "I just overheard a really disturbing conversation."

"Oh? Between whom?" Vivien pushed aside her papers, giving Pandy her full attention.

"It was between Otto and Doug. There was a special board meeting called to discuss who would become the next permanent CEO. Apparently there was a video shown of you talking shortly after baby Lily's death, saying you were finding it difficult to focus on the business."

Vivien's breath left her. It suddenly dawned on her. *Rebecca. She was recording me at the party.* It felt like someone was strangling her.

"Otto was lobbying hard for Duncan and Doug violently disagreed with him, but when it came to a board vote it sounds like Duncan won." Pandy bit her lip.

Vivien shook her head in disgust. "Thank you for sharing that with me, Pandy. I don't know how things are going to play out now. We can only hope for the best."

Even though Women's Apparel had outgrown Men's Apparel recently, Vivien was beginning to feel uneasy.

*

With some reluctance the board made Duncan the permanent CEO of Smart Sports as of March 1. For the first time in its history the company had a new CEO. That gave Duncan the green light to implement sweeping decisions he'd been planning.

Duncan's first order of business as CEO was to make some organizational changes that would send shock waves throughout Smart Sports. He called a company-wide meeting to share his decisions.

Standing tall upon the stage, Duncan was in his element. "I'm really excited about these org changes, which will strengthen how we lead this company. First, Johnny O'Connell is being promoted to the new role of COO, reporting to me. In terms of the divisions, Tim Kelley will continue to be president of Women's Footwear, and we'll begin a process to find my replacement for Men's Footwear. Vivien Lee remains president of Women's Apparel. And the highly talented Rebecca Roche will become president of Men's Apparel."

Huh? The last announcement was one that everyone in the company had difficulty swallowing.

Vivien recognized the game plan–Duncan was drawing his circle in more tightly, closing it off to others who weren't in his clique. He was putting people he trusted into key positions of power. Though she was still one of the top executives, the rules had changed and now she'd have to figure out how to play the game all over again.

*

At the first executive staff meeting with Duncan as CEO, things were different. As the executives walked into the room, Duncan's assistant, Marla, handed them a sheet of paper.

"What this?" Tim asked.

Marla replied, "A seating chart for how Duncan wants the room organized."

Duncan's closest allies sat near to him, while outcasts like Vivien, Tim, Klaas, and CIO Norm were seated at the far end of the table.

Rebecca breezed in and air-kissed everyone on both cheeks.

"Ooh, I'm so excited to work more closely with you guys," she squealed. Rebecca gave Vivien a slight smile, just for show.

Tim whispered to Vivien, "What on earth is she wearing?"

As a professional woman, the sight horrified Vivien. Rebecca wore a sheer cream-colored blouse with a lacy blue bra underneath that was clearly visible. On the bottom, she had an extremely short pair of Kelly green shorts, ivory pearlized stockings, and black high-heel pumps that added at least four inches to Rebecca's short stature. She was dressed more appropriately for appearing in a music video than for work.

Vivien smirked and whispered, "Lindsay Lohan called and she wants her outfit back."

She and Tim chuckled softly, while Rebecca made herself comfortable in the seat next to Duncan's. Her bizarre attire didn't seem to bother the other guys, whose eyes skimmed over her body, especially Duncan, whose gaze lingered a bit too long. Rebecca seemed to soak it all up, using sex to her advantage.

After droning on about mundane items, Duncan fidgeted uncomfortably. "Well, we've had a request from *Fast Company* to do a profile on Smart Sports. They asked to speak to a few executives, but given the company is in a state of upheaval now, it's best that I handle the interview. You guys focus on keeping your teams running the business properly."

"Sounds great, Dunk. I'm sure you'll make us all proud," Rebecca cooed.

There was no discussion. Duncan was his own PR machine.

CHAPTER 26: UNSPORTSMANLIKE CONDUCT

Vivien noted Duncan's new and annoying habit of making impossible demands.

"Guys, I want you to move up the launch of the Speed Demon shoe. As the new CEO I need to have a big win in the market and show Wall Street that we're back on track."

Johnny O cocked his head. "But, Dunk, the shoe isn't ready."

"We're still having problems perfecting the fit," Tim said.

Duncan stood up and leaned on the conference table. "Look, the ad time has already been bought; we have no choice. You guys need to just make it happen."

No one said it out loud, but they knew the Smart brothers would never deliberately launch a shoe that was ill fitting. Duncan was already making bad calls.

*

After the meeting, Klaas grumbled his concerns to Vivien.

"You know what I find even more annoying?" she said. "Duncan's on a power trip when it comes to time." Vivien scowled. "He's never on time–for anything. Have you noticed? In the beginning he'd show up twenty minutes late for a meeting, just to show he was the MIPR."

The Dutchman huffed, "*Ja*, I know. What's the MIPR?"

Vivien said, "That's my acronym for the 'most important person in the room.' He makes everyone wait for him."

Klaas giggled, "Hoo-hoo, that's a good one. I've been in meetings where we've waited for him for forty minutes! And last time I had a one-on-one touch-base with him, there was a huge line. I got home after dinner that night."

*

"There's a row of club chairs in the hallway outside Duncan's office," Vivien said as she chopped up garlic cloves with more force than necessary. "It's like a principal's office, where executives have to wait for their turn to see the new CEO. A colossal waste of time."

Clay took the cutting board and dumped the garlic into a pan, where it sizzled in olive oil. "Duncan wants to know that you showed up for your meeting at the appointed time, right?"

She leaned against the counter. "Right."

He grabbed a wooden spoon. "If I were you I'd check in with his assistant and then leave." His blue eyes held a look of intensity.

"That's perfect." Vivien rubbed her hands. "I'll see how late he's running and then leave my notebook, which has my name on the cover, and my water bottle on one of the club chairs. That way it will look like I just walked away for a minute."

Clay laughed, "Yeah, meanwhile you can head back to your office to get some work done. Then just go back to his office when he's close to being ready for you." He stirred the garlic around in the pan.

Vivien took a sip of wine and let out a sigh. "That's so much better than being forced to sit outside his office for an hour or more."

She started using that tactic and wasn't late for a meeting with Duncan once.

*

Regardless of Duncan's boorish behavior, Vivien managed to stay under the radar...until he started pulling his *I've a favor to ask* move.

One day Duncan came to her and said, "V, I've a favor to ask of you."

"Okay," Vivien replied, taking the bait. "How can I help?"

"I need you to do a rather intricate analysis of the problems we're having with some wholesale accounts."

"Sure, no problem."

Dutifully, Vivien completed the work—in addition to her other priorities—and brought a pile of bound presentation books to share at the executive staff meeting. Despite having her on the agenda to present the analysis, when they ran short of time Duncan said, "Oh, bugger. V, mind if we bump you to next week?"

This happened week after week. Then Duncan would forget about his last request and pull his *I've a favor to ask* move again, giving her another onerous assignment. Vivien finally caught on. Duncan was wasting her precious time and diminishing her importance in front of the other executives. Another game. She started bringing a folder of bound books which were actually a bunch of blank sheets of paper with a cover sheet. Eventually Vivien even stopped that charade.

The next time Duncan gave her an extra assignment, she agreed but simply neglected to do it. This cycle continued until she ran into a hiccup. When Duncan was again about to skip over Vivien's latest analysis, Johnny O interjected.

"Hey, Dunk, why do we keep bumping V off the agenda? Let's give her a chance to share her analysis, I'm sure she's got some good stuff to show us." Johnny O smiled supportively.

Duncan looked surprised, Vivien doubly so. She had zilch.

Ever the quick thinker, she said, "Why, thanks, Johnny O. I happen to have my presentation on a thumb drive back in my office. I can ask Pandy to set up the projector and bring the thumb drive. Shouldn't take more than ten minutes to set up, and I have about thirty minutes of detailed material. Of course, if there are more pressing things you want to cover I can find another time to share it. Your call, Dunk."

She knew Duncan's decision would be to put it off indefinitely. In the end, Vivien stopped doing the bogus work and never presented her extra assignments to the executive team.

*

In the month and a half since becoming CEO Duncan had led Smart Sports on a spending spree–a big-ticket item on Duncan's shopping list was the purchase of another corporate jet, intended solely for his use. His rationale was that as CEO he needed the freedom and flexibility to travel at a moment's notice.

"Another jet? That's an expensive toy," Vivien said as she ran alongside Tim.

"Did you hear he also bought some land in Maui? I heard him saying he intends to build a magnificent second home there worthy of a CEO…more grand than Oprah's retreat."

Vivien rolled her eyes. "Oh, please."

"So, what do you think Duncan has in store for this year's Smart Sports Games?"

"I have no clue, Tim. Maybe some events he can actually win." She gave a wry smile.

*

Vivien couldn't have been more right. Duncan hadn't fared well in the last Smart Sports Games, so this year's contests were tailored to suit his strengths: skiing, tennis, and golf–never mind this was a company founded by runners.

As usual, there was a Red Team and a Blue Team, but only the top fifty executives were invited to compete, so every contestant would have to participate in every event. There were grumblings from the rest of the employees about the exclusivity of this year's games–a sharp contrast to previous years, where the focus had been on building team spirit. Zac Archer handpicked the teams, and it was clear the deck was stacked in favor of Duncan's Blue Team. No surprise, Vivien, Tim, and Klaas were on the Red Team.

The games kicked off on an overcast April day with Steele revving up the crowd to greet their guest athlete, Justin Stewart. Justin was even more massive and muscular than the last time Vivien had seen him; his bulging neck veins appeared poised to burst with steroid-saturated blood.

Justin bumped fists with Steele and Duncan. His constant on-court antics made him unpopular with women and people of color, so as Justin said a few words to the crowd most employees listened without enthusiasm.

The first event was a roller-ski race along the banks of the river, in which contestants wore elongated inline skates. The event was fun to watch as there were some spectacular crashes. Fortunately each contestant wore a helmet, knee pads, and wrist guards. Because no one, with the exception of Duncan, had ever tried roller skis, there was a lot of awkwardness involved.

Vivien had a bad tumble at the beginning of the race but managed to recover. The big surprise was that Klaas was an excellent skier and clocked in the fastest time by far. The final heat came down to Duncan and Klaas.

As the two men crouched at the starting line, Duncan whispered something to him. The cheerful expression left Klaas's face and his lips turned white. As the gun went off, they scrambled to get a good start and transitioned into a smooth pace. Klaas was building a comfortable lead, but as they neared the finish line he grabbed his hamstring and came to a stop. Duncan whooshed past him, crossing the finish line, arms raised in victory.

Vivien ran up to her teammate. "Klaas, are you okay?"

His face reddened. "Ah, yes. I just got a cramp in my leg here."

"Oh really? That's too bad. It looked like you had it in the bag."

"*Ja.*"

From the sheepish look in Klaas's eyes, Vivien could tell exactly what had happened.

She frowned. "Klaas, I hope Duncan didn't make you throw the race."

Klaas stared at the ground.

"Well, you better get some ice for that leg, my friend."

Duncan's Blue Team took the skiing event and was in the lead.

*

The next event was a timed golf event. Each contestant was given a large bucket of balls and had to hit as many balls as possible into various wooden targets with a netted hole in the middle, all with the same point values. The time allotted was thirty seconds. Duncan's teammates weren't following any sort of strategy and were splaying golf balls everywhere.

Vivien watched the first few contestants, who tried hitting balls into each of the various targets. With every new target, they'd have to adjust their stance and their aim. A waste of precious time. When her turn came, she'd be more strategic–pick one target and just drill balls into that one. Vivien executed her plan and got the most balls into the target in the shortest amount of time. She advised her teammates to use the same strategy. While Duncan and Johnny O performed well, Rebecca was hopeless. The Blue Team couldn't make up the point deficit, so the Red Team handily took the golf event.

*

The last event was held on the tennis courts–an automatic ball machine launched tennis balls, which the contestant had to volley back into huge buckets with different point values. Since the Red and Blue teams were tied, the final event would determine the winner. Tennis balls shot out of the launcher at lightning speed. Tim and Klaas stood close to Vivien, watching the event, as Johnny O flailed around trying to return every ball. It was comical. Rebecca did a bit better but screeched a couple of times when she was hit by flying tennis balls.

Points were awarded for the number of balls hit into the different-point-value buckets in one minute. Managing time was important, but more critical was accuracy. With the speed of the balls coming out, Vivien realized it wasn't possible to hit every ball well.

"Tim, there's no penalty for not hitting every ball, is there?" Vivien asked.

"Nope. Doesn't seem like these folks remember that detail, though," he chuckled.

"Know what? I'm just going to hit every other ball." Vivien squinted. "I'll aim for the highest-point bucket."

Klaas nodded. "Great idea, V, that should give us a better chance of winning."

When Vivien's turn came she did as she planned and was more accurate with her shots. Klaas and Tim followed suit, and the final contest came down to a tiebreaker between Duncan and Vivien.

Waiting for his turn, Duncan smiled at Vivien, looking supremely confident. For the tiebreaker they changed things up a bit. There was only one bucket to hit into, but the one-minute time frame was the same. As Duncan started his turn, the tennis ball launcher was noticeably slower, making it easier for him to hit the balls into the bucket.

As emcee, Steele gave live commentary, along with Justin. "Great performance from our CEO, Duncan. He hit forty-two of the fifty total balls into the bucket." Duncan flashed a grin in triumph as his Blue Team buddies crowded around him, high-fiving their boss.

Vivien stepped onto the tennis court and looked back at her team. She noticed Klaas wringing his hands. Clutching the tennis racket, she stood ready for the contest.

Steele proclaimed, "Start the clock."

Indeed the big clock started counting down the time, but no balls came out of the machine. Five seconds went by…then another three. The entire crowd protested loudly.

"What's going on?"

"Start shooting the balls!"

"Come on, guys."

Finally the tennis balls came out, but at a snail's pace.

Vivien glanced at the clock and realized time was running short with just over forty-five seconds remaining. She called out to the ball machine operator, "Hey, Bill, triple the speed!"

With that the dial was cranked up and a barrage of balls hurtled toward Vivien. She concentrated so hard she didn't even hear all the cheering. She hit her forty-fourth ball into the bucket just as the buzzer signaled time was up.

Vivien had beaten Duncan's score by two points to clinch the victory for the Red Team. Tim, Klaas and the rest of the Red Team rushed in to congratulate her. But instead of announcing the winner, Steele was huddled in a discussion with Duncan, Zac and Justin.

Steele announced, "The judges need to confer about this event. We'll take a short break and get back to you."

*

Pandy ran up to congratulate her boss on her performance in the tennis event. "That was some clutch shooting, V!" She gave her a hug.

"Oh, thanks, Pandy. I'm still recovering from the first event." Vivien rubbed the bruises on her shin.

Pandy and Vivien chatted as they watched Duncan, Steele, Zac, and Justin retreat to the glass-enclosed conference room in the Stadium, visible to all the employees. They talked for a bit until Duncan signaled someone outside the door.

Marla came out and walked over to the two of them. "Vivien, they'd like to speak with you inside."

Vivien shrugged at Pandy and made her way into the Stadium.

Pandy and every other Smart Sports employee watched attentively. Vivien entered the conference room and, still standing, listened to what Steele had to say. Duncan sat at the end of the table and threw up his arms as he spoke. Vivien gave a slow nod and left the room. A keen observer would have had difficulty assessing what happened based solely on watching her unflappable display; even Pandy didn't have a clue.

The four guys came back outside and Steele stepped up to the microphone.

"After the judges reviewed the last event, the conclusion is that one of the contestants had an unfair advantage."

Obviously! Duncan had a huge advantage since there were no balls to hit for the first fifteen seconds of Vivien's turn, Pandy thought, nodding her head in approval of her boss's triumph.

Steele continued, "Because the ball machine was operated at a faster rate for Vivien, that gave her an unfair advantage and enabled her to hit more balls into the bucket. The judges have decided to disqualify her from this event, and that means the winner is Duncan Doric. It also means the Blue Team takes the title. Congratulations, Blue Team!"

There was some cheering, limited to Duncan and a handful of his teammates. Pandy crossed her arms. This wasn't fair. And this sure wasn't the Smart Sports she knew.

*

After the whole Smart Sports Games debacle, Vivien tried not stand out too much or do anything to publicly challenge Duncan.

One Sunday night in early June just before she and Clay were going to bed, their home phone rang. The caller ID indicated it was a local number.

Who could be calling me at this time?

"Oh, hallo, V. How are you?" Duncan sounded like he'd had one too many beers.

Too late, she remembered that the prior week Marla had collected a bunch of personal information from each of his direct reports: their home address and phone number, the name and occupation of their partner/spouse, and a detailed résumé.

"I'm fine, Dunk. How are you?"

"Good, good. What are you up to?"

"Well, it's late, so I was about to go to bed. Is there something you need?"

Vivien tried sounding friendly but she was annoyed he'd intrude on her privacy. Still, she had to appear cooperative. Just last week Duncan had cut her marketing budget, so she didn't want to provoke him into making any more damaging decisions.

"As a matter of fact, V, I've a favor to ask of you."

Not the dreaded phrase. What is it this time?

"I just realized I'm to give a presentation to the entire group of summer interns, and I'm double booked, so I can't do it. As CEO, my schedule is totally swamped."

"I'm sure it is, Dunk. So do you need me to help with the presentation?"

"If you can give the presentation in my place, V, that'd be great. It's already written, you just need to present it."

"Okay, no problem."

"Wonderful, thanks."

She could hear him sigh in relief.

"When's the presentation, Dunk?"

"Oh, tomorrow at eight a.m."

Nothing like some advance notice, boss.

Duncan continued, "I put the presentation on a flash drive so you can pick it up from Marla tomorrow morning, before you head over to the Stadium. Thanks much, V. Cheers."

Doing this "favor" meant shifting around her busy schedule and getting to work earlier so she could at least look at what she was supposed to present. She fired off an email to Pandy on what meetings to move, and she sent a message to Marla to arrange getting the flash drive.

First thing in the morning, Vivien stopped by Duncan's office to see Marla in a state of panic.

"I can't seem to locate Duncan's thumb drive–I'll have to call his cell."

Vivien responded calmly, "Okay, I'll head over to the Stadium and greet the interns, since it's getting close to seven forty-five. Would you please bring the presentation and load it up on the system while I'm stalling for time?"

"All right, Vivien, I'll run over and get it set up ASAP."

Vivien would have no chance to review what she was presenting before she got up onstage–she'd have to wing it. That made her cross. She grabbed a few Smart Sports goodies from her office and rushed over to the Stadium.

The auditorium was now packed with two hundred summer interns eagerly waiting for the program to start. Zac Archer was hosting the day.

With his deep tan and slicked-back hair, Zac said, "Welcome, everyone. I'm sure you're all thrilled to be here on campus." He gave them a blinding white smile. "You're so fortunate to be part of our amazing company. Unfortunately, our CEO, Duncan Doric, had something urgent come up so instead we have the president of Women's Apparel, Vivien Lee, here to give the presentation. I promise, you guys are in for a real treat."

Vivien walked out onstage and greeted the crowd. To buy some time and engage the audience, she asked the interns some Smart Sports trivia questions and threw prizes out to the crowd for the correct answers.

"Who knows the name of the woman who designed the Smart Sports logo?"

"How many countries around the world do we sell our products in?"

"What was the name of the first running shoe model we sold?"

Then Vivien looked up. In the control room, Marla was waving at her frantically. Obviously, Vivien couldn't hear Marla, so she subtly pointed to her phone, indicating that Marla should text her.

Marla bent over her smartphone, thumbs flying. Her text read, *Duncan's thumb drive is blank. No presentation on it!!! What should we do?*

She almost laughed out loud when she read the question "What should *we* do?" After all, Vivien was the one standing onstage in front of two hundred people waiting to see a presentation. And she had nothing. *Nice move, Dunk.* She had to come up with something, anything, to say to these folks.

"Listen, you're going to be seeing lots of presentations during your orientation, so I'm not going to bore you with a bunch of PowerPoint slides. Instead, I'm going to share with you something far more interesting and useful...the Smart Sports Seven."

The audience leaned forward, their curiosity piqued. Even Zac tilted his head, eager to know what Vivien was talking about.

"The Smart Sports Seven is my own invention, but you'll find it valuable. It's the three things that make this a unique place to work and the four critical factors you'll need to succeed here."

The audience murmured with excitement. Vivien then laid out the Smart Sports Seven: three differentiators—integrity, ingenuity, and inclusion, and four factors needed to succeed—passion, performance, perspective, and pluck. She explained each in detail, peppered with captivating anecdotes of people in the company who demonstrated each one. The interns were rapt with attention, taking copious notes on what she shared.

Vivien wrapped up. "Good luck to all of you and I look forward to working with you this summer."

Thunderous applause and the buffalo-stampede sound of the seats flipping up was their response. Not bad for a speech she'd made up on the spot. When Vivien looked up at the control booth, she saw Marla jumping up and down and clapping. It made her smile.

On the way back to her office, however, Vivien's smile vanished as she came to the realization that Duncan had set her up–to fail, to look stupid, to be embarrassed, or possibly all of the above. Playing dirtier than ever. What could she do when she loved her job but couldn't tolerate her boss?

*

Vivien walked down the hall toward her office early one morning and heard a big commotion going on in Duncan's office.

Against her better judgment, she poked her head in. "Hey, guys, what's up?"

Duncan was wringing his hands as Johnny O and Steele stared in disbelief at his computer screen. They looked panicked.

"Bloody hell! I just made an utterly daft mistake. Bugger!" Duncan pounded his fists on the table.

Johnny O met Vivien's inquisitive gaze and said, "The CEO of Dick's Sporting Goods sent a message to Duncan and some others to express his great displeasure about a mistake we made. We messed up on a big order and shipped the product for Dick's to the Sports Authority instead." Johnny O rubbed his head. "The CEO's message really pissed off Duncan, who fired off an email to our team about the issue. And he included a few choice words about the Dick's CEO."

"Not everyone's style, but what's the problem?" Vivien asked.

Johnny O explained, "Duncan inadvertently copied the Dick's CEO on the message–he hit 'reply all' by mistake."

"Oh. Not good."

"Yeah, especially when he called the guy a wanker…and worse."

This was a bona fide disaster. Dick's was one of Smart Sports' largest customers.

"It's a bloody catastrophe! What can I do now?" Duncan wailed in a very un-CEO-like manner.

The guys sat there in silence.

"The only saving grace is that CEO is old-school and doesn't check his email until he gets into the office, where he can sit down with his reading glasses. So, you've got a couple of options, Dunk," Vivien said.

He raised his head in interest.

"First option, you can call his cell, admit you sent an email in error, and ask him to just delete it."

Johnny O said, "Scratch that; this guy will want to read it."

She said, "Second and best option, you call his assistant now and tell her you sent an email by mistake. Ask her to delete it from her boss's inbox before he gets in. Then I'd send her a nice bouquet of flowers to thank her."

"Hmm." Duncan looked deep in thought. Then his pupils contracted and his left jaw muscle twitched. Vivien had seen this signal before; the last time was right before he tried feeding her to a shark. Something bad was coming.

"Got it!" A huge smile came across Duncan's face. "I'll call the CEO on his cell, but I'll tell him I sent an email with a computer virus. I'll say it's wreaked havoc on our systems, and he should delete the email unopened and shut down their systems so the virus won't spread. Yeah, that's the ticket!"

"Dunk, that is brilliant! You're awesome, man." Steele clapped his boss on the back.

Johnny O shifted his weight and stared at the floor.

"Um, well, there's just one problem with that, Dunk," Vivien said.

"Problem? What problem?"

"Lying to the CEO of our biggest customer about a fake computer virus is not only immoral, but causing them to shut down their company's computer systems…that's also illegal."

Duncan blinked. "Illegal?"

"As in it's against the law."

His eyes narrowed to slits. Duncan boomed, "The law? Do you

know who I am? I'm the leader of the coolest company on this planet. I'm the CEO of Smart Sports. I *am* the law."

Vivien physically took a step back upon hearing Duncan's statement. *Has he completely lost it? He's not the CEO, he's the dictator of Smart Sports.*

Even his buddy Johnny O raised an eyebrow. "Dunk, you sure you want to do that, man?"

"Everybody out, I need to get on the phone and handle this now," Duncan said, rubbing his hands together in glee as he ushered them out of his office.

*

The issue of Fast Company with the in-depth profile of Smart Sports and its new CEO caused a stir, not only across the sports industry, but with the general public.

Hand over her mouth to stifle her laughter, Pandy brought the magazine into Vivien's office. "V, have you seen this yet?"

Vivien got up. "No, let's take a look. I'm curious to see what Duncan said that's causing all the fuss." They sat down at her conference table.

"I just looked at one of Duncan's quotes in a side bubble...it's a doozy." Pandy pointed.

Skimming over the parts about the history of Smart Sports and Duncan's ascension to the throne after the Smart brothers' accident, Vivien came to the meat of the article–Duncan's take on the business and his plans for the future.

We market to fit, athletic, attractive people. We don't want overweight, lazy slobs wearing our brand...that tarnishes our reputation as an authentic sports brand. We want our Smart Sports logo on real athletes–the ones who've earned the right to wear it.

"Ouch," Vivien said. "That's not going to go over so well."

Eyes wide, Pandy shrugged. "I can't believe he'd say something like that. Don't we want all types of people wearing the Smart Sports brand? Isn't it about getting everyone to be more active?"

Nodding, Vivien said, "Well said, Pandy. That was the Smart brothers' vision exactly. They should have interviewed you instead!" They shared a giggle.

✳

Duncan was particularly frustrated at the next executive staff meeting, which he had moved to Thursday to suit his schedule.

In the past four days there had been major headaches he had to deal with. First was the backlash from Dick's Sporting Goods. Their CEO was still angry about the poor service from Smart Sports and the computer virus debacle–he'd cut their orders by half. Second was that silly magazine article. Somehow certain people found his comments offensive and now some consumers were boycotting the Smart Sports brand. To make things worse, the Speed Demon, their premier running shoe, which had just launched, was being returned in droves by runners complaining the shoe gave them blisters. Retailers were irate.

Uncharacteristically, Steele chastised his boss. "Dunk, your comments in that article about who should wear our brand really threw a wrench into things. I think you need to make some kind of public apology on our website. We're getting killed on social media."

Groaning, Duncan rubbed the back of his neck and frowned. "Okay, guys, I can fix this. I'll record some kind of video apology today. Steele, can you set that up for after lunch?"

Rubbing his shaved head, Johnny O piped up, "Dunk, I just got the updated sales report and Dick's is canceling more orders–this is going to lead to a disastrous quarter. Can you get on the phone with the Dick's CEO and apologize personally or appease him somehow?"

Bloody waste of my time sucking up to these accounts, Duncan thought. He shook his head but replied, "All right, all right. I'll give the CEO a call."

"Another thing," Johnny O added, "the returns on the Speed Demon shoe are really high. It's not good." He held up the returns report for Duncan to see.

Tim tossed his pen on the table. "Remember, Dunk, we warned you about launching the shoe before the fit was perfected. We anticipated having problems with the Speed Demon."

What, so everyone was piling on now? He was the CEO; didn't anyone appreciate him? Why weren't they more supportive? Well, he was still the one calling the shots.

"Listen, Johnny O, I made you COO. I need you to step up and do your job, smooth things over with retailers about the new shoe. Figure out how to solve this." Johnny O gave him a dubious look, which Duncan ignored.

Duncan looked down at his printed daily schedule. "Marla, get the corporate jet fueled up and ready for me to leave by four p.m."

*

It was getting more and more common for Vivien to say less and less in the executive staff meetings. She looked around the room as the other executives stared at the floor.

Duncan's recent screw-ups were costing the company money and destroying millions of dollars of shareholder value. No one had to ask where Duncan was flying to; he was headed to Maui to oversee the construction of his vacation retreat. Duncan was making a mess of things and expecting the others to clean it up.

*

That Friday in late June, when she had her regular Skype call with her Smasher friends, Vivien shared a whole slew of anecdotes about Duncan's megalomania.

"That's bonkers," Andi said. "The guy is a complete power freak. How long can he possibly last as CEO, especially when he's doing such a terrible job?"

"Who knows?" Vivien sighed. "He could be there for a while. He's got the backing of the board of directors."

Sofia chimed in, "You mean his father-in-law? Isn't he aware of the problems Duncan is causing? There's been some pretty serious stuff. What happened when he told that lie to Dick's Sporting Goods?"

Vivien grimaced and shook her head. "His actions caused our biggest customer to shut down their entire computer system for two days while their IT department swept their systems looking for a phantom virus. Who knows what it cost that company in terms of lost productivity?"

Grace shook her head. "All due to Duncan's lie, just to save face." Then she let out a guffaw. "But the worst was his video apology on the Smart Sports website for his outrageous comments in that article. I've never seen a CEO tear up like that!"

"Or be so insincere. You know, he never actually apologized for his comments," Sofia observed, "he just whined about feeling misunderstood. Meanwhile the stock is tanking."

Andi smacked her hand on the table. "How much worse can it get, Vivi? Are you sure you want to stick around?"

"I have no idea," Vivien said drily, not sure which question she was answering.

CHAPTER 27: PLAYING HARDBALL

Duncan made an announcement at the next executive staff meeting. "Our top executives will be accompanying me on a market trip to Europe in mid-July." He adjusted his glasses and looked around the table. "That includes the COO, our three presidents, and Steele." Duncan still hadn't hired a replacement for president of Men's Footwear, so Tim's workload was double these days. *Too bad, so sad,* Duncan thought.

Way at the end of the conference table, Klaas looked stoic.

Duncan continued, "We'll visit several European cities to assess market attractiveness and look more closely at some newly opened Smart Sports stores. The plan is to visit London, Berlin, Paris, and then wrap up our trip in Milan. We'll all take the larger corporate jet."

Vivien raised her hand. "Dunk, just a reminder, I'll be in Asia visiting apparel factories and gearing up to launch our new product line. So I'll fly from China to meet you guys in London. Okay?"

"Fine, fine," Duncan said. "It will be a great opportunity for us to bond further as a team, so I'm looking forward to a great trip." He was also looking forward to a little alone time with Rebecca in Paris and Milan and having a bit of fun.

*

The day before she was supposed to fly to London, Vivien received a cryptic email from Marla relaying a message that Duncan wanted to meet two days later than planned. Grateful to spend the extra time with her team and the factories, Vivien had Pandy adjust her travel plans.

Two days later the Smart Sports executives were scheduled to meet in the lobby of Grosvenor House in London at nine a.m. Vivien was there promptly and sat alone for some time. Finally, around ten forty-five a.m. the executives showed up with the local team. Given their chummy interactions, Vivien assumed they must have bonded over breakfast...without her.

"Hey, guys," Vivien said.

"Oh, Vivien, I forgot you were even coming!" Rebecca said in a shrill voice.

Vivien shrugged and said, "Well, I'm here and ready to get started on our European tour."

Rebecca smirked and Tim gave her a strange look.

"What's up, Timmy?" she asked as he hugged her.

"Fill you in later," he said under his breath.

While the group began their market tour, Vivien and Tim hung back a little.

"What's going on?" she asked.

"Duncan rearranged our itinerary and we all traveled to Paris first, then Berlin. We arrived in London last night," Tim said.

So they'd been bonding as a team without Vivien, plus she'd missed all the retail visits in the first two cities. Day one of the trip and she was already behind the eight ball. Great.

The team was walking to their third destination when Tim's cell phone rang. He chatted a bit and said to the caller, "Hang on, let me get Duncan for you." Covering the microphone, Tim said, "Hey, Dunk, Ethan would like to speak with you."

Duncan snapped, "Ethan? Who the hell is that?"

"Um, he's your lead footwear designer for tennis."

"Oh, right, right." Duncan took the phone from Tim. "Ethan, buddy, what's up?"

Toward the end of a long and tiring day, some of the team returned to the hotel while others splintered off to do a bit of shopping.

Exhausted and jet-lagged, Vivien relished just having a few minutes to rest. When she opened her eyes, it was over an hour later. Still no word from Duncan on team dinner plans. After another thirty minutes she was famished and pinged Tim to see if he wanted to grab a bite.

He texted back, *V, where are you? We're all downstairs at the restaurant. Come join us.*

The rest of the guys seemed welcoming when Vivien showed up, while Duncan appeared to not notice she was there. He was deep in conversation with Rebecca, who wore a low-cut gold tank top and a tight black leather miniskirt.

When dinner was over, Vivien escaped to her room. As she was shutting her door, she heard Rebecca giggling and peeked out to see her and Duncan going into their hotel room together.

✳

Vivien called her fiancé for moral support. "Thankfully, Tim is here, but this trip has been terrible, Clay. I'm left out of things, and whenever I try to fit in with Duncan and his clique I'm rejected."

"Those guys are assholes. Just try to stay positive and upbeat, babe. The trip's almost over, right?"

"Yeah. Just one more stop."

Clay said, "Maybe things will be better in Italy."

✳

Her voice sounded jubilant the next time they spoke. "Clay, you were so right. Milan has been fantastic!"

"Aww, that's wonderful, Vivi. What changed?"

"Well, I was getting settled in my hotel room when my phone rang. It was Duncan inviting me to come have a glass of wine in the piazza."

"Now, that's a surprise. What made him so friendly all of a sudden?" Clay sounded puzzled.

"You wouldn't believe it. His wife, Giovanna Utz, the WNBA star, decided to surprise him and showed up in Milan."

"No way!"

"Duncan was having drinks with Rebecca when Giovanna suddenly arrived, so to avoid suspicion he immediately called me and acted like I was supposed to be there. Made up some story about how with all the male bonding, he felt it was proper to spend regular time with the female executives to get our perspective over a glass of wine. He was sweating bullets."

Clay laughed. "Would've loved to see that. What a jerk. So, what was his wife like?"

"Smart, beautiful, multilingual, and really tall. Great personality. I can't imagine what he sees in Rebecca, who's totally annoying. Anyway, the best part was having Giovanna join us for our team dinners the next couple of nights, so I got to know her pretty well…all under Duncan's watchful eye. Man, was he on high alert."

"That's hilarious, babe. Glad you had some fun. When are you heading back?"

"Giovanna left this morning and the plan was for all of us to take the jet back home today. But Duncan told us to go ahead and he'd have his jet pick him up so he could head back to Paris with Rebecca for a couple of days to study the market. He was probably trying to appease her."

"God, can he be any more obvious? I wonder what the other guys think of all this."

"Well, just to needle him a bit I said, 'Dunk, wouldn't it make sense for me to join you guys, since I missed the Paris market visit the first time around?' I knew he'd never go for it, but I enjoyed seeing him squirm."

"Nicely played, babe. I'll see you tonight. Can't wait."

✳

Feeling like an embattled soldier on weekend furlough, Vivien was thrilled to get home and spend a relaxing weekend with Clay. The night she arrived home he cooked filet mignon and uncorked a great bottle of Pinot.

She was still jet-lagged when she returned to the office that Monday and was confused when she pushed the elevator button for the fourth floor and it didn't work. She pushed it again. What was going on? Just then her phone rang. Pandy.

"Hi, V. Welcome back from Europe."

"Thanks, Pandy. I'm trying to get to our floor but the elevator isn't working."

"I know. Come meet me on the third floor way in the back." Pandy sounded unsettled.

Reaching the end of the hallway, Vivien peeked into a vast room with two tiny windows and saw her assistant seated next to a pile of boxes. She walked through the door. The room housed two small cubicles.

"Where are we, Pandy, Siberia?"

"Pretty much," she sighed. "While you were away in Europe, Duncan had the floor plan of the entire building redone. He's taken over the entire fourth floor. Marla said he renovated and redecorated his floor and had soundproof walls and floors installed. Plus he had electronic locks put on the elevator and stairwells, so you need a special key code to get to the CEO's floor now." Pandy scrunched up her face.

"Okay. So what happened to all the stuff in my office?" Vivien asked.

Pandy pointed to the cubicle with boxes piled everywhere.

"Is this a joke?" So Vivien, who ran the second-largest business at Smart Sports, was now relegated to a cubicle in a huge, empty storage room.

"Apparently Zac Archer was in charge of deciding who would get which office, so he ended up with a primo office, and, of course, Johnny O, Rebecca, Steele, and Charl got the largest and most luxurious offices overlooking the river."

"Hmm," Vivien mumbled.

"Don't feel too bad, V. Tim and Klaas got moved to cubicles, too, and you should see the size of the CIO and chief counsel's cubes–they're smaller than ours!"

One thing Vivien had learned from her boxing trainer was to bob and weave. "Wait a sec, Pandy, we have this entire space, right?"

Her assistant nodded.

Vivien rubbed her chin for a minute and her resilience kicked in. "This may not be too bad after all. Let's lose the cubicle walls and move the desks to the corners of the room. We can grab some of the spare furniture and set it up like a lounge–you know, a casual, open workspace."

Pandy's eyes lit up. "Ooh, we can add some sofas and pillows and funky lamps. Maybe even set up a bar!" The two giggled. "We'll make it the coolest workspace on campus, V. And I'll make sure to get your name on the door."

Their conversation was interrupted by a muffled sound that came from a speaker above.

"Hallo, everyone, Duncan here. I'd like anyone director level and above who's working on the Sports Authority inventory issue to report to the fourth-floor conference room in ten minutes. Call Marla for today's elevator code."

Vivien laughed. "You've got to be kidding. Duncan installed an intercom system?"

"Yup. He can press a button and be heard in every building on campus, just like a high school PA system." Pandy rolled her eyes.

Over the next half hour more Duncan announcements came through.

"Anyone who knows details about Nike's new running shoe launch, call my office straightaway."

"Whoever is leading the marketing campaign for the new tennis shoe, call my office in ten minutes."

And so on.

The only way Vivien would maintain her sanity was to beat these jerks at their own game.

CHAPTER 28: THE FULL-COURT PRESS

The last quarterly Strategic Business Review had been run as normal because Duncan didn't want to signal to the board that anything had changed. But, by early August Duncan was feeling an unprecedented level of clout and decided to do as he wished.

"I'm changing things up a bit," Duncan announced. "We're holding our next SBR in two weeks at the Sunriver Resort near Bend, Oregon. It will be preceded by a two-day executive off-site at Sunriver. All senior executives plus Charl will be attending."

"Sunriver is a four-hour drive from here," Steele said. "How are the board members going to get out there?"

Duncan smiled. "I've arranged for SUV limos to fetch the directors and drive them to the meeting site in style."

"Sweet," Steele replied.

Given the long drive, Vivien wasn't looking forward to making the trip alone. After the meeting broke up she said, "Hey, Timmy, what do you think? Wanna drive out together?"

Tim nodded. "You bet. Of course Duncan, Johnny O, and Rebecca will drive together, and Zac and Charl will buddy up. Steele mentioned he's going to be out there already, so that leaves you, me, and Klaas." The off-site hadn't even started and they were already negotiating political land mines about how to get there.

As if on cue, Klaas ran up to them. "Guys, can we ride together, please?"

In the "outcasts" car, the first part of the drive was quiet. Tim looked pale and thinner than normal. A result of the stress, maybe? Vivien's weight had also dropped recently from all the extra hours of work, and from all the stress. Lately when they ran together, Vivien had noticed Tim's pace and stamina were not what they had been a year ago. But she attributed that to exhaustion.

Tim drove his SUV with Vivien in the front and Klaas dozing in the back.

"The last ten months have been a bear, V. I'm swamped with work, running both Men's and Women's Footwear, and I've got key open positions I'm desperate to fill." He scowled. "I've told Zac I need at least a dozen great footwear designers but he's just sitting on his ass. He spends more time getting himself in magazines than actually doing his job. It's ridiculous."

Vivien snorted. "Are you surprised? Zac's not exactly the Roger Bannister of recruiting." They chuckled.

"I'm thinking about saying something to Duncan," Tim said. "It should matter to him that we don't have the right talent in place for the footwear business. Maybe he can get Zac to move more quickly. I'm also going to give Zac a piece of my mind. Smart Sports has always been a place where honesty is paramount."

Vivien put her hand on his arm. "Timmy, you might want to rethink that one. This is now an entirely different company and in the new Smart Sports it's not always wise to speak your mind. You're right, Zac deserves to be chastised. But will your feedback make him do anything differently? And do you really think Duncan's going to criticize his buddy? He's the one who hired Zac into Smart Sports and promoted him. Sure, you'll feel better, but anything negative you say to Zac will get back to Dunk, so I'd use more caution. There's no upside."

Tim beat his fist softly on the steering wheel. He shook his head and repeated, "No upside, no upside. Yeah, V, you are right. Thanks for the advice, my friend."

They rode silently for a few minutes.

"You know, it just burns me up," Tim said. "Duncan never did anything to earn the CEO role. The only thing he did was not screw up the largest business in the company, that's all. Did he make the business better? No. Did he inject new ideas? Not a chance. Did he create a winning strategy? Nope. Was he great at leading and developing people? No way. The only thing that earned him the role was his relationships and his time in the job."

"Don't forget, Dunk's responsible for 'fourteen major footwear launches,' as it says in his email signature line," Vivien quipped. "I couldn't agree with you more, but welcome to corporate America. It's often not the most qualified individual who gets the CEO role, it's the person with the right relationships, or the most fortunate timing. That's the sad truth."

As they drove on, Vivien tried to lighten the mood. "Okay, Timmy, pop quiz. What was Duncan's phrase of the week?"

Tim's blue eyes brightened. "'Special sauce.'" He nudged her. "Remember you told me that if I used Dunk's favorite phrase of the week he'd be more receptive to my ideas?"

"Yeah."

"Well," he said, grinning, "I was pitching a new product line to Dunk and he was disinterested until I dubbed the line the 'special sauce' of our training shoe offering. Duncan immediately gave his approval. Ha ha!"

"Hey, Klaas, nap time is over. We're here," Vivien said.

Klaas sat up and rubbed his eyes as they pulled into the curved driveway of the Sunriver Resort. They checked in and made their way to their assigned rustic cabins.

*

A team dinner was scheduled that evening, and as Vivien walked into the bar she noticed Duncan holding court with Rebecca, Johnny O, Steele, Zac, and Charl. All conversation ceased when they saw Vivien approach.

"Hi, guys, mind if I join you?" she greeted them brightly.

"Oh, hey, V. We're actually working on something," Zac said.

Trying to get rid of her? Stubbornness kicked in. She refused to be excluded, certainly not by Zac Archer.

"Great, maybe I can help!" Vivien maintained a smiling, friendly demeanor and looked straight at Johnny O.

Her stare prompted Johnny O to say, "Have a seat, V. Can I get you a beer?"

After the team dinner that night, Vivien strolled back to the cabins with Tim. "Ugh, that whole meal was so depressing."

Tim paused to gaze up at the stars. "Yeah, same old same old. Duncan sharing his many inside jokes with his clique, while we sat at the other end of the table. At least we've got each other, V."

*

On the next morning's agenda was to brainstorm the critical priorities for Smart Sports to address over the next two years. Everyone settled into their seats in the conference room while Duncan explained the task for the first half of the day.

He said, "I need someone to take notes on the flip chart. V, would you?" He held out the marker.

She stayed put for a moment. "Actually, Dunk, I'd prefer to focus on participating. Would you mind asking someone else? For some reason, women are always asked to be the scribes and frankly my handwriting's not that great."

"Aw, come on, V, be a team player," Charl said out of left field.

Why was Charl even there? He really didn't have a clear role, and his prodding was irritating.

"I'd rather you do it, Vivien," Duncan said, stepping toward her. His look conveyed that he didn't like being challenged, least of all by her.

She smiled and tried to look cooperative. "Sure, no problem. Just remember, I warned you about my writing."

"I'm sure it will be fine," Duncan snapped.

Vivien grabbed a handful of colored markers, then set up the flip charts. Duncan asked Johnny O to facilitate, and the team threw out ideas for areas they needed to focus on to succeed as a company. Ideas flowed and Vivien wrote fast in a cursive style; the loops of her letters resembled a stretched-out Slinky. She used abbreviations where necessary.

The team brainstormed for ninety minutes before taking a break.

Vivien took a step back. "Oh, wait, I wanted to capture a few more thoughts."

She scrawled additional items in the margins, numbered all the flip chart pages, and lined the markers up in a neat row. As she walked over to the refreshment table she saw Johnny O signal Duncan. She couldn't hear what they said but could make an assumption. Vivien had cheerfully taken notes exactly as she was instructed–but what good were notes that were illegible? Johnny O pointed to the flip charts while Duncan scrutinized them, trying to decipher the writing. Finally he shook his head and took off his glasses.

As the team reconvened Vivien bounded back over and picked up the markers.

Placing his hand on her shoulder, Johnny O said, "V, thanks for taking notes. Why don't you take a break and we'll have Rebecca be the scribe for now. All right?"

"Oh, okay." Vivien sat down pretending to be disappointed.

Tim leaned over and whispered, "I've seen your writing before, V, and it's never that bad." He raised an eyebrow.

Vivien winked. She wasn't asked to take notes again.

After a couple more hours of brainstorming the team had filled ten flip charts. Rebecca put her own stamp on things by indicating with hearts, stars, or flowers the ideas she liked best. In another skimpy outfit of short shorts and high heels, Rebecca was openly enjoying prancing around in front of everyone. The guys groaned at Rebecca's embellishments on the flip charts while they checked out her legs.

Duncan stood up. "Now we have to choose our FINO priorities–our 'failure is not an option' priorities–to keep Smart Sports a dominant player. I'll give everyone three stickers…put your stickers on the priorities you think should be the top three. You can put all your stickers on one idea if you like. Here you go," he said as he tore off sets of three stickers from a page and handed them to each executive.

Everyone dutifully studied the pages and placed their stickers. Where people couldn't read Vivien's writing she translated, so at least everyone knew what they were voting for. Steele put his three stickers on an idea that read, "Make Smart Sports the coolest brand ever." Groan. With all the stickers on the pages, the team took a short break while Duncan, Johnny O, and Rebecca tabulated the results.

They returned from break and two new flip chart pages were in the center of the room with the acronym *FINO* written on top. Duncan talked them through the two pages, with most heads in the room nodding. Vivien's was not one of them. She couldn't help herself: she had to speak up.

"Dunk, I have a question."

Duncan paused. "What is it, V?"

She pointed at the pages. "The items on this list are supposed to be our key priorities, the ones we're focusing on for the next year, right?"

"That's correct." He placed his hands on his hips.

"Maybe I'm just a simple person, but when I have more priorities than fingers to count them on I find it confusing. We have twenty-four

FINO priorities–that's two priorities per month. How can we have that many? Which ones are we supposed to focus on?"

She noticed Johnny O move to say something, but he stopped in his tracks.

Duncan scoffed, "All of them. We have to focus on all of them."

After a lunch break, Duncan started assigning a task leader to each of the twenty-four FINO priorities. With eight people, the average number assigned to each should have been three.

Duncan gave out the assignments. "I'm overseeing the list, so I didn't assign myself as a task leader. Johnny O, you have these three. Klaas, this one's for you. Rebecca, here are your two." Duncan pointed and wrote people's initials next to their assignments. "Timmy, these are your three. Steele and Charl, you've each got two. V, the rest are yours."

Vivien quickly counted and shot back incredulously, "Eleven? You want me to be task leader for *eleven* FINO priorities, Dunk?" Ludicrous.

Did he want her division to fail?

"Well, V, you've had a successful career up to this point. And you're the only executive at Smart Sports with an MBA from the prestigious Wharton School of Penn State. With your fancy education and expertise, this should be easy for you." Duncan gave her a self-satisfied smile.

She didn't bother correcting him on the school name. Instead, Vivien took an acquiescent breath and said, "Okay, Dunk, I'll give it a shot."

*

Hired guides called nature walkers led the executive team on a hike that afternoon, pointing out different plant species and any wildlife they came across. Duncan's clique kept close to him, while Klaas stayed just behind the main pack, with Tim and Vivien bringing up the rear. They hardly spoke at all; they were just trying to get through this off-site. Perhaps this was the one activity they might enjoy.

They reached a vista point, where the Smart Sports executives were asked to sit in a circle and the nature walkers were dismissed.

Zac's eyes twinkled. "We're in for a real treat. I asked Dunk for some latitude to try something new. We're going to do an Inspiration Circle."

Vivien shot a glance at Tim, who shrugged.

"Here's how the Inspiration Circle works," Zac said. "We all chant while a talking stick is passed around. Whoever gets the talking stick holds it up and says a few words about the Smart Sports person who inspires them the most. Then we chant some more and the next person gets the talking stick."

Zac taught the chant and kicked off the Inspiration Circle. He was the first to hold up the talking stick, silencing the group chant. "I don't want to seem like a kiss-ass, but I have to be honest and say my inspiration is none other than Dunk. We've been through a lot, buddy, and we're leading the most amazing company in the world. Your brains, energy, and drive are exactly what we need. You were destined to be our leader, and in my book, you were the only choice for CEO."

Oh god, this is going to be painful. Vivien cringed.

Zac droned on about what a great leader Duncan was, in addition to being a cool guy. Finally he finished and the group resumed the chant until the talking stick was passed to Rebecca. She said solemnly, "Dunk, you're the Steve Jobs of the sports world, only you're more of a genius."

Please. Vivien felt as if they were prying her throat open and forcing her to swallow molten tar.

Steele piled on the Duncan-admiration bandwagon even further. Next was Charl. In keeping with the regularly scheduled programming, Charl picked Duncan as his inspiration.

"Man, you've supported me no matter what, and I really appreciate that, Dunk." Charl wiped away a tear. "You so deserve to be CEO and you're setting a new direction for the company, one that I support a thousand percent."

Duncan smiled appreciatively.

"It's important to me to do work that I'm proud of and work with people I'm proud of, and, Dunk, I'm so proud of you, man," Charl said.

All of Duncan's allies seemed to be driving home the point that he was the right choice for CEO. Did they even have a clue that he was not the Smart brothers' first pick?

Seated next to Charl was Klaas who had been fairly quiet during the off-site so far. Klaas held up the talking stick.

Don't do it, Klaas, Vivien thought, *don't suck up to Duncan like everyone else.*

Klaas cleared his throat and looked at the ground. "For me, there are a lot of inspiring people in the company. For example, the people who come up with new product ideas."

Heads nodded in agreement.

"I even see some inspiring people in our finance and accounting departments."

No heads nodded on that one.

Klaas adjusted his wire-rimmed glasses. "But, if I have to think about the one person who truly inspires me the most and is the soul of Smart Sports, I have to say it is Duncan."

Wimp.

As if his livelihood depended on it, Klaas piled on the compliments, while Duncan pretended to be modest.

The Duncan accolade parade continued until the talking stick came to rest with Tim. He looked like he was dreading what he felt forced to say. On the one hand, he had to play the game, but the internal struggle was obvious. Tim talked about one of his footwear designers who really inspired him. Then he quickly followed with a mumbled comment about Duncan's inspirational leadership.

Everyone was folding like cheap lawn chairs.

Lastly it was Vivien's turn for the talking stick. Did they even care what she had to say? Could she manage to fawn over Duncan? Not her style. She couldn't bring herself to do it and still look herself in the mirror.

"Who inspires me? My team," Vivien said. "My team inspires me every day with their ideas, their dedication, and their joy. Also, the Smart brothers, with their brains, humility, and values, have been a great inspiration to me. But honestly, I want to say that I've found something in each person in this circle that inspires me in some way, so I want to thank each of you for that."

People looked surprised at what they perceived as a compliment from Vivien, and they even smiled.

They inspired her, all right–to triumph over them all.

Afterward Zac declared the Inspiration Circle a victory. And so it was–the Inspiration Circle would go down in the corporate annals as the apex of ass-kissing.

Vivien's biggest disappointment was Klaas, whose vein of thinking seemed to be if he was accepted by Duncan and his clique, no matter the cost, he'd be able to save himself.

*

Elated by the successful first day of the off-site, Duncan gathered his team the next morning and explained how day two would unfold. The executives sat in a U shape around him while Duncan shared his demands.

"Right then, listen up." Duncan leaned back and flexed his biceps. He felt invincible. "We'll spend today preparing for the SBR. Each president will sit individually with me and Klaas for thirty minutes. We'll review a hard copy of your presentation slide by slide so I can give my approval. Then each of you can go to a corner of the conference room and make the changes I want. Any questions?" He adjusted his glasses. "Okay, first up is Tim, then Rebecca, and Vivien last."

Duncan grumbled about Tim's forty-seven slides. "This is pretty long, mate."

Tim scratched his head. "Yes, Dunk, but this covers both Men's and Women's Footwear and includes all the information you requested."

"Well, try and get it down to around forty slides, Timmy. All right?"

Tim gathered up his pages and slunk over to a corner.

Rebecca was up next for Men's Apparel with a presentation thirty slides in length. She sidled up to him and sweetly asked Duncan for his input on the best headlines for each slide, taking copious notes. What a doll. Rebecca craved his opinion, and it made him feel especially clever. And she smiled and did exactly as she was instructed. So easy.

Finally Vivien came over and sat down to review her presentation. She had put together a twenty-five-page overview of the business, sharing financials, growth rates, marketing activities, and new products, and gains versus the competition. Judging from her smile, Vivien felt confident about her presentation. Duncan knew exactly how to wipe that smile off her face.

"You have way too much material here, V," he stated in a clipped tone. Duncan grabbed his Sharpie and started marking pages with huge X's.

Vivien replied, "Actually, Dunk, this is less than I've presented in past SBRs and as it stands it's the shortest presentation of all the divisions." Maybe it was a mistake to have everyone sitting in the same conference room–Vivien had heard his remarks to the other presidents and she knew exactly how long their presentations were.

"We need to cut out the extraneous material. Right, Klaas?" He stared at the Dutchman, knowing he would buckle.

Klaas looked confused and to lighten the mood he joked, "*Ja*, sure, we could cut out the financials." He gave a nervous laugh.

Perfect. Why should Duncan give Vivien the chance to show off with all the great financials for her division? He was the CEO and the spotlight should be on him.

"Good thinking, Klaas." Duncan tapped his finger against his head. He noticed Vivien shooting a death look over to Klaas.

Duncan was on a roll. "I think we can also cut the new-product slides. And how the business is faring versus competition; the board has already heard that before. Let's not bore them with repetitive stuff."

In less than ten minutes Duncan had slashed her presentation down to just six pages. No financials, no exciting new-product news, no information about the major gains in market share versus the competitive field. Now her presentation was exactly the way he wanted it.

*

Vivien leaned back in her chair, feebly watching the train wreck unfold. This was a business review and her chance to show the rapid growth of the division to the board of directors. Now her boss was telling her not to share any numbers? It made no sense.

Her head pounded, a stress headache in full bloom. Vivien felt almost too drained to fight. She hunched forward and said in a quiet tone, "Okay, Dunk, so we're cutting out a bunch of stuff. Won't the board find it odd that mine is the only presentation without *any* financials?"

Duncan looked at her and seemed to be thinking.

"All right then, don't add any slides back, but you can cover the content," he instructed vaguely.

Vivien tossed her pen onto the table. "Share the numbers, but don't put them on a slide? That's what you want, Dunk?" She shrugged.

Duncan got up to get more coffee. "Yes, talk about the numbers but don't show them. Don't add any more slides."

Klaas stared at the floor, avoiding eye contact with Vivien. She had just witnessed him cave in to Duncan–it was the path he'd taken and there was no turning back now.

Walking into an SBR with only six slides would make Vivien's overview look like a light-beer version of what should have been a martini-strength presentation. Was Duncan trying to make her look unprepared in front of the board by eliminating all the meaningful information from her presentation? And what was this bullshit about "talk about the numbers but don't show them"? Her division was turning in the fastest revenue growth in Smart Sports history; as CEO, wouldn't Dunk want to take some credit for that?

Duncan returned and sat down. "All right, V, I think we're done here."

"Okay," she sighed, and retreated to a corner to make the changes.

Each presenter was required to give Marla their final presentation by end of day, so it could be reviewed one last time by Duncan and loaded onto the presentation computer for the next day. No one was allowed to run their presentation from their own laptop.

＊

To close out the executive off-site, Duncan gathered his executive team one more time to talk about what competitors were doing that they might learn from.

People threw out different examples of what the competition was doing well.

Vivien offered, "The launch of Nike's new lightweight training footwear collection in Europe was handled well–they used a clever marketing campaign with product seeding and social media to bring attention to the product."

Duncan snorted, "I wouldn't praise anything that comes out of Nike's European business. I don't think the GM, Julia St. James, is particularly strong–only an idiot would think she was doing something of note."

A slap in the face. It was abrasive for Duncan to disregard Vivien's input so strongly in front of all the others. Smirks were shared among Zac, Rebecca, Steele, and Charl.

＊

That warm August evening Duncan peeled off from the rest of the team to join the board of directors for a private dinner. Vivien was at her limit, having suffered through two excruciating days with the others, so she ordered room service, spoke with Clay, and watched a movie called The Shawshank Redemption. She empathized with the protagonist, Andy Dufresne, who was wrongly imprisoned for years. He kept up his spirit despite savage conditions and plotted his escape over time. It occurred to Vivien that she had the luxury of being free. She was free to choose what she wanted to do, even free to leave Smart Sports if it got to be too much. But she couldn't abandon her team... and she still had much to do, much to prove. Also there was the matter of her stock options–by the end of August her shares would be fully vested and worth millions. Surely she could grind it out a bit longer and try to stay a few moves ahead of Duncan and his band of bullies.

＊

Shortly before the start of the SBR meeting, the board of directors milled about near the refreshment table.

Doug Hawke gave Vivien a hug, aware that others were watching them. "I heard about the Inspiration Circle you guys did. Sounds very uplifting." His eyes held a mischievous twinkle.

"Oh yes, very uplifting. Guess Duncan filled you in on our off-site at dinner?"

"Sure did. Anyway, I'm excited to see your presentation, V. You've got the best financials of all the divisions, so I'm sure the board will be duly impressed."

Vivien looked down and said quietly, "Doug, yesterday Duncan cut my presentation from twenty-five slides down to six. And he took out all my financials. I'm allowed to 'talk about' the financials but not share any numbers. How can I talk about financials without numbers?"

Doug narrowed his eyes and shook his head. "Don't let him stop you from sharing the critical results about your business. I've got you covered." He gave a wink of encouragement.

"Just having you here is a big boost for me, Doug." She smiled.

Vivien had noticed Doug looked a bit drained lately–ever since the Smart brothers' accident, in fact. Maybe all the politics were getting to him, too.

She hadn't slept much the night before and was grappling with how to share her financial results. Vivien stared at the giant spread of fruit on the refreshment table, searching for an idea. Then something clicked and she went off to find someone from the catering staff.

✳

When Vivien walked into the large conference room, she noticed Duncan speaking to Rebecca and Charl in the back corner. Typically only the presidents, the COO, and sometimes the CFO attended. Why was Charl even there?

Duncan gave an overview of the company financials and key highlights. He also showed his usual adrenaline reel of high points over the last quarter. As the video played he leaned back, smiling in his bicep-flex pose, and then self-assuredly gave the rest of his presentation.

Tim masterfully reviewed all of the footwear businesses. Rebecca got up in yet another getup of short shorts and high heels and squeaked through her review of Men's Apparel. She vacillated between adamant statements about her business and giggling about the numbers, which she flubbed but got through with a few assists from Duncan and Klaas.

During the lunch break, as everyone was eating, Duncan suggested that Vivien start her presentation. While she normally kicked things off with some physical activity, her boss told her to skip it since everyone was eating.

"No worries," she said brightly. She had only six slides and plenty of time to fill, so she took her time going through the slides and adding interesting anecdotes about the business. The board seemed genuinely engaged. She wrapped up her last slide.

Then Doug said, "Wait, we're missing something here. Where are your financials? The board has seen them from all the other divisions, and I know I speak for everyone when I say we're interested to hear yours. I assume that's all right with you, Duncan."

Even Otto looked confused.

Vivien gave a shrug and explained, "My financial slides actually got cut, but I can talk about the numbers."

She looked over at Duncan, who nodded in approval.

The catering staff had provided fruit, a chef's knife, a cutting board, and some glass bowls. She placed an apple on the cutting board and sliced it. "I'm going to talk about our business using what I call fiscal fruit."

"The fruit symbolizes our financials. See this sliver of apple?" Vivien held up a thin slice. "This represents the revenues for Smart Sports Women's Apparel at the beginning of this year. And over here"–she pointed to a glass bowl filled with apples–"is what our revenues will look like by the end of this fiscal year. Significant growth, as you can see."

Eyes widened in admiration.

Vivien went on, "Our revenue increased at a growth rate of about four hundred percent. Now, let's move over to bananas. This little slice of banana is what our profits looked like at the start of the year. These bananas show where we will end up profit-wise." She pointed to a stack of bananas on a plate. "Again, a significant jump in performance, as we nearly quadrupled EBITDA."

The directors nodded appreciatively.

"Now, I can't finish the discussion about fiscal fruit without talking about oranges. This orange represents our budget at the beginning of the year. Unfortunately, that budget was slashed severely, so this thin wedge of orange shows what our actual budget looks like." Vivien held it up. "What's the significance of all this? Women's Apparel is on track to deliver the biggest increase in top-line revenue and profits this year, while also having the biggest budget cuts of any Smart Sports division. I'd say that's pretty appetizing." She popped the orange segment into her mouth and ate it.

"Ha ha, fiscal fruit, I love it! This is much better than a lot of numbers on a slide," Otto Utz said, clapping his hands. "Vivien, how did you manage to achieve these amazing results on a shoestring budget? You squeezed more growth out of your division than anyone else."

Vivien explained they'd revamped their website and in-store execution to focus on selling outfits, which increased average spend. They modified the cadence of store deliveries, flowing in product more frequently, to drive store traffic. Lastly, the team set up a temporary flash-sale microsite to sell off markdown inventory to customers in their database, which expanded their maintained margin. "And those were just a few of the efforts we executed."

"Once again, you knocked it out of the park, Vivien," Doug said matter-of-factly as the other directors just smiled. Doug shot a knowing look at Otto Utz. Even Johnny O gave a thumbs-up.

"Excellent work," Otto echoed. "And this is even more impressive compared to our other business units, which are all seeing softness in sales."

Vivien stole a look at Duncan, who shuffled papers and avoided her glance. He shouldn't have been cross with her–after all, she'd followed his explicit instructions. Still, whenever she did something creative to captivate the people in the room, the mere fact that she flourished under taxing circumstances got under his skin. He was the

CEO and didn't want anyone upstaging him.

The last agenda item was an update from Doug.

Doug stood. "As employee number one, I've seen Smart Sports go through struggles and also tremendous successes. And I've served on this board for nearly twenty years." His voice dropped in volume. "But now I have to say good-bye. Due to some serious health issues, I can no longer serve on the board, so I am resigning my post effective immediately. It's been a helluva ride."

"Oh no, that's terrible news," Vivien whispered to Tim.

"I know," he replied. "Doug's such a standout employee and director."

And he had been invaluable as Vivien's ghost mentor. Doug was a seemingly healthy man in his sixties.

Vivien pulled him aside after the meeting. "Doug, what's going on? Are you okay?"

In his typical direct style Doug responded, "I've got the pain in the ass of having prostate cancer. But I have some great doctors at OHSU treating me, and they say my prognosis is good." He put his arm around her. "Don't worry, V, I'll keep you posted."

She couldn't stop the tears from welling up and she hugged him.

"All right, Doug," she said, smiling and stepping back. "And when you're up for it, let's tee it up at the Reserve. I can't tell you how much you'll be missed."

Doug put on a cheerful face, but his eyes held a grave look. Vivien prayed he'd be fine.

*

Vivien and Tim had a relatively quiet drive back to Portland that afternoon, since Klaas hitched a ride with Steele. As Sunriver got smaller in their rearview mirror, the two of them breathed a sigh of relief.

"Thank god that hellish experience is over," Tim said, puffing his cheeks out.

Vivien shook her head. "Timmy, I was this close to losing my mind. That bizarre Inspiration Circle, the over-scripted SBR, and spending all that time with Duncan's clique–it was worse than being forced to watch a marathon darts competition."

Tim laughed. "You said it, V. I can't wait to get home to Chris and the kids. I'm going to pour myself a nice glass of wine and forget it all happened."

PART SEVEN

CHAPTER 29: THE "TOUCH-BASE"

It was sports award night at the MAC Club, only this time Vivien was a known entity and she enjoyed catching up with industry friends.

People expressed sorrow about Alex's death and concern over Malcolm's condition. Unfortunately, since that horrific day in February Malcolm had remained in a coma, and by now it was nearing the end of August. Vivien visited the health care facility regularly to check in on him and share news about Smart Sports. She had no clue if he was even aware of her visits.

When they sat down to dinner at the Smart Sports table it was the usual–Duncan surrounded by his loyal posse. Vivien wondered if the people at the Nike, Under Armour, and Adidas tables were having more fun.

Finally the time arrived for the big award announcement. The athlete presenting the award this night was baseball legend Derek Jeter, who was impeccably dressed in a gray bespoke suit.

Even Klaas murmured, "Wow, what a handsome guy."

Vivien giggled. Derek Jeter was charismatic and articulate. She was so mesmerized by his presence she barely caught what he was saying.

Derek said, "This year's Premier Product Award goes to a first-time winner…Vivien Lee of Smart Sports, for the Electrify track skin." He flashed a brilliant smile.

The audience erupted in applause as a video played Waverly Brown's Olympic moment, when the Electrify track skin was revealed to the world.

Someone elbowed Vivien in the ribs. *Huh?* "V, you won! Go get your award." Tim hugged her, pulling her up out of her chair.

Vivien walked unsteadily in her heels and when she tripped on the first step, Duncan rushed to her side. He smiled and escorted her up the stairs. When they got to the stage Derek gave her a respectful peck on the cheek and handed her the award. Meanwhile, Duncan stepped up to the microphone.

"Hallo, everyone. I'm Duncan Doric, CEO of Smart Sports. I'd just like to say a few words about this win and about Vivien Lee."

Surprised by the win, Vivien stood smiling and felt the weight of the trophy in her hands.

"What Vivien Lee accomplished was nothing..." He paused. "Nothing short of astonishing."

She breathed a sigh of relief.

"The moment Vivien arrived at Smart Sports she changed the game. She turned around a tough business, injecting ideas, innovation, and a can-do attitude. Vivien made hers the most successful division at Smart Sports through her relentless pursuit of excellence. I'm thrilled she's won this award tonight and wanted to take this opportunity to congratulate her." He turned toward her. "Vivien, I hope you continue to inspire the people at our company to strive for new heights."

Duncan Doric was saying this in front of everyone? Was she dreaming? To the audience it must have sounded like a lovefest.

Stunned, Vivien said, "Wow, Duncan, thank you." He hugged her and stood aside so she could speak. "This award was made possible by the incredible talent and effort of my entire team. A year ago we sat at that table"–Vivien gestured–"and Malcolm and Alex predicted we'd win this someday. I guess 'someday' is today, and I'd like to dedicate this award to the Smart brothers and to our entire company. This is amazing, thank you."

Had they turned a corner? Perhaps Duncan had recognized Vivien was an important talent to keep around, that it was in the best interest of the company to finally accept her. Maybe he'd realized she could help him succeed. His public display of respect indicated to everyone that he valued her. Vivien felt a renewed sense of optimism about Smart Sports and her future there.

*

Vivien admired the huge balloon bouquet tied to her desk as she dialed her friend. "Hey, Coop, thanks so much for the balloons. They're awesome and brighten up my workspace."

"Congratulations on your big award, sweetie. I'm so proud of you," Coop said. "Are you taking any time to relax and bask in the glory?"

She huffed. "I wish. This week's going to be crazy. Tuesday morning I head to San Francisco for a two-day off-site with my leadership team, then I return late Wednesday evening. Thursday morning I get on the corporate jet to Napa with the executive team for a Smart Sports retreat for our key accounts for two days. Who knows when I can even do my laundry!"

Coop gave her sage advice: "Don't forget to take time for yourself, Vivi, and realize what you've accomplished. It's a big deal. Enjoy it, okay?"

Vivien chuckled, "Okay, Coop. Thanks again."

*

"I'm off, Clay," Vivien called out. Her fiancé was working from the West Coast for a couple of days, taking conference calls from their Portland condo that day and heading to San Francisco the next, then back to New York.

"Okay, babe, have a great trip. I'll miss you." Clay came over to give her a kiss. "Listen, when you get back there's some stuff we should talk about."

"Stuff?" Vivien was rushing to get out the door but paused for a moment. His tone gave her a funny feeling.

Clay took a step back. "Um, you know, wedding plans, that kind of stuff," he mumbled.

"Okay, sounds great!"

*

Vivien planned to get to campus early and squeeze in a workout before her travels started. As she drove out of the parking garage her windshield was splattered with rain. Strange to have such a soggy day in late August.

Outside, the winds were whipping the rain sideways, making it impossible to stay dry. The gym was warm inside and moist with sweat; the scent of chlorine from the Olympic-sized pool permeated the air. The early morning powerlift class, a combination of weight training and cardio, was Vivien's favorite, and she quickly changed into her workout gear. As she put her phone in her locker she saw a text from Pandy: *Don't forget the van's taking everyone to the airport promptly at 9:30 am. Okay?*

Halfway into the high-intensity class, the director of the sports complex peered through the large windows and made a beeline for Vivien.

"What's up?" she asked, breathing heavily. She stopped and wondered if there was some kind of emergency.

"Duncan's assistant is trying to track you down. She said he wants to see you right away."

"All right, let me at least finish my workout," Vivien panted.

The director said in a low voice, "It sounds pretty urgent; maybe you should give her a call. You can use the phone in the hallway."

Annoyed by the interruption, Vivien set down her barbell and grabbed her towel. Sweat dripped from her brow. She stepped outside the classroom to dial Marla. She was still catching her breath when Marla picked up.

"Oh, Vivien, what a relief. I'm sorry to disturb you, but Duncan emailed me early this morning and said he needed to see you immediately for a touch-base."

"A touch-base? About what, Marla?"

She sighed, "I have no clue. He just indicated there's an urgent issue he needs to discuss."

"I was just in the middle of a gym class. Okay, let me get changed and I'll head up to his floor to see him."

"All right, he said he wants to see you by seven thirty." *Jeez.*

Vivien ran back to grab her water bottle and locker key and made a hasty departure from the workout class. She showered quickly, got dressed, and briefly ran the blow dryer over her bangs so she could get to the executive building by seven thirty. The rest of her hair was dripping wet when she walked into the building.

*

She punched in the security code Marla had given her and pushed the button for the fourth floor, which was now referred to as "Duncan's floor." The elevator stopped on the second floor and Rebecca got on.

"Good morning, Rebecca," Vivien said.

Rebecca gave her an evil sneer. "It sure is." Then she turned abruptly and got off on the third floor. So rude. Rebecca's undeserved promotion to president and continued attachment to Duncan made her more dangerous than ever. Her ego had ballooned and her behavior was insufferable. Recalling J. J.'s line, Vivien repeated it: "A little Rebecca goes a long way."

Their elevator encounter was bizarre and it gave Vivien a bad feeling in her gut. When she reached Duncan's floor, Marla escorted her to one of the conference rooms. On her way there, Vivien ran into Klaas, who was walking with Fred from Finance, who had the misfortune of being Rebecca's fiancé. Vivien felt pure pity for the guy.

"Hi, Klaas, hi, Fred, how's it going?" she asked.

Fred gave her a warm greeting, while Klaas looked startled.

"Klaas, let's grab ten minutes this morning before I head to my off-site. I've updated my quarterly forecast and I'd like to share the improved numbers with you."

The Dutchman hesitated, then replied, "Oh, wow, that is so great, Vivien. Why don't you call me and I'll come to your office." He did not make eye contact.

Vivien turned the corner and entered the conference room. When she walked in, she was surprised to see Zac Archer sitting there. He had a stack of manila folders placed neatly in front of him and greeted her with a toothpaste-commercial grin.

She was about to ask Zac why he was there when Duncan walked in. He took the seat farthest away from her, the one closest to the door. He looked pale. Oddly enough, he was wearing a button-down white shirt today. What, was he trying to appear more corporate?

"Good morning, Dunk. Why did you need to see me so urgently?"

He cleared his throat. "We need to speak with you about an HR issue. Isn't that right, Zac?" Zac nodded emphatically.

"What HR issue are you talking about?" Vivien asked.

Duncan's jaw tightened and his pupils contracted. He was either lying or scared or both. Scared of what? He continued with a non sequitur. "I think we should keep this conversation as professional as possible."

"Sure, of course." For someone who'd demanded to see her immediately he was taking his sweet time getting to the point.

"Uh, I'm…well, I'm just going to say it. We've decided to make a change in the leadership of the business." Duncan looked down at his papers.

Vivien wondered, who "we" was and what "business" he was talking about. She looked at him blankly and waited.

"We've decided to make a change in the leadership of the Women's Apparel business, and you will no longer be the president. Effective immediately. We're terminating your employment today, as a matter of fact." Duncan plowed ahead, not waiting for a reaction. "We're offering a very generous severance agreement that I think you'll be pleased with." He wouldn't look at her.

What the…? What was Duncan talking about? Was he nuts?

Vivien maintained her composure. "I don't understand. I'm being fired? For what reason?"

For the first time, Duncan made eye contact. "Remember, we agreed to keep this conversation as professional as possible. We need a new leader to take the business forward."

"I agree about keeping it professional, Dunk," she said, holding his gaze. "But this is certainly unexpected. I've never been fired before and I'd like to understand why. The business is doing great and the product, marketing, and team are all performing at their peak. We've been executing a compelling strategy that's been working incredibly well."

Duncan scoffed, "Oh, so are you saying you're the one who's done all the work, V? You can't take all the credit."

"Of course I'm not saying I did it all. I have an entire team who's been working hard to deliver what we've achieved. But I did create the vision and strategy, and made thousands of decisions that got the business to where it is today." Vivien spoke in an even tone.

"Well, I for one haven't seen enough improvement. It's my belief more progress could have been made."

Had Duncan lost his mind? What planet was he living on? Vivien had turned around a business that had been failing for years, and in record time. No one had ever been able to accomplish that. No one. And their growth in revenues and profits had far surpassed that of any other division. A simple glance at the business metrics would confirm Vivien had accomplished a herculean task. And what about Zac? How could any HR professional support such a wacky decision?

Vivien was incredulous. "I don't understand what you mean, Dunk. We're having the best performance in the history of the division. Why would you fire someone when the business is doing so well? That makes zero sense."

Duncan tugged at the neck of his shirt as if it were strangling him.

She was not going to make this easy for him. "You yourself said at the sports industry awards dinner last week, 'Vivien made hers the most successful division at Smart Sports through her relentless pursuit of excellence.' One week I'm doing fantastic, the next week I'm being fired. Tell me, Dunk, what has changed in the last week?"

The CEO furrowed his brow and blinked hard. Zac shot him a quizzical look. Despite his lack of competence, even he seemed to be questioning Duncan's decision.

"Um, well, I have some other concerns. Grave concerns." Duncan clasped his hands together. "Issues with your team management skills."

"What are you talking about? I've always prided myself on my leadership and coaching skills. I ask my team for feedback regularly and it's been nothing but positive. Can you give me some specifics?"

"I cannot give you particulars."

"But you've spoken with members of my team and gotten feedback about some issues?"

"No, no. I didn't speak with them directly. I wouldn't think that would be professional," Duncan said through tight lips.

Vivien threw up her hands. "Does anyone else find this baffling? You're making a judgment call about my team management skills with no feedback from my team? How can you have an informed opinion about my skills as a leader when you have no facts?"

"It's my own opinion I've formed based on my own observations."

The conversation was Kafkaesque in its circular logic.

Duncan said, "I've heard negative comments about your leadership style."

From whom? Rebecca? They hadn't worked together for some time.

Vivien took a breath and placed her hands on the table. "In well-run organizations, if there's a specific concern about an executive they're told about it and given an opportunity to make changes. I wasn't even given that chance. I've never received negative feedback from you about my leadership skills until now."

A rather concerned-looking Zac spoke up. "Dunk, you did give V feedback on this stuff before, right? At least a few times?"

Duncan rubbed the back of his neck and began to stammer, "Um, yeah. I believe I made at least a comment or two about it earlier this summer, V. Anyway, it's simply too late, you just haven't performed up to expectations."

She was not about to back down. "Duncan, we both know that's not true. There's a minimum level of decency with which you are supposed to treat people; you've not shown that to me or many others. If you continue to run the company in this manner, you will destroy it. What you're doing is not right. Or do you think you can do anything you want?"

With a glint in his eye, Duncan said, "I'm the CEO, I have the power to make these kinds of calls. I am the successor to the Smart brothers."

Vivien scoffed, "Yeah, Dunk, *success* being the operative word in *successor*. Sales have declined steadily under your leadership. You've alienated our consumers and our most prized accounts. You launched a shoe that had the highest returns in company history. The stock is down seventy percent since you took over, which means you've destroyed billions of dollars in shareholder value. I'm sorry, exactly which part of your tenure are you calling a success?"

His look darkened. "It's my decision and it's final. This conversation is over, Vivien."

With that, Duncan abruptly got up and practically sprinted out of the room.

Vivien looked at Zac who, judging by the beads of sweat on his upper lip, was fearful–whether he was afraid of her or the unintelligible situation surrounding her termination, she couldn't be sure.

"This is crazy, Zac. Surely you don't agree with this decision."

"I have to support Dunk's decision." Of course he wouldn't go against his boss.

"How? I didn't even hear a real reason for my getting fired."

"Perhaps you weren't listening closely enough. Duncan gave clear reasons."

Vivien leaned forward. "I was listening, but I heard no facts."

Zac sniffed. "Legally he doesn't have to give you a reason for your termination, V."

"What are you talking about?"

"Oregon is an at-will employment state, so you can be fired for any reason or no reason, at any time. That's just how it works."

Vivien paused for a beat. "So that means you and all the other Smart Sports executives have at-will employment contracts as well?"

He replied accommodatingly, "Yes, I have one, too. But this meeting isn't about me, it's about you. And unfortunately your time here has come to an end."

"Then I'll just say good-bye to my team and be on my way."

"No, Vivien. Dunk and I don't think that would be a good idea. We'll handle the communication to your team about the situation."

"You mean I don't even get to say good-bye to my team? They're going to think I've done something wrong to be fired suddenly, and with no chance to speak with them."

"We'll inform them of the decision." Zac sounded like a robot.

"What about all my stuff?"

"We'll take care of it. All your computer files, papers, and personal belongings will be delivered to your home. Don't worry, you'll get everything."

"I have my purse and briefcase sitting on top of my desk. I need to go back and at least get those things."

"All right, V. I'll escort you to your office and you can take only your most important personal belongings. We can sit for a few minutes and review the papers we need you to sign, including your severance agreement. Joe from Security is waiting outside. He'll walk us to your office, then escort you to your car."

This is nuts, I'm being treated like a criminal.

Numbly she stood up, hair still dripping beads of water from her post-workout shower onto the surface of the birch conference room table. Ironic. Despite all she'd contributed to the company, it had taken under nine minutes for her career at Smart Sports to come to an abrupt end. The conversation hadn't even taken long enough for her hair to dry.

Outside the conference room, Joe the burly security guard shifted his weight. Joe and Zac both looked uneasy as they made their way into the elevator and down the hall to Vivien's workspace.

They opened the door.

"Wow, I didn't know you turned this into an open workspace, V. It's really cool," Zac remarked, insensitive to the situation.

They walked in and Pandy looked up, alarmed to see her boss with the strange entourage. Vivien stopped and said, "Just a sec, I need to use the restroom."

From the look she gave Pandy her assistant would know to come and meet her. Vivien was pacing around the restroom when Pandy burst in.

"What's going on, V?"

"Something crazy happened, Pandy. Duncan just fired me."

"What? No way! Why would he do such a thing? He can't just fire you."

"He can and he did. Honestly, it's just politics. Duncan's seen me as a threat for a while, and now that he's CEO he has the power to get rid of me, even if it makes no sense."

"Oh my god, no, no, no." Pandy's eyes started to fill with tears.

Vivien put her hand on her assistant's shoulder. "Listen, Pandy, I need to get back. These guys just escorted me up here to pick up a couple of personal things. If I need to call you I'll use your cell number, not your work line. Please do me a favor and pretend we didn't talk. Duncan and Zac are going to make an announcement to our team to let everyone know that I'm gone." She gave her assistant a warm smile. "And thanks for everything, Pandy. I've really enjoyed working with you. You're the best." Vivien gave her a big hug.

"This is totally insane, V. I can't believe this is happening. You're the best boss I've ever had, I don't want to work for anyone else. Oh my god!"

"Just remember, Pandy, you need to appear as if you don't know anything, okay?"

Vivien returned quickly to her workspace, where Zac was holding the signed shoes she received from Mackey Keeyes. Apparently he was taking an inventory of her belongings and deciding which ones to keep for himself. Vivien collected her purse, briefcase, and picture of her and Clay, then sat down at her conference table with Zac.

He pushed a manila envelope toward Vivien that held a few documents. The first was her termination letter, which she flipped through, and she was shocked to see who'd signed it: Klaas van der Hooft. When she'd bumped into Klaas moments before her meeting with Duncan, he'd known full well what she was walking into, and he didn't warn her or try to help her. Coward. After all she'd done for him?

Zac also pulled out a severance agreement and a noncompete contract.

Vivien set the papers aside. "Zac, I can't believe how poorly this is being handled."

Zac's back stiffened. "Well, I, for one, am disappointed in all this, V. I had my reservations about your being hired, but eventually I supported you. I was hoping you would succeed as our first female leader."

Vivien responded curtly, "You're missing the point, Zac. I did succeed. That's exactly why Duncan's getting rid of me. He's eliminating the competition."

Their terse conversation was interrupted by a loud scraping noise outside her door.

From the hallway she heard Pandy shout, "Hey, wait a minute! What do you think you're doing?"

Vivien walked to the door of her office area to discover the source of the noise. It was the maintenance guy, Danny, scraping Vivien's name off the door. In addition to firing her brutally, they couldn't wait to remove all evidence that Vivien Lee had ever worked there. This was absurd.

Calmly, Vivien said, "Hi, Danny, I'm sure someone sent you to take care of this, but would you mind coming back in ten minutes, please?"

Danny replied, "I'm sorry, Vivien, I was just doing what I was told." Even he could see she had gotten canned. He added quietly, "I don't agree with what they're doing to you. If my daughter's employer treated her this way...well, it's shameful."

"Thanks, Danny."

He gave her a sympathetic look and skulked away as Vivien returned to wrap things up with Zac.

"I'm curious, Zac, how do you expect to retain the best talent when people see arbitrary decisions made, like this one? Do you think people will feel good about their future here?"

Zac frowned, knowing that she spoke the truth. "I'm sure you're still in shock, V. Please look over the papers and sign and send them back within two weeks. As I said, I'm disappointed that it had to end this way."

"*Disappointed* doesn't do a good enough job describing what I'm feeling right now."

Vivien gave him a withering look that cowed Zac into silence. Then Joe the security guard escorted her out of the building. Vivien got into her car and took a moment to call Clay. "No signal" flashed across her phone screen. *You've gotta be joking. Those assholes cut off my cell phone already?* It wasn't even eight thirty in the morning, and so far she'd been fired, kicked out of her office, and cut off from all communication. She took a few deep breaths to regain her equilibrium and put the car in gear. For the last time Vivien drove away from the Smart Sports campus, as sheets of rain pelted her car.

＊

The Women's Apparel leadership team had already boarded the van to the airport. Duncan sent Marla ahead to tell them he wanted to address the entire team and bring them back inside.

Duncan, with Zac alongside, walked in and stood at the end of the conference table. Of course, none of the jokers had a clue what this little meeting was about. Someone muttered a question about whether there might be news about Malcolm. They must have realized Vivien was notably absent.

Duncan said a few words about how phenomenally well the division was doing, the best in its history. He congratulated the team. Then he dropped the bombshell. "We've made a change in the leadership of the business and Vivien Lee is no longer the president."

There was an audible gasp.

He continued, "We will be determining a successor, but in the interim I shall be taking a more active role in this division." Then he turned and walked out, Zac following him like an eager puppy.

He gave them no chance to ask any questions.

＊

Resilience. It was a trait that always helped Vivien deal with setbacks. Ever the pragmatist, she figured since she had some spare time she'd stop by the grocery store on the way home. It gave her time to clear her head and let the reality of what had just occurred sink in.

Clay looked up in surprise when she walked through the door. He got up to take the armful of groceries.

"Hey, babe, what are you doing back home? Did you forget something?"

She pulled him into the living room and sat down.

"You're not going to believe this, Clay...Duncan just fired me."

"What? That's outrageous!" He put his arms around her and gave her a long, supportive hug.

She felt herself melt into his arms.

"Come on, let me take you out to breakfast and you can tell me what happened. I'll cancel all my calls."

Clay quickly put away the perishables and led Vivien out the door. They huddled under a large golf umbrella and walked to their favorite eatery, where the first thing Clay did was order a half bottle of their favorite champagne.

He poured a glass for each of them. "Hey, it's not like either of us has to go into the office later." He winked. "Tell me what happened, Vivi."

Clay recoiled when he heard about the irrationality that both Duncan and Zac displayed.

"I can't believe those assholes wouldn't let you say good-bye to your team!" He slammed his hand down.

Still numb, Vivien murmured, "They're probably meeting with my team now and making the announcement. People are going to be surprised."

Clay shook his head in disgust. "Horrified is more like it. This is the dumbest business decision I've ever heard. After all you've done for the company? Political bullshit. We need to get you a good employment attorney–don't sign any papers until a lawyer's checked them out."

"Okay. You know they cut off my cell phone already? That's why I couldn't call you."

"Imbeciles!" Clay spat.

"On the bright side, I have a lot of free time to spend with you, honey." It was the first time Vivien had smiled all morning.

Clay took her hands in his. "Listen, babe, you've been working your ass off and you deserve a break. Relax a bit, spend time with your friends, maybe travel a little. But my perspective is only a handful of people can do what you can. I think you need to give yourself the chance to do something great–you can do anything you choose."

That only deepened Vivien's conviction that she was engaged to the right guy. It also confirmed what her father had always told her about a true life partner–that person should lighten your burdens and double your joys.

*

Vivien used her home computer to compose an email message to Pandy, asking her to forward it to the team.

It read, "As you may have heard, I was fired from Smart Sports today for reasons even I don't understand. I want you to know how grateful I am to have worked with each of you. We should all feel proud of what we accomplished together, and I hope you'll continue to fulfill the vision we set out to achieve. Keep in touch. All my best, Vivien."

She looked it over and hit "send." Then she took a deep breath and called her father, Coop, and her Ceiling Smasher friends to share the news.

Her dad said, "Vivi, you know you were a success and so does everyone else. Don't take this situation to heart. Come home and spend some time with your dear old dad soon, okay?"

Coop huffed, "That is the wackiest thing I've ever heard. What a bunch of idiots!"

Andi, Sofia, and Grace were equally shocked and supportive. "Bastards!" Andi spat. "You should sue their asses."

By noon Vivien had run down to Pioneer Place and acquired a new cell phone and number. She gave her new contact information to Pandy, who shared it selectively.

J. J. was the first to call. "This makes absolutely no sense!" He described their meeting with Duncan. "The most bizarre business meeting I've ever seen. For him to say, 'Congratulations, this business has never done better and, oh yeah, now your fantastic leader is gone,' was ridiculous. Everyone was like, 'What do we do now?' Obviously our leadership off-site was canceled."

Vivien let out a big sigh. "I don't know what to say, J. J. I was as stunned as you guys."

He grunted. "You know, there's no question in my mind Rebecca was part of the whole evil plot to dethrone you."

Vivien reflected on her elevator encounter with Rebecca that morning–she must have known Vivien was on her way to meet Duncan to get the axe. That explained the malicious tone.

"Yes, this reeks of Rebecca's handiwork. She is tightly bound to Duncan in ways you can't even imagine, J. J. Anyway, it's a terrible political environment there, so it's safer for you to keep our communication on the QT. I'd love for you to keep me in the loop on the business, though. We'll get together for drinks when things calm down, okay?"

J. J. said, "Everybody's in shock and they're worried about you. What should I tell them?"

"Tell them I'll be fine. I'll bounce back."

"Okay, V. For the record, it's going to suck not having you as our leader. I can't imagine working on this business without you."

∗

Vivien spent the afternoon fielding calls from concerned team members and various colleagues who called to offer their support. Tim Kelley told her to use him as a reference and wondered aloud if he was next on the chopping block. She didn't hear a peep from Klaas. No surprise.

Doug Hawke phoned up and, in his own expressive way, conveyed his disgust with Duncan and the whole situation. Apparently, no one on the board knew of Duncan's plan to fire Vivien.

"You don't think Otto knew? After all, he's chairman and Duncan's father-in-law. Duncan isn't brave enough to make such a bold move without some support."

"Maybe you're right, V. In fact, you should reach out to Otto and set up a meeting–put him in the hot seat. Even though I'm no longer on the board, I still have a cordial relationship with Otto. I'll clear the path for that to happen."

"Thanks, Doug. You've always been a fantastic source of advice and support. I hope you know how much I appreciate all you've done for me."

Doug joked, "Whoa, let's not get too carried away."

"Well, the highlight of my week was hearing that your cancer treatments are going so well. When you get the all-clear sign from your doctor let's play some golf."

Before the close of business her Ceiling Smashers network came through for her. One Smasher was a district court judge, extremely well connected in the legal world. She put Vivien together with two top employment attorneys, her introductory email reading, "Please help my friend Vivien, who's the most talented business executive I know."

Both attorneys responded right away, and Vivien scheduled calls with them for the following morning. True to his word, Doug used his influence with Otto–Vivien received a phone call from his assistant to set up a meeting in the next few days.

✳

In the evening, as Clay was in the kitchen preparing dinner, Vivien sprawled out on the living room sofa. She tried to wrap her head around the events of the last twelve hours. It was still unbelievable. Her normal level of confidence was shaken–why didn't she see this coming? What could she have done differently?

Their home phone rang and the caller ID said Private Number, but she answered it anyway.

"Hey, V, pretty crazy day, huh?"

Johnny O, Duncan's supposed best buddy. Why would he call her?

"Yup, crazy day. Didn't see it coming," she replied cautiously.

"Look, off the record, I feel terrible about what happened to you, V. I knew Dunk wanted you gone, but I didn't agree with him at all. I can't believe he actually went through with it."

"Me too." She chuckled a bit.

Johnny O sounded earnest. "You deserve better than this, especially since everyone knows it was all you–you turned around the business, came up with all the creative ideas, and you're the one who made it so successful. I, for one, thoroughly enjoyed working with you."

Astonished, Vivien replied, "Why, thanks, Johnny O. I really enjoyed working with you, as well. We had some fun times together. And despite your attempts to prove otherwise, I think you're truly a good guy."

She could hear him take a deep breath.

"It took me a while to figure out what's so different about you, V. You're a good person and somehow you've found a way to make integrity interesting."

Vivien was speechless. Perhaps she'd succeeded in winning him over after all. "That's one of the nicest things anyone's said to me, Johnny O."

"I've often wondered, can a nice, high-integrity person be a successful executive in this industry?" He turned serious. "I genuinely hope so."

Vivien allowed herself a little smile. "Hey, I appreciate your reaching out to me. Who knows, maybe we'll find ourselves working together again someday."

Johnny O promised to keep in touch, though realistically Vivien knew it would be awkward for them to maintain a friendship. Still, it had taken guts for him to call and say what he really thought, and for that he scored major points in her book. Perhaps his bond with Duncan wasn't as tight as it seemed.

Her pre-bedtime ritual was to plan out her tasks for the next day. It was second nature for her to prepare her thoughts on new product ideas, marketing strategies, and meeting objectives. Her tooth brushing slowed when she came to realize she had nothing left to plan. Everything she had been working on was suddenly erased. Her job had been snatched away in an instant, but it would take much longer for her passion for the business to die.

∗

As much as she tried to sleep, her head was spinning with thoughts about her unfinished tasks, her worries about the team, and her outrage over her dismissal. The Duncan meeting kept running through her head, and his treachery and cowardice infuriated her. Then her thoughts shifted to Rebecca, who'd clearly been plotting her demise. Who else was in on the scheming– Charl? Zac? Steele? It sickened her. And what about Klaas? Wasn't he supposed to be her friend? Bitter tears rolled onto her pillow.

Maybe she had focused too much energy on doing a fantastic job– she should have paid more attention to the politics and played the game better. The silver lining was that now she had the luxury of time. And she'd have complete control over her schedule. It was a tiny sliver of positivity from an otherwise horrendous day, and with that thought Vivien finally succumbed to a fitful sleep.

CHAPTER 30: THE END?

Clay took an early flight while Vivien slept in a little the next morning. She leisurely sipped her coffee and perused the paper. Then she flipped on the TV and channel-surfed the morning news shows. There she was...Elizabeth Atwood, Clay's ex-girlfriend. Vivien had to admit she looked pretty good. She turned up the volume.

Grinning, the coanchor said, "This is huge, Lizzy. Oh my gosh, congratulations on your engagement! You're going to break a lot of hearts. Who's the lucky guy?"

Elizabeth just smiled. "He's a wonderful man and we're really happy."

Hmm, so Clay's ex was officially off the market. His mother would be chagrined. Maybe this meant she'd finally accept Vivien as her future daughter-in-law. With no job to worry about, Vivien would have plenty of time to plan all their wedding details.

*

She made a few notes before taking her calls with the employment attorneys, both of whom came from top-notch firms. Her first call was helpful, then she explained the circumstances surrounding her termination to the second lawyer, Jeffrey.

Jeffrey drew in a breath. "I'm familiar with at-will employment contracts, but being terminated when your performance was unquestionably stellar is nonsensical. I haven't seen a case like yours in my entire legal career. So, do you want to sue these guys for wrongful termination?"

"Well," Vivien said, "even though I don't respect the current leadership, I feel loyal to the founders of the company, the Smart brothers. I wouldn't feel right about suing the company after all the opportunities the Smarts gave me."

"That's your prerogative, Vivien." Jeffrey sounded like he was flipping through pages. "I looked over your severance agreement and there were some questionable clauses: First, the hush clause prohibits you from disclosing any details surrounding your termination. Second, the nonretaliation clause states that even if certain parties may have acted wrongly toward you, you cannot take action against them. Lastly, the nondisparagement clause means you cannot say anything remotely negative about certain executives whose names are listed."

Wow, this guy is quick and thorough. "Yeah, I've never been fired before but all that sounded odd to me."

"These are highly unusual clauses and I'd advise you to get them removed before you sign, although there is a financial incentive attached. You would forfeit that if you ask them to change these clauses."

Vivien said, "On principle I don't agree with those three clauses, so I want them taken out. I don't care about the money."

"You also have a yearlong noncompete contract, which prevents you from working in the industry, but you'll be fully compensated."

"So they're paying me not to work?" Vivien shook her head.

"That's right. They're paying you one and a half times your salary, plus bonus. If I had that deal I'd be out playing golf every day!" He laughed. "Can you think of anything else we need to address?"

Her head was spinning. "No, I don't think so."

Jeffrey said, "Look, Vivien, I want to help you because you've been treated so unfairly. This shouldn't take much time so I'll waive my fee and make a call to Smart Sports if you'd like me to negotiate on your behalf."

Vivien decided to move ahead with Jeffrey because he was so

knowledgeable and responsive. The fact that a top attorney would be calling about Vivien would surely get Zac's attention.

Jeffrey negotiated Vivien's contract to remove the three questionable clauses, but she lost a $150,000 incentive to have those changes made. That was a big price to pay. But it came down to morals or money... and Vivien chose the former.

*

Two days after her sudden departure, Vivien was set to meet with Otto Utz for a morning coffee and a chat. She looked around the rustic coffeehouse at the collection of long-haired, tattooed patrons. Everyone wore oversized headphones and crouched over their keyboards. Otto's assistant had picked a place that was a known hangout for local musicians and artists, making it unlikely that Vivien and Otto would be seen together by anyone in their industry.

Vivien arrived early and, taking advantage of the free Wi-Fi, sent out an email to her entire address list updating her contact information. Her computer pinged, alerting her to a new email. It was from Tim. It read, "V, the weirdness continues. We're here at the executive retreat in Napa and Zac announced that you left the company. Duncan refuses to even speak your name. Losing my mind, but the wine is helping."

Arriving a few minutes late, Otto apologized in his clipped German accent and shook the beads of water from his raincoat.

Vivien extended her hand, saying, "Thanks for meeting with me, Otto. First, I want to set your mind at ease. I haven't signed the severance agreement yet, but I want you to know I don't intend to sue the company. What I want is simple." She opened her hands, palms turned up. "I just want to know why I was fired."

Otto sipped his espresso pensively. "Vivien, you know I have nothing but admiration for you. You achieved tremendous things at Smart Sports, so I am very impressed with you. I think you're an extremely talented and bright executive. In fact, I would be more than happy to serve as a reference for you."

It was an offer she wasn't expecting. So kind of him.

He leaned a bit closer. "But, about your leaving, that was Duncan's decision. He is the CEO and he needs the freedom to make the decisions he sees fit. I did not agree with the decision, but in the end I must support him. Could I reverse the decision, get Duncan to change his mind? Possibly, but–"

"Oh, no," Vivien interjected, "I wouldn't want you to do that, Otto. I never want to work with Duncan again." Her resolute look seemed to surprise him. "I just want to know what reason he gave you for firing me, when all evidence indicated I was doing a great job."

"You weren't doing a great job, Vivien." He reached across the table and patted her arm. "You were doing a phenomenal job."

She gave a little laugh in appreciation.

Otto scratched his head, as if trying to recall specifics. "Duncan mentioned you weren't responsive to his feedback. He said over the past year he'd given you lots of feedback on your leadership style, but you were unwilling to change. I believe there was also a person who worked on your team who complained that morale was low."

Rebecca. Despite wanting to address the inaccurate comment about morale, Vivien knew better than to come across as defensive. But she had to set the record straight where Duncan was concerned.

"Actually, Duncan's statement about giving me feedback isn't true–I never received any feedback from him until the day he fired me."

Otto frowned. A conundrum. Who should he believe, his son-in-law or this woman sitting across from him? The chairman was an intelligent, analytical man, and the divergent stories weren't adding up. Vivien could see the whole thing was perplexing to him.

He puckered his lips a bit.

Otto explained, "Obviously I am not deep into the day-to-day business details. While this outcome is one neither of us is comfortable with, ultimately I have to put my trust in his judgment. Duncan is CEO and he's running the company. I'm sorry, Vivien. Who knows? In the end, I may regret supporting this decision."

She wasn't getting the closure she needed–perhaps she never would. It was obvious Duncan had lied to Otto, but he was too far removed from the business and the people to have a sense of what was really going on. Did he know about the countless unethical things his son-in-law had done? How would he react to learning his son-in-law was not only having an affair with his direct report Rebecca but had fathered her son? He'd blow up.

Vivien sighed. She believed in karma. Eventually, all Duncan's sins would come out, especially if he continued to act with such hubris. Evil people often fashioned their own demise.

At least she had the support of the chairman of the board. When she started looking for a new job, to be able to cite him as a reference would be tremendous.

Vivien rested her chin on her hand. "I'm concerned about my former division and my team–we worked so hard to get the business to where it is. I still care about Smart Sports and most of the people there." Vivien looked into Otto's eyes. "I hope what's so great about the company does not die."

"I wish for the same."

She took the opportunity to plant a seed. "You strike me as a good leader, and I know you've successfully built and run businesses. It could really benefit Smart Sports to have more involvement from you in the future."

He seemed to mull it over.

Vivien checked her watch. "Anyway, I'd like to thank you for your time, Otto, and I wish you the best." She stood, hand outstretched.

"Please keep in touch, Vivien. I have a feeling our paths will cross again. And, don't forget, when you need a reference, don't hesitate to call me." Otto smiled, shaking her hand and enclosing it with the other.

The morning after her meeting with Otto, eager to put everything behind her, Vivien signed the revised severance agreement, stuck it in a FedEx envelope, and sent it off. She was glad to be done with the whole mess.

Later that day, while she was out running errands, her cell phone rang. It was the organizer of a *Fortune* magazine business conference she'd agreed to speak at–six months ago. The woman wanted to confirm Vivien's attendance. Her airfare and hotel were already booked and paid for, and the program was already printed. It would be poor form to back out now. Vivien told the woman she'd be there and hung up.

She was fishing for her car keys when her phone rang again. Rick, her investment advisor, had been unable to reach her until he received her email with her updated contact info. "I have a few things to review with you, Vivien, but why aren't you in the office today?"

She explained in a weary voice the highlights of her departure.

"So, then what's the situation with your stock options?" Rick sounded alarmed.

Oh god, with all of the stress of her abrupt termination and lack of sleep this was something she'd missed completely. That was out of character. "Umm...I don't know. Let me check."

Like all the top Smart Sports executives, Vivien had stock options with a two-year vesting period, which was right around now. She raced home and rummaged through her financial papers, locating the original stock agreement she signed when the company went public. It stated the date her options were scheduled to vest fully–August 30.

She dropped her head into her hands and groaned. Duncan had fired her on August 28, two days before she was fully vested. In all of the termination papers she signed, there was no mention of stock options, but one short clause stated that as of August 28, Vivien relinquished any additional financial claims. That meant she lost all her stock options and couldn't sue them for the loss.

That explained why Duncan was in such a hurry to fire her. He wanted Vivien to suffer. It wasn't enough to take away her title, her livelihood, and her dignity–he was out to inflict pain. Why did he have it in for her so badly? If she had been let go just forty-eight hours later, she would have walked away with a financial windfall. Vivien hadn't thought it possible to feel any worse about her termination... until now.

She read and reread the stock agreement, learning some interesting tidbits that she kept in the back of her mind. But that didn't change the fact that the money she'd worked so hard for had vanished.

*

Joe, the security guard from Smart Sports, called Vivien that week about having the contents of her office delivered. He and Zac had personally packed up her office, and he wanted to know when her belongings should be sent over.

Vivien figured there would be at least four boxes of files, three boxes of her books and notebooks, and then another three boxes of stuff like memorabilia, product she had purchased, photos, samples that had been made for her. She cleared out some space in their storage room to be ready for all the things she had accumulated at Smart Sports.

The next day a delivery van pulled up outside her building as Vivien was returning from the gym.

"Hi, can you load the boxes onto a hand truck and help me get them upstairs?" she asked. "I want to put them in our storage room."

The delivery guy, dressed in shorts despite the rain, nodded. He disappeared for a moment and then came back from behind the truck with a single box loaded on his hand truck.

A bit impatient, Vivien put her hands on her hips. "Shouldn't we load on as many boxes as possible, to minimize the number of trips?"

The delivery guy looked perplexed and he consulted his clipboard, which was quickly accumulating water droplets from the gray skies. "Miss, this is the entire delivery."

"Wait a minute, this is just one box. I had way more stuff than this," she said, dumbfounded. "I was expecting, like, nine more boxes."

"This is all they approved to be delivered to you. A single box. See the requisition?"

He showed her the order, signed by Zac Archer.

Vivien's stomach tightened. "Hang on a sec, let me see what's in the box."

She tore off the lid, flabbergasted to find what Zac deemed appropriate for her to keep. A box of Altoid mints, a hairbrush, a box of tissues, her Wharton coffee mug, a few business books, and her Rolodex with all the business cards removed. Unbelievable.

They wouldn't allow her to take a single notebook or any of the files she had brought with her when she started? They'd even emptied the business cards from the Rolodex; what was that about? All the things she'd received as a Smart Sports executive–the autographed shoes from Mackey Keeyes, signed Olympic apparel, photos of her with her team and various professional athletes, her Smart Sports MVP Award and Premier Product Award, and even her own bag of workout clothes that she'd paid for–all of it was missing. What the heck?

Vivien emailed Zac directly, asking about the rest of her belongings.

"Your personal items have been returned to you. All other items in your former office are company property and have been dispensed accordingly. We consider this matter closed." Nice.

Before she signed off her email a ping notified her of a new message in her inbox. It was from Greg, the scuba diver she'd met on the Australia trip.

"Hi, Vivien, good to hear from you. How are you? I'm guessing from your updated contact info that you've left Smart Sports? If that's the case, don't forget I still have that shark video of you and your 'buddy' Duncan. Let me know if you're okay with me trying to sell it. Thanks! Take care, Greg."

She stroked her chin like a villain from a James Bond movie and smiled wickedly, then typed, "Go for it, Greg."

CHAPTER 31: THE GREAT DIVIDE

It was the most prestigious stage upon which a businesswoman could walk. *Fortune's* Most Powerful Women Summit was about to commence and an electrifying buzz emanated from the three thousand people in the audience. The luxe hotel in New York City boasted a humongous, chandelier-lit ballroom jam-packed with professionals seeking career tips from successful female leaders.

Vivien stood by the side door nearest the stage and groaned. She was a featured panel speaker but right now she'd have opted for being smothered in honey and lowered into a pit of fire ants. Reeling from her recent work catastrophe, for the first time in her professional life she had no clue what to do next. But Vivien had committed to this conference long ago and couldn't back out now even if she felt like a fraud for being there. She steeled her nerves and swung open the ballroom door.

Just get through this, you can do it. She swiftly walked backstage.

Behind the curtains the panelists greeted each other warmly and proceeded to get mic'd up. The composition of this panel was unique. It featured four female executives from male-dominated industries: a chief technology officer from a hot tech company, a former astronaut and now COO for an aerospace company, an MBA PhD biotech entrepreneur whose company was developing a vaccine for HIV, and lastly, a president from the sports industry. The four women were engaged in animated conversation when the conference organizer rushed toward them.

Breathless, she said, "I have some bad news. We had a last-minute cancellation from our keynote speaker. Ellen Rose, CEO of a major food company, had to deal with the *Listeria* food poisoning scare affecting their consumers. But we pulled some strings and got a terrific replacement." She smiled, glancing nervously at her watch.

There was a commotion as the ballroom doors were flung open and the replacement speaker bounded in. It was Mike Price, the infamous CEO who, for years, had led one of the largest conglomerates in the world. Nicknamed the Butcher, Mike could dissect a business (and a business leader) in seconds flat with gruff but clever comments.

Mike's booming voice seemed mismatched with his diminutive size.

"This must be my lucky day," he said. "To be the only guy in a roomful of beautiful and accomplished women."

Deborah, the biotech CEO, whispered to Vivien, "Ugh, I wish he would've left out the 'beautiful' comment." They shared a grimace.

Mike was tanned and exuded confidence in his midnight-blue, custom-tailored suit with its light blue silk pocket square. He introduced himself, shaking hands with each panelist.

At stage right was a lectern where Mike would be speaking, and on an elevated platform at stage left sat four dark velvet overstuffed chairs for the panelists.

A chime sounded, silencing the audience. Moderating the conference was a top female reporter for *Fortune* magazine. She said a quick hello to the speakers and then dashed onstage to kick off the program.

"Welcome, everyone, we're so excited about our program today. First, I must tell you that Ellen Rose, our original keynote speaker, had a company emergency and had to cancel. But we not only have a fantastic replacement, we have four amazing panelists for you today."

The moderator signaled for Mike and the four panelists to come out onstage. The panelists took their seats in the overstuffed chairs while Mike stood beside the moderator looking imperious.

She gushed, "Mike Price is a legend in the business world who's now retired. For two decades he was CEO of 3M, the global conglomerate that produces everything from sticky notepads to medical devices. His leadership of such a broad set of businesses required vision, attention to detail, and the ability to make quick decisions. He's known for being a sharp, no-nonsense executive who speaks his mind, and we're thrilled to welcome Mike today." She paused for applause.

The moderator motioned to the four women onstage. "You've read the bios of our panelists. These four pioneers not only chose to work in male-dominated industries, they all broke through the glass ceiling in their respective fields. I know you'll find their stories inspiring. Let's get started with Mike and his words of wisdom on how more women can become CEOs."

The all-female audience gave Mike a warm reception, and the silver-haired CEO stood at the lectern and placed his reading glasses on his nose.

"Thanks for having me here today. I know the theme of this conference is 'How More Women Can Make It to the Top,' and I'm happy to share my thoughts. For years, I ran and grew one of the largest and most complex businesses in the world."

He talked about the myriad challenges as CEO of a complex company, sharing a few entertaining anecdotes about his experiences. Finally he shifted to the topic of how more talented female executives could move up the corporate ladder.

"Over the years it wasn't uncommon for me to have a dozen or so direct reports. I've personally conducted hundreds of performance appraisals and provided career advice to countless male and female executives. So, what's the difference between the people who make it to the top and the ones who flame out? I can tell you in simple terms what it takes."

He arrived at the meat of his speech, the good stuff. This was the reason everyone had come to hear the speakers, to learn the secrets for getting to the top. The audience leaned forward.

Mike smiled confidently. "When you look at the successful leaders at the top of any Fortune Five Hundred company, you'll recognize a single common characteristic. Of all the people, male or female, who make it to the top, the one consistent trait is..."

The audience held their breath.

"...they get results. That's it, pretty straightforward. No big mystery. You get results, you move up. You consistently get great results, you move to upper management. You get the best results in the company, and ultimately you can become CEO."

Huh? All the women knew this wasn't reality. If this were an Olympic performance the Russian judges would have given him a 1.7.

He pressed on, "Doesn't matter if you're a man or a woman, it's the same for everyone. Any woman who gets fantastic results is able to become CEO. There are no so-called barriers. Now, I'm getting a little tired of hearing women say it's too difficult to get to the top. What's all the fuss? My advice for all of you? Stop making excuses. Don't waste time complaining...just focus on getting results. Do that and you're guaranteed to make it to the top."

Mike didn't pause or look up. He should have. Irritated murmurs rumbled through the crowd, building like an angry tsunami about to come crashing down on the guy. The growing cacophony finally caused him to take in the sea of enraged faces. The tension was as thick as the New York City traffic outside.

Vivien let out an involuntarily chuckle and under her breath said, "That is so not true."

Suddenly Vivien had the unsettling feeling that all eyes in the room were upon her...they were. It was then she realized her microphone was switched on.

Before she could elaborate, Lisa, the former astronaut, said, "I agree with Vivien. What you said is not accurate, Mike. Just look at the statistics on the dearth of female CEOs–less than two percent. I don't think your comments match up with reality."

Deborah, the biotech CEO, blurted, "Seriously, Mike, can you be that out of touch?"

Piling on, the CTO of the tech company said, "That advice is totally useless."

Vivien's shoulders tensed up and she felt a drop of sweat snake its way down her back. She'd committed a gaffe that initiated the wave of criticism from the other panelists; she had to think of a way to repair this–and fast.

"Mike, I apologize for the interruption," she said. "We appreciate your being here and offering your remarks. You're a CEO with a storied career. But with all due respect, your comments about what it takes for a woman to get to the top–that's just not how it works."

The burst of applause showed the audience's support. Vivien held her hand up to quiet them. She wanted to be nice to Mike and treat him with respect, but also help him understand that his comments were way off the mark.

"My intent isn't to embarrass you, Mike. Can we talk this through together, so you can see where I'm coming from?"

Mike removed his reading glasses and rubbed the bridge of his nose. "Sure, go ahead."

"Has your corporation ever had a female CEO?"

"No," he scoffed, then instantly caught himself.

"You've got eleven major business units. How many are run by women?"

"Well, er, none…to date."

"And of the twenty or so senior executives, how many are women?"

"One. No, wait, two!" Mike's face lit up a little.

Vivien gave a wry smile. "Let me guess: one heads up HR, one's in charge of diversity."

"Great guess. That's correct."

Deborah interjected, "Predictable."

Vivien continued. "Mike, you ran the company for nineteen years, and during that time how many women led a major business?"

Mike leaned on the lectern, chin in his hand. "Not many. Honestly, I'd have to say most top spots went to men. The guys were more aggressive about going after a job when it opened up. Many positioned themselves for a role even before the job became available. I played golf with these guys and got to know them well–that helped me assess what businesses they'd be good at leading."

"Okay, and how many high-potential women did you play golf with?"

Mike wrinkled his forehead, searching his memory. Finally he answered, "Come to think of it, none. I'm not even sure if any of the female executives played golf."

"So, here's where we agree, Mike. You say a woman who wants to get to the top has to deliver results. That's true. But as you've just explained, there's more to getting to the top than doing a stellar job. You've got to have someone at the top pulling for you. You've got to have informal interactions with the decision makers so when a key spot opens up they immediately think of you. You just said you afforded those informal interactions only to men. As a result, only men were promoted to the top spots. How many talented women in your organization never got the chance to be considered for a key role? An unfortunate outcome is that the male senior executives in your company will likely follow your example, so what chance is there really for a woman to become CEO? How can you say CEO opportunities easily exist for women, Mike, when they were lacking in your own company?"

Vivien had laid out a sound argument. Although her last question was rhetorical, Mike stood there shaking his head. Then he did something unexpected. The famous CEO gathered up his speech, crumpled it into a ball, and threw it on the floor. "You know what, Vivien? Thank you. Your comments are completely fair. Upon reflection, I'm ashamed I didn't do a better job for the talented women in my own organization. So instead of spouting off when I clearly have no clue, I'm going to shut my trap and listen to what you all have to say. Maybe I'll learn something."

Applause erupted in support of Mike for listening and handling the situation with class. He stepped off the stage and took a seat among the attendees.

The moderator collected herself and stepped up to the lectern.

She said graciously, "Mike, your comments elicited a lively response and it's important that we have this dialogue. And, Vivien, you bring up great points about the real challenges women face as they move up the corporate ladder. What did you do to break the glass ceiling? What pointers can you give us?"

Now that the attention was focused on her job, Vivien shifted in her seat.

The moderator quickly added, "On second thought, let's open that question up to all the panelists."

Vivien breathed a sigh of relief and let the other panelists have the spotlight.

After the others spoke, Lisa added, "It's been tough. At times I've felt like someone's put concrete boots on my feet and thrown me into the ocean–in the middle of a shark feeding frenzy."

"Oh, that reminds me," the moderator interjected, "last night my kids were watching Shark Week on Discovery Channel. There was a story about Smart Sports executives on a scuba diving trip. They showed a video of a guy using his female colleague as a human shield to protect himself against a shark! Vivien, do you happen to know the people involved?"

Vivien was unaware the video had already aired.

"Well, yes, I do." She hesitated. "Actually…that was me in the video. And the guy trying to feed me to the shark was my former boss."

Every person gasped. Even Mike Price covered his mouth in horror.

The moderator got the three thousand people in the audience to settle down. "You said the guy in the video was your 'former boss.' Does that mean he's no longer with the company?"

"No." Vivien let out a bitter chuckle. "It means I'm no longer with the company."

The confused crowd rumbled.

"That's a very recent development. I'm guessing it was your decision to leave, perhaps to achieve a better work/life balance? I understand you're trying to have a family."

The diplomatic moderator gave Vivien an out, a painless way to explain her sudden departure from Smart Sports. Until that moment failure had been a foreign concept to her. But now she'd stumbled in such a public way…it was the ultimate humiliation. Should she save face or be honest?

"Yeah, I decided to leave the company so I could spend more time with my family. Isn't that what everyone says?" She looked intrepidly out at the audience. "But that's not the truth. The truth is…I was fired, despite turning in a record performance."

A hush fell across the great ballroom.

The moderator couldn't mask her shock. "What? Why?"

Vivien said, "Let's just say it had nothing to do with results and everything to do with politics. Sad, but true."

"Well, Vivien, with your talent you can surely do anything, so please keep us posted."

After the panel concluded, her fellow panelists hugged her and Mike Price made a beeline for Vivien, shaking her hand firmly.

"Sorry to hear about the difficulties at Smart Sports, Vivien." His eyes twinkled. "But I have no doubt you'll make a fantastic CEO someday soon." Mike clapped her on the shoulder and looked surprised at the solid muscle Vivien sported. "Only a fool would try to mess with you!"

As Vivien was leaving she spotted a familiar face–Kay Wyskowski, the *WSJ* reporter who'd interviewed her a while back.

"Kay, how are you doing? How's your baby?"

"Wonderful to see you, Vivien. My daughter's almost a year old and doing great."

A pang of sorrow pierced Vivien's heart—Lily would also have been around a year old by now. She mustered a smile. "I'm happy for you, Kay."

Kay squeezed Vivien's arm. "I'm so disappointed to hear about your leaving Smart Sports, you were such a ray of hope for the industry. What's next for you?"

Vivien sighed. "I have absolutely no idea."

*

Pandy walked into the commissary at the peak of the lunchtime rush. What rotten timing. The hubbub was bigger than normal. The four big-screen TVs near the cashiers' stations normally played different sports channels. But today, someone had turned all the televisions to the Discovery Channel. She put down her tray and took out her wallet. "What's up with that?" She pointed to the TVs overhead.

"Word has it a Smart Sports video is going to be on Discovery Channel." The cashier rang up the purchase and took Pandy's money.

Pandy took her tray to a nearby table and sat down to eat.

Sure enough, once the volume was turned up the voice-over introduced a Shark Week program, telling viewers to stay tuned for some unbelievable footage from a Smart Sports dive trip. People shushed each other's conversations so they could watch and listen. Indeed, those watching saw the camera pan across the deck of a dive boat as divers prepared for their dive. They recognized the familiar faces of their top executives, some of whom waved to the camera.

"Look! There's the Smart brothers!" someone yelled excitedly.

"Oh my gosh, I can't believe it's Malcolm and Alex."

"And there's Vivien!"

Pandy put her sandwich down. Poor Alex. And Malcolm, still in a coma. And V. It was like a one-two-three punch.

The excitement was intense as they all watched their former leaders get into the crystal-blue water and start their dive. The abundant marine life and varied colors of coral were mesmerizing and captured vividly on digital video. The divers were leisurely exploring the underwater sights of the Great Barrier Reef until the camera cut to the dive master giving a signal to the divers.

"Whoa, that's the signal for a tiger shark," someone shouted.

They saw the divers seek shelter just as the enormous tiger shark came into view and then disappeared just as quickly. The camera followed the shark into the deep waters. Blackness filled the screen for a few seconds, then the gigantic beast ascended powerfully through the water, headed toward two of the divers, who were hugging a wall.

Pandy's heart beat faster.

*

Duncan rushed into the commissary with Steele Hamilton in tow. It was Duncan's custom to obtain his food, then cut to the front of the line to pay, so he could get out quickly. After all, his time was so much more valuable than anyone else's. As he and Steele grabbed their lunch and pushed in front of everyone at the cashier, there was total silence in the commissary. Even the people they'd cut ahead of were too distracted to notice.

Everyone's attention was on the TVs.

"Oh dear god," Duncan blurted as he identified the video from that diving trip he wished could be wiped from his memory.

Everyone in the room witnessed the female diver struggling to free herself from the grasp of her dive "buddy" and the sheer mettle she displayed as she faced the tiger shark head-on.

"Holy shit."

That was the general consensus as the viewers saw the male diver thrust his female buddy toward the shark and then glimpsed the quick downward tug on her leg.

The cameraman also captured the postdive activity. If there was any question about who those two divers were, their identities were clearly revealed when they were back on board the boat.

After Vivien Lee was whisked away by the rest of the divers, the camera zoomed in on a lone individual. It was the hunched-over figure of the cowardly diver, the faint tattoo on the back of his neck still readable.

The voice-over said, "For those of you who don't know Latin, that translates to 'Strength Under Pressure.' I'd call that false advertising, wouldn't you?"

Not everyone at Smart Sports knew about Duncan's neck tattoo, but he was easily recognizable from the video. A grave hush fell across the commissary.

Then someone whispered, "Look, Duncan's standing right over there."

Like a herd of animals sensing imminent danger, all the employees turned their heads in unison toward Duncan. Mortified, he snatched up his food without paying and, avoiding all eye contact, dashed out of the commissary as quickly as possible. Steele Hamilton followed close on his heels.

✳

Pandy watched them go, her stomach quivering so much she couldn't even think about eating.

V had seemed a bit unsettled when she returned from that diving trip, but she never said a word about the shark attack.

A couple of tables over, Johnny O was having lunch with Tim Kelley. Johnny O chuckled and softly said, "Payback's a bitch, Dunk."

*

Duncan was in a prickly mood as he sat down for his next meeting. It was to review plans for the launch of a new tennis shoe, specifically designed for athlete Justin Stewart.

He scrutinized the product and demanded, "Who decided to go with an embroidered logo instead of the TPU logo I wanted?"

The footwear designer Ethan responded, "I did. We tried the thermoplastic polyurethane logo on the sample shoe and it didn't pass the wear test. It kept delaminating, so we couldn't execute it. I decided it would be better to go with embroidery." What nerve.

"You decided, Evan?" Duncan bellowed. "You? Decided?"

The entire room was silent. No one dared correct Duncan on the name.

Duncan said, "I specifically asked for TPU, not embroidery. This footwear was created under my watch and as the CEO of Smart Sports I have final say. Change it back."

"But I'm trying to explain, Duncan, that isn't going to work..." Ethan trembled. "A TPU logo on top of the toe box will be unstable. Also, it's too close to the product launch date to make this kind of change. It will delay our deliveries to stores."

"Well, then, I've made my next decision. You're fired, Evan."

Everyone sat there in shock. Ethan was speechless. "Seriously?" the footwear designer meekly asked.

"Get out of my sight," the CEO snapped. There was an awkward fifteen seconds as Ethan picked up his belongings and shuffled out of the room, his face red with anger.

*

It was a two-day trip to New York for Vivien, enough time to do the Fortune conference, spend time with her dad and with Clay, and catch up with her friends. On day two, after some much-needed retail therapy, Vivien sat alone in a café drinking tea and reflecting.

She was no longer the president of a company…she was nothing. For the first time in her life she felt like an utter failure. Uncharacteristically, she let a tear fall, and it plopped into her tea. She released a bitter sigh. The Smart Sports ordeal had taken so much out of her. Would she ever be prepared for something like that again? Well, at least her personal life was happy–she was engaged to a wonderful man and they were planning their wedding. Vivien gently set her cup down and checked her watch, then headed out to meet her friends.

A strong breeze swirled about and pedestrians tried to avoid the debris kicked up by the warm September winds. Vivien shielded her eyes as she crossed the street and noticed someone on the opposite corner who seemed to be waiting for her: Miles Zabriskie, her former SCP colleague. The last person on the island of Manhattan she wished to see.

"Vivien, hello," he said. Even those two small words managed to annoy her.

"Hi, Miles, how's it going?" She tried to sound upbeat.

He smirked. "That's a question I should be asking you. I saw the news on the Internet about *Fortune's* Most Powerful Women Summit. Guess you're no longer in that set, given your termination from Smart Sports."

He pursed his lips, trying to suppress a smile. God, was he ever irritating.

"Yup, no longer with Smart Sports. *C'est la vie.* Well, gotta go." Vivien tried making her exit, but he wasn't letting her get away that easily.

This was a nightmare moment for Vivien–she was downcast, jobless, stripped of her stock option payout, publicly humiliated, and now Miles Zabriskie was ridiculing her.

"I tried to warn you about how tough it'd be, Vivien." Miles pushed his glasses up at the bridge of his nose with his middle finger. "Sorry it didn't work out for you."

He wasn't.

Miles kept on. "I have to admit, even I was shocked to hear the great Vivien Lee got the axe!" He guffawed.

Vivien's patience evaporated in the arid winds and she snapped, "Miles, just because I got fired doesn't mean I wasn't successful." Hmm. Even as she said it she was aware it sounded nonsensical. That embarrassed her even more in front of this jerk.

"So what're you going to do now? Pop out a few kids and be a stay-at-home mom?"

He was a human scalpel, so deft at getting under her skin.

Vivien snapped, "Sure, Miles. Maybe being a mom is the one occupation where I have a shot at being a success. Great to see you." It wasn't.

She darted away and left him standing on the corner. Vivien was kicking herself over her mistakes–she had been too trusting of the other Smart Sports executives and too much of a Goody Two- Shoes. If she had played the game better she wouldn't have been out on the street now, humiliated.

✳

"Aren't you guys are a sight for sore eyes!" Vivien called to her friends. Her spirits lifted as she hugged her Ceiling Smasher buddies–Grace, Andi, and Sofia–and Coop. They were having cocktails at the Royalton hotel, enjoying the strong air-conditioning and the quirky Philippe Starck interior of whimsical accents and bold geographic shapes. They were just catching up on all their latest news when someone called out.

"Andi, I knew I'd find you here. Hi, everyone! Vivi, great to see you." It was Courtney Greene, a Wharton chum and member of the Ceiling Smashers crew. Courtney was one of those brilliant people who could perform complex math problems in their head in seconds flat. Vivien always marveled at what a skilled networker Courtney was: she seemed to know everyone. That made her the perfect partner for Andi, as the two of them were starting up a private equity firm, called BC Capital, which stood for "Bold Chicks."

"What a nice surprise, Courtney. I haven't seen you since our last Smashers dinner." Vivien gave her a hug. "Love the new do."

"Oh, yeah, I was going for a Halle Berry look." Courtney gave a hearty laugh. "So, Vivi, are you at least a little relieved to be done with Smart Sports? Andi told me it was a really tough environment."

Vivien sighed. "Well, my departure was unexpected, but there were some high points."

She recounted how exciting it was, especially when the Smart brothers were in charge, to turn around and grow the Women's Apparel business. Vivien also shared some painful anecdotes–the bad advice she got, the poisoned sake, the awful off-site and Inspiration Circle. When she saw Courtney's horrified look she realized how much she'd endured in the past two years.

Courtney ordered a drink and then turned to Vivien. "That's brutal. I-banking was challenging, but not as bad as what you went through. Why'd you stick it out that long?"

Knowing Courtney was a Detroit Pistons fan, Vivien invoked the words of manager Joe Dumars: "'Real leaders don't talk about the pressure of the playoffs. They see it as an opportunity, a chance of a lifetime, to show who they are and what they can do.' No matter how difficult it was, I wasn't going to let those guys beat me. I wanted to show them what I was capable of."

Andi nudged her. "And you kicked ass, Vivi. You got fantastic results. You were the first female president in the industry and achieved success in record time."

"Yeah, but I never imagined I could be fired while doing a 'fantastic' job." Vivien shook her head and sipped her drink. "Well, at least now you guys can't say I've never failed at anything." She laughed bitterly.

Grace put her arm around Vivien's shoulders. "You should be proud of what you accomplished, no matter how things turned out or how unfairly they treated you. This is just a setback."

The appetizers arrived and Coop popped one in his mouth. "Don't let it get to you, Vivi. People get fired every day for totally random reasons. We'll just find you another business to run, that's all. Next."

Vivien cherished her friends. They were all doing their best to build her back up.

"I'd love to go back to running my old division, just not as part of Smart Sports anymore," Vivien sighed. "To have my team back and to lead the business the way I see fit–that would be perfect."

"Hey, that's an interesting idea." Courtney's brown eyes sparkled, indicating her brain was revving up. "Are you proposing doing a corporate carve-out of the Women's Apparel business from the company? Would the board go for that? What size deal could that be potentially?"

Vivien hadn't been thinking about that specific idea and wasn't even familiar with the term *carve-out*.

"That could be very intriguing," Andi murmured, "very intriguing."

"Guys, I was just thinking out loud," Vivien said, "or dreaming is more like it. I don't think the CEO would be up for it."

Courtney leaned forward. "Listen, Vivi, even though the economy's been tough, I think savvy investors are looking to snap up bargains– buy distressed businesses they can turn around. In the private equity world there's a shortage of talented executives who know how to turn around businesses and they're always looking for talent. It would be good for you to get to know some PE firms."

Sofia, who had been quiet so far, said, "Courtney's right, Vivi, you should get to know the private equity world. Your talents would be appreciated and well compensated there." As she lifted her glass to her lips Vivien was momentarily blinded.

"Hang on, what's that, Sofi?" Vivien's jaw dropped. "That bling."

Everyone's eyes moved to Sofia's left hand, where a huge diamond ring sat.

Sofia gave a sheepish smile and announced, "Jasper and I got engaged." Whoa, this from the woman who'd said she would never marry?

Her friends whooped and cheered, firing off questions to Sofia. Vivien ordered a bottle of champagne to celebrate.

"The wedding's going to be in early December." Sofia paused for effect. "In Paris."

Vivien forgot all the misery she felt about her job–or lack thereof–and was overjoyed with her friend's news.

"So, when are you and Clay getting married, sweetie?" Coop raised an eyebrow.

"Hopefully soon, now that I have time to focus on it." Vivien smiled. "I did a little shopping this afternoon and I think I've found the perfect wedding dress!"

"So exciting!" Sofia said. "We'll have to compare notes on styles."

While they munched on appetizers, Grace was deep in thought. "Vivi, why don't you make another trip out here soon? Meet some private equity people, see what opportunities exist, maybe explore this carve-out idea further. Can't hurt to have options, and you need to get back on the horse."

"But I have a non-compete," she protested.

Grace sniffed, "Who cares? Work in a different industry. I'm sure there are tons of opportunities for someone like you."

"Plus if you get a new job quickly you can earn two salaries at once!" Andi raised her glass.

"Okay, okay." Vivien held up her hands in surrender and then did something she typically found difficult; she asked for help. "Courtney, do you think you could make some introductions for me? Maybe to PE firms that specialize in retail and consumer goods?"

Slapping her thigh, Courtney said, "Done and done. I'll start with email introductions, then you can do phone calls with these folks, and then we'll get you set up with in-person meetings in the coming months."

The conversation with Courtney had sparked her interest. Vivien felt she had unfinished work to do with her old division. Could a corporate carve-out work? Would Duncan even consider it? Her gut told her no. He'd rather run the Women's Apparel business into the ground than give Vivien a second chance at success. It wasn't about making a good business decision, it was about preserving his ego. And he had the full backing of the board of directors, so it was unlikely she could pitch the idea to them successfully. No, the conditions didn't exist for that to happen, so she mentally shelved the idea. But it sure was nice to fantasize about it.

*

Instead of going to her father's apartment, on impulse Vivien headed to Clay's place even though it was well past midnight. She had a nice buzz from the champagne and the wine that she'd enjoyed with her friends at dinner. Now she was in an amorous mood. I'll crawl into bed naked and surprise him.

When she entered Clay's apartment it was quiet. Figuring her fiancé was asleep in bed, she disrobed and pulled back the covers. The bed was empty. Huh? Where was Clay at this hour?

She grabbed his cashmere bathrobe and rang him on her cell.

Clay's voice was a bit scratchy and he sounded sleepy. "What's up, Vivien?" Weird; he rarely called her that.

"I'm at your place, honey. Thought I'd surprise you. Where are you?"

"Oh, um, working late. Must have fallen asleep at my desk," he said hastily. "Listen, I'll grab a cab and be home in fifteen minutes. Can you wait up for me?"

Vivien said sweetly, "Sure, honey. Can't wait to see you!"

He just said, "Okay," and hung up. Odd.

*

She was on the sofa about to doze off when she heard the front door open. Clay rushed in and looked a mess. His suit was rumpled and his eyes bloodshot–despite that, he still looked handsome with that chiseled face. She wanted him to swoop her up and take her into the bedroom. Instead of kissing her, he plopped down next to her on the sofa and dropped his head into his hands.

"Vivien, I have to talk to you about some stuff." He looked at her, his eyes darkened.

She sensed something was wrong and immediately sat up, fully alert. "What is it, honey? You're scaring me."

He looked at the floor. "Listen, babe, we've been through so much together. I want you to know that I love you…I'll always love you."

Vivien sat silently waiting for the *but*.

"But we can't be together anymore."

"What are you talking about, Clay? Why can't we be together?" Her heart raced.

"Vivi, I'm so, so sorry. It's all my fault. I started seeing Elizabeth again some time ago. It started off as a friendly thing and it just took off from there…I didn't mean for it to happen."

This wasn't going to be a problem. Elizabeth Atwood was already engaged.

"Well, Clay, I hate to break it to you, but Elizabeth just announced on national television that she's engaged."

He closed his eyes and his body tightened up, as if he were in physical pain. "Yes, I know. She is engaged…to me." Clay's eyes filled with tears. "And, well, she's pregnant. I'm so sorry."

Her heart smashed onto the floor in a thousand pieces. The one thing she had been sure of had suddenly evaporated. How could something so strong vanish in an instant?

"I tried to tell you earlier, but that whole mess with your job happened..." He wiped away tears. "Vivi, I know it's too much to ask your forgiveness. I've made such a mess of things. I never planned for it to work out this way."

All the warmth left her body and she pulled the robe closer around her. She said evenly, "Let me get this straight. While you were engaged to me you started an affair with Elizabeth Atwood, got her pregnant, and proposed to her. You're engaged to two people at the same time and now you're breaking up with me? Do I have that sequence of events correct, Clay?"

He winced and nodded.

"So in addition to having backups for all your stuff, you had a backup fiancée, as well?"

How much humiliation was it possible for a person to suffer in a single day? Vivien's face reddened. She refused to let Clay see how much he'd hurt her. Vivien had to get out...go somewhere she could catch her breath.

She stood. "Well, I hope you, your mother, and Elizabeth will all be very happy together. You know, someday you'll have to stop letting your mother make all your decisions for you. Good-bye, Clay." Still clad in his robe, she grabbed her clothes off the floor and hastened to the door.

"Uh, babe...my robe?" Clay cocked his head, giving her a timid look.

"Use your backup, Clay." She slammed the door.

✳

Vivien left Clay's building and walked, still clad in his bathrobe, the forty blocks home to her father's apartment. She looked so disheveled that even homeless guys skirted around her. She tried to slip in quietly, but her dad was a light sleeper and came out of his bedroom to greet her.

He rubbed his eyes. "It's late, Vivi. Are you okay?"

SHAZ KAHNG

As much as she tried keeping her feelings locked inside, when Vivien saw the look of concern in her father's eyes, she lost it. She buried her face in her hands and sobbed in uncontrollable heaves. As she shared the news of her broken engagement, her father held her tight, her tears soaking his Brooks Brothers pajama top, a Christmas gift from her.

"Oh, my darling daughter, I'm so sorry," he sighed, and held her tight. Then he thought for a moment. "But...if you weren't meant to be together, maybe it's better to know now than a few years into the marriage." Her dad always found a bright side to every situation, no matter how bleak.

Vivien mumbled, "Yeah, I guess so, Dad."

Dr. Lee ushered his daughter into the kitchen to sit down and brought her a glass of water.

Pulling up a chair, he took a breath and put his hand on his heart. "Honestly, Vivi, I'm a little relieved."

"Why?"

"Clay's mother was such a coldhearted witch, wasn't she? Now we don't have to worry about spending every holiday with her for the rest of our lives–I'm so glad!" He giggled.

Vivien couldn't contain herself and soon father and daughter were crying with laughter.

*

Taking Vivien's suggestion that he get more involved in the business, Otto decided he'd attend the company-wide meeting called by Duncan Doric that Monday morning. As he walked from the parking lot, Otto checked his watch and quickened his pace to be on time.

At ten o'clock Smart Sports employees ambled into the Stadium to hear what was coming next. Otto had snuck in the back entrance unnoticed and took a seat in the last row of the balcony. Music blasted over the sound system and then Steele Hamilton bounded onstage to greet the audience. He asked them to give their CEO, Duncan, a hearty welcome.

Otto noted that applause was minimal as Duncan came out. He spoke about the proud history and promising future of Smart Sports, but it was obvious the employees were growing restless. It was no secret that the business was in terrible shape and the stock had been on a sustained decline. When Duncan explained the need to make some changes in the leadership of the business, some employees snickered.

"Johnny O'Connell has been our COO for the past year and he'll now take on the additional title of president of Smart Sports. Also, we're streamlining our organizational structure, so instead of having four presidents over the divisions, we'll simply have a president of Footwear and a president of Apparel. I'm pleased to announce the president of Apparel will be someone with tremendous apparel experience…Charl Davis."

Duncan waited for applause that did not come as the audience sat in silence. Otto thought, *Wait a minute, isn't Charl the guy who failed at running Women's Apparel the first time around?*

Then Duncan unveiled the biggest bombshell. "And our president of Footwear will be a talented product expert, Rebecca Roche."

Audible gasps echoed across the Stadium, followed by loud grumbling.

Way back in the balcony within earshot of Otto, one footwear employee said to another, "Who the hell is Rebecca Roche?"

His friend responded, "She's that annoying blond chick, the one with the 'special relationship' with Duncan, if you know what I mean. Rebecca screwed up Women's Apparel, then Men's Apparel. And she doesn't know a damn thing about footwear, so this is moronic. Another bullshit move from the omnipotent Duncan Doric. Time to dust off my résumé."

Otto cocked his head, alarmed at what he just heard. Could Duncan be having an affair with this woman Rebecca Roche? *Nonsense,*

Duncan is a good son-in-law and a good husband to Giovanna. He's lucky to be married to my daughter–is it possible he'd ever stray? As if coming out of a bad dream, Otto shook his head and chuckled. No, that employee was simply wrong. Still, he couldn't help but hear what others were saying.

"More crazy corporate changes."

"It'll all change again in six months' time."

"They should do the smart thing and bring back Vivien Lee to run things."

Rubbing his chin, Otto felt perplexed. Duncan had been the safest choice for the Smart Sports CEO role and he was surely making the right decisions for the company…wasn't he?

✳

A couple days later Vivien was back in Portland, where she met up with Tim Kelley for drinks and to hear firsthand about all of the org changes. Neither of them could believe the CEO of a public company would promote his mistress to head up a business about which she knew nothing.

Tim looked terrible–even more gaunt than when she'd seen him last. He must have been feeling a tremendous amount of strain these days, and it showed.

"So when you were sitting in the auditorium that day and heard Duncan announce Rebecca as president–that was when you realized you would be reporting to her? Duncan gave you no warning?"

He frowned. "Nope."

Vivien shrugged. "How crazy is it that you, with decades of footwear experience, have a boss who doesn't know the product and wears high-heel pumps every day?"

Flicking his hand, Tim shifted the conversation. "You know, V, I discovered where your MVP and Premier Product Awards ended up," he said, an entertained look on his face.

Vivien scoffed, "Where, the trash? Or as Duncan says, 'the rubbish bin'?" She imitated his fake British accent and bicep-flex pose.

"Actually no. I noticed them last week when I was having my touch-base with Duncan. They're sitting on a glass shelf in Duncan's office. But your name is covered up with electrical tape," he said, laughing for the first time in ages.

She let out a snort and her drink nearly shot out her nose. Then Vivien put her hand on Tim's arm.

"Seriously, Timmy, how are you doing? You don't look so great, if you don't mind my saying so. I'm worried about you. If the job is making you this miserable, you don't have to stay there."

Unsmiling, Tim toyed with his wedding band. "The practical issue is that Chris is at home with the kids and thinking about starting a business. Right now, I'm the main breadwinner…and the only one with health care coverage for the family."

"I understand, but I can see this job is just wearing you down."

"To tell you the truth, V, I don't think I'm going to last much longer." He had a sad, faraway expression. "But I appreciate your concern, my friend. What about you? How are you doing?"

"Other than getting fired and having a broken engagement? Fabulous!" Vivien rolled her eyes and exhaled. "You know, I read an interesting *Sports Illustrated* article on the plane. It said when a sports champion looks back over their career the thing they remember most isn't the championships won or the awards. It's the big losses where they failed to convert. That sting of defeat never wears off."

Tim looked pensive. "And that's how you feel about your departure from Smart Sports, V?"

"It is, Timmy. As much as I try to forget about my division and my team and stop worrying about its future, I can't put it out of my mind."

Now Vivien had no job, no fiancé, and tons of free time. *Guess I'll relax and make the most of it.* She soon came to appreciate her newfound freedom and open schedule. She'd work out when the gym was empty, meet a friend for lunch and go shopping, and pick up groceries when no one was around. *So convenient.* And with her noncompete agreement she was making more money than she had when she was working.

Vivien was running on the treadmill when her phone rang. It was Scott Abelman. Members of Vivien's former team were constantly calling and asking for advice on issues ranging from distribution strategy to product offering. She had to gently prod them to ask these questions of their new boss, Charl.

"How's it going, V?" Scott tried sounding casual.

"Great, just finishing up my run. What's up, Scott?"

He sighed. "I'm pulling my hair out trying to get Charl to deal with some major crises we're having. We've been begging for his help and he finally sat down with our leadership team yesterday. We did a round robin discussing all the problems and proposed solutions."

"Mmm-hmm, how'd that go?" Vivien toweled off her sweat.

Scott snorted. "We were desperate for some advice, to have Charl step up and be a leader...what did he do? He said, 'Okay, guys, fix it,' and got up and left."

Vivien couldn't help but chuckle softly. *Poor Charl.* This time around as president he also had Men's Apparel in his realm and was in way over his head.

"He either makes terrible decisions or no decisions at all," Scott complained. "And at our staff meetings Charl doesn't want to hear any bad news, so we're not allowed to discuss the poor business results... it's such a mess."

On the one hand, Vivien felt exonerated to hear how ineptly Charl was handling things. On the other hand, it was agonizing to see the business she and her team had worked so hard to build up spiraling into the abyss in such short order.

*

J. J. called, expressing nothing but disgust. "This is a classic case of not knowing how good someone is until they're gone. No one realized how difficult it was to turn this business around, because you made it look so easy. Charl is a nice guy, but we didn't realize what a poor leader he was until we worked for you. We sure wish you could come back and run things, V."

"Me too," Vivien said wistfully.

Her life at Smart Sports seemed so distant now. While she was enjoying her hiatus, Vivien couldn't sit idly by…she'd have to find a new purpose, and soon.

CHAPTER 32: A FRESH START

Just as Vivien stepped off the plane in LaGuardia she got a text from Andi: *Time to get back on the horse, Vivi.* Andi and Courtney had set up in-person meetings for her with eight private equity firms specializing in retail and consumer goods. Vivien had spoken with most of the firms prior to coming to New York and was excited to explore things further.

She took a taxi to her father's apartment. October leaves flew up as the cab sped through the streets. People rushed around Manhattan with vibrant energy, a welcome change from the deliberate pace of Portland. She dialed up Andi to check in.

"So my agenda in these PE meetings is twofold: First, to impress them with my expertise so they can envision me leading one of their portfolio companies. And, second, for me to get a sense of chemistry and vet the firms and people I want to work with. Sound good?"

Andi said, "That's perfect. We've briefed these firms on your experience and track record and the partners are eager to meet with you. Also we arranged the meetings over three days so you can get your feet wet first. Once your comfort level is higher you'll meet with the more prestigious firms."

"Sounds great," Vivien said. "I can't thank you guys enough."

Courtney added, "Happy to help, Vivi. You're gonna do great. Let's get together after your second day and regroup, okay?"

It had been a while since Vivien donned a business suit or even attended a meeting, and she felt oddly out of practice.

✳

The two days were a blur–rushing from meeting to meeting and dealing with all the different personalities.

Vivien collapsed into an overstuffed chair in Courtney and Andi's offices at BC Capital. "This is exhausting. Who knew just sitting around and talking to people could be so tiring?"

Andi laughed, "Vivi, you've only been out of the work force for a few months. You've got to get your stamina back. Here, have some coffee." She poured cups all around.

Pulling out her notebook and pen, Courtney got down to business. "Okay, what were your impressions of the firms you met with over the past couple of days?"

Vivien concentrated. "Day one, my breakfast meeting was a write-off–the partner I met was a cheapskate and their firm only looks for bargains. Not a good fit." She flipped through her notes. "Second meeting, at the Cornell Club, was good; the partner was friendly and intellectually curious. His firm was buying an alpine sports company that would have been a great fit for me...except for my noncompete. He said he'd keep me in mind for future opportunities."

Courtney sighed. "Sometimes the fit is great but the timing's off. And the third meeting?"

"Great people who make smart deals and seem very collaborative. They had a few CEO opportunities: a high-end pet retailer, an isotonic sports beverage company, and a chain of hair salons specializing in blowouts. None were the perfect fit, but I agreed to look at the position specifications and keep in touch."

"Okay." Andi leaned back in her chair. "What about today's meetings?"

"My meeting with the new PE firm down in the Financial District was odd...the partner was smart but quite rude, and it was clear he found himself impressive."

Andi snorted, "Yup, sounds just like Sebastian."

"I could tell he was a micromanager–no chance in hell I could envision working with him. But he isn't the kind of guy you want to piss off, so I agreed to stay connected. After that was a lunch meeting at Brasserie. We hadn't even ordered our food yet when the partner immediately plunged into asking my advice on turning around some of their portfolio businesses; he wanted step-by-step specifics on how to solve their problems and brought an associate along to take notes."

Courtney frowned. "Remember, Vivi, I mentioned some guys might view your meeting as a chance to get free consulting advice from an expert. I hope you didn't give too much away."

"No, I steered the conversation toward what I was looking to do. Then when I got up to use the restroom I ran into the Cornell Club partner from the previous day and said hello. When I returned to our table the partner sensed he had competition and said, 'Vivien, are you also talking to that firm over there about opportunities? You seem pretty well connected in the PE world. We'd love to work with you in some capacity, maybe get your help evaluating companies we're thinking about buying…on a paid basis, of course.'" Vivien chuckled. "Said I'd think about it."

She wrapped up the highs and lows and told her Smasher friends about her gut feel for the people–who she'd like to work with and the jerks she wanted to avoid.

"Good, good." Courtney took notes. "There are deals happening all the time. Now that these guys know you I'm sure they'll be calling on you. Let's prepare for tomorrow's meetings."

Vivien took a breath. "Hey, thanks again for all your support. The whole Smart Sports ordeal was a nightmare. This process is helping me regain my footing…and giving me hope."

"Good to hear, Vivi. Just don't screw it up." Andi punched her arm in jest.

They all shared a laugh.

"Anyway, isn't that why we formed our secret Ceiling Smashers society–to help each other do what none of us could do alone? And to have each other's backs?" Andi said. "That's exactly what we're doing here."

They strategized on the meetings for the next day, then Vivien looked at her watch and jumped up.

"I promised my dad I'd meet him for dinner. I'd better get going." She gathered her things.

Andi and Courtney got up to show her out.

"Let us know how tomorrow goes," Courtney said. "By the way, have you given any more thought to the corporate carve-out idea? Smart Sports stock has tanked. Maybe they'd be open to a discussion at this point."

Vivien paused. "Honestly, Courtney, I still think it would take a dramatic change to the business for them to even consider the idea. But I'll keep tabs on it and let you know if anything changes…or when pigs fly," she chuckled.

Courtney nodded. "All right, sounds good. We've raised a new fund and we're set to make some investments. BC Capital has a fair bit of cash in our two limited partner funds. This carve-out idea is one I'd still be eager to do."

Typical Courtney Greene; once she seized upon an idea she clung to it like a pit bull. It was one of the characteristics that made her a success. Her cell phone rang and as she moved away to take the call Andi nudged Vivien.

"I see you're still wearing some old hardware, Vivi." She pointed to the engagement ring. "What's up with that?"

Vivien brushed it off. "Oh, it's nothing, Andi. Clay's history." She sounded flippant, though her heart would take some time to recover. She looked at the ring. "I just felt it would be better not to walk into these meetings as a single woman, so I wore it for them. Anyway, sporting a nice rock can't hurt, right?"

The last day she'd be meeting with the two most prestigious firms in the PE world, Crane Capital and Gaius Capital.

Vivien was duly impressed when she walked into the lavish offices of Crane Capital. The firm owned the entire building and it was an architect's dream. Their offices were housed in a spacious four-story town house nestled in between midtown skyscrapers. An airy atrium with abundant skylights was at the center, and Vivien looked up to see interior glass walls partitioning each floor. It was open, modern, and light, with high end finishes.

"Nice view, isn't it?" the receptionist said in a friendly voice.

"Heck yeah," Vivien responded. "I could live here."

The receptionist laughed and showed Vivien to the conference room, where there was a large spread of breakfast items, coffees, teas, and bottled water. "Please, help yourself to anything you wish."

Vivien showed some restraint, taking only a bottle of water. She sipped it and strolled around the room appreciating the artwork.

"Vivien, is that you?"

She whirled around. It was Reed Franklin, a Wharton classmate.

"Reed, great to see you!" Vivien smiled. "I had no idea you were with the firm."

"You look wonderful." He hugged her. "Yeah, I've been with Crane for six years now and am loving it."

It would be a much better meeting with Reed there; the fact that he already knew her gave her instant credibility. Crane Capital had made the news lately with some sizeable deals.

Vivien's discussion with the partners was stimulating and all of them seemed impressed with her talent and accomplishments–they alluded to an upcoming opportunity that might interest her.

Reed told her after the meeting, "Excellent job, Vivien. My partners thought you were awesome–I'll keep you posted on the CEO role they mentioned. We're working on something that could be the perfect fit for you."

"Thanks, Reed. I'm not in a big rush to find a job; I really want to find the right role."

"Okay, Vivi. Also, if you end up considering a different role with another PE firm, feel free to use me as a sounding board. I'm happy to share my insights on other firms out there."

"I really appreciate that, Reed."

They hugged and said good-bye.

＊

Her final meeting was at the downtown offices of Gaius Capital, the most elite firm in all of private equity. It was the oldest and largest firm, with the best track record of making first-rate deals and growing outstanding companies. The outside of the building was relatively nondescript, but that changed as soon as Vivien stepped off the elevator.

The private elevator opened to the reception area of Gaius Capital, and it was stunning. Vivien caught herself midgasp when she realized that was the desired effect of the design. The décor was mostly stark white and ultramodern, and in the middle of an enormous room was a white marble desk. An attractive woman sat there, dressed in Kelly green–the color of money, Vivien noted–with a sleek brown ponytail.

Her eyes moved up and up–the vaulted ceiling must have been more than sixty feet high and a massive chandelier hung at the center, while a curved staircase led up to the partners' floor.

When you make a boatload of money I guess this is how you spend it. Vivien mused.

The cordial receptionist asked Vivien if she'd like a drink and offered her myriad choices of water–domestic or imported, sparkling or still, chilled or tepid, flavored or plain. Based on the multitude of options she guessed the firm owned a beverage company.

Vivien made herself comfortable in the sitting area, where the plush ecru furniture looked like it had never been used. After she took a few sips from her crystal goblet of sparkling, refrigerated, plain water, another executive assistant appeared to guide her up the grand staircase. Vivien noted the woman's Christian Louboutin pumps. *Wow, even I would think twice about buying such pricey shoes.*

The entire upper floor consisted of only three partner offices and five executive assistants' cubicles. Vivien was led to the corner office of the partner in charge. Upon entering, she was mesmerized by the breathtaking view overlooking the water.

"Now, *that* is a million-dollar view," she joked.

The partner swiveled around in his Herman Miller Embody chair and said in a slightly jaded tone, "Yes, everyone loves the view. But I spend most of my time looking at my computer screen."

He was a tall, athletic-looking man attired in an elegant business suit. The partner introduced himself as Howard, the chairman of Gaius Capital, and sat down at his marble-topped conference table with her. Obviously bright, but somewhat socially awkward, Howard dispensed with any small talk and delved immediately into the details of her background and what she was looking to do.

Diligent about making tons of money, this partner had to be efficient with his time, as Vivien noticed most PE partners were. The conversation took a while to flow naturally, but she turned on the charm and offered tidbits that piqued the top partner's interest.

After a relatively short time Howard stated, "I'm ready to share my conclusion. I can see that you're incredibly bright and have expertise that is, frankly, difficult to find. Hiring executives to run a stable, mature business is easy, but it takes a different skill set altogether to turn around and grow a company."

"Thanks," Vivien replied, "and I agree, turning around a business is a whole different ball of wax."

"I think it would make sense to work together if we can find the right opportunity. I've got you on my radar now, so that's good." Looking at his watch, Howard said, "Thank you for coming in, Vivien, I'm glad we had this opportunity to meet."

With that, the meeting was over. She hadn't even walked out the door yet before Howard was already sitting in front of his computer screen. Not warm and fuzzy, but certainly focused and efficient.

*

Outside, Vivien rang up Courtney and Andi to give them the lowdown on her meetings.

When she heard about Vivien's meeting at Gaius Capital, Courtney laughed, "I forgot to warn you that Howard has a somewhat robotic personality. Eventually, he warms up. He's a brilliant guy and a good person to do business with. The fact that he liked you and gave you as much time as he did is a great sign."

"Ooookay," said Vivien. She assured her friends she'd inform them of any developments. When Vivien wrapped up her call, she saw she'd received a message from an unfamiliar number with a 503 area code. Portland. She walked out onto the busy sidewalk and checked her voice mail.

It was Tim Kelley's spouse, who'd left a short message asking her to call back as soon as possible. She rang up Chris immediately.

"Vivien, I have some terrible news. It's about Tim." Chris's voice was almost a whisper and quivered with emotion. "Timmy passed away today."

Vivien stopped in her tracks, causing a near collision with an oncoming pedestrian. "Oh my god, what? What happened, Chris? I just saw Timmy not long ago."

"Tim didn't want anyone to know, but he's been fighting a serious illness for the past couple of years, and he finally succumbed to it. Maybe you figured it out."

Vivien had noticed a steady decline in his health, but she'd attributed Tim's haggard appearance to the stress of working at Smart Sports. Chris didn't elaborate and Vivien didn't feel it appropriate to press for more details.

"The only saving grace was that Tim went peacefully with his family all around him." Chris choked back a sob.

Vivien was overcome with a wave of sorrow and had to steady herself against a building–Tim was such an amazing person, so vibrant and talented. And now he was leaving behind a spouse and two young children. "Oh, Chris, this is devastating. I'm so sorry. I can't believe Timmy's gone."

"I can't either. I'm a total mess, but I'm trying to keep it together for the kids." Chris sniffled.

"What can I do to help?"

"Well, I know Tim would love to have you at his memorial service. It's happening on Tuesday. Can you come, V?"

"Of course I'll be there. Absolutely."

Chris hesitated for a minute. "I should let you know there will be some other Smart Sports executives there…like Duncan Doric. His assistant said he wanted to pay his respects."

Ugh, just the person Vivien did not want to see. But this wasn't about her.

"Listen, Chris, don't worry about me. This is about honoring Tim. I'll definitely be there for him and for you. I'm in New York now but will call you when I get back to Portland on Sunday. In the meantime if you and your family need anything, I'm here for you."

"Thanks, Vivien, you were always Tim's best friend from the company."

*

Vivien headed back to Portland on Sunday morning, and by early evening she had delivered a roasted chicken, mashed potatoes, sautéed haricots verts, and chocolate ice cream to Chris and the kids.

When she asked about Tim's memorial service, Chris said wearily, "Tim's sister, Sloane, has been a tremendous help in getting it organized." Vivien had met Sloane one time–she was a footwear designer who worked in the Innovation Kitchen at Nike. "The rest of his family and I want to keep it to a couple of speakers at the service, but Duncan's assistant told Sloane he'd like to say a few words. I guess that should be all right." Resignedly, Chris sighed. The events of the last week had clearly taken their toll.

"Don't worry, Chris," Vivien offered reassuringly, "Duncan is a very good public speaker, so I'm sure his comments will be fine."

CHAPTER 33: SAYING GOOD-BYE...
AND HELLO

The Tuesday of Tim's memorial service, bleak skies appeared overhead and driving rain only added to the melancholy mood. Vivien wore a black pantsuit and lavender blouse, arriving early to the funeral home. It felt surprisingly chilly for late October.

She shared her condolences with Tim's family–his parents and his sister, Sloane.

"Vivien, thank you for coming. Tim always spoke so highly about you and he really admired you," Sloane said. "He was the one who prodded me to get my executive MBA at Stanford a couple of years ago. My brother thought I had a future in management."

Vivien smiled. "Sounds just like Tim. If you ever want to chat about careers over coffee, just let me know."

Then she spotted Chris and the kids. Vivien gave them all hugs and told them how much she'd miss Tim.

When she entered the chapel a few people were scattered about the pews, so she took a seat in the back and perused the program. More people filed in and Vivien glanced over to see Johnny O sitting across the aisle five rows ahead.

Just as the memorial service was about to begin, two men rushed in and slid into the pew directly in front of her. They didn't have to turn around for Vivien to instantly recognize them: Duncan Doric and Klaas van der Hooft. So Klaas was even tighter with Duncan these days?

"Bugger, I didn't even have a chance to pay my respects to Tim's spouse. Chris, isn't it? Haven't met her, I only spoke with his sister,

Sloane, over the phone."

"Uh-huh," Klaas said.

"Damn tragedy to lose Timmy, and at only forty-two years old. Stomach cancer, what a bitch." Duncan shook his head.

"Yes, it's terribly sad Tim is gone. I will surely miss him," the Dutchman replied, and turned his head slightly. That was when he caught a glimpse of who was sitting behind him. "Oh, Vivien," he said awkwardly, "um, hello."

"Hello, Klaas," she replied without emotion.

She could see Duncan's back stiffen up when he heard her voice, but he refused to turn around and acknowledge her presence. Coward.

The preacher started off the ceremony and then introduced Tim's sister. His parents were too grief stricken to speak. Trying to keep her emotions in check, Sloane first thanked everyone for coming to honor Tim. She shared a couple of stories of her fondest memories of her brother.

At that point in the ceremony, Sloane asked Tim's spouse, Chris, to come up and say a few words. A big, muscular guy who looked like an NFL linebacker stood up and approached the lectern. His leaden pace and broken posture conveyed his sorrow so completely, words weren't necessary.

A few people exchanged confused glances. The man began with a statement that took many in the room by surprise.

"For those who have heard my name but never met me, I'm Chris. Tim was my partner, my husband, and the love of my life. We were together for sixteen years and raised two beautiful kids." Then Chris revealed another bombshell. "Some of you heard that Tim was battling stomach cancer. It was his wish to keep his illness private. But before he died he said, 'Honey, I'm tired of all this nonsense. I want people to know the truth, whether they like it or not.' So the truth is we lost Tim not to stomach cancer, but to complications from the AIDS virus."

Chris paused a minute to let the news sink in. Some were stunned

SHAZ KAHNG

to learn that Tim was gay, but Vivien had grown close to Tim and was one of the few from Smart Sports who knew about this aspect of his life. In fact, Vivien was the only work friend ever invited over to Chris and Tim's home.

Duncan elbowed Klaas and demanded, "Did you have any idea that Tim was a poofter?"

Klaas recoiled, taken aback by the ugly inquiry, but shook his head in the negative.

Chris continued, "Tim and I met years ago at a barbecue a mutual friend was throwing. I hadn't even finished my first beer when I knew this was the man I wanted to spend my life with. We had our first date shortly thereafter and have been together ever since. We've raised two wonderful children, Matthew and Cassie. Tim loved me and our family, but even more he loved creating things. He was so passionate about his work at Smart Sports and obsessed with designing shoes-excuse me, I mean 'footwear'-that often in the middle of the night he'd flick on the bedside light and start sketching a shoe. You may find that endearing, but after you've been awakened like that for sixteen years it wears on you-when I think about it now it still irritates me."

Chris let out a tender chuckle and it was the first time the rest of the folks laughed.

"While Tim loved working in the sports industry, he recognized it was a macho industry and he didn't think coming out would serve his career well."

Vivien's heart wrenched as she grasped that for his entire career not only was Tim afraid to tell his colleagues who he really was, he was probably terrified they'd somehow discover his illness. Wasn't suffering through AIDS agony enough? Tim's misery was compounded by the necessity he felt to hide his condition from his colleagues. Vivien wished that Tim had been more open about his illness; certainly people would have been compassionate and supportive. Well…maybe not everyone.

Upon hearing these revelations, Duncan made an indignant snort, stood up, and exited the chapel, nearly knocking over a large floral arrangement in his haste. *Seriously, did he just* leave *in the middle of Tim's funeral?* Vivien could barely contain her rage and had to take a few deep breaths to calm down.

Chris concluded his touching eulogy and by then everyone was sobbing. Then he said, "Tim's boss has asked to say a few words, so I'd like to invite Duncan Doric up here now." Chris scanned across the pews. "Duncan, where are you?"

Indeed, that was the question.

A long, uncomfortable silence followed. All the Smart Sports employees looked around and realized their CEO was now absent. They sat frozen in panic. Without Duncan to deliver his prepared remarks, who from the company would get up to speak?

Chris waited a few more beats and then somehow sensed that Duncan had gone missing. "Um, would one of Tim's friends from Smart Sports like to say a few words?" Crickets. Chris looked hopefully at the audience.

Vivien jumped up and strode purposefully down the aisle, powered by sheer fury. She swiftly reached the front of the room, satisfied by the mere fact she'd arrived at the lectern. Turning to face the crowd, it suddenly dawned on her she was required to speak–she had no idea what to say. All eyes looked expectantly at her and she noticed Johnny O giving her a little wink of encouragement.

Vivien cleared her throat, stalling for time.

"What can I say about Tim..." Long pause. "Tim was one of the first people who befriended me at Smart Sports, and we got into the habit of running together a couple times a week. Because I was usually trying to catch my breath, I'd ask him questions about footwear, and I learned it was a topic for Tim that was limitless. So he'd talk the entire time and I could just enjoy running and breathing."

People chuckled. This was followed by another long pause. Vivien clasped her hands, trying to concentrate.

"Tim was…he was a great runner…"

She was off to a pretty weak start.

Sloane looked at Vivien with an open, encouraging expression.

Focus. Vivien wracked her brain trying to think of something more meaningful to say at this crucial moment. This was her one chance to pay tribute to Tim. The audience shifted in their seats, probably praying for brevity at this point. Suddenly reality hit Vivien…she'd never see her dear friend again, never see Tim's smile or laugh at one of his silly jokes. She was overcome with a crushing sense of loss.

Finally, inspiration struck and Vivien remembered something worthy of sharing.

"I'm sorry, there are so many wonderful things about Tim I can talk about, I'm having difficulty deciding what to say. While I have many fond memories of Tim, there's one story that really stands out. Last year, Timmy and I were volunteering at one of the public elementary schools in a low-income section of the city. We participated in a Career Day and talked with the kids about working in the sports industry. Together, Tim and I explained how footwear and apparel are designed, constructed, and manufactured and showed what the product looked like along the way. We were about to pack up and head out when the principal stopped us in the hall, asking for some business advice. She was preparing a financial case to request more funding from the board of education to add more classrooms. The school was extremely overcrowded with over fifty-five students in each classroom. The principal told us she and her staff had made this request before and were denied. She thought they'd fumbled their previous request and she appealed to us for help. Tim turned to me and said, 'V, we've got to do this.' We knew we had to do two things: present the numbers to the board more effectively, and make a more compelling case. So, instead of showing a PowerPoint deck and a bunch of spreadsheets, we made up a small card that explained the situation mostly in pictures with a few key numbers. Tim and I came up with what we thought was a brilliant strategy, but Tim made it even better. Along with the principal, we invited the board members to meet us in the hallway of the school, just ten minutes before a scheduled classroom change. We thought the best way to show them the problem was to let them experience it themselves. Our plan was to present the case for more space and then let reality do the rest. The board members gathered around us as we handed out the cards and started our discussion. The ringing of the bell interrupted us. A roaring stream of students flooded the hallways and we were nearly trampled by the stampede of kids rushing to get to their next class. The board members witnessed the chaos and overcrowding firsthand. We got the funding request approved before they left that day."

People applauded and Vivien smiled.

"That's not even the best part of the story. Tim had a trick up his sleeve. Earlier that morning he'd announced to the students that during that particular class change, the first two students in their seats in each of the classrooms would win a Sony PlayStation. The prospect of winning such a coveted prize made the class change even more frenzied. As a result of Tim's creativity, the kids finally got the expanded classroom space they deserved and a good number got the PlayStations. I know that's just one story, and it's impossible to sum up a person's life with one anecdote. But I think it demonstrates the qualities that made Tim so special, as a person and as a professional: his intelligence, his creativity, his kindness, and his impact on others. I'm grateful to have worked on that pro bono project and at Smart Sports with Tim, and I'm even more grateful that I had the privilege of calling him my friend. Muhammad Ali once said, 'The man who has no imagination has no wings.' Tim had wings."

Contented with her comments, Vivien stepped down from the lectern. As she made her way back to her seat, Chris and the rest of Tim's family stretched out their hands in gratitude. Johnny O gave her a high five as Vivien passed him.

After the ceremony concluded and the mass of people crowded into the reception area for coffee and sandwiches, Johnny O came up to say hello.

"Awesome job, V, especially having to do it off the cuff like that," he said, hugging her. "How are you?"

She gave him a genuine smile. "Great to see you, Johnny O. Things are good with me. How are you?"

He shrugged. "Oh, some changes afoot. Actually, I submitted my resignation to Duncan two days ago."

"Wow. That's big news."

That explained why he and Duncan had sat apart at the memorial service. Neither of them mentioned Duncan's departure.

Johnny O rubbed his shaved head. "Yeah. Honestly, V, I got tired of Duncan's antics and needed to make a clean break. I don't like how he treats people. You, of all people, know what I mean."

"Sure do," Vivien said. "Well, good for you. What are you going to do next?"

With a tilt of his head, he said, "I'm thinking about it. Maybe take some time off. Although, Patagonia offered me a job heading up their apparel business. Maybe we should both go down to SoCal."

"But don't you have a noncompete contract you'll have to honor?"

"Here's the thing, V." Johnny O winked and leaned in close. "Noncompetes are illegal in California. Can't be enforced." He threw his head back and laughed as Vivien giggled in delight.

"Nice."

"Well, V," he said, "the truth is that I think someday we're all going to be working for you. And you know what? I look forward to seeing that happen."

"We'll see, Johnny O, we'll see."

Could there be more defections to come?

Vivien turned to head out and saw Klaas standing by the door. She was about to wave, but he pretended not to see her and left. Perhaps he was worried about being seen speaking with her; it might get back to Duncan. Was Klaas still so afraid of him?

She grabbed her raincoat and umbrella off the coatrack and said good-bye to Chris, who gave her a big bear hug, and then Vivien ran out in the pouring rain. She slammed the car door shut and was about to start the engine when she heard a tap on the window. Klaas. He stood there in the rain without an umbrella, a typical Portlandian. She cracked the window.

"Uh, hey there, Vivien." He tried sounding casual and put his hand on the roof of her car for support. "I wanted to say that you did a great job in there with your speech."

"Thanks, Klaas."

"How are you doing these days, V?"

"Fine, Klaas." She would let him say whatever he wanted, but she felt no compulsion to make it easy on him.

"You may have wondered, *Why haven't I heard from Klaas all this time?* And that's a good question. To tell you the truth, V, I was too ashamed to call you."

Vivien looked at him and let him squirm.

His steel-rimmed eyeglasses were speckled with raindrops and water dripped from his hair. "I'm sure you realized I was the one who signed your termination letter."

"I noticed that."

"Well, I didn't feel good about that. But Duncan was my boss and I felt he was my friend, so I couldn't go against my friend."

Vivien responded flatly, "That's funny, Klaas, I considered us to be friends at the time. Have you forgotten the time Duncan tried to have you canned and I helped save your butt?"

Klaas blinked.

"Oh. I forgot about that completely. I am a big jerk. I'm sorry about all of it, V, truly. I took your friendship and didn't return it in kind. I've been wanting to apologize for a while but haven't had the guts to do it. Will you please, please forgive me?"

By now Klaas's hair was soaked along with his suit–he looked like a forlorn stray dog.

"You know, Klaas, you really pissed me off." She scowled.

He continued to give her the sad puppy-dog eyes. Vivien let out a sigh.

"Oh, okay, Klaas, I forgive you. But if you want to be friends with me, then you have to make the effort. Moving forward, the quality of our friendship will be determined by what you put into it."

A goofy grin came across Klaas's face, along with a look of relief. "Thank you, V, I won't let you down. How about drinks next week? My treat. I'll email you."

"All right, Klaas."

He walked away soggy but with a spring in his step.

*

Despite being emotionally drained, Vivien made her biweekly visit to Malcolm Smart. It took all her strength to share the news of Tim's passing with the man lying on the hospital bed.

"It was a lovely memorial service and all of Tim's family and friends were there." Then Vivien mentioned what she suspected Malcolm already knew and had accepted without issue–that Tim was gay and died from AIDS. "The only low point of the ceremony was when Duncan, upon learning Tim was gay, got up and left. Didn't even stick around to pay the tribute he was supposed to…made my stomach churn." She couldn't contain the resentment in her voice.

Out of the corner of her eye, she noticed a familiar signal. Malcolm's right hand rubbed his left forearm…what he did when he heard something he didn't like. *See, Duncan,* she thought, *even Malcolm's disgusted with you. Wait a minute–he moved his hand?* Vivien's gaze traveled from his arm to his face, and for the first time in ages Malcolm's eyes were wide open.

"Malcolm, can you hear me?" she asked.

He blinked and smiled.

Her heart jumped. Vivien leaned over and hugged him. "Oh my gosh," she said, "we've all missed you so much. I'll go get your family."

In the history of sports comebacks, this would rank high.

Within minutes, Malcolm was speaking softly but monosyllabically. He conveyed to his wife and kids, mostly with his eyes and limited arm movement, how over the moon he was to be back with them. This man, who had been in a coma for eight months, comprehended his family's reaction of unbounded joy at seeing him awake and alert.

Because the sudden change in Malcolm's condition was unexpected and his outlook uncertain, his wife, Sheri, asked Vivien to keep things under wraps.

*

Much to Vivien's surprise, Klaas remained true to his word and invited her for drinks the following week. Barely seated at the bar for a few minutes, Klaas downed his pilsner and seemed quite comfortable by the time he finished his second beer.

"Ugh, V, I can't tell you how taxing it is at work. You're lucky you got out when you did." Being at Smart Sports was wearing on him; it was evident from the dark circles under Klaas's eyes. "Duncan's exceedingly irrational these days—firing people at will, demanding the impossible...he's the Kim Jong-il of the sports industry."

"Jeez, that sounds terrible." Vivien wasn't surprised.

Klaas lifted his glass to his lips. "Oof, *ja*. He fired a footwear designer over a minor issue...that kind of thing is happening every day. Duncan thinks he's a creative person, but the only creativity he's shown is on his expense reports." The Dutchman half laughed and ordered another beer. "No one is safe, V. Who knows, Duncan may decide tomorrow he wants to fire me. But given what I know, maybe he'll think twice about it."

Vivien's ears perked up. "What do you mean, Klaas?"

He explained, in his slightly inebriated state, that over the years Duncan had had a number of serious expense "irregularities"–meaning violations–for which he could be terminated. There were many unusual purchases he'd submitted on his expense reports–Vivien recalled the Prada wallet that Duncan bought in Tokyo and she'd later seen in Rebecca's hands–and questionable travel he'd taken with the corporate jet, like the side trip to Paris and his visits to Maui.

Surely these things would have caught up with him by now? It seemed no one knew about these issues except for Klaas and his finance director Fred. They both thought bringing Duncan's expense irregularities to the attention of the board would backfire on them. Since Duncan's control over the board of directors was tightly locked down, Klaas and Fred had concluded taking any action would only result in their losing their jobs.

The Dutchman laughed bitterly. "After all, Duncan's the boss... when you're the boss, who can fire you?"

The wheels in Vivien's mind turned.

She recalled a small but crucial detail from rereading the stock options agreement after Duncan fired her. It was a clause regarding termination buried in the legalese. It stated that if an employee was terminated for cause, they would immediately forfeit all their stock options–both vested and unvested.

Terminated for cause...

"Listen, Klaas, keep that information in your back pocket and don't tell anyone else about it. There might be a time when it could be useful to us both. Now, I'm calling you a cab. There's no way I'm letting you drive home tonight."

PART EIGHT

CHAPTER 34: THE GAME PLAN

The following week Vivien received two messages–catalysts that would change everything. The first was from Sheri, Malcolm's wife, saying he'd like to spend an afternoon with her.

The second was an email from Jodie, the SCP consultant she'd mentored on Shadow Day. Jodie asked how Vivien was doing and explained that Mahesh had been good enough to share her contact information. Then came the part that triggered something profound in Vivien.

Jodie wrote, "I'm not sure what you're considering next in your career, but I expect and hope it's something great. You were a legend at SCP, so I was distressed to hear what Miles Zabriskie said about you at the firm's cocktail party. In fact, many of us were upset by it. Miles said he ran into you recently, and you 'admitted' the only thing you could succeed at now was being a stay-at-home mom. Vivien, I hope that's not true, because you're a role model for so many of us…we're rooting for you. Your success inspires us."

Miles. He'd taken her sarcastic comment and turned it into an admission. What a rat.

It dawned on her that the choices she made had an impact on other women. Vivien owed it to herself, and to others, to take another shot at a leadership role and not give up until she was satisfied with the outcome. Miles's brush-off not only strengthened her resolve to succeed, it made Vivien defiant. No way she'd allow people like Miles Zabriskie and Duncan Doric to demean her–she was done with that.

✳

Vivien called Sheri Smart and set up a time to meet Malcolm. When she arrived, Malcolm was vastly improved since even a week ago. He was sitting upright in a wheelchair and was surprisingly articulate. It hadn't taken long for him to regain his ability to speak, and his memory seemed as sharp as ever.

"Let's sit together for a while, V." Malcolm smiled, motioning for her to come beside him. "I know you've been visiting me all this time and updating me on what was happening at Smart Sports. Your support means the world to me. But I need to hear things again... From your perspective, what happened with the company?"

"Sure, Malcolm." Vivien pulled a chair close. She chronicled all that had happened from the day of the helicopter accident forward. At some points in her description, Malcolm flinched. Occasionally, he asked her to repeat something for him. It took over two hours to tell the whole story.

He sat there shaking his head. It was obvious that power had been placed in the wrong hands, with disastrous results.

Finally, Malcolm said, "Hearing all that is devastating. Alex and I once had a great company, with the right values and wonderful people, and now what was great about Smart Sports has been obliterated."

Vivien nodded in agreement.

Malcolm put his hand on her arm. "Tell me, Vivien, would you be interested in going back to Smart Sports?"

"Sorry, Malcolm, but no. I would never go back to the company in its current form. I'm still recovering from the PTSD." She twitched as if being electrocuted.

Malcolm let out a laugh. "You do know, Vivien, you were our first choice for CEO. Do you remember that? Because I certainly do."

"I remember, Malcolm."

"I understand you're exploring other opportunities. Sheri

mentioned you've gotten a few offers to run private equity-backed companies. That's exciting." But Malcolm couldn't hide his disappointment.

"Yes, the opportunities are appealing," Vivien said. "But I still care deeply about Smart Sports and I'm still passionate about my division and my team."

Malcolm asked the million-dollar question. "So, what do you want to do next, V?"

A bolt of lightning hit her...all this time she'd been thinking too small. Her confidence was so sapped she focused only on a sliver of the real opportunity. But now things had changed.

Vivien smiled. "Malcolm, while there are many things I can do, there's only one thing I really want to do." She explained the idea about doing a corporate carve-out, only this time took it one step further and appealed to Malcolm for his help.

Inside of ten minutes, one piece of the puzzle was fashioned.

Malcolm clenched his fists and said, "V, it's time for us to take back our company."

"Let's go for it," she said, feeling jubilant. They sketched out next steps. "I'll get the ball rolling."

Outside of the health care facility, Vivien phoned up Courtney and Andi.

"Guess what, my friends? Pigs are flying."

✳

An intricate puzzle was forming in her head, and Vivien strategized on a game plan. There were three critical pieces needed to complete the puzzle: key people, financial backing, and crucial information. She'd have to bring all these elements together at the same time.

Part of her plan required significant private equity funding, so she enlisted Andi and Courtney to give her a critical assist. Her top two choices were the premier PE firms, Crane and Gaius. She would have liked to work with Crane Capital and Reed, but his firm had just inked a deal in the same industry, knocking them out of contention. That left Gaius Capital. Vivien would need Courtney and Andi to facilitate the meeting.

Vivien flew to New York and sat down to dinner with Andi and Courtney to devise an approach for the meeting. The next morning, feeling as prepared as possible, the three women arrived at the offices of Gaius Capital to meet with the founding partner.

Howard was waiting for them and swiveled around in his chair. He greeted Courtney warmly, met Andi for the first time, and welcomed Vivien back.

He got right down to business. "You asked for this meeting, Vivien. I'm assuming you have something specific in mind you'd like to discuss?"

"That's correct, Howard, actually a couple of ideas. Let me explain the first one." Vivien shared the first option, a corporate carve-out of the Smart Sports Women's Apparel business, and laid out the reasons why it made sense. She'd barely finished her explanation when Howard jumped in.

"Courtney, Andi, the two of you vetted this idea and you like it?" he asked.

"This is a stellar opportunity and one that doesn't come along often," Courtney said. "We believe it's attractive from both a strategic and financial perspective."

He stood up and asked them to sit tight, then he left the room. When he returned, the other two senior partners accompanied him.

"Let's continue our discussion," Howard said.

Vivien shared her idea again and the rationale for doing it. The other partners tried remaining poker-faced, but based on the enthusiastic glances they shared, she figured they were interested.

Courtney seized the opportunity. "Guys, let's start hashing out some numbers to see if it makes sense. We can start with the high-level investment thesis and growth strategy that Vivien has put together." She passed out copies of a handout. The plan was to whet their appetites, then unveil the big idea.

After a bit of group number crunching, Howard leaned back from the table. "As you know, our deal size is typically at the higher end of the range."

That was an understatement. Gaius Capital was known for making the biggest deals out there.

"I like you, Vivien, and I like this space. The corporate carve-out idea is intriguing. However, I'm afraid it may be too small a deal for us."

Vivien sat back in her chair and shot a surreptitious look at her friends.

"Well, there's another option you might find more appealing. It would be an all-encompassing approach." Vivien threw down the gauntlet.

Just like the women had strategized the night before, Courtney interjected. "Howie, what Vivien's alluding to is a way to make this work for everyone. We could go for the whole enchilada. Buy the whole thing. That would make the investment size and the return worth your while. Our firm, BC Capital, would partner with you and invest alongside you–we can work out the details. We have the means to get to a majority ownership stake extremely quickly. Timing-wise, the price of the investment couldn't be better, given the depressed stock price."

Howard was already checking the stock price on his computer. He whistled in appreciation while his partners punched numbers into their HP 12C calculators.

Courtney said, "Of course, the vital piece to making this work is having Vivien run it."

Howard gave her a penetrating look. "And, Vivien, you're comfortable with that?"

"One hundred percent. And I'll earn you a fantastic ROI."

For the first time, Howard laughed. "All right, I like the sound of that."

Then Vivien went in for the kill, pulling out a handwritten note and passing it to Howard. "I thought this might help."

He unfolded the note and scanned it. The handwritten note from Malcolm Smart read, "Vivien Lee always was and remains our number one choice for Smart Sports CEO. This deal cannot be consummated without her talent, brains, integrity, and leadership. She's the key." Howard simply said, "Wow," and handed the note to his partners.

Courtney shot Vivien a triumphant look. Andi gave her a wink.

"Let's get this deal done." Howard slapped his hands on the table. "We need to put a little more meat on the bones and run a few different financial scenarios. Vivien, we'll need you to help fill in the blanks."

Vivien pulled out a second set of handouts for everyone. "This pro forma should help us build the scenarios."

One of the other partners said, "This is excellent."

Visibly excited, Howard said, "Let's set up a conference call for later today to get moving on this. One of my assistants will contact you. Courtney and Andi, I'm looking forward to teaming up with you, and thanks for bringing this opportunity to me." Howard stood up and shook Vivien's hand. "We're not only investing in this idea, Vivien, we're investing in you. You're the one who will make it happen. I'm looking forward to a great ride." A broad grin broke across Howard's face.

After the meeting, Vivien and her friends stepped outside and celebrated with high fives. Pulling themselves together, the women walked over to the lobby of a nearby luxury hotel. While Vivien sat in a corner to make some calls, Andi and Courtney hunkered down over a coffee table to work out details.

Vivien whipped out her phone and called Malcolm.

"Looks like we've got ourselves a deal–to do the whole thing,"

Vivien said. "Your note worked like a charm, Malcolm. Sure you're ready for all this?"

"Absolutely. It's time." Malcolm sounded resolute.

They shared a triumphant chuckle and planned out next steps. Two pieces of the puzzle were set–Malcolm's endorsement and the private equity backing needed. Vivien's game plan was on track. The only puzzle piece left was to get rid of Duncan in the most efficient way possible. That was where Klaas came into the picture.

Vivien made one more call. "Klaas, things are moving forward. Now's the time to pull together that information we discussed."

✳

Back in Portland, Malcolm called a clandestine meeting of the board of directors, plus Doug Hawke. He explained in detail all that had happened under Duncan's rule.

"Duncan Doric destroyed the Smart Sports culture, damaged the brand, deceived our customers, and made a catastrophe of the business." Malcolm fumed. "But the worst part about his time as CEO is the suffering he inflicted upon our most talented, hardest-working, and most honorable people."

He shared a few choice anecdotes.

The directors listened and Malcolm took in their expressions of shock and outrage.

"Now let me explain what's going to happen next," Malcolm said.

Because he controlled the majority of shares, he could force a board vote, although that proved unnecessary. The board unanimously agreed to be dissolved, paving the way for a take-private transaction. Not only did chairman Otto Utz support the changes, he apologized profusely to Malcolm for making such a mess of his company.

Otto shook his head. "Obviously, I backed the wrong executive."

The disgust on his face was clear.

Malcolm said, "Indeed. I want to inform you that Duncan Doric will be fired for cause at the upcoming company meeting."

CHAPTER 35: WHAT GOES AROUND...

Typical of his reign, Duncan called a company-wide meeting to announce yet another reorganization. On a Friday afternoon in late November all employees were summoned to the Stadium. By now Otto grew wise to the fact that Duncan was shuffling around his cronies into new roles with more imposing titles.

Otto invited Doug Hawke to sit with him at the back of the auditorium.

"You were so right, Doug. Duncan was absolutely the wrong choice for CEO," he said in a soft voice. Otto rubbed his face with his hands. "The company is about to close its books on the most disastrous year in its history, all because of Duncan...and because of my terrible decision. Duncan is still as confident as ever, but I have to admit even I've heard people say they're embarrassed to work for Smart Sports these days. It's all because of me not doing my job properly as board chairman."

"Hmm," Doug said, "we all make mistakes, Otto." He patted him on the arm. Doug was too classy to say *I told you so.*

Otto shot Doug a grateful look.

Doug glanced at his watch. "Well, I'd better go take care of things."

✳

Pandy noticed that Duncan had cleverly arranged for his few remaining supporters to sit in the front rows of the auditorium. Of course, she was stuck in the back with the rest of the crowd. As the employees filed in, only a select few were invited by the ushers to occupy seats in the roped-off area near the stage. The intent was that when Duncan came out onstage, he could be assured of some hearty applause. What a phony.

An up-tempo soundtrack blasted over the speakers, and a video loop of inspiring Smart Sports images played on the huge screen. The music came down in volume and Steele walked out to work the audience.

"Hello, Smart Sports!" Steele greeted everyone. "Isn't this the coolest company around?"

He was met with a tepid response.

Steele introduced their CEO, like an announcer trying to rev up a basketball arena as the star players ran onto the court. Halfhearted applause was offered. People were weary of hearing the same thing from Duncan and just wanted to get the meeting over with so they could go back to their desks and comb the Internet for new jobs; maybe another sports company was hiring.

Duncan stepped out into the spotlight, waving at the crowd and smiling a broad smile that revealed recently whitened teeth. He wore his trademark dark deep-V-neck T-shirt and jeans, with the latest style of Smart Sports shoes. As he prepared to speak, Duncan ran his hand through his wavy silver hair, which was now long enough to conceal the tattoo on the back of his neck.

"Hallo, everyone," he said, rubbing his hands together with glee. Duncan leaned on the lectern, like a king surveying his minions. It didn't seem to matter how terribly the company was performing; this was a man who relished being in the spotlight, however undeserved it was.

Duncan made an attempt to be witty but his joke fell flat. Pandy rolled her eyes. Mercifully, he got to the meat of his comments. His ersatz English accent was amped up a few notches as he addressed the audience.

"Right then, I've called you all here to announce some important changes in the organization structure. As you know, the role of president has been vacant since the recent departure of Johnny O'Connell. We've decided to eliminate that position altogether. I will be distributing those responsibilities to various members of my executive team. Taking responsibility for–"

All of a sudden a loud rumble came from the audience, and Duncan stopped speaking to see what was happening. Walking toward him on the stage was a trim, energetic-looking Doug Hawke. All the employees hooted and clapped with delight.

Doug waved and flashed a huge grin as he walked up to Duncan, who looked perplexed.

Nudging Duncan aside, Doug leaned into the microphone. "Sorry to interrupt your little meeting here, Dunk, but I have a surprise for everyone. I'd like to bring out a special guest, someone who needs no introduction."

He gestured toward the wings, and when the special guest appeared the room fell silent.

Pandy blinked and stood, amazed at the sight.

Malcolm Smart, moving with the aid of a cane, walked purposefully onto the stage. The founder was greeted with a standing ovation and stamping, whistling, and shouts so loud the walls shook. The excitement was palpable.

"Oh my gosh, what a miracle!" Pandy was overjoyed to see Malcolm alive and well.

The cheering and deafening applause for Malcolm continued interminably, despite his many attempts to quiet things down.

∗

Duncan stood aside, bewildered. He had never received that kind of welcome. His face reddened and he rubbed the back of his neck. It took a moment for him to regain his composure, then he walked over to give Malcolm a hug. Duncan's attempt was deflected by a Heisman move when Malcolm put his arm out to stop him. Instead, the founder gripped Duncan's shoulder and placed him off to the side. Huh? Duncan couldn't understand the cold reception. Maybe Malcolm wanted to say a few words to thank him first.

Malcolm stepped up to the lectern and leaned on both forearms. "Hey, everyone, it's so great to be back. You know, I really missed all of you. I only wish Alex were here as well."

The response from employees was an explosion of supportive applause.

Malcolm bowed his head. "Let me get right to it. I'm here to announce some major changes to Smart Sports. First, the biggest news is that we are going through what's called a 'take-private transaction.' That means a small team of private-equity firms that I've approved has purchased the outstanding shares of our company. That, combined with my majority holdings, has allowed us to take this company private, and we have dissolved the board of directors. We will no longer be a public company and can go about fixing everything that is broken"–Malcolm gave a sideways look to Duncan–"out of public view."

Duncan snorted. *These employees are too stupid to understand the details of what Malcolm's talking about.*

Malcolm said, "It's amazing to witness the impact one person can have on a company–good or bad. I have to say the amount of damage that's been done to Smart Sports in the last nine months is staggering–almost beyond belief. It just kills me. Having the wrong person in charge can completely destroy a business, a company, a culture, and the lives of many people–and that's just what Duncan has done to this company. My company."

The founder's words made Duncan flinch. He shoved his hands in his pockets and cast his gaze downward. What about the things he had done right? Didn't he deserve some credit for stepping into the CEO role at such a difficult time? Surely Malcolm would thank him for that.

Malcolm continued, "The second piece of news I want to share is another reorg, but this time for the better. Effective today, Duncan Doric is no longer CEO of Smart Sports." Malcolm turned to Duncan, who stood there, head hanging down, and said, "Duncan, you're fired."

The audience erupted in applause and cheers. Unbelievable.

How could this be happening? To him? Two big, burly security guards came onstage and stood on either side of him. Duncan jerked his head around in a daze, his mouth agape. They swiftly escorted him offstage.

Malcolm smiled at his employees. "The measure of a man–or person, I should say–isn't just what he achieves, but how he does it. Our new CEO is a person who has proven they can not only do an extremely difficult job exceptionally well, but do it with integrity, humility, and the quality of kindness."

Duncan reached the space behind the curtains and, with a start, saw who was waiting in the wings. "Oh, it's you," Duncan said haughtily. "What are you doing here, V?"

Vivien Lee stared right at him. "You'll see."

Duncan narrowed his eyes. "Well, I've got news for you. It doesn't matter what happens to me today; I've got connections in this industry–deep connections that span years. I have loads of people backing me...now, that's power. It's the kind of power no one can touch. I'll be back on top of another company in no time. You watch."

Vivien shot him a skeptical look. "Duncan, from your 'Strength Under Pressure' tattoo, I know you're a fan of Latin. So, here's some more Latin for you: '*Veni, vidi, vici.*'"

"Huh? What does that mean?" he scowled.

"It means 'I came, I saw, I kicked your ass.' Stick around and enjoy the show, Dunk."

With a smile of satisfaction, Vivien walked away.

Malcolm continued, "The new CEO of Smart Sports is not only the most impressive business executive I've ever known, but also a good human being and great leader. It thrills me to present your new CEO, Vivien Lee."

As she joined Malcolm onstage Duncan heard the sound of a buffalo stampede as hundreds of chairs seats slammed into seat backs. A standing ovation. They'd never done that for him.

Malcolm and Doug hugged her. She walked to the lip of the stage, microphone in hand. "Hi, everyone, it's so great to be back and to see all of you. Let's return Smart Sports to a place we're proud of–where integrity, ideas, talent, and teamwork are valued. Together, we can move forward and restore Smart Sports to greatness. Are you with me?"

A tidal wave of cheers echoed across the Stadium, and across the campus.

✳

Duncan was ushered out the door and directly to his BMW. Did that really just happen? How could his fortunes have changed so swiftly?

One of the well-muscled security men pulled two envelopes from his inside jacket pocket and handed them to Duncan.

"What's this?" Duncan snatched them away and ripped them open.

Inside one envelope was his termination letter, stating that, in addition to his abysmal performance as CEO, he was being fired for cause due to egregious expense violations over the years. It also informed him that being fired for cause meant he forfeited all his stock options, vested and unvested. *What the...? My options were worth a bloody fortune.*

He pulled out the second letter.

Duncan blinked back the tears. It was an invoice from Smart Sports–an order to repay $972,920.11 in unauthorized expenses to the company.

His shock turned to rage and then to bewilderment. How was it possible for Vivien Lee to swoop in and take his job?

*

When Duncan drove home to his gated community, he saw mounds of debris scattered across the yard in front of his house: his clothes, some cut into shreds, and his hundreds of pairs of athletic shoes. Giovanna had emptied his closet, throwing Duncan's belongings from their second-floor bedroom window.

Oh, no. Otto must have told her everything…especially about the expense reports for his trips with Rebecca.

As he tentatively came up the walkway, Giovanna poked her head out the window and yelled, "Game over, Duncan! Get the hell out. And here are the divorce papers for you to sign."

She stuffed an envelope into one of his running shoes and hurled it at his head. He didn't react quickly enough. It caught him smack in the eye.

Duncan sank to the ground, sobbing. "Giovanna, darling!"

The window slammed shut. Silence.

After a while he started crawling around on his hands and knees, picking up the pieces of clothing and shoes he could salvage.

*

Vivien's phone rang. She glanced at the screen and grinned. "Hi, Johnny O, what's up?"

"Well, V, I'm looking out my living room window across the street." He described the whole sorry scene–the flying shoe, the pleading, and Duncan crawling around collecting his crap. "Payback's a bitch, Dunk." Johnny O snickered. "Now he's got another black eye…that's karma."

Vivien laughed. "*Veni, vidi, vici*, baby."

CHAPTER 36: FLYING HIGH

It didn't take long for the electrifying news about Smart Sports' change in leadership to get out. Within a week Vivien had gone from being a little-known executive to being the first female CEO in the history of the sports industry.

Fortunately, Vivien would have a short reprieve. Sofia was having her wedding in Paris and Vivien was glad to get out of the country for a bit. She caught her flight from Portland to JFK and was to meet her friends at the gate. As she walked past the newsstand, something caught Vivien's eye. It was her. The reporter who hosted the *Fortune* conference had called her the previous week for an interview. She told Vivien she was doing a profile on her and wanted to talk about her new role. But, *holy crap*, Vivien had had no idea she'd be the lead story. Her face was on the cover of *Fortune* magazine.

Vivien stood there, blushing. Her appointment as CEO of Smart Sports was getting more attention than she'd expected. She grabbed a copy of the magazine and placed an issue of *Sports Illustrated* on top, to hide her photo. The cashier robotically rang up the purchase and handed Vivien the bag, not noticing her face was on one of the magazines.

She made a detour to the restroom and hid herself in one of the stalls to see what the article was all about. The article was entitled, "How an Outsider Became a Trailblazing CEO."

Not only was Vivien shocked to see her entire career, educational background, and personal history laid out on the pages, but there were quotes–all highly positive; she breathed a sigh of relief– from former clients, colleagues, and classmates. The conclusion of the article was that the sports industry was in need of a shake-up, and the reporter was betting on Vivien Lee to do something extraordinary.

Nothing like setting high expectations before she even started the job.

The sidebar about Duncan made Vivien guffaw. Titled "The Worst Boss in America?," it described how far Smart Sports declined on Duncan's watch and the wave of talent that left the company under his reign. An anecdote was included about a speaking engagement that occurred toward the latter part of Duncan's time as CEO. At an industry conference, during the Q&A session that followed his speech, a provocative question was thrown out from an audience member.

"Duncan, as CEO what grade would you give yourself on the job you've done for Smart Sports, a C? Or a D, perhaps?"

Duncan responded huffily, "Certainly not. I'd grade myself higher than that, much higher. I'd give myself an A, maybe an A minus."

The person who asked the question stood up. "Well, I worked for you at Smart Sports until recently and I'd give you an F. And a U. You were not only the worst boss I've ever had, I truly believe you are the worst boss in America."

That audience member was Ethan, the tennis footwear designer whom Duncan fired on a whim. Ethan borrowed his material heavily from a *Saturday Night Live* skit, but it was perfect for the occasion.

Closing the magazine with a chuckle, Vivien suddenly realized the time. She raced through the airport to meet her friends, who stood waiting at their gate. Although they wanted to sit together, Sofia had finagled first-class upgrades for all of them, so they were separated a bit. Sofia was up front. Coop ended up in a seat across the aisle from Vivien, with Grace and Andi in the pair of seats behind Vivien's row. There was an empty window seat next to Vivien, which Coop hoped to snag once the cabin doors closed.

Moments before the flight to Paris was about to take off, there was a rush of activity in the doorway of the first-class cabin and a few muffled shrieks. The passenger who was to sit beside Vivien appeared, escorted by a customer service rep.

"I do apologize, miss, but would you mind if I squeeze past?" The man had a polite, twangy Australian accent.

Vivien looked up from her book directly into the mesmerizing brown eyes of Hugh Jackman, one of her all-time favorite actors.

Outwardly cool and collected, Vivien said, "Sure, no problem." Inside she kept a nervous giggle from bubbling up.

She stood to let the versatile actor/singer/dancer pass and looked over to see Coop's jaw drop.

Hugh flashed his high-wattage grin. "Thanks ever so much." Hugh shuffled past her to his seat–he smelled like a crisp morning breeze in a verdant forest. "How are you going?"

From her visits to Australia, Vivien recognized this phrase as the Australian version of "How are you doing?" She shyly responded she was fine.

As Vivien sat down, she glanced back at Grace and Andi eyes wide with excitement. Her friends gawked through the gaps in the seat backs to get a better glimpse. Meanwhile, Coop was craning his neck.

Guessing correctly that the actor might not want to engage in idle chitchat, Vivien resumed reading her book. The flight attendant made the requisite announcements and the plane taxied for takeoff. Upon reaching its cruising altitude, the plane leveled off and cocktails were served.

Vivien held up her champagne glass to toast all her friends. Curious about her seat-mate, she stole a couple of surreptitious glances in his direction but tried her utmost to respect his privacy. It must have been tough to have everyone recognize you and want to talk to you. Coop was being too obvious about checking out Mr. Jackman and Vivien had to motion to him to settle down.

After a while the white noise of the humming aircraft started to lull the passengers into a state of relaxation. Vivien was so engrossed in her book, she barely noticed someone tapping her arm.

A small voice said timidly, "Excuse me. May I have an autograph?"

A young girl stood next to her, holding out a pad with a pleading look in her eyes.

"Hi there." Vivien whispered, "You know, it might work better if you say 'please.'" She gave the girl a wink of encouragement.

In a slightly more confident voice, the girl asked, "May I have an autograph, *please*?"

Vivien looked over sympathetically at Hugh Jackman, who was fishing around in his jacket pockets for a pen. The girl's wide-eyed gaze passed from Hugh to Vivien and back again.

Vivien took the pad and passed it to the actor. "This must happen to you all the time."

"Aw, it's all right. For the kids, I don't mind one bit." Hugh signed the pad and, with a friendly twinkle in his eyes, said a few kind words, handing the pad back.

Strangely, she didn't reach for it. In fact, the girl stood there looking confused.

Maybe she's starstruck.

Finally the girl blurted, "Thank you, sir, but, actually, it was your autograph I wanted." She looked at Vivien. "You're Vivien Lee, the new CEO of Smart Sports, right? My mom and I were just reading about you in her business magazine. We were excited to see you when we got on board. Someday I want to run my own business, and my mom says I can do it, just like you." The girl gave her a toothy smile. "May I have your autograph, Miss Lee, please?"

"Oh please, call me Vivien."

Someone in the row ahead of Vivien's overheard the exchange and stood up to investigate. Holding up his copy of *Fortune* so all could see Vivien's face on the cover, he pointed at her and shrieked in a French accent, "Oh my god, it's you! It's you!" Then he noticed Hugh Jackman and said, "And it's Hugh, it's Hugh!" Which sounded exactly like his previous statement.

Vivien smiled wanly and sank down in her seat.

Hugh collected himself, gave a tight smile, and handed the pad to a stunned Vivien.

It was her first time fielding a request for an autograph. "I'd be happy to give you an autograph. What's your name?" Vivien said in a soft voice.

"Katrina."

"Great name." Vivien smiled. She wrote a short message and signed her name, handing the pad back to its beaming owner.

Hugh joked, "By the way, Katrina, I'm her bodyguard." He pointed to Vivien as the girl smiled.

Standing there, Katrina said, "Vivien, do you have any advice for me?"

Vivien paused for a moment. What advice would be helpful to a ten-year-old girl?

"Well, Katrina, my father used to tell me something that always helped me keep things in perspective. He'd say, 'Don't let your successes go to your head, and don't let your failures get to your heart.' If you keep that in mind, I'm sure you'll do great."

"Thank you so much, Vivien!" Katrina pranced back to her seat, clutching her autographed treasure in both hands raised exuberantly over her head.

"Would you mind signing one for me, Vivien?" Hugh asked with his trademark grin. "My wife and kids would be tickled that I sat next to a business trailblazer. Sometimes my kids think my job can be a bit of a yawn."

God, was he ever charming.

Vivien let out a nervous chuckle, while Andi gave her friend's seat a good-natured kick.

Settling back in her seat, Vivien took in a deep breath and exhaled slowly. For the first time in what seemed like forever, a powerful sense of possibility grabbed hold of her. Vivien felt the delicious anticipation that she was about to embark on a journey whose outcome she could not predict…and she was game.

ACKNOWLEDGMENTS

Many people, in ways large and small but always significant, helped me bring this book to life.

I'm forever grateful to my family, especially my husband Bill for all his support and encouragement along the way. Thanks to my father, the late Dr. Anthony Kahng, and my mother, Dr. Young-Hee Lowe, who taught me that nothing is impossible.

Thank you to my editor, Kristen Stieffel, who helped me hone my story and was an uplifting writing coach.

For providing sage advice or invaluable help along the way I'd like to thank:

Karen Bakos, David Ebershoff, Suzie Ivelich, Michael Pogozelski, the Reedsy team including Aja Pollock and Mark Thomas, Paul A. Slavin, and Bradley West. Also, thanks to my friends, colleagues, and my network of Wharton women (and men).

Finally, thank you to all the amazing, positive women out there who are demonstrating every day that sometimes the best man for the job really is a strong woman.

∾

THE CLOSER: QUESTIONS & TOPICS FOR READING GROUP DISCUSSION

1. What did you like best about this book? What was unique/original about it?

2. What aspects of the story could you most relate to and why?

3. What was it about the main character that you liked the most?

4. The Closer is about Vivien Lee's experience in joining Smart Sports as the first female senior executive. Have you ever been a "first" or in a situation where you were one of the only women leaders? Share your experiences.

5. When Vivien moves from NYC to Portland, Oregon she leaves her safety net of family and friends behind. Have you ever made a major change (moved cities, switched jobs or industries) where you felt like an outsider? What was it like?

6. In the book Vivien handles a myriad of challenges in her role as president of Smart Sports Women's Apparel? What stood out to you?

7. One of the themes in this book was the bond between women. What aspect of that subject resonated with you?

8. Which character in the book would you most like to meet and have dinner with? What would be an interesting topic of conversation?

9. What's your favorite quote from the book and why?

10. What do you think the author's purpose was in writing this story? What ideas or concepts was the author trying to convey?

11. If you could ask the author one question about the book what would it be?

Made in the USA
Coppell, TX
25 September 2020